ECONOMI
Made

The Mac
has been
especially
but can eq
be used as
an aid to group study.
However complex the subject,
the reader is taken
step by step,
clearly and methodically,
through the course. Each volume
has been prepared by experts,
taking account of
modern educational requirements,
to ensure the most
effective way of
acquiring knowledge.

In the same series

Accounting
Acting and Stagecraft
Additional Mathematics
Administration in Business
Advertising
Anthropology
Applied Economics
Applied Mathematics
Applied Mechanics
Art Appreciation
Art of Speaking
Art of Writing
Biology
Book-keeping
British Constitution
Business and Administrative Organisation
Business Economics
Business Statistics and Accounting
Calculus
Chemistry
Childcare
Commerce
Company Law
Computer Programming
Computers and Microprocessors
Cookery
Cost and Management Accounting
Data Processing
Dressmaking
Economic History
Economic and Social Geography
Economics
Effective Communication
Electricity
Electronic Computers
Electronics
English
English Literature
Export
Financial Management
French
Geology
German
Housing, Tenancy and Planning Law
Human Anatomy
Human Biology
Italian
Journalism
Latin
Law
Management
Marketing
Mathematics
Modern Biology
Modern Electronics
Modern European History
New Mathematics
Office Practice
Organic Chemistry
Personnel Management
Philosophy
Photography
Physical Geography
Physics
Practical Typewriting
Psychiatry
Psychology
Rapid Reading
Retailing
Russian
Salesmanship
Secretarial Practice
Social Services
Sociology
Spanish
Statistics
Transport and Distribution
Twentieth-Century British History
Typing
Woodwork

ECONOMIC HISTORY
Made Simple

Bernard J. Smales, BA, BSc (Econ)

Made Simple Books
HEINEMANN : London

Made and printed in Great Britain
by Butler & Tanner Ltd, Frome and London
for the publishers William Heinemann Ltd,
10 Upper Grosvenor Street, London W1X 9PA

First Edition, September 1975
Second Edition, August 1981

SBN 434 98479 5

Preface

For most of the world's history, except for the very privileged, the most important problem has been that of survival. Most people who live in an economically advanced country can now confidently expect to survive and to have a basic minimum of comfort and security. This is because since the mid-eighteenth century the momentum of economic change has increased in many countries, and the kind of advance which might formerly have taken thousands of years to accomplish has been achieved in a matter of decades.

Great Britain was the first country to experience a sustained increase in the rate of economic change, which helps to explain why a relatively small country managed to achieve a position of wealth and influence in the world. This book endeavours, in a concise and logical form, to trace this achievement from about 1760 to the present day, and to assess the impact of technological change on our lives.

The book covers the syllabuses for GCE 'A' Level economic and social history and undergraduate degree courses in British economic and social history since 1760. The book should also be useful to any students of economics who wish to explore the realities of economic life in historical perspective. This Second Edition deals in more depth with the period following the Second World War, and since modern economic history is in fact applied economics, the book should therefore be particularly useful to students of that subject. Emphasis has been placed in the latter chapters on more recent economic, social and industrial policies which is relevant to the subject matter covered in many B.E.C. National and Higher National Diploma and Certificate courses. The book will also provide sound background reference for more elementary studies as well as being of value to any reader who seeks a greater understanding of the world in which we live.

B. J. S.

Acknowledgements

I would like to acknowledge the help given to me by the following persons in the preparation of this manuscript: Mrs Marion Lock, who typed the manuscript; my colleague Mr Michael Rendell, who helped with some of the diagrams; and Mr Robert Postema of Made Simple Books, who guided the book from its inception to its completion.

B. J. S.

Contents

SECTION THREE: WAR, DEPRESSION AND RECOVERY, 1914–39

SECTION FOUR: BRITAIN'S ECONOMIC AND SOCIAL DEVELOPMENT SINCE 1939

SECTION ONE

THE EMERGENCE OF THE FIRST INDUSTRIAL NATION 1760–1830

CHAPTER ONE

INTRODUCTION

What is Economic History?

The study of economic history, as an academic discipline, attempts to provide a systematic and integrated explanation of our economic past. It portrays man's efforts to provide himself with goods and services in order to satisfy his basic needs of food, drink, clothing and shelter. This involves a study of agriculture, industry, trade and commerce, both from the point of view of economic trends and institutional changes.

Economic history frequently spills over into the allied fields of political and social history, particularly when it is concerned with the wellbeing of different groups during the course of economic change, but invariably it is much less dependent upon personality. Sir George Clark's definition of economic history is that it . . . 'traces through the past the matters with which economics is concerned. These are the thoughts and acts of men and women in those relations which have to do with their work and livelihood, such relations as those of buyers and sellers, producers and consumers, town dwellers and countrymen, rich and poor, borrowers and lenders, masters and men or, as we say nowadays, employers and employees, and unemployed too. In economic history there is never a definite starting point.'

The Concept of an Industrial Revolution

Most people refer to the 'Industrial Revolution' in Britain when describing the striking economic changes that took place in the British economy in the second half of the eighteenth and early part of the nineteenth centuries, when Britain was transformed from being mainly an agrarian and rural society to being increasingly an industrial and urban one. It must be remembered, however, that this period only witnessed the rise of modern industry, not the rise of industry as such, since slow and sporadic growth had been taking place long before the eighteenth century. Even as early as the tenth century there was an expansion on a small scale of European commerce and a significant growth of certain cities and towns. This trend was greatly stimulated during the fifteenth century with the discovery of the New World and new routes to the East. The influx of precious metals from the New World to the Old resulted in a general rise of prices which created favourable economic opportunities.

A closer look at the evidence in Britain reveals that large-scale industry was common in mining and manufacture long before the middle of the eighteenth century. A period of increased economic activity began during the sixteenth century, and continued throughout the seventeenth and early eighteenth centuries. During the late sixteenth century new industries such as sugar refineries and saltpetre works were introduced into this country from abroad. A typical industrial transformation occurred in urban brewing during the seventeenth century in London, when the industry was changed from a handcraft basis, involving individual families and publicans brewing their own beer, to one where commercial brewers, producing possibly 10,000 barrels a year in specialised places of manufacture, supplied dependent publicans whose economic function became reduced to simple retailing. For many years Barclay's brewery was one of the sights of London for those who wanted to look at large-scale, power-driven industry. On the other hand, some industries retained their medieval form of production and structure of organisation until the later nineteenth century, such as flour milling, glove-making and shoe-making. It would therefore be more correct to define the rise of industrialism in Britain as having been a slow process going back to the sixteenth century and possibly before, rather than confining it to the economic events of the late eighteenth century. This does not mean that we should no longer regard the late eighteenth century as being an important historical watershed. On the contrary, the period is of immense significance to the economic historian because it represents the first great speeding up in modern times of industrial development, the momentum of which was maintained and increased.

The term 'Industrial Revolution' was not in use when this speeding up of economic change took place in the period approximately between 1760 and 1830, but was used later by an economic historian, Arnold Toynbee, in a series of lectures given in 1881 and published in 1884. The suitability of this terminology has been questioned since the word 'revolution' implies that what happened took place suddenly, whilst in fact the actual process of industrialisation was a slow process taking place over a number of decades.

Rostow's Theory of Economic Growth

Professor W. W. Rostow has attempted to explain England's and other countries' experiences in industrialisation by identifying five stages in the growth of an economy. He has done this by examining the sweep of modern economic history in terms of economic trends and fluctuations rather than by describing institutional changes. The five stages of growth which he referred to are:

(*a*) *The Traditional Society*. According to Rostow this stage occurred before men came to accept that the world was under the power of a few knowable laws which were capable of systematic and productive manipulation. Many changes occurred in these societies—for example, in trade and agriculture—but there was a limit to these changes, because men lacked the necessary know-how to make invention a regular flow.

Most of the labour force was employed in food production, whilst any income above minimum consumption levels was usually wasted on such extravagances as the building of monuments or the waging of wars.

(*b*) *The Preconditions for Take-Off*. This is the period when 'the insights of modern science began to be translated into new production functions in both agriculture and industry. . . .' This stage was first experienced by Britain between the Middle Ages and the mid-eighteenth century, and was due to her favourable geographic position, her resource endowment, her relatively enlightened social and political structure, and the widening of her markets and extension of trade. During this period, according to Rostow, 'new types of enterprising men came forward—in private economy, in government, or both—willing to mobilise savings and to take risks in pursuit of profit or modernisation. Banks and other institutions for mobilising capital appear. Investment increases, notably in transport, communications and raw materials. . . .'

(*c*) *The Take-Off*. This is usually a short period of between two and three decades when economic growth becomes more or less automatic. During this stage there is a rise in the proportion of net investment to national income from under 5 per cent to over 10 per cent. Resources become concentrated in one or two industries which Rostow refers to as 'leading sectors'.

Britain's leading sector in 'take-off' was in the cotton textile industry. The difference between this increase in economic activity and earlier economic upsurges is that it was self-sustained. Innovation and development became a systematic flow rather than the ebb and flow of isolated achievements which had been the case in the past.

It is important to realise that there are many flaws in Rostow's model of economic growth, as with all generalisations. For example, Britain did not achieve a net investment ratio of 10 per cent until the railway boom of the 1840s. Nevertheless, the theory has been extremely valuable if only by provoking considerable controversy over the important issue of economic growth.

The last two stages of Rostow's growth model—the drive to maturity, when there is a rapid expansion of major industries, and the age of high mass consumption, when large numbers of people begin to enjoy the comfort of modern existence—are irrelevant to this section of the book, and will be referred to later.

The Philosophical Rationale for Sustained Economic Growth

A natural corollary of change is for man to attempt to understand what is happening and to provide a rationale for it; therefore such a dramatic change as the Industrial Revolution was inevitably followed by new ideas in economic and social affairs. Thus Industrial Capitalism came to be justified by the so-called 'political economy' of a group of thinkers often referred to as 'the classical economists'. 'Classical economics' was an expression originally used by Karl Marx, and refers to the writings of a group of philosophers, the most prominent of which were Adam Smith (1723–90), Jeremy Bentham (1748–1832), Thomas

Malthus (1766–1834), David Ricardo (1772–1823), James Mill (1773–1836), and his son, John Stuart Mill (1806–73). These classical economists all believed basically in the philosophy of laissez-faire, or economic freedom with the minimum of government intervention, and it was this philosophy which provided the basis on which the nineteenth century classical liberal economy was built.

The ideas of laissez-faire were originally formulated by Adam Smith in his monumental work, *The Wealth of Nations*, published in 1776. In this great work Adam Smith encouraged men to pursue their individual self-interest, which he thought was the same as material gain, and concluded that the aggregate effect of everyone pursuing their self-interest in competition with each other would be for the common good. He also thought that the role of the State should be minimal, though he realised that the State had to provide public services such as defence, law and order, and certain other institutions, which no individual alone could maintain.

It is interesting to reflect that nowadays it would be very difficult for a country to experience an Industrial Revolution without the full backing and support of its government, yet the extraordinary thing was that the Industrial Revolution in Britain was not brought about by government planners or economists. The very opposite was true because governments in Britain showed an increasing resistance to most forms of government control over economic and social life from the late eighteenth century onwards. This was reflected in the gradual abolition of such things as tariffs on imported goods, regulation of wages and prices and monopoly trading rights. In fact, government for a long time chose to ignore the evil consequences of industrialisation such as poor working and living conditions, and bad sanitation.

Suggested Further Reading

Ashton, T. S., *The Industrial Revolution 1760–1830*, O.U.P., Oxford and London, 1948.

Rostow, W. W., *The Stages of Economic Growth*, O.U.P., Oxford and London, 1960.

Wilson, C. H., *England's Apprenticeship, 1603–1763*, Longmans, London, 1965.

Taylor, A. J., *Laissez-Faire and State Intervention in Nineteenth-Century Britain*, Macmillan, London, 1972.

Exercises

1. In what respect does economic and social history differ from political history?
2. Trace the main economic developments of the sixteenth century.
3. How does a theory of economic growth help you to understand economic history?
4. How would you justify the use of the term 'Industrial Revolution' to describe the economic changes of the late eighteenth and early nineteenth centuries?
5. Outline what you understand by the term 'laissez-faire' and assess the extent to which the concept influenced economic and social policy in the early stages of industrialisation.

Summary

1. Economic history, which frequently overlaps with political and social history, provides an explanation of our economic past.

2. The process of industrialisation was speeded up in the eighteenth century and momentum of change was maintained and increased.

3. The term Industrial 'Revolution' is misleading because it implies that the striking changes beginning in the mid-eighteenth century took place suddenly, when in fact they were spread over several decades.

4. W. W. Rostow has attempted to explain modern industrial development by identifying five stages of economic growth.

5. The philosophical rationale for economic growth was 'laissez-faire', which was based on the premise that the best government was the one that governed least; therefore the Industrial Revolution in Britain was not brought about by government planners or economists.

CHAPTER TWO

THE PREREQUISITES FOR SUSTAINED ECONOMIC GROWTH

Many theories have been put forward to explain why the pace of economic development quickened so markedly about the middle of the eighteenth century, and there is some controversy concerning which were the most important factors. Obviously, the synchronisation of a group of prerequisites to produce unprecedented economic development was no accident. There had to be increases in the factors of production: land, labour and capital. These factors had to be co-ordinated by entrepreneurs, i.e. by people who organised the work and resources of others. These entrepreneurs had to be keen to find new markets and new ideas. They also had to be free to operate in a country which had a government capable of maintaining law and order, and willing to accept some responsibility for building up social capital such as roads.

It is interesting to consider why Britain was fortunate enough to gain a generation start over other countries in the process of industrialisation. France, after all, had a bigger population than Britain during the eighteenth century: therefore potentially she had a bigger labour force and a more extensive home market. She also had a flourishing overseas trade, particularly with the Levant and her colonies in the West Indies. High standards of craftsmanship were achieved both in the domestic industries and the state factories where tapestries and porcelain were made.

French scientists made important progress and applied scientific knowledge to solve industrial problems; for example, Clouet made cast steel, Jacquard invented the silk loom and Leblanc produced artificial soda. In addition, the State actively promoted manufactures.

Germany also had high standards of industrial skill and large resources of coal were available in the Ruhr, Saar and Upper Silesia. The Fairs of Leipzig and Frankfurt were of international importance and large quantities of goods were carried on German rivers.

Why, then, did Germany and France not industrialise before Britain? In France wealth was very unevenly divided before the French Revolution of 1789, and inadequate coal resources hampered the growth of heavy industry, a disadvantage which was still hindering French industrialisation even in the twentieth century. In Germany the division of the country into a large number of separate states and the failure to establish colonies overseas adversely affected industrial growth. The national resources of both countries were dissipated in the long wars of the eighteenth century, and internal customs barriers and road and river tolls acted as impediments to both industrial and commercial expansion.

Britain alone had all the right prerequisites in the mid-eighteenth

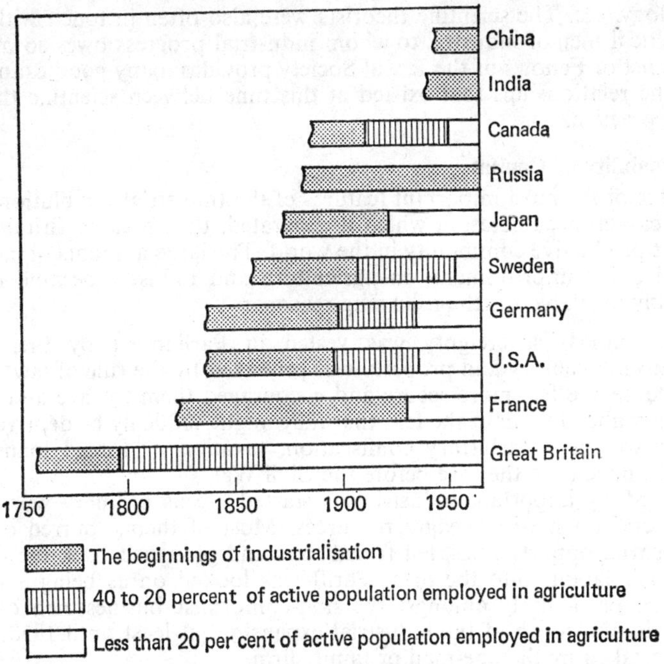

Fig. 1. The spread of the Industrial Revolution.
(courtesy Penguin Books Ltd)

century, and was thus poised for rapid economic growth, the momentum of which was sustained and increased. The following factors played a critical part in this process of growth.

Favourable Background Conditions

For two or three hundred years before the so-called Industrial Revolution of the eighteenth century people began to enquire more into the nature of Man's existence. A more rational outlook and approach began to evolve in the late sixteenth century, and the importance was realised of quantitative measurements and careful testing of ideas by experiment. There was an increasing interest in statistics, as was illustrated by Gregory King, who made estimates of English population during the late seventeenth century and provided us with the most precise picture of England's economic and social structure in the years immediately before the Industrial Revolution.

The scientific work of men in the sixteenth and seventeenth centuries, like Francis Bacon, Robert Boyle and Isaac Newton led to important developments. Newton, for example, did not concern himself too much with whether or not his ideas were immediately useful, but his methods, together with those of some of his contemporaries, provided the sound basis upon which industrial progress could subsequently be achieved.

Gradually, scientific enquiry became more specific as natural philosophy was split up into the separate disciplines of chemistry, physics, geology, etc. The scientific theorists were also often in touch with the practical men of industry, to whom industrial progress owes so much. The list of Fellows of the Royal Society provides many good examples of the relationships that existed at this time between scientific theory and practice.

Availability of Capital

One of the most important features of the Industrial Revolution was the capital accumulation which it generated, thus making Britain the most productive community in the world. The large amounts of capital needed for improvements in agriculture and industry became more readily available for the following reasons:

1. Political sovereignty was vested in Parliament by the mid-eighteenth century and property was protected by the rule of law. This made people feel more secure and encouraged them to save and plan further ahead without the fear that they might suddenly be deprived of their wealth by arbitrary confiscation, taxation or forced loans, as might have been the case before the Civil War.

2. Many important industrialists started life as ordinary workmen and craftsmen with meagre resources. Most of them, spurred on by improved opportunities, led frugal lives and ploughed back the fruits of their labour into the firm. Thrift was looked on as being a great virtue, particularly amongst the non-conformist businessmen of the North, and much of the industrial expansion, at least until 1850, was undertaken by the one-man or family firm.

3. Profits from agriculture were also used to finance industry. The improved farming methods of the eighteenth century, together with rising prices caused by increasing demand and wartime inflation, led to many farmers making large profits. This surplus capital was often lent through the country banks to the growing manufacturing centres, which were constantly in need of cash and credit.

4. It was common for trading profits to be invested in industry by successful and enterprising merchants. Amongst the industries to benefit from this form of finance were the South Wales coal and iron industries, and the Lancashire and Yorkshire cotton industry.

5. The founding and growth of numerous insurance companies and friendly societies collected together large sums of money from many small savers. This money was then available for profitable but safe investment.

6. Britain was a net borrower from abroad up to the end of the eighteenth century and did not start being a vigorous exporter of capital until after 1815. This meant that investment was in fact being undertaken by foreigners in Britain, mainly the Dutch. Nearly half the British National Debt was held by foreigners in 1776. This situation was rapidly changed after 1781 when Holland became involved with Britain in war, resulting in most of the debt being transferred to the well-to-do classes in this country.

Thus by 1830 avenues of finance had been firmly established to see Britain through the 'take-off' period, and whilst the scale of industry remained generally small, the facilities proved to be adequate. It must be remembered that the country between 1750 and 1850 depended very much on the private owner of risk capital, and whilst the Stock Exchange widened its interests towards industrial investment, it was not really until the railway boom of the 1840s that there was any appreciable increase in the number of investors who resorted to it.

Impersonal investment was greatly inhibited by the restrictive legislation affecting the formation of joint stock companies. The Bubble Act of 1720 laid down that there could be only six partners in a company and each one of them had to have unlimited liability. This was a most unfortunate measure because it meant that, until the middle of the nineteenth century, most manufacturing enterprises were unable to seek public capital as a company by issuing shares on the Stock Exchange. It is true that joint stock companies could still be formed by the rather cumbersome and often expensive process of obtaining a private Act of Parliament or a Crown Charter, and certain canal promoters, turnpike trusts, dock makers, insurance firms and railway builders did go to the trouble of obtaining private Acts of Parliament.

Joint stock companies were, nevertheless, very much the exception rather than the rule before 1850, and certainly changes in company law were necessary if Britain was to shoulder the gigantic capital burdens of building up large-scale industry in the future.

Growth of Population

The increase in the size of England's population from about 1760 onwards acted as a strong stimulant to industrialisation and economic growth, though an expanding population by itself without any of the other prerequisites for growth could have been a disaster, as was illustrated in Ireland during the middle decades of the nineteenth century. More recent examples of the consequences of population growth unaccompanied by other changes may be found in many of the underdeveloped regions of the world at the present time. Conditions in England, however, during the second half of the eighteenth century and early part of the nineteenth, favoured an increase in population since it tended to move towards the sectors where there were increasing returns and advancing productivity, as in manufacturing, mining, trade and industry.

The Causes of Population Growth

It is very important to realise that the causes of population growth during the period 1760–1830 are controversial due to the shortcomings of the available information; dogmatic statements are therefore impossible and a balanced point of view can be reached only by evaluating the various arguments and theories on the subject.

The major contemporary sources used in compiling population statistics up to 1830 were the parish registers and the decennial censuses begun in 1801. It was not until the second half of the nineteenth century, after the passing of the Registration Act in 1836, which provided for compulsory registration of births, marriages and deaths, and the introduction of the Annual Reports of the Registrar General in 1838, that we can say with any accuracy exactly what were the causes and the nature of the changes in the size and structure of population.

Statistics are available for the period before 1800 since the 1801 census required parishes to supply details of baptisms, burials, and marriages for 1780–1800, and in 1836 John Rickman, the administrator of the early censuses, attempted to push the pre-census history of the population back to the late sixteenth century by asking the parishes to submit further details from their registers. Much of this earlier evidence though was inaccurate due to the fallibility of information from parish registers. The Methodists, for example, in the late eighteenth and early nineteenth centuries did not practise Anglican baptism or burial, and there was a growing number of private cemeteries, thus introducing the possibility of error in the calculation of births and deaths.

Table 1 shows Rickman's estimates for population growth between

Table 1. Estimated Population of England and Wales (1750–1800)

1750	6,467,000
1760	6,736,000
1770	7,428,000
1780	7,953,000
1790	8,675,000
1800	9,168,000

Source: B. R. Mitchell, *British Historical Statistics.*

Table 2. Population of England and Wales According to Census Reports (1801–31)

1801	8,893,000
1811	10,164,000
1821	12,000,000
1831	13,896,000

Source: B. R. Mitchell, *British Historical Statistics.*

1750 and 1800 and Table 2 shows population growth from the census reports between 1801 and 1831.

This phenomenal growth of population from approximately 6½ million in 1750 to nearly 14 million in 1831 inspired the population theorist, Thomas Malthus, to publish the essay in 1798 in which he argued that population would tend to increase in geometric progression, whilst the production of food would only increase in arithmetic progression, or, in other words, the population would grow faster than food supplies.

Malthus, who came from a predominantly rural part of England, and who drew evidence from other contemporary societies like Sweden and Norway, which were mainly agrarian, had every reason to anticipate diminishing returns, but he was probably not fully aware of the great technical revolution that was going on in England, and therefore underestimated the possibility of increasing food supplies. In any case, after

1850 Britain obtained an increasing proportion of her food supplies from abroad, though Malthus would most likely have taken the view that this would only postpone the evil day, and eventually all the cultivable soil would be fully employed. No doubt he would have been very surprised to learn about the problems of over-production in primary products which occurred during the inter-war years of the twentieth century.

Population changes come about through variations in the birth and death rates or migration, but since the pattern of immigration and emigration did not contribute towards the growth of population in the late eighteenth and early nineteenth centuries, the increase must be explained in terms of changes in birth and death rates.

Birth Rates

As can be seen from Table 3, birth rates probably rose slightly in the 1770s and then remained fairly constant until 1810. During the decade 1811–20 they fell, probably due to the influence of the Napoleonic Wars, and then recovered again during the 1830s.

Table 3. Estimated Birth Rates (1751–1840) in England and Wales

	(per thousand)
1751–60	36·9
1771–80	37·5
1791–1800	37·3
1811–20	26·6
1831–40	36·6

Thomas Malthus was of the opinion that the Allowance system, by which the Poor Law Authorities paid benefits to the sick and unemployed and made up the wages of the employed men to a reasonable subsistence level, caused people to be irresponsible about the size of their families, as poor relief was paid in proportion to the number of dependants.

Another major contribution to the debate was that the growth of industries like cotton, in which child labour could easily be used, stimulated the demand for children, as they were self-supporting from an early age.

On the other hand, it should be remembered that child labour was commonly used long before the Industrial Revolution.

T. H. Marshall, in an article written in 1929, thought that the rise in the birth rate, which he considered was a minor factor in population growth, may have been caused by a decline of the apprenticeship system. With the growth of such industries as coal and cotton, where there was no apprenticeship at all, a man would be earning as much by the age of eighteen as he would probably ever earn, whereas under the guild system a man would only be earning his full income several years later in life. This would most likely have applied to peasant farming also, since a small independent cultivator might have been reluctant to marry early and have a large family due to the difficulty of obtaining a living from the land.

A further possible reason for the rising birth rate was a fall in the death rate, for as more women survived the full child-bearing period, so the number of children they were likely to have would increase. As late as 1850 only two thirds of women reached the child-bearing age, and only half completed it.

Death Rates

The death rate during the 1730s and the 1740s was very high, mainly on account of the excessive consumption of spirits, particularly gin. The output of spirits in Britain reached their peak in 1742–3 when 8 million gallons were produced. Some people feared that the steep rise in the number of deaths and the degradation which drink brought to both the rich and poor alike would jeopardise not only the future of civilised life in Britain, but even the continuance of the human race. The gin age came to an end in 1751 when distillers were forbidden to sell by retail and both spirit and licence duties were raised. Gradually the high consumption of gin began to fall, and during the second half of the eighteenth century more tea was consumed. Water was a very noxious substance at this time, and the boiling of water to make tea resulted in the use of sterile water which was not dangerous.

Table 4. Estimated Death Rates (1751–1840) in England and Wales

	(*per thousand*)
1751–60	30·3
1771–80	31·1
1791–1800	26·9
1811–1820	21·1
1831–40	23·4

Infantile mortality was very high in the eighteenth century. This is an important aspect of population change because by reducing infantile mortality, future birth rates were affected. In London between the following dates:

1730–49, 74 per cent died before reaching the age of five years.
1770–89, 51·4 per cent died before reaching the age of five years.
1810–29, 32 per cent died before reaching the age of five years.

Some idea of the chance of early death can be acquired by a glance at Edward Gibbons' autobiography written in 1792: 'The death of a new-born child before that of its parents may seem an unnatural, but it is strictly a probable event; since of any given number, the greater part are extinguished before their ninth year, before they possess the faculties of mind or body. Without accusing the profuse waste or imperfect workmanship of Nature, I shall only observe that this unfavourable chance was multiplied against my infant existence. So feeble was my constitution, so precarious my life, that in the baptism of each of my brothers, my father's prudence repeated my Christian name of

Edward, that in the case of the departure of the eldest son, this patronymic appellation might be still perpetuated in the family.'

The main changes in midwifery during the eighteenth century which could have reduced mortality were the introduction on a substantial scale of institutional delivery and a change in obstetric technique and management, though it was probably not so much a change in obstetric technique as an improvement in hygiene which caused a fall in maternal mortality.

The opinion has been put forward that it was better food and a more varied diet and better supplies of coal rather than a change in health and medicine which led to a fall in the death rate. There seems little doubt that a more efficient agriculture brought about by technical change and enclosure of fields did lead to an improvement in the quality and quantity of food supplies. The introduction of root crops made it possible to feed more cattle in the winter months, thus providing a supply of fresh meat throughout the year. The resistance to disease was strengthened through the substitution of wheat for inferior cereals, an increase in the consumption of vegetables, the preserving of fruits and the importation of sugar and citrus fruits. Also the growth in the demand for food was an effective demand since the rising manufacturing and trading regions offered higher and more regular money wages than agricultural areas did. Therefore, as a response to higher money incomes an improvement in diet could take place even though environmental conditions deteriorated with the growth of the new industrial towns. This probably had a profound effect on birth rates since better nutrition on the part of mothers would lessen the incidence of miscarriage and babies would be born stronger.

It is possible now to assess more accurately the contribution of medical improvements to a reduction of the death rate during the eighteenth century, and it seems likely that even though a fall in the death rate influenced population growth more than a change in the birth rate, this was not due to any specific medical innovations. Until the use of anaesthetics after 1846, surgery was greatly inhibited because surgeons, and probably patients to an even greater extent, were reluctant to undergo long and complicated operations. Before the introduction of anaesthesia, operations were more or less limited to amputation, lithotomy, trepanning of the skull, incision of abscess, and operation for cataract. The success rate of these operations was generally low. As late as 1874 the senior surgeon to University College Hospital, reviewing thirty years' experience in surgery, showed that mortality following all forms of amputation was between 35 and 50 per cent, and following certain forms it was as high as 90 per cent. These figures were based on the work of the most expert surgeons, working in the largest hospitals, and are probably no worse than would have been obtained elsewhere: indeed, in continental hospitals in the same period, mortality was even higher.

Results of other types of operation were also bad. It was not until the introduction of antiseptic procedures, in the third quarter of the nineteenth century, that surgery became relatively safe. The medical practitioner may have acquired more knowledge of anatomy, physiology and morbid anatomy in the late eighteenth and early nineteenth centuries, but this proved to be of no value to the patient until later.

Medicine became more institutionalised as the number of hospitals greatly increased after 1700. In 1700 there were two public hospitals in London (St Bartholomew's and St Thomas's) and only five in the whole of England. Between 1700 and 1825, 154 new hospitals were founded, and the hospital accommodation in London was nothing to be ashamed of, even by modern standards, though this had little influence on the falling death rate, since with the exception of vaccination against smallpox, the decline of the death rate during the nineteenth century was almost wholly attributable to environmental change, and owed little to specific therapy. Only the very worst cases were admitted into hospitals, and being sent to hospital was almost the equivalent of being sentenced to death, because of the greatly increased possibility of contracting infectious diseases. It was not until the second half of the nineteenth century that the importance of segregating infectious patients was appreciated. It was believed that infectious and non-infectious cases could be mixed in the ratio of one to six, and as recently as 1854 persons infected with cholera were admitted to the general wards of St Bartholomew's Hospital.

The dispensary movement, started in 1769, brought treatment within the reach of a great number of poor persons, and whilst they were probably no better in administering treatment than were the hospitals and private practice, they did contribute to improved standards by teaching the importance of cleanliness and ventilation. They can be compared with the obstetricians who added nothing to the safety of the act of delivery, but justified their presence in the labour room by insisting on better standards of hygiene.

The extent of the knowledge of medicine in the eighteenth century was of a low standard and diagnosis was poor as can be seen from the following 'Weekly Bill of Mortality'.

London's 'Weekly Bill of Mortality'
(from the 'Reading Mercury', 1757)

Abortive	2	Convulsion	308
Aged	45	Dropsie	25
Apoplexy	1	Evil	1
Asthma	1	Fever	63
Childbed	4	Gout	1
Chrisms	2	Grief	2
Griping in the Guts	23	Rising of the Lights	2
Headmouldshot	4	Smallpox	56
Jaundies	6	Stillborn	25
Imposthume	2	Stone	2
Livergrown	2	Stoppage in the Stomach	3
Looseness	7	Suddenly	1
Measles	6	Teeth	76
Palsie	2	Tissic	8
Purples	1	Thrush	3
Mortification	1	Vomiting	1
Rickets	4	Water in the Head	3
Consumption	60		

The important breakthrough seems to have come more through improvements in personal hygiene than through medical improvements. Most people in the eighteenth century had lice, which increased the incidence of disease. After about 1790 the use of soap increased as people began to wash more, with the result that they became less 'lousy'. Another way in which people were ridding themselves of lice was by the more frequent washing of their clothes. The cheap manufacture of cotton cloth as a result of the Industrial Revolution made cotton clothes more plentiful, and therefore encouraged people to wash them more often. Previously clothes were made of wool and were less plentiful, which discouraged people from washing them often, due to the tendency of wool to shrink and rot with frequent washing. Cotton clothes on the other hand could be boiled without damaging the fabric.

Environmental factors obviously played a critical part in the reduction of the death rate. The use of brick in place of timber in walls and of slate or stone in the roofs instead of thatch, reduced the number of disease-carrying pests.

Bubonic plague, carried by rats, seemed to have died out by the eighteenth century. One explanation put forward is that the old English black rat, which preferred living near human company in houses, was destroyed by the Norwegian brown rat which entered the country via the ports and preferred to live near docks or granaries rather than in human company.

Another factor lessening the incidence of disease was the removal of many noxious processes of manufacture from the homes of workers.

Malaria, also known as ague, died out during the eighteenth century, probably as a result of enclosure and the drainage of marshes, which resulted in the extinction of the mosquito.

Smallpox was treated from the 1720s onwards by the process of inoculation, and was the only disease in the eighteenth century upon which specific preventive therapy could conceivably have had a substantial effect. Throughout the century about 10 per cent of the deaths recorded in the London Bills of Mortality were attributed to smallpox, and a marked reduction in its incidence would undoubtedly have been reflected in national mortality trends.

Inoculation involved using infected material from patients with smallpox, and therefore it was a dangerous as well as an expensive practice. It was first tested on convicts, and its subsequent use was mainly restricted to the upper classes until the later years of the eighteenth century, by which time charitable funds made it possible for large numbers of persons of all classes to be inoculated. It seems unlikely though that inoculation in the eighteenth century can have reduced the incidence of smallpox sufficiently to have had a substantial effect on national mortality trends. The process was eventually superseded by vaccination, introduced in 1778, and finally made illegal in 1840.

The remaining killer diseases were cholera and typhus, and since these were water-borne diseases remedies for them were not found until the public health reforms of the late nineteenth century.

Migration was not a factor responsible for the growth of population since the number of emigrants exceeded the number of immigrants. During the eighteenth century probably as many as a million people left Britain to seek a living overseas, mainly in the colonies. Among them some 50,000 criminals were transported to Maryland or Botany Bay, and even though it was illegal, until the early nineteenth century, some workers took their technical skills to Europe where there was a growing demand for them.

Official attitudes towards migration have varied over the years according to whether or not there seemed to be a danger of over- or under-population. In Elizabethan times, when there was a high level of unemployment, colonisation was favoured as a remedy but by the eighteenth century the shortage of skilled workers resulted in laws being passed forbidding them to emigrate. Fears arising from over-population, no doubt as a consequence of Malthus's Essay, caused official attitudes to change once again during the 1820s.

After considering all the important evidence, it is fairly safe to conclude that the growth of population, which was probably the most critical factor in the 'take-off' stage for Britain in the eighteenth century, was more a result of a fall in death rates rather than an increase in birth rates, though birth rates undoubtedly rose mainly due to a change in the age of marriage.

The Agrarian Revolution

The rapid increase in population, particularly after 1750, meant that there were many more mouths to feed, and therefore agriculture had to become more efficient if it was to cope with the increase. Certainly, if an industrial revolution was to proceed very far and if there was to be sustained economic change, a much higher productivity was essential in farming. Also, since there was a greater proportionate increase of urban population, the country areas round about the manufacturing districts had to produce more for them. This was particularly the case after 1793, when the war against France broke out and seriously disrupted food supplies from abroad, making Britain more dependent on her own farms.

At the beginning of the eighteenth century farming had hardly changed since the middle ages. In the North and West, where the land was hilly and where sheep and cattle rearing were more important than crop growing, farms were generally enclosed and consisted of compact fields separated by fences and hedges, whilst further south, over much of the really fertile arable region of the country, open-field farming was still carried on. Villages in these areas usually consisted of three large fields divided into strips, one field being allowed to lie fallow, while the other two were planted with grain. The village animals were grazed on the common land, and the villagers had their ancient rights of grazing pigs, collecting wood and cutting turf on the waste, the rough marsh, and the scrub and woodland which lay beyond the common pasture.

This system of open-field farming was very inefficient but with a relatively small population of 6½ million people living in England, Scotland and Wales at the beginning of the eighteenth century these subsistence farming methods were sufficient to provide the nation's food requirements. With the rapid growth of population in the second half of the eighteenth century drastic improvements in farming methods were called for. The inefficiency of the system can be seen by the fact that the strips in the big fields were separated from each other by small walls of earth, and these, together with the pathways threading through the fields wasted an enormous amount of good land. Leaving a field fallow each year to recover its goodness was also very wasteful, and meant that only two thirds of the village land was really productive. The absence of hedges and fences allowed weeds to spread easily from one strip to the next and encouraged animals to stray into the growing crops.

Problems were also caused by the joint ownership and use of the common. Since a farmer did not own the common land he was reluctant to spend his time and money improving it; hence the village pasture land was frequently undrained and of poor quality. This often led to diseases among the livestock, and on unfenced common such diseases spread like wildfire. Hence the yield from an open-field village tended to be very low, probably about half the yield obtainable from an enclosed village of the same size.

If there was to be economic growth then there had to be agricultural change. Agriculture provided many of the raw materials for industry and the labour force, in many regions of the 'putting out' system, whereby people performed light industrial tasks in their own homes, was really a joint labour force with agriculture. Also capital and credit flows between the land and non-farming activities were intimately linked.

Fortunately, change on a massive scale in the eighteenth century was possible because of certain favourable background conditions.

1. *The ownership of land had, between 1500 and 1800, become much more highly concentrated in the hands of those who for various reasons were more likely to adopt the most efficient techniques.*

(a) The dissolution of the monasteries had taken away land from what had become a very conservative element in English life.

(b) The economic difficulties of the crown and the nobility between 1540 and 1640 resulted in much land passing into the hands of the gentry, who were much more likely to adopt new methods.

(c) The growth of estates during the early eighteenth century encouraged improvement. By the eighteenth century the English countryside was studded with estates, each with its hall or manor house. These family seats were most numerous in the home counties, but were also sprinkled around the country as a whole.

(d) Another influence bringing about concentration of ownership in the hands of a go-ahead group of people was the tendency for both successful merchants and professional men to buy large amounts of land to raise their social position. City men and manufacturers moved to the country for various motives; sometimes for the amenities it offered, sometimes as a step to Parliament, but often because they hoped that one day they might be on equal terms with the squires.

The traditional point of view of the effects of all this was that the peasantry in the eighteenth century in England, i.e. the class of small owner farmers, often called yeomen, declined rapidly. Care should be exercised in the interpretation and presentation of this point since recent research suggests that it is improbable that there was any disastrous decline of small farmers after the late eighteenth century. Professor Mingay says that the belief that there was a considerable decline in the numbers of small farmers working on the land from the later eighteenth century onwards rests on the exaggerated view of the effects of enclosure and the technical advantages of large units. He doubts how far the economies of scale in agriculture were important before the middle nineteenth century. However, there does appear to have been a fairly drastic decline of small owner-occupier farmers between the later seventeenth and eighteenth centuries. Socially, no doubt, this would have had its disadvantages, but economically this could have been of enormous benefit to the country because peasant farmers are nearly always resistant to change.

2. *The development of more scientific and commercial attitudes to farming encouraged agricultural change.* This brought about a more critical attitude to such problems as the breeding of animals and the growing of crops. The farmer immigrants who had gone with Charles II to France during the Civil War brought back many new ideas from the more advanced continent, and bodies like the Royal Society were founded soon after the Restoration. These ideas eventually permeated down to agricultural practice.

A number of new techniques were tried out by certain enterprising landlords whose success did much to change British agriculture. Amongst the most notable were:

Jethro Tull (*1674–1740*)

Tull was one of the first exponents of scientific farming, who, by observation and experiment, found the best level to sow seed, realising that carefully planned sowing as opposed to the traditional broadcast method was much more productive. This actually caused a strike among his field labourers who thought that seed ought to be sown as described in the Bible. In addition, he emphasised the importance of clean farming, and techniques such as deep hoeing and ploughing to get rid of the weeds, to break up the soil properly and to expose it to the air. For this purpose he developed a horse-hoe, which would have been too expensive and difficult to use under the open-field system.

Viscount (*Turnip*) *Townsend* (*1674–1738*)

Viscount Townsend was a notable politician who devoted his later years to improving farming. He had been British Ambassador in Holland, Lord-Lieutenant in Ireland, and a Secretary of State, and but for a quarrel with the Prime Minister, Robert Walpole, he might well have spent all his life in politics. Instead, he retired to his estate at Raynham in Norfolk, and spent the last eight years of his life putting it in order. He laid stress on the value of turnips both as a means of enriching the soil and as a valuable winter food for cattle. Perhaps his most important contribution was the Norfolk Four Course Rotation (for example, wheat, turnips, barley, clover), i.e. alternation of corn and root crops thus avoiding leaving the land fallow, which had previously been necessary in order to restore its full fertility. This led to a sharp increase in productivity on those farms where this rotation was practised.

Robert Bakewell (*1725–1795*)

Bakewell was the greatest early exponent of the scientific breeding of livestock. He used turnips as winter food, and this made possible fatter and better stock and the consequent increase in manure improved the land. His most important contribution was to develop the technique of carefully controlled selective breeding. He concentrated mainly on the breeding of sheep, and was most successful with the 'Leicester Shorthorns', choosing, for example, beasts which had short legs and heavy shoulders and flanks, and breeding only from these. By concentrating on quality of flesh and fatness, i.e. for meat rather than wool, spectacular increases in the average weight of sheep marketed were achieved. He also did some breeding work with cattle and horses.

His example soon encouraged progressive stock breeders all over the country to improve their stocks and herds by selective breeding, and their success can be seen from the following table of average weights of beasts sold at Smithfield market in London:

	1710	*1795*
Oxen	370 lb.	800 lb.
Calves	50 lb.	150 lb.
Sheep	38 lb.	80 lb.

Arthur Young (*1742–1820*)

Young was an unsuccessful farmer—in fact, his attempt to become a farmer ended in financial failure. However, in some ways, he was even more important than the innovators themselves for bright ideas had been practised locally for centuries, and what was really needed was a real diffusion of knowledge on a large scale. Through a long series of books, pamphlets and articles begun in 1767 he did much to influence better methods in agriculture. He travelled all over the country collecting information about up-to-date farms and persuaded leading farmers, including George III, to contribute articles to his farming magazine, *The Annals of Agriculture*. In 1793 he was appointed Secretary of the new Board of Agriculture, and collected evidence about agricultural conditions, appointing agricultural commissioners to do this work in the field. He aimed to spread knowledge of latest practices, and to stimulate interest in modern farming by such devices as ploughing matches, agricultural shows and farmers' clubs. He also wanted to see the tenant farmer having longer leases. In the last twenty years of the century, leases of seven, fourteen or twenty-one years became more common. He also advocated larger farms and heavier capital expenditure since the small farmer could not afford such items as heavy use of manure, high prices for good livestock and expensive drainage systems. Thus, Arthur Young made an important contribution to agricultural progress by giving publicity to the agrarian revolution.

Coke of Holkham (1752–1847)

Coke of Holkham was chiefly notable as a great exponent of successful farm management, and was probably the most famous farmer of his day. He emphasised the value of heavy manuring, and was able to produce wheat even on very sandy soil. His farm was transformed from a badly drained property into one of the most up-to-date farms in the country. Coke proved to be a model landlord, laying great stress on the need for improving farm cottages and encouraging his tenants to sink their own money into farm improvements by granting them longer leases. Each year at sheep-shearing time, from 1818 onwards, he held great house parties at which the latest techniques were demonstrated.

As a result of all this he enjoyed a great commercial success, and managed to raise his income from £2,000 to £20,000 a year.

3. *The Enclosure Movement, the idea of which was not new, was intensified during the eighteenth century.* Enclosure made possible the adoption of the best modern methods such as cattle-breeding, elaborate expenditure on drainage, the four-course rotation, and the use of machinery, like the horse-hoe. Moreover, it made possible a careful choice of tenants for whom capital expenditure was worthwhile. Enclosure was thus the most important single factor affecting land use because it made most of the other innovations possible.

The Enclosure Movement

As can be seen from Fig. 2, Britain in the first half of the eighteenth century was a net exporter of corn under the protection of the Corn Laws and the stimulus of corn bounties or subsidies after 1589. Thus, even in the first half of the eighteenth century, much hitherto waste land came to be used, and English farming was fairly prosperous. According to Clapham, country folk did well and their standard of living rose so that they were regularly eating fresh meat and wheaten bread. Moreover, Lord Ernie described Britain as the granary of Europe in the first fifty years of the century.

After 1760 the stimulus of the rise in population produced profound effects on British agriculture, and the country became a net importer of wheat after 1775. Moreover, the price of corn rose very sharply, and with new methods lowering the cost, really large profits could be made by a man of initiative. To take advantage of these new opportunities, it was usually essential to change over from the open-field system to enclosed land. Also, many of these developments needed large amounts of capital and so it was the owner-farmer or the substantial tenant who benefited at the expense of a declining peasantry.

After 1760 the pace of the enclosure movement, as measured by the number of enclosure acts, increased enormously, seven million acres being covered by parliamentary Enclosure Acts passed between 1760 and 1800 and a further 800 between 1800 and 1815. The pace of enclosure is therefore a very good guide to the progress of the agrarian revolution which, as Table 5 shows, speeded up around 1750, and reached a climax during the Napoleonic Wars when the demand for home grown wheat was at its height.

We should be wary in the interpretation of these figures about the rapidity of the changes, since enclosure might have taken place by private agreement without any Act and without leaving any contemporary record available to the historian. It should be remembered that

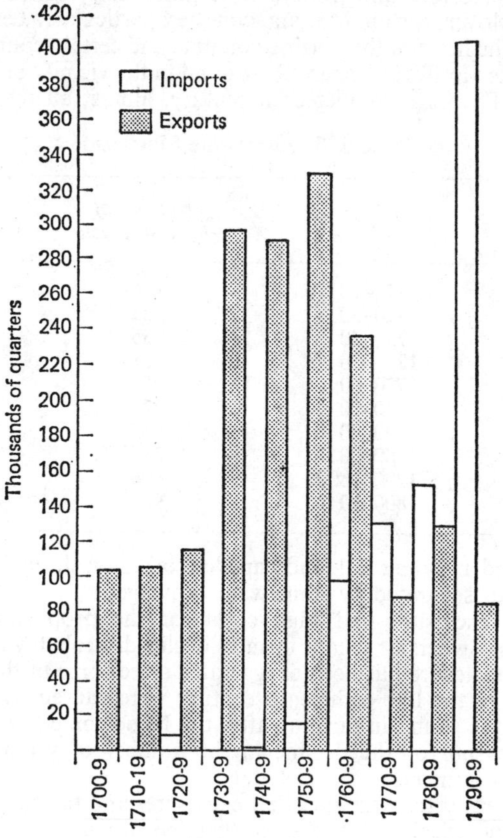

Fig. 2. The British corn trade (1700–1800).

enclosure by private Act of Parliament only gradually established itself as the normal procedure, and therefore, if the progress of enclosures is measured in terms of the Enclosure Acts passed, the quickening of the movement might tend to be exaggerated. Before 1750 most of the early enclosures were done by agreement or by purchase, or occasionally by fraud.

It was not until after 1750 that the Private Act of Parliament became the main method of enclosure. After the passing of an Enclosure Act specifying the land to be involved, enclosure commissioners were sent to visit and survey the parish and re-allot the land in an award that was legally binding on all parties. If the small peasant farmer could not afford his contribution to the joint cost of enclosure, then he lost the land. As a result, many tenants were evicted without any compensation.

There was a certain amount of enclosure in many parts of Britain but it was particularly intense in several areas. The East Anglian counties of Norfolk and Suffolk were particularly suited to growing wheat and clover; certain Midland counties, particularly Leicestershire, which was the heart of the grazing country; and certain counties around London, like Hertfordshire and Essex and in the vicinity of other growing towns. By the mid-nineteenth century, almost all the open fields

Table 5. The Enclosure Movement

Year	*Number of Enclosure acts*
1714–20	6
1720–30	33
1730–40	35
1740–50	38
1750–60	156
1760–70	424
1770–80	642
1780–90	287
1790–1800	506
1800–10	906

had vanished and the rural landscape had taken on the modern appearance of fields separated by stone walls or hedges.

Socially, enclosure had high costs for the proportion of small independent owners or tenant farmers declined. Probably the hardship caused by enclosure has been exaggerated since some of the difficulties in farming in the late eighteenth century were caused by the French Wars, and the slump in farming after the Napoleonic Wars was probably the reason for the decline in the number of yeoman or small independent farmers.

It is important to remember that enclosures and the agrarian revolution were inextricably linked since they led to the adoption of better methods, and hence higher productivity. Without this increased productivity the growth of a large urban population, in days before massive food imports were practicable, would have been impossible.

Availability of Essential Raw Materials

The vital raw materials in the early stages of the Industrial Revolution were iron and coal. Without these materials a country's economic development would have been severely handicapped, as was the case with France on account of her lack of coal resources.

Britain was fortunate, however, in having plentiful supplies of both iron and coal, and these resources were conveniently placed with regard to waterways, which were the cheapest means of transport for bulky materials before the development of railways. The technical inventions that facilitated the working of iron and coal resources will be dealt with later.

Improvements in Transport

Improvements in transport facilities were essential to the Industrial Revolution, since not only did the quantity of goods produced by capital and labour increase, but also there was a much greater degree of regional specialisation. Before the eighteenth century internal transport was confined to roads and trackways and to rivers and sea transport, and in this respect Britain was fortunate because inland water transport was provided by a number of rivers, and no place was more than 100 miles from the sea. Furthermore, Britain contained no dense forests or impassable mountain barriers.

Roads

The engineering of roads with a 'hard' surface, which the Romans had superimposed upon ancient trackways in Britain, became a lost art after their departure, and was not resurrected until the eighteenth century. For many centuries English roads were in a most unsatisfactory condition, thus greatly emphasising regional differences, so that when travellers left their native homes their distinctiveness became obvious both to themselves and to those whom they met. This was reflected in their speech, folklore, customs, diet and forms of recreation. Since the amount of travelling undertaken in the Middle Ages was insufficient to warrant the construction of a good system of roads, the authorities, both national and local, paid little attention to the problem.

Sometimes road maintenance was encouraged by the Church or monasteries, but no State action to improve the roads was taken until 1555, when a law was passed placing responsibility for the repair of the roads in each parish upon two surveyors appointed by the parishioners. Under this law each parish was expected to repair its own portion of the main road by ensuring that the men of the village did from four to six days unpaid work each year maintaining the roads. There were obvious weaknesses in this system, namely:

(i) The parishes were not large enough for the task and indifferent to the comfort of travellers passing through.

(ii) There was a real lack of expert knowledge since it was impossible to expect a person to attain proficiency in a task which occupied him for only a few days in the year. Hence unskilful work was performed under inexpert supervision.

A proper method of road repairs and maintenance was no one's concern. Ploughing them up, putting sand, gravel or pebbles on the surfaces and smoothing them over, constituted the maximum of maintenance achieved. People were thus invariably ignorant or indifferent when it came to the maintenance of the roads, and it was this system of parish-maintained roads which created the sort of conditions described by Arthur Young and many other eighteenth-century writers:

'Of all the cursed roads that ever disgraced this kingdom in the very ages of barbarism, none ever equalled that from Billericay to the King's Head at Tilbury. It is for near twelve miles so narrow that a mouse cannot pass by any carriage; I saw a fellow creep under his waggon to assist me to lift, if possible, my chaise over a hedge. The ruts are of an incredible depth—and a pavement of diamonds might as well be sought for as a quarter. The trees everywhere overgrow the roads, so that it is totally impervious to the sun except at a few places. And to add to all the infamous circumstances which concur to plague a traveller, I must not forget the eternally meeting with chalk-waggons, themselves frequently stuck fast till a collection of them are in the same situation, and twenty or thirty horses may be tacked to each to draw them out one by one.'

Arthur Young, *Six Weeks Tour*, 1768

Road improvements only became possible with the introduction of turnpike trusts, which were private companies that took over stretches of road from parishes, put them into a good state of repair and then, by charging tolls, ran them as profit-making concerns.

The first Turnpike Act was passed in 1663, but it was not until the second half of the eighteenth century that they became common, more than 450 such acts being passed between 1760 and 1774. By 1830 no fewer than 2,450 turnpike acts had been passed. This resulted in an improvement of the main roads towards the end of the eighteenth century, making it possible for large towns to be linked up by regular coaching services, but the by-roads and country lanes continued to remain in a state of poor repair, and Arthur Young even criticised the condition of some of the turnpike roads. The trouble with the managers of the turnpike trusts was that they were often more eager to collect tolls than they were to repair the roads, and they caused great inconvenience to the traveller by interrupting his journey at a multiplicity of toll gates where he had to pay cash.

The money which became available through tolls enabled the trusts to employ full-time paid workmen as road builders and menders, as well as architects and engineers who studied the problems of road foundation and shape, surface composition, gradients and other technical details. The three most famous engineers were:

1. *'Blind Jack' Metcalf* (1717–1810), who came from Knaresborough in Yorkshire, and had been blinded by smallpox at the age of six. Despite his disability 'Blind Jack' was a remarkable person who lived an unusually full life, being at various times soldier, farmer, publican, and road engineer. Between 1765 and 1792 Metcalf constructed 180 miles of turnpike road, mostly in Lancashire and Yorkshire, tapping his way across the moors with his hollow stick. Metcalf pioneered drainage, digging ditches along the sides of his roads and giving them a convex surface so that rainwater could run away easily.

2. *Thomas Telford* (1757–1834) was probably the greatest of all

British civil engineers. As engineer to the Government Commission for Highland Roads and Bridges he constructed nearly 1,000 miles of road and more than 100 bridges in Scotland. The magnificent Menai Straits Suspension Bridge and the Caledonian Canal were among his many engineering achievements. The most famous road which he built was the London–Holyhead road, begun in 1815, and renowned for its strong foundations, its gentle gradients, its moderate curvature, and the width of surface.

3. *John Macadam* (1756–1836) is perhaps the most well known of the road engineers because he developed a method of surfacing roads with small granite chippings, a system that still bears his name. Much of his work consisted of repairing and strengthening old roads with his new kind of surface rather than constructing new roads.

As a result of the introduction of turnpike roads and the achievements of road engineers there were by 1830 more than 22,000 miles of good road in the kingdom, resulting in a considerable saving of time on many journeys. For example, in 1750 a journey from London to Edinburgh undertaken in favourable conditions took ten days: by 1830 it could be done in two.

Canals

Navigable rivers, which had been used for generations to transport heavy goods, were deepened and widened in the early eighteenth century to increase their usefulness. But rivers were not always in the right place to serve industry, and they were liable to flood or drought, depending upon the time of year. These problems were overcome by the construction of artificial waterways.

The first English canal of the eighteenth century was the Sankey Navigation, completed in 1757, and stretching from the coalfield of St Helens down to the River Mersey at Warrington. This construction was financed by a group of Liverpool merchants and was originally planned as a river improvement enterprise.

The first English navigation route to be planned from its inception as a canal was the Bridgewater Canal, built by James Brindley between 1759 and 1761. The Duke of Bridgewater financed the project in order to transport coal from his mines at Worsley to Manchester, a distance of eleven miles. The canal proved to be a complete success resulting in the cost of coal in Manchester being halved. Brindley, who was semi-illiterate, was a remarkable man indeed. His aqueduct carrying the canal across the River Irwell was considered by some to be the eighth wonder of the world.

The completion of this canal opened an era of canal building. Between 1758 and 1802, 165 Acts of Parliament were passed authorising the construction of canals, this creating the chief arteries of the first phase of the industrial revolution. The trunk lines, started in the 1770s, created interior lines of communication connecting important industrial areas with the ports, and through them the outside world and export markets. The areas benefiting most were the South Wales coalfield, Lancashire, the West Riding of Yorkshire, the North Staffordshire potteries and the area around Birmingham, which became the hub of the English canal system. These new waterways made possible the transportation of raw materials, fuel, manufactured goods and farm produce in ever-increasing quantities and at lower cost.

The Growth of Markets

During the eighteenth century Britain's exports and imports expanded faster than ever before, as Table 6 indicates.

Care should be taken in interpreting these statistics since they are figures based on fixed prices and the import figures do not of course take account of the smuggling which was quite considerable at this time.

Wool was the most important export in the sixteenth and seventeenth centuries and imports were mainly luxuries like sugar, tea, tobacco and spices. Cloth exports doubled during the eighteenth century, and by 1800 new exports characteristic of an Industrial Revolution, such as iron and copper goods and steam engines, became important.

Under the pressure of a growing volume of trade and more peaceful trading conditions the old trading policies began slowly to change. The

Table 6. Total Trade, England and Wales 1700–90 (£ million)

	Imports	*Exports*	*Re-exports*
1700	5·8	3·7	2·1
1710	4·0	4·7	1·6
1720	6·1	4·6	2·3
1730	7·8	5·3	3·2
1740	6·7	5·1	3·1
1750	7·8	9·5	3·2
1760	9·8	11·0	3·7
1770	12·2	9·5	4·8
1780	10·8	8·0	4·6
1790	17·4	14·1	4·8

world markets were no longer thought of as limited and to be monopolised, and during the eighteenth century unlimited markets were visualised in Europe, America and the East which could be exploited if only trade were freer. This growth in trade, however, was not steady, and there were times when business fell off sharply: for example, between 1775 and 1780 because of the American War of Independence. It should also be noted that the rate of growth was much faster in the second half of the eighteenth century rather than the first, particularly after 1780, as Table 7 shows.

Being an island, and being geographically well placed for trade with Europe and America, Britain was in a good position to benefit from increased trade. She was also able to take advantage of the widespread Colonial system by forging new trading interests in the East and in the new colony of Australia.

Adam Smith's book *The Wealth of Nations*, published in 1776, provided the ideological basis for thinking men who were looking towards freer trade. Smith believed that the most powerful stimulus to growth was free enterprise and intense competition rather than government initiative. Some steps were taken in the direction of lower tariffs during the eighteenth century, but these efforts were frustrated by the outbreak of war with France in 1793.

Certain parts of Britain particularly benefited from the growth of

Table 7. Destination of Exports and Sources of Imports England and Wales (1700–1800)

(*Figures in £ million Official Values; annual average for each 5-year period*)

Area		*1701–5*	*1726–30*	*1751–5*	*1776–80*	*1796–1800*
North Europe	Exports	3·12	3·53	5·13	3·9	11·77
	Imports	1·35	1·53	1·22	1·6	2·68
Baltic	Exports	0·3	0·2	0·29	0·37	0·34
	Imports	0·48	0·61	0·97	1·61	3·19
Portugal and Spain	Exports	0·63	1·55	2·14	1·25	0·92
	Imports	0·41	0·79	0·68	0·75	1·22
Mediterranean Countries	Exports	0·6	0·85	1·00	0·75	0·74
	Imports	0·56	0·93	0·91	0·64	0·39
Africa	Exports	0·1	0·2	0·23	0·24	1·00
	Imports	0·02	0·04	0·04	0·06	0·07
East Indies	Exports	0·11	0·11	0·79	0·91	2·21
	Imports	0·55	1·00	1·12	1·30	4·83
British West Indies	Exports	0·31	0·47	0·71	1·24	4·38
	Imports	0·55	1·00	1·12	1·30	4·83
North America	Exports	0·27	0·53	1·30	1·30	6·79

Source: P. Mathias, *The First Industrial Nation.*

overseas trade. Bristol and Liverpool, for example, flourished on the African slave trade, which provided a profitable triangle of trade across the Atlantic; England exported trinkets, etc., to West Africa; slaves were then shipped to the West Indies and the profits of this trade were used to purchase sugar and tobacco, which were then imported into England. The prosperity that this trade brought is illustrated by the increase in Liverpool's population, which grew from 5,000 in 1700 to 77,000 in 1800.

Suggested Further Reading

Ashton, T. S., *An Economic History of England: The 18th Century*, O.U.P., Oxford and London, 1955.

Beales, H. L., *The Industrial Revolution, 1750–1850*, Cass, London, 1928.

Chambers, J. D., and Mingay, G. E., *The Agricultural Revolution, 1750–1880*, Batsford, London, 1966.

Court, W. H. B., *A Concise Economic History of Britain from 1750 to Recent Times*, C.U.P., Cambridge, 1954.

Deanne, P., *The First Industrial Revolution*, C.U.P., Cambridge, 1965.
Flinn, M. W., *Origins of the Industrial Revolution*, Longmans, London, 1966.
Glass, D. V., and Eversley, D. E. C. (editors), *Population in History, Essays in Historical Demography*, Edward Arnold, London, 1965.
Hartwell, R. M., *The Industrial Revolution and Economic Growth*, Methuen, 1971.
Hartwell, R. M. (editor), *Causes of the Industrial Revolution*, Methuen, London, 1967.
Mathias, P., *The First Industrial Nation*, Methuen, London, 1969.
Pressnell, L. S. (editor), *Studies in the Industrial Revolution*, Athlone Press, London, 1960.

Exercises

1. Why was England the first country to experience rapid and sustained economic growth?
2. Where did the money come from to finance the Industrial Revolution?
3. Discuss the view that population growth in the eighteenth century triggered off the Industrial Revolution.
4. For what reasons did British agriculture become more efficient in the eighteenth century?
5. Outline the most important improvements in transport between 1760 and 1830.
6. What advantages did England gain from her overseas trade in the eighteenth century?

Summary

1. Britain was the first country to have all the right ingredients for rapid and sustained industrialisation.
2. Parliamentary sovereignty and the rule of law provided the right background for increased savings and investment.
3. The rapid growth in population from 6½ million in 1750 to nearly 14 million in 1831 provided potentially more purchasing power, and therefore a wider home market. This increase in population was probably due more to a fall in death rates rather than an increase in birth rates, though birth rates did rise as a result of earlier marriages.
4. Massive food imports were impracticable in the eighteenth century; therefore improvements in agricultural techniques were essential to provide for the growth of a large urban population.
5. Britain had large supplies of iron and coal which were conveniently placed for transportation by water.
6. Road improvements in the eighteenth century were undertaken by a number of talented engineers, the most famous being Metcalfe, Telford and Macadam, and were financed mainly by the levying of tolls.
7. Before the advent of railways, canals made possible the transportation of bulky commodities such as raw materials, fuel, manufactured goods and farm produce.
8. Britain benefited in the eighteenth century from increased trade with Europe, America and the East, and some steps were taken before the end of the century to stimulate trade by reducing tariffs.

CHAPTER THREE

THE GROWTH OF INDUSTRY

As we have seen, significant changes took place in economic development during the second half of the eighteenth century, resulting in a far greater number of workpeople and a far larger amount of capital being drawn into a bigger scale of enterprise, than ever before. This took place against a background of minimal state intervention.

The Influence of the State on Economic Development

A modern society would find it extremely difficult to achieve an Industrial Revolution without the energetic support of its government, yet in Britain the Industrial Revolution was not a product of government planners or economists. The State did not consciously promote innovation or investment, except through its military ventures, which only involved the construction of a few dockyards and ordnance works. The State also chose, for a long time, to ignore the evil consequences of economic growth such as bad sanitation and poor living and working conditions. In fact, after 1750, there was a growing hostility towards most forms of government control over economic and social life. This could be seen in the movement towards the encouragement of self-help in the provision of welfare, which was an attempt to reduce the dependence of the poor on the State. The hatred of monopoly and the desire for competition were reflected in the lapsing of most of the monopoly privileges granted to the early chartered companies. The first step taken towards a free trade policy was the Trade Treaty with France as early as 1786, though the Napoleonic Wars delayed any further extension of the free trade idea.

Certain government measures hampered and restricted economic enterprise, as was the case with the Bubble Act of 1720, which restricted partnerships in joint stock companies to six, all of whom had unlimited liability. This measure was harmful to industrial growth and resulted in the emergence of an unbalanced banking system during a period of critical development. That is not to say that government in Britain deliberately sought to obstruct the Industrial Revolution: on the contrary, governments endeavoured to help the owners of property, who after 1688, were no longer at the mercy of absolute monarchy. They also helped economic development by extending markets and sources of raw materials through their policies of war and diplomacy. On the home front the patent laws encouraged innovation and Parliament became the authority for the granting of legal powers for enclosures, turnpike trusts and canals.

The Pioneers of Industrialism

The early pioneers of industrialism in the eighteenth century came from every social class, including the nobility, and from all parts of the country. George III himself, who was known as Farmer George, was keenly interested in agricultural improvements. Agriculture produced many textile manufacturers. Some prosperous yeomen had old textile connections through domestic weaving, and others on a higher social scale worked the minerals on their properties, or contributed, as the Duke of Bridgewater did, to new forms of transport. Men from all walks of life found in manufacture possibilities of advancement far greater than in their earlier occupations. The famous cotton spinner, Richard Arkwright, was originally a barber, whilst the leading figure in the North of England iron industry, Samuel Walker, had been a schoolmaster. Samuel Smiles later on in the nineteenth century was to extol fully the virtues of individual enterprise. The experience of the Industrial Revolution was to provide him with numerous examples of self-made men who started life penniless, and later achieved great wealth and influence.

The development of a keen interest in improvements in industry was helped by the exclusion of religious dissenters from jobs in universities, politics, the Civil Service and the Armed Forces, which meant that talented and enterprising non-conformists had to look for career opportunities elsewhere. People who were bold enough to seek out new forms of worship were often the types who were attracted towards new and unconventional careers in industry. Non-conformists were also usually better educated, particularly Scotsmen, for the Scottish education system in the eighteenth century was greatly superior to the English. Moreover, non-conformist religious beliefs encouraged the essential virtues of thrift and hard work, and a much stronger sense of economic values.

New Technology

New techniques and methods of production enabled Britain to produce commodities at a fraction of their former cost, in terms of the amount of land, labour and capital devoted to their production, as well as making it possible to produce new products which no amount of effort and resources could have produced in the past. The development of technology was one of the most important features of the Industrial Revolution, since certain key inventions set the pace of its progress, but it is important to remember that ingenious minds have existed in every age and technological progress is not a new phenomenon. Some of the most fundamental breakthroughs, such as the invention of the wheel or the control of fire, were made many thousands of years ago and compare favourably in their impact with anything that the modern age can offer. What was unique about the period since the eighteenth century was the rapidity, depth and constancy of the flow of new technology. Technological progress became systematic and dependable, not just a store of ad hoc achievements inherited from the past.

It would appear from the evidence that the wave of inventions during the Industrial Revolution were probably more due to 'practical tinkerers' experimenting on the basis of trial and error than a product of the educational system of the country.

The people who made the greatest contribution seem to have been the inspired amateurs or craftsmen, such as the clocksmiths, wheelwrights or blacksmiths rather than the professional inventor. Obviously there were exceptions, such as James Watt, a mathematical instrument maker, who benefited from contacts with a Scottish university, and whose work therefore had a scientific basis.

In considering the accelerated pace of technological invention in the eighteenth century it is important to note that inventions are cumulative, and that they tend to interact upon one another. Entrepreneurs anxious to extend their demand frequently cut their prices, and thus sought new innovations to cut costs. Often an invention that transforms one phase in a long series of processes of production breaks an equilibrium and necessitates further innovation. The cotton industry of the eighteenth century provides the classic example of this process. The adoption of Kay's flying shuttle, enabling one weaver to operate a loom previously requiring two, created a growing shortage of cotton yarn, as the weavers now worked too quickly for the spinners to keep them supplied. This generated an incentive to develop an innovation in spinning, the result of which was Hargreaves' spinning jenny.

The numbers of patents sealed (Table 8) give some indication of the growth of technical experiment and progress.

Table 8. Numbers of Patents Sealed (1750–1850)

Decade	*Totals*
1750–9	92
1760–9	205
1770–9	294
1780–9	477
1790–9	647
1800–9	924
1810–19	1,124
1820–9	1,462
1830–9	2,453
1840–9	4,581

Source: Robin M. Reeve, *The Industrial Revolution 1760–1850.*

The most important invention, shaping the whole course of industrialisation, was the steam engine, since it became the means for applying basic innovations in so many industries and transport.

The practical use of steam power had been known to the ancient Greeks, but it was not until the seventeenth century that an effective method of harnessing it had been devised, when Thomas Savery demonstrated his 'atmospheric' fire engine. This engine was used successfully for pumping water from Cornish copper mines, but unfortunately the engine had no safety valve and therefore was a dangerous device and explosions did happen.

The first engine that was commercially useful was developed by Thomas Newcomen in 1706 and put to work in a colliery in 1712. This engine had only a reciprocating, as distinct from a rotary motion action, and therefore was used for pumping water from coal mines rather than for turning machinery in industry. One of its most serious drawbacks was its wasteful fuel consumption.

It was James Watt who found the remedy for excessive fuel consumption by inventing in 1765 a separate condenser which immediately doubled the thermal efficiency of the Newcomen engine. Watt's experiments were financed by Dr John Roebuck and, after Roebuck's bankruptcy, by the Birmingham hardware manufacturer, Matthew Boulton. The steam engine patented by Watt in 1769 was a reciprocating type, the same as Newcomen's, but in 1781 he devised a system of gear wheels, called a 'sun and planet' motion, which was particularly well

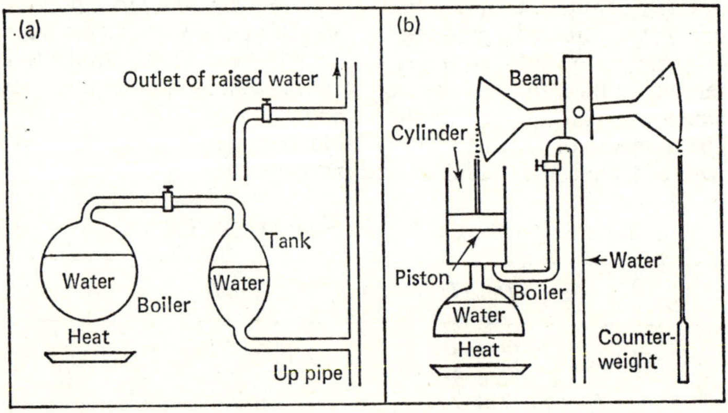

Fig. 3(a). Thomas Savery's engine (1698).

The water in the boiler is heated to make steam, which passes, when the valve is opened, into the tank. The tank is then doused with water from a pipe above, and the steam condenses, creating a partial vacuum. Thus, water is drawn up the pipe, and forced out.

(b) Newcomen's engine (1706).

Water is heated in the boiler to make steam, which passes into the cylinder and forces the piston up, assisted by the counterweight. Water is then admitted into the cylinder. The steam condenses and creates a partial vacuum, thus drawing the piston back down again. A seesaw motion is set up which is used to drive a pump.

suited to the driving of machinery and which was eventually applied to a whole range of manufacturing industry, as well as to transport.

Despite the obvious advantages of Watt's engincs over the Newcomen and Savery types, research has shown that large numbers of both types were produced as late as the nineteenth century, though after this the Watt engine became supreme. The reason for this was that the Watt engines, protected by patent, were expensive to instal due to the monopoly of Boulton and Watt in their manufacture, and since fuel waste was not a critical factor on the coalfields, colliery owners for a time found it cheaper to instal Newcomen engines. Also it is sometimes overlooked that Newcomen's engine, like Watt's, could be adapted to a rotative motion by means of a crank and flywheel, and many were so adapted after 1780, but the Newcomen engine's motion proved to be less regular than that of Watt's and the fuel consumption was greater. Nevertheless, in many operations, such as winding coal from pits, grinding corn and crushing seeds, these drawbacks were not considered to be important.

The adoption of the steam engine was a slow process, and it is important not to exaggerate the rate at which steam power was adapted for use by industry (see Fig. 4). The early steam engines were mainly

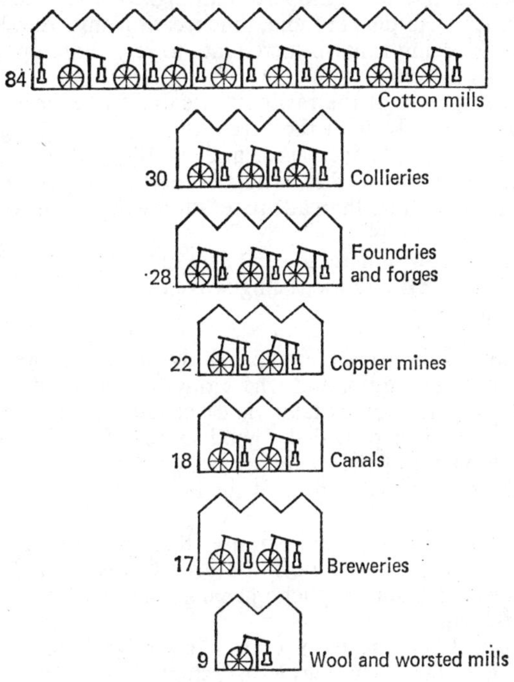

Fig. 4. Use of Boulton and Watt steam engines in Industry (1775–1800).

employed in the mining, iron and textile industries, and their widespread use in manufacturing industry did not not come until the second half of the nineteenth century. The cotton industry, for example, from which the greatest demands for steam engines came, still used 30 per cent of water power in 1830 to drive its mills whilst the weaving side of the woollen industry employed hardly any steam power at all. It must be remembered that the early steam engines were individually made, and there were no standardised spare parts. If a machine broke down, as often happened, it had to be repaired by skilled engineers from the original makers, which was a costly and inconvenient process.

Development of the Basic Industries

Textiles

Cotton

The Cotton Industry became much more important during the second half of the eighteenth century due to a number of new developments.

1. It was stimulated by the imposition of duties on imported cloth from India.
2. The death of the Mogul Emperor Aurangzeb in 1707 caused a long period of political disorders in India, thus creating unfavourable trading conditions and forcing English merchants to rely more upon the products of English industry.
3. Before 1790 most of the raw cotton came from the West Indies, but from then onwards, with the invention of the cotton gin, cotton imports from the U.S.A. increased, and by 1850 80 per cent of our imports came from the U.S.A. This meant that by the end of the eighteenth century a more than adequate supply of cotton was available from this source.
4. Population growth increased and demand for clothing, and cotton proved to be a versatile fabric, being woven and printed into a great variety of forms.

The new cotton industry grew up mainly in Lancashire, where the climate was cool and damp, and where raw cotton could conveniently be imported from the United States via Liverpool. Also, the fast-flowing streams of the Pennines provided a good source of water power whilst, with the development of the steam engine, proximity to vast quantities of coal facilitated the switch-over of the industry from water to steam power.

The cotton textile industry, to use Rostow's terminology, was Britain's leading sector in 'take-off'. In other words, it was the industry which spearheaded Britain's phenomenal economic development since the eighteenth century.

Up to about 1780, the early cotton industry was almost entirely organised as a cottage or domestic industry where weaving was men's work, women spun and children prepared the material. This specialisation within the family would have been idyllic had it not been for the fact that a single weaver used as much yarn as three or four spinners could provide. This meant that weavers who lacked an adequate number of female dependants had to make up the deficiency by employing unattached spinners or spinsters.

The first of the great inventions was Kay's flying shuttle, invented in 1733. This shuttle was designed for use with the ordinary handloom, and consisted mainly of a picking-peg contrivance which enabled the weaver to jerk the shuttle to and fro through the warp, using one hand. This speeded up the work of the weaver, and enabled him to weave a wider cloth.

This was an invention affecting weaving and not spinning, and was not a very logical development since weaving was already a quicker process than spinning. Hence it was rather ahead of its time, and therefore not widely adopted.

As a result of the scarcity of yarn in the cotton industry, the family economy began to break down. It also provided incentives for the introduction of improved machines and a factory system in spinning.

An early attempt to mechanise the spinning process was made by Lewis Paul in 1738, but failed because of mechanical defects.

The really important innovation in spinning began with Hargreaves' spinning jenny of 1765. By the 1760s there was a pressing need for more thread and Hargreaves' machine met this need. This machine was based on a comparatively simple extension of the principle of the spinning wheel, and did not at first involve either the use of power or the introduction of a factory system. Whereas the spinning wheel turned only one spindle, and spun only one thread at a time, the jenny carried several spindles on a simple framework, and spun several threads. This invention did not involve a revolution in the manufacture of cotton goods, because the jenny could still be used in private houses, as it was worked by hand. At first the jenny may have helped to revive the domestic industry, since it made it easier for the weaver to supply himself with yarn by the labour of his wife and family.

The next spinning invention, Arkwright's frame (1769), took the industry out of the cottage into the mill since it was a machine which proved to be too heavy for human motive power, and had to be driven by a water wheel. The water frame consisted of four pairs of rollers rotating with progressive rapidity, so that the thread became finer and finer as it was drawn through the rollers, finishing up by being wound onto spindles at the far end of the machine. This machine worked faster than the jenny, and the product was much stronger, providing the warp for an all cotton cloth, whereas previously a linen thread had been used. This invention meant that cloth was now being made in England entirely out of cotton, and within half a century the manufacture of cotton cloth had replaced woollen manufacture as the country's most important and prosperous industry.

Having no capital of his own, Arkwright made a contract with two merchant manufacturers of hosiery, Need of Nottingham and Strutt of Derby, who enabled him to establish in 1771 his first factory in Derbyshire where he used the swift-running streams as his source of power. In the late 1770s he returned to Lancashire, and this gave the local industry a tremendous boost.

Although Arkwright patented this invention, his claim to have invented it is doubtful since his forte was as a businessman rather than an inventor, and evidence does seem to indicate other possible sources of origin.

When the patent for the machine eventually lapsed in 1785, which meant that the water frame could be used by any manufacturer, Arkwright continued to prosper, and in spite of his humble beginnings as a travelling barber and wigmaker, he became the owner of great factories and was probably worth about £500,000 at the time of his death.

Samuel Crompton's 'mule' (1776) was the third spinning invention of importance. It was a cross between the jenny and the water frame in which Arkwright's rollers were combined with Hargreaves' moving carriage, the result being a thread of unprecedented fineness, suitable for muslin and other delicate fabrics. The machine was for some years used only in cottages, and did not really begin to take its place as the most important spinning instrument until about 1790, when it was adopted on a large scale for use with a water-wheel. From then on the cottage industry in spinning began to die out, and there was the employment of a larger proportion of adults in factories.

By the 1790s spinning output was far outrunning weaving, thus creating incentives for the development of improvements in weaving. The first of these was devised by an enterprising clergyman in 1785, Edmund Cartwright. His power loom, a clumsy contrivance of weights and springs, was not technically very successful, and the numbers of handloom weavers continued to expand rapidly, particularly during and just after the Napoleonic Wars, when money for new enterprises was scarce. It was not until 1813 that the first practical power loom was developed by William Horrocks of Stockport, by which time the supply of weavers had adjusted itself to the supply of yarn, and their high earnings were beginning to fall, with the result that power was not extensively employed before the 1830s. As late as the 1840s, in spite of the rapid mechanisation of the textile industry, there were still as many as 200,000 poverty-stricken handloom weavers in existence competing against the more productive machines.

Thus, from the 1780s onwards, numerous millstone grit factories were constructed alongside streams in the beautiful valleys of Lancashire and Derbyshire as the factory system replaced the domestic system in textile manufacture.

After the Napoleonic Wars tall chimneys, which contaminated the clear air of the Pennines, began to appear in ever increasing numbers as steam power was quickly adopted. Before the advent of steam power, cotton manufacture continued to be mainly a rural industry and the need for water power during the early stages of industrialisation led to the further dispersion of the industry to rural settings, particularly in Lancashire. Steam power reversed this trend, and led to the expansion of urban centres of cotton production within easy access of ample coal supplies, such as Manchester, Bolton and Oldham.

The Woollen Industry

This industry is the oldest of the great manufacturing industries of this country, and until the early years of the nineteenth century woollen and worsted goods were the largest item among the exports of British manufactured commodities. It was located mainly in the West Country, East Anglia and the West Riding of Yorkshire, though before the Industrial Revolution cloth was woven almost everywhere in the country.

The woollen industry was slower than the cotton industry in adopting mechanisation, mainly because it was much older and therefore had a stronger craft tradition which resisted technical change. Halevy observed that: 'Whatever desire they might feel to force the rate of production, the capitalists were obliged to consider the attachment shown by the workmen for their old organisation and old plant.' Also, the industry was encouraged to remain labour intensive after 1815 because of the abundant supplies of labour available due to population growth, demobilised soldiers, and large numbers of Irish immigrants.

The two main forms of woollen production are worsted, which uses the long fibre, and wool, which uses the short and so proved less adaptable to machinery.

By 1815 worsted spinning was done in the mills, but the worsted industry as a whole did not become predominantly a factory trade until about 1860. Power looms replaced handlooms only very slowly and handloom weaving in the woollen section did not cease to be of substantial importance until the last quarter of the nineteenth century. Meanwhile, Yorkshire, being more progressive than the other centres of woollen production and endowed with ample supplies of wool, coal and cheap labour, became the most important area for the manufacture of woollen cloth.

Iron

Iron has been in common use since early times, and even in the middle ages iron-making was based on capitalist methods, since primary iron production could not be undertaken by the small craftsmen, partly for technical reasons and partly because they could not afford the large sums of money that would be needed.

Until the middle of the eighteenth century charcoal was used for the smelting of iron, and thus contributed towards the depletion of the forests which formerly covered a large part of the country. As a result of a growing shortage of wood in the sixteenth and seventeenth centuries the industry became very dispersed, the main areas being the Sussex Weald, the Forest of Dean, and the Wrekin district of Shropshire. Because of the importance of timber for naval construction, restrictions were imposed on the use of timber for smelting, resulting in only 18,000 tons of iron being produced per year around 1750.

A number of technological advances during the eighteenth century resulted in a vast expansion of the industry.

1. The Quaker, Abraham Darby, was the first man to use coke for smelting iron ore at his works at Coalbrookdale, thus freeing the industry from dependence on diminishing and expensive supplies of wood. The reason why coke was appropriate for smelting as distinct from coal was that coal contains sulphur which makes iron brittle. Hence, Darby burnt off the sulphur in the coal to make coke.

Darby had used coke successfully in his blast furnace as early as 1709, but the adoption of this process was slow due to a basic failure to understand the chemistry of iron manufacture. Not every coal made a coke suitable for smelting iron ore, and it took several decades to achieve a knowledge of mix and finished product that made it possible to make use of less favourable materials.

2. Coke smelting required a stronger blast, which was achieved in 1776 when John Wilkinson combined the cast-iron blowing cylinder developed around 1760 with Watt's rotative steam engine.

3. Nielson's hot air blast (1828) made it possible to achieve very high temperatures in the blast furnace by the use of waste gas from the furnace. The process economised greatly in the use of fuel, which particularly benefited the Scottish iron industry. By 1830 it was possible to obtain a ton of pig iron with three and a half tons of coal, compared with one ton of pig iron to eight tons of coal in the 1790s.

4. Between 1740 and 1742, Benjamin Huntsman, a Sheffield iron manager, improved the process for making high-grade steel by more accurately controlling the quantities of carbon used in its manufacture through the use of the crucible. The big drawback to this development was that only small quantities could be made in this way and a real advance in steel-making had to wait until the second half of the nineteenth century, when a series of technical advances made the cheap mass production of steel a reality.

5. The production of cheap and abundant wrought iron, a malleable iron, from cast iron, was due to Henry Cort, who in 1784 perfected the processes of puddling and rolling, whereby the pig iron was heated with coal and stirred, or puddled, until the impurities had been removed. The metal was then passed between rollers which turned the iron into the desired shape.

These technical advances in the iron industry turned iron for the first time into a cheap commodity available for a variety of new purposes. Elegant iron bridges crossed rivers; graceful iron balconies adorned Georgian houses; iron provided the basic raw material for the steam engineering industries; and the Black Country metal trades and machines, which previously had consisted of wood or leather with only their working edges made of metal, could now be constructed wholly in iron, thus adding to the precision of their functioning.

These technical advances, together with the heavy duties on imported iron from abroad, and the growing demand for iron generally, as the Industrial Revolution progressed led to a rapid expansion of the industry. The output of iron trebled between 1780 and 1830, from 200,000 tons to 600,000 tons, and then more than trebled again during the next twenty years. As the industry expanded during the early nineteenth century the older centres of production declined and South Wales became the most important iron producing area.

Coal

The industrial developments of the eighteenth century required a rapid expansion of the coalmining industry, but even before this coal was already taking the place of charcoal in a wide variety of industries. During the sixteenth and seventeenth centuries, when output rose from less than a quarter million tons to three million tons, mining was carried on in a rural rather than an urban setting, and the miners combined their work in the pits with work on the land during the months of harvest. Coal deposits were discovered when they outcropped on the surface, so that the mining of it required simple digging or tunnelling into the side of hills, but as early as the eighteenth century miners were compelled to exploit lower layers of coal and pitshafts often reached depths of 200 ft.

The growing demand for coal in the sixteenth and seventeenth centuries was brought about mainly by the growth of population and the expansion of such industries as brewing, distilling, brickmaking, pottery, sugar refining, soapboiling, cutlery, nailmaking and glass. This was in a country that was almost denuded of its forests and therefore in great need of new sources of thermal energy.

Demand was further boosted during the eighteenth century when coke was introduced as a substitute for coal, which meant that it could be used in place of wood in important industries such as iron smelting. The developments that took place in steam power during the eighteenth century provided further demands for coal, but these were modest compared with the demands made from this source in the nineteenth century.

As the demand for coal grew, and pits became deeper, the technical difficulties of mining increased and a number of problems had to be overcome by technical advances.

1. Flooding underground became a serious problem. To sink a pit is to dig a well, as water from the surrounding soil drains into the pit, making it impossible to work a coal seam unless continuous pumping is carried on. Before the eighteenth century water was pumped from the mines mainly by hand, but sometimes in the deeper pits the pumps were worked by various contrivances, such as windlasses, treadmills, horse gins, windmills and water-wheels. The solution to this problem was found in the development of the steam engine. As early as 1698 Savery produced a primitive steam pump which was improved upon by Newcomen in 1712, which in turn was followed by Watt's engine after 1769. It should be remembered that even though Watt's engine was much more efficient than Newcomen's, the Newcomen engine continued to compete with Watt's steam engine on the coalfield until the late nineteenth century since the economy of fuel achieved by the use of the Watt engine was not an important consideration to the colliery owner.

2. The miner's life was also threatened by suffocation and fire through problems of ventilation. Without a good supply of fresh air miners could not work properly, and poisonous and explosive gases were liable to collect underground. This was dealt with at first by the use of two shafts, with burning coals creating a draft through convection, so that fresh air was blown down one shaft and stale air expelled by the other. This was an unsatisfactory form of ventilation though, because gas drawn out of the mine frequently ignited when it came into contact with the burning coals, and serious accidents resulted. By the 1840s the problem had been solved by using powerful steam driven fans.

3. Lighting below ground was a difficult problem due to the danger from explosive gases. The chief cause of the trouble in the earlier and smaller pits was chokedamp, or carbonic acid gas. The danger here was not so great since chokedamp put out the miner's candle, but in the larger and later pits the main risk arose from firedamp or marsh gas, which exploded without warning when it came into contact with the miner's candle. Explosions were frequent and caused great loss of life.

Various attempts were made to produce light below ground. Flint and steel and putrescent fish were all tried as illuminants, but without success. The problem was that it was dangerous to use naked flames in a mine, yet a flame cannot be entirely enclosed since a supply of oxygen is necessary for its maintenance. This difficulty was overcome by Sir Humphrey Davy in 1815, when he constructed a lamp which by the use of wire gauze made it possible for air to reach the flame, and as the flame would not pass through the cold gauze, the outside gases could not be ignited. This did not lead to any considerable decrease in the number of colliery accidents since one of its primary effects was to encourage the working of deeper and more dangerous pits, but it did have the effect of causing an increase in the output of coal.

4. The transport of coal, both on the surface and underground, created still further problems. This was dealt with by the construction of railways and the introduction of winding gear in the deeper pits for bringing coal to the surface. The transportation of coal over a distance of miles was greatly facilitated before 1830 by the development of the canal system and the expansion of coastal shipping.

As a result of overcoming these supply problems in order to meet the increased demand, coal output rose from $4\frac{3}{4}$ million tons in 1750 to 16 million tons in 1830.

When studying industrial developments one should be careful not to view particular industries in isolation. The cotton industry was the first industry to be industrialised but the expansion of the iron and coal industries and the improvement of the steam engine as a source of industrial power were indispensable to widespread industrialisation. The connection between the various industries usually was very close. For example, the steam engine was originally used to produce more coal, coal produced more iron, and iron produced more engines.

Suggested Further Reading

Ashton, T. S., *Iron and Steel in the Industrial Revolution* (2nd ed.), Manchester University Press, Manchester, 1951.

Ashton, T. S., and Sykes, J., *The Coal Industry in the 18th Century* (2nd ed.), Manchester University Press, Manchester, 1964.

Hartwell, R. M., *The Industrial Revolution in England*, Historical Association, London, 1966.

Mantoux, P., *The Industrial Revolution of the 18th Century*, Cape, London, 1961.

Mathias, P., *The First Industrial Nation*, Methuen, London, 1969.

Pollard, S., *The Genesis of Modern Management: A Study of the Industrial Revolution in Great Britain*, Methuen, London, 1965.

Reeve, R. M., *The Industrial Revolution 1750–1850*, London University Press, London, 1971.

Robson, R., *The Cotton Industry in Britain*, Macmillan, London, 1957.

Exercises

1. In what ways did the government help, and how did it hinder economic development in the period 1760 to 1830?

2. Trace the contribution of new technology to industrial progress in the eighteenth century.

3. What factors made innovation a regular and dependable flow as distinct from a collection of isolated and unrelated achievements from the past?

4. Britain's take-off between 1783 and 1802 into self-sustained growth was in the cotton textile industry. Discuss.

5. To what extent did Britain's economic growth after 1760 depend upon the development of her coal and iron industries?

Summary

1. There was a growing hostility after 1750 towards most forms of Government control over economic life; consequently industrialisation took place against a background of minimal state intervention.

2. The pioneers of industrialism came from all walks of life, though the non-conformists made a special contribution mainly because of their better education and their exclusion from important jobs connected with the State.

3. Technological progress in the eighteenth century became systematic and dependable rather than a store of *ad hoc* achievements inherited from the past.

4. The cotton textile industry spearheaded Britain's rapid economic development in the late eighteenth century and became the leading sector in 'take-off'.

5. The woollen industry adopted machinery more slowly than the cotton industry because it was an older industry with a stronger craft tradition which resisted technical change.

6. A number of technical advances in the eighteenth century turned iron into a cheap commodity and made it available for a variety of new purposes.

7. The increased demand for coal in the eighteenth century was met by the solving of a number of supply problems, the most prominent of which were the underground dangers arising from water, poisonous air and explosive gases.

CHAPTER FOUR

WAR AND THE INDUSTRIAL REVOLUTION

The early stages of the Industrial Revolution took place at the same time as a number of momentous wars. The most important of these were:

1. The Seven Years' War (1756–63), resulting in both India and Canada developing under British rather than French rule.
2. The American War of Independence (1775–83), involving the loss of important colonies.
3. The long wars with France between 1793 to 1815, known as the Napoleonic Wars.

During the American War of Independence, command of the sea was temporarily lost and trade declined, but during both the Seven Years' War and the Napoleonic Wars there was an expansion of overseas trade.

Britain's influence in the Caribbean was extended during the Seven Years' War by acquiring the greater part of the West Indies, and in the wars against Napoleon continental trade was disrupted, which shifted the pivot of European Atlantic commerce towards Britain, resulting in an expansion of exports of nearly 4 per cent per annum, which was a higher rate of growth than either before or after the Wars.

The Napoleonic Wars influenced the course of Britain's economic development, during a critical period of the industrialisation process, in the following ways:

1. Small farmers, who were threatened by the changes brought about by the agrarian revolution, were in a better position to survive during the inflationary period of war, since all but the least efficient producers could show a profit. The number of smallholdings did not decline until after the war.
2. The shortage of grain encouraged rapid enclosures and the utilisation of waste and marginal land.
3. War demands created a high level of employment and stimulated industry generally. Amongst the industries to benefit were the metal and textile industries, though the French wars were, on the whole, more favourable to the metal industries than to the textile manufacturers. Because of the demands for weapons and war equipment, the iron industry did particularly well. There was the general introduction of the improved puddling and rolling processes and inventions were induced such as John Wilkinson's device for boring cannon. Certain areas of the economy, however, were adversely affected by the wars. Iron exports, for example, suffered, and there was a decline in the construction of workshops, canals and highways.

4. The most important single economic effect of the wars was the impact of inflation. This was caused mainly by the considerable increase in Government spending, which was paid for in the first few years by money raised through the Bank of England rather than through taxation. This helped to cause a drain of gold from the Bank, which in 1797 was compelled to suspend cash payments, which were not resumed again until 1821. This meant that in future payments were made by an ever increasing supply of notes issued by a rapidly growing number of small country banks. This resulted, of course, in inflation.

Inflation increased economic buoyancy and the level of employment, which in turn improved our capability to bring the war with France to a successful conclusion. It also adversely affected the welfare of the workers since prices, profits and wages rose, but wages did not rise as fast as prices and profits, and, moreover, wages rose unevenly over the country as a whole and in different sorts of jobs. Hence, during the war, much distress was experienced by many of the workers, who were in addition having to cope with the structural upheavals brought about by the Industrial Revolution.

Post-War Distress

For the farmer and the manufacturer war had meant high prices for their commodities, and the immediate economic consequences of peace were disastrous for them both. As prices fell after the war the number of bankruptcies among farmers rose enormously and this naturally meant a higher level of unemployment for the labourers.

Prices generally in 1814 as a result of inflation were about twice what they had been before the outbreak of the war, but by 1816 they were about one and a third times the pre-war figure, and apart from a temporary recovery in 1818 they continued to fall. The reaction of the landlords and farmers, who dominated Parliament, was to pass the Corn Law of 1815, completely banning the importation of corn unless the price fell below the high level of eighty shillings a quarter. This aroused considerable anger among the free traders and the industrialists and their workers, who saw the measure simply as a means whereby the landlord could keep the price of bread high. The landowners, on the other hand, argued that cheaper bread would simply mean a chance for industrialists to pay their workers less money.

The falling prices also adversely affected industry because they checked the expansion of business and discouraged the borrowing of capital. Also, the coming of peace meant the end of a considerable market for the iron, munitions and textile industries, leading to the closing of many factories. Unemployment rose as 300,000 men from the armed services were demobilised and thrown onto the labour market, thus increasing the burden of welfare relief on the rates.

During the war the National Debt had swelled from a level of £228 million in 1793 to a total in 1816 of £876 million, which meant that taxes had to remain high after the war in order to pay the interest, and the burden of that interest obviously became greater as a result of the fall in prices.

Furthermore, the abolition in 1816 of Income Tax, imposed by Pitt as a wartime expedient, meant that the poor had to make a disproportionate contribution to the Exchequer since the bulk of the ordinary revenue was raised by means of indirect taxes on such goods as sugar, tea, beer, spirits and tobacco of which the lower classes were big consumers.

Not surprisingly, therefore, the years after 1815 were a time of desperate discontent and turmoil, and were marked by an increase in violence. This discontent and violence only strengthened the Government's determination to defend the position of their own class, believing that if they gave an inch there would be no knowing where the changes might end.

Suggested Further Reading

Ashton, T. S., *Economic Fluctuations in England, 1700–1800*, O.U.P., Oxford and London, 1959.

Derry, T. K., *Britain Since 1750*, O.U.P., Oxford and London, 1965.

Redford, A., *The Economic History of England 1760–1860* (2nd ed.), Longmans, London, 1960.

Exercises

1. What do you consider are the predictable effects of any war on a country's economic development?
2. To what extent were wars responsible for social distress in the early stages of industrialisation?
3. Assess the gains for Britain, if any, of the long wars with Napoleon between 1793 and 1815.

Summary

1. The early stages of the Industrial Revolution coincided with the Seven Years' War (1756–63), the American War of Independence (1775–83) and the Napoleonic Wars (1793–1815).
2. Trade declined during the War of American Independence but during the Seven Years' War and the Napoleonic Wars there was an expansion of overseas trade.
3. The Napoleonic Wars stimulated agriculture and industry and brought about a high rate of inflation, all of which increased economic buoyancy and the level of employment.
4. The post-war deflationary period between 1815 and 1822 was characterised by growing unemployment, discontent and violence.

CHAPTER FIVE

THE HUMAN RESULTS OF THE INDUSTRIAL REVOLUTION

Mobility of Labour

The increase in the population from the mid-eighteenth century tended to move towards the sectors where there were increasing returns and advancing productivity, as in manufacturing, mining, trade and industry. Table 9, which is subject to margins of error, was produced by Deanne and Cole to compare the distribution of the working population between industries for each census year.

Table 9. Estimated Percentage Distribution of the British Labour Force, 1801–31
(as percentages of the total occupied population)

	Agriculture, forestry, fishing	*Manufacture, mining, industry*	*Trade, transport*	*Domestic, personal*	*Public, professional, all others*
1801	35·9	29·7	11·2	11·5	11·8
1811	33·0	30·2	11·6	11·8	13·3
1821	28·4	38·4	12·1	12·7	8·5
1831	24·6	40·8	12·4	12·6	9·5

Source: *British Economic Growth 1688–1959*, by Deanne and Cole.

As can be seen from the table there was an estimated drop in the percentage of the labour force employed in agriculture, forestry and fishing, whilst Table 10 shows that absolute numbers employed in these industries did not decline, but tended to move slightly upwards.

Table 10. Estimated Industrial Distribution of the British Labour Force, 1801–31
(millions of persons)

	Agriculture, forestry, fishing	*Mining, quarrying, manufactures, and building*	*Trade, transport*	*Public service, professional*	*Domestic, personal*	*Total*
1801	1·7	1·4	0·5	0·3	0·6	4·8
1811	1·8	1·7	0·6	0·4	0·7	5·5
1821	1·8	2·4	0·8	0·3	0·8	6·2
1831	1·8	3·0	0·9	0·3	0·9	7·2

Source: *British Economic Growth 1688–1959*, by Deanne and Cole.

If the land available in Britain had had to support a much larger population there would have been lower output per head, and diminishing returns after a certain point. As it was, the absolute numbers employed on the land did not substantially increase during the early nineteenth century whilst the increase in agricultural productivity resulting from the agrarian revolution enabled the non-agricultural workforce to continue to grow.

Usually people tended to move only a short distance from the immediate hinterland into the manufacturing centres, as for example from the Yorkshire Dales into such places as Darlington or from one valley of South Wales to the next. This often resulted in a shortage of labour in the areas from which the migrants moved, which caused wages to rise and thus encouraged the movement of people from further afield, resulting in a long wave, rolling from the South and East, towards the coalfields of the Midlands and North, where power-driven industry was being developed during the nineteenth century.

The Rise of the Industrial Town and the Growth of the Factory System

Industrial Towns

The increase in the size of the population not only provided a bigger labour force, the greater proportion of which was able to move towards industrial employment through improvements in agriculture, but it also provided potentially more purchasing power, and therefore a wider market. It was necessary for this growth to be biased towards urban growth since employment in industry was usually at higher incomes

Table 11. Urban Growth, 1801–31

	1801	*1811*	*1821*	*1831*
Birmingham	71	83	102	144
Bradford	13	16	26	44
Halifax	12	13	17	22
Huddersfield	7	10	13	19
Leeds	53	63	84	123
Liverpool	82	104	138	202
Manchester	75	89	126	182

Source: B. R. Mitchell, *Abstract of British Historical Statistics.*

than agriculture, and was not insulated from the market economy as those in agriculture were, usually being employed in self-sufficient households. Table 11 shows the rate of urban growth in thousands of some of the principal industrial towns between 1801 and 1831.

The social consequences of the growth of these towns were grim. At the beginning of the nineteenth century, each of the big towns had slum areas in which the working classes were to be found. These people, who were separated from the better off sections of the community, were left alone to struggle through life as best they could.

The slum areas of towns were unplanned, usually consisting of rows of one- or two-storied terrace houses, built close together and without proper regard for adequate air and light. The sanitary arrangements were appalling since there were neither gutters nor drains to carry away animal and vegetable refuse.

It was common for most working-class families to live in only one room, which was invariably damp, badly lit, and with poor ventilation. Very often these rooms were located below ground level.

Some improvements in sewerage were made during the eighteenth century, and this was reflected in the death rate, which was falling up to the 1820s and 1830s. The death rate then began to rise as the deterioration of town conditions overtook and soon far surpassed the rate of improvement. Between 1831 and 1841 the death rate per thousand of Leeds shot up from 20·7 to 27·2; of Manchester from 30·2 to 33·8; and of Liverpool from 21 to 34·8. Conditions tended to be worst in the growing industrial towns which had to cope with the problem of disposing of large quantities of industrial waste.

The Factory System

Industry, unlike agriculture, is subject to a law of increasing returns or diminishing costs, and everything combines to encourage large-scale production. Closely allied with this tendency goes a movement to increase the size of units of production, and the factory tends to replace the workshop. Consequently, the tendency grew for large numbers of workers to be employed under one roof by a single capitalist master or by a partnership or company of capitalists.

The factory system first made an impact on the cotton spinning industry partly because the first machines were spinning machines, and spinning was mainly a woman's employment, and women showed less reluctance than men to submit to factory discipline. The system offered to the capitalist the advantages of power-driven machinery and better supervision of labour.

Conditions within the factories created a whole series of new problems. The workers became more dependent on the employer than they had been before. Under the domestic system the capitalist had been concerned with the purchase of the raw material and the sale of the finished product rather than with the actual processes of manufacture, which were carried on mainly in the workers' homes. Long hours for low wages were worked in the factories by men, women and young children. Discipline was severe since the factory owners believed that the only way they could make a profit was to drive their workpeople to the limit, which meant the need to start punctually, to work regular hours and to do the job systematically. Fines were imposed for such offences as leaving factory windows open or singing at work, which must have appeared particularly harsh to those workers who had been accustomed to cottage industry.

Factory production was predominant in the textile, metal and mining industries by the 1830s. The average factory employed between 50 and 1,000 workers, who had few prospects of advancement and who were destined to dreary and monotonous work as well as appalling living conditions in the towns. It must be remembered though that the general diffusion of the factory system into manufacturing did not take place until the second half of the nineteenth century. Until then many aspects of industry remained small, based on manual methods such as farming, nailmaking, shoemaking, blacksmiths, leather tanning and the Birmingham hardware trades.

The Beginnings of Working Class Organisation

Working class organisation up to the mid-nineteenth century was largely confined to the skilled artisan rather than the industrial worker. Until then working class organisation tended to be a reaction to changes in the structure of industry which had been taking place since the late seventeenth century and which involved the breaking up of a system that had been regulated by the State, by guilds and by long centuries of custom. Unionism was an attempt on the part of the skilled worker to prevent the gap between worker and master growing ever wider as the Industrial Revolution progressed.

During the eighteenth century many workers became associated with trade clubs that were organised to run sickness and burial funds for their members and to restrict the number of apprentices in certain trades. These trade clubs became more and more like trade unions as the century progressed.

In 1799 and 1800 the Government passed the Combination Acts, making combinations both of employees and employers illegal. These were in many respects panic measures in response to the fear of revolution on the French model.

The effect of these laws on trade unions was quite varied. Some unions went on quite happily without interference by the authorities, whilst others were cloaked in a veil of secrecy. Life was made especially difficult for those who for economic reasons were most completely at the mercy of their employers. In unskilled work, where there was always a reserve of men to take the place of those dismissed, or in trades where skilled artisans were threatened by the introduction of machinery, it readily degenerated into violence both against employers and against workmen unwilling to support the combination. Thus by making trade unions illegal the Government intensified the conflict between capital and labour, particularly in the bitter years after 1815.

The person most responsible for the repeal of the Combination Laws in 1824 was the Radical leader, Francis Place (1771–1854), who was a master tailor in business at No. 16 Charing Cross Road. With the help of a radical M.P., Joseph Hume, he managed to get a parliamentary committee appointed to investigate the combination Acts.

Francis Place had a flair for practical politics, though he made the mistake of believing that unionism would assume a passive role once it was legalised. This did not happen since the 1824 Act legalising trade unions coincided with a period of good trade, which encouraged workers to seek higher wages through strike action. The result was another Act in 1825 which confirmed the 1824 Act that Combinations were legal, but which also laid down that the workers should confine their activities to peaceful bargaining about hours and wages and that they were not allowed to 'molest', 'obstruct', or 'intimidate' their employers or other workers. The inclusion of these vague words in the Act left trade unions in a very doubtful position as far as the law was concerned until the third quarter of the nineteenth century.

Trade unionism during the next decade became associated with the Utopian Socialism of Robert Owen (1771–1858), a man whose life spanned extraordinary times. He reached manhood when the Industrial Revolution was increasing in momentum and when Britain was embarking on the war with Napoleon. As a man he lived through the economic crises and industrial disturbances following the peace of 1815, as well as the long agitation for parliamentary reform and the working class movements, industrial and political, which followed the Reform Acts of 1832.

Owen started life with few advantages, and until the age of eighteen worked as a shop assistant. Then with the help of a loan of £100 plus his personal qualities he became by the age of twenty-nine head of the great cotton mills of New Lanark.

Owen attempted to create at New Lanark not so much a factory as an industrial community where he undertook the care of the social life of his workers as well as their work as producers. Owen said, 'I can make manufacturing pay without reducing those whom I employ to misery and degradation.' He did in fact make New Lanark pay and showed how it was possible to reconcile philanthropy with exploitation.

After an abortive attempt at founding a 'Village of Co-operation' in America, Owen returned to Britain where he found a new opportunity to put some of his ideas into practice in the trade union movement. This involved the creation of a giant trade union, the Grand National Consolidated Trades Union, which was to include all kinds of workers. This revolutionary organisation was aimed ultimately at replacing private employers by a system of workers' control and the idea was that eventually parliamentary government was to be superseded by the rule of the 'Grand National'. The long-term aims of the 'Grand National' were to rationalise the structure of combinations, to achieve a general control of movements for an advance of wages, and to coordinate assistance for strikes, especially strikes against a reduction of wages.

Both the Government and the Press supported the employers against Trade Unions. The Government was particularly concerned because of rural unrest in the southern counties, which manifested itself in rick-burning and machine-breaking. Hence the Home Secretary, Lord Melbourne, chose to make an example of six men of the Dorset village of Tolpuddle who were charged with uttering an illegal oath contrary to an act of 1797 when planning to join the Grand National Consolidated Trades Union, and in March 1834 they were sentenced to seven years' transportation.

The Grand National Consolidated Trades Union, which may have been a good idea, was far ahead of its time, and after the example of the Tolpuddle Martyrs it foundered and disintegrated. As a result, the working classes became temporarily disenchanted with trade unionism during the next few years and sought to bring about political reforms through the Chartist Movement.

The Development of the Poor Law up to 1834

During the Middle Ages there was extensive help available for the needy. This was mainly because the family, which was a closer-knit unit than it is today, invariably accepted responsibility for the sick and old. Help was also available from the Church which gave alms; from the monasteries which provided lodgings for travellers; and from the guilds which provided the modern equivalent of friendly society benefits to their members.

There arose the need during Tudor times for a new system of poor relief due to growing economic and social stresses. This was embodied in the Elizabethan Poor Law Act of 1601 which put together the essentials of the poor relief system and remained in force until 1834. This law was designed to provide relief for the 'lame, impotent, old and blind, and such others being poor, and not able to work'. Children were to be apprenticed, boys until they were 24 and girls to the age of 21. To provide work for unemployed adults, 'a convenient stock of flax, hemp, wool, thread, iron and other stuff' was to be purchased. Stress was laid on family responsibility and those unwilling to work were to be harshly punished.

The parish was to be the unit legally liable for its own poor. Each parish was to have its 'overseers of the poor', appointed by the county J.P.'s who were ultimately under the supervision of the privy council in Westminster.

Many attempts were made towards the end of the seventeenth century to meet the cost of poor relief by 'setting the poor on work' in workhouses. This practice was extended to a much wider number of places by an Act passed in 1723.

With the onset of the Industrial Revolution in the eighteenth century the problems of providing poor relief became more serious. This was due to the upheavals caused by the population explosion, the displacement of the people due to enclosures, the break-up of the domestic system and the growth of the factory system. In addition, inflation during the period of the long wars with France between 1793 and 1815 made the situation even worse. Thus, magistrates found it difficult, in a steadily worsening situation from the 1790s onwards, to maintain public order. Their response was, invariably, to give more generous support in order to appease the masses. This was done in the following ways.

1. The Gilbert Act of 1782 laid down that parishes could, if they wished, combine to form poor law unions. This Act also provided that no person should be sent to such poor-houses except the aged, sick, or otherwise impotent poor. This implied that some form of outdoor relief was to be provided for able-bodied persons. According to the Act, poor persons 'who shall be able and willing to work but who cannot get employment' were to be found employment by the guardians as near home as possible. The guardians received the wages of such poor persons as a contribution to their keep and made up any deficit out of the poor rate. Hence, the labourer was guaranteed a minimum of subsistence.

2. The Speenhamland system, which made wages up to a minimum

subsistence level, was introduced in Berkshire in 1795 when a group of magistrates resolved that 'the present state of the poor does require further assistance than has been generally given them'. This 'further assistance' was based on the price of bread and the size of a person's family (Table 12).

This system spread rapidly so that by 1818 it was being used by all counties in the South of England and parts of the Midlands.

As a result of the more generous treatment of the poor the cost of poor relief rose from £2 million in 1786, to £8 million in 1818. Between 1815 and 1830 the general price level fell by almost a half and yet the cost of poor relief remained approximately the same. Contemporaries

Table 12. The Bread Scale

Gallon loaf (8 lb. 11 oz.)		*Minimum wage*	*Wife*	*Each child*
1/-		3/-	1/6	1/6
When price of loaf rose to 1/4	*minimum wage rose to*	4/-	1/10	1/10
,, ,, 1/6	,, ,,	4/6	2/-	2/-

claimed that farms and even whole villages had to be abandoned since the burden of the rates made it impossible for many people to make a living.

Thus, there was mounting opposition amongst the ratepayers at the cost of providing relief through the allowance system. The system was also attacked because many people considered that it encouraged the growth of large families at a time when there was a danger of over-population. This growing opposition led to the Government setting up a Poor Law Commission in 1832 to investigate the whole problem of poor relief. This was followed by the passing of the Poor Law Amendment Act of 1834, which set up a system of poor relief that remained more or less intact until the early years of the twentieth century.

Standards of Living

The question which naturally arises is: 'Were people better or worse off as a result of the tumultuous changes which industrialism brought?'

This is a very difficult question to answer since it involves not only considering whether a person's material possessions increased but also whether or not the worker willingly gave up a rural, pre-industrial way of life for the way of life of an urban industrial society.

Professor Ashton has observed that most people consider the period 1760 to the setting up of the Welfare State in 1945 as being marked by little but toil, sweat and oppression. This point of view has been reinforced by contemporary writers such as Marx and Engels who painted a very black picture of the consequences of industrialism on the quality of life of the masses. It must be remembered, however, that such writers were motivated by the desire for social reform rather than to provide posterity with an objective appraisal of the facts as they were, and many of the orthodox opinions which look on the Industrial Revolution as having been a disaster, have changed. For one thing, there has been a change in the type of evidence looked for. For example, too much reliance may have been placed on information given in the official enquiries of the nineteenth century whose purposes were to expose abuses rather than to describe the entire economic system in normal working order. Also, many of the hardships blamed upon industrialisation, may have been caused to some extent by the long wars against the French Revolutionaries.

Many people now believe that industrialisation, especially in the long run, was an immense gain for everyone, rich and poor. Mrs Gilboy, the statistician, showed that over the eighteenth century, the labourers in the textile regions of the North became better off. It is true that as a result of inflation many poor people became poorer after 1793, but before the war ended in 1815 industrial wages in England had caught up with retail prices, and in the 1820s the gain was pronounced. In 1831 the cost of living was more than in 1790, but over this span of time urban wages had increased by no less than 43 per cent.

It must also be borne in mind that the products of the Industrial Revolution were not in general luxuries, but necessities and capital goods. By 1822, the effects of the Napoleonic Wars were passing away and the increasing quantities of cotton and woollen goods and food and drink were being consumed not by the few but by the masses. Also, our imports, which were mainly paid for by our industrial exports, consisted in the main of sugar, grain, coffee and tea, for the people at large and not luxury goods.

Thus, the Industrial Revolution provided the means to feed and clothe and employ the growing population, which otherwise undoubtedly would have faced disaster.

Suggested Further Reading

Cole, G. D. H., and Postgate, R., *The Common People 1746–1946*, Methuen, London, 1968.

Hobsbawm, E. J., and Hartwell, R. M., 'The Standard of Living During the Industrial Revolution: A Discussion', *Economic History Review*, 2nd series, 1957, **10**, No. 1.

Marshall, J. D., *The Old Poor Law, 1795–1834*, Macmillan, London, 1968.

Redford, A., *Labour Migration in England, 1800–1850* (2nd ed.), Manchester University Press, Manchester, 1964.

Taylor, P. A. M. (editor), *The Industrial Revolution: Triumph or Disaster?* Heath, Boston, 1958.

Exercises

1. 'Flight from the land'. Is this an appropriate description of the period 1760–1830?

2. Account for the appalling conditions in the growing industrial towns during the early nineteenth century.

3. To what extent had the factory system replaced the domestic system in the manufacture of goods by 1830?

4. Why was it foolish to make trade unions illegal during the period 1799–1824?
5. Outline the events leading up to the Poor Law Amendment Act of 1834.
6. In what ways was the quality of life for the masses influenced by the Industrial Revolution.

Summary

1. The increase in the population from the mid-eighteenth century tended to move towards the sectors where there were increasing returns and advancing productivity, whilst the increase in agricultural productivity resulting from the agrarian revolution enabled the non-agricultural workforce to grow.
2. Rapid urban development resulted in appalling conditions in the towns which were reflected during the 1820s and 1830s in a rising death rate.
3. The factory system was predominant in the textile, metal and mining industries by the 1830s but was not extended to manufacturing in general until the second half of the nineteenth century.
4. Trade unions were illegal between 1799 and 1824, but even when they were legalised they were for a long time in a doubtful position as far as the law was concerned.
5. The difficulties of maintaining public order during times of tumultuous change in the late eighteenth century led to more generous provision of poor relief, though there was mounting opposition against this generosity in the early nineteenth century.
6. The rather gloomy point of view that the Industrial Revolution was a disaster for the masses has given way more and more to the belief that industrialisation, especially in the long run, was an immense gain for everyone.

SECTION TWO

BRITAIN AS THE WORKSHOP OF THE WORLD 1830–1914

In 1830 Britain was undergoing the transition from being a primarily agricultural and commercial economy to becoming the first modern industrial state in the world, an experience which brought fundamental changes both to her outlook and physical appearance. By 1914 railways had welded the country into one economic unit, green country had been turned into towns and suburbs, the population had grown in leaps and bounds, and the North of England became for the first time the most densely inhabited part of the Kingdom.

Manufacturing became relatively more important than the primary sectors of the economy, and services directly supporting industry such as transport, trade, banking, insurance and finance were developed.

Vast sums of money accumulated for profitable investment both at home and overseas. Thus Britain played a vital role in the development of the international economy, which in turn stimulated foreign competition and created a challenge to her economic supremacy in the last quarter of the nineteenth century.

The material progress made in this period was firmly based on the belief that the best results were achieved in an atmosphere of free competition and laissez faire. Resourcefulness, determination and 'self-help' were advocated as the key to success in an industrial world. In this laissez faire atmosphere great progress and riches were made, but the wealth was very unevenly distributed, and there was much social injustice, as well as considerable pollution of the environment.

1830 – 1914

CHAPTER SIX

POPULATION GROWTH

Population grew rapidly during this period, rising from approximately 14 million in 1830 to 37 million in 1914. This growth of population stimulated British industry by providing her with a larger labour force and a bigger domestic market.

Table 13. Population of England and Wales

Year	*Population* (millions)	*Birth rate*	*Death rate*
1838	15·3	30·3	22·4
1841	15·9	32·2	21·6
1851	18·0	34·3	22·0
1861	20·1	34·6	21·6
1871	22·8	35·0	22·6
1881	26·0	33·9	18·9
1891	29·1	31·4	20·2
1901	32·6	28·5	16·9
1911	36·1	24·3	14·6

Source: B. R. Mitchell, *British Historical Statistics.*

The causes of population growth during this period are much easier to explain than population changes up to the 1830s due to the passing of the Registration Act in 1836, which provided for the compulsory registration of births, marriages and deaths. In this period the birth rate rose continually up until the 1870s, after which it fell, whilst the general trend of the death rate was downward, with upward deviations from time to time, the fall being particularly pronounced from the 1880s onwards.

The Population Cycle

A population cycle involving four stages of development can be identified in a mature economy. This experience of population growth in England and Wales since the mid-eighteenth century (Fig. 5) is typical of that in many Western European countries.

Stage I represented the normal state of mankind before the tumultuous changes associated with the Industrial Revolution. Both birth rates and death rates were high and population growth was slow and irregular. BR + DR High – Pop Growth slow

Stage II lasted in England and Wales from about 1750 to 1880. The most significant features of this period were that the death rate began

BR High DR Slow

to fall rapidly for most of the time, whilst birth rates remained fairly constant, resulting in a trebling of the population.

Stage III saw a rapid fall in the birth rate from about 1880 onwards and a continuation in the fall of the death rate.

Stage IV represents the situation as it is at present with fairly stable birth and death rates resulting in a small but steady growth of population.

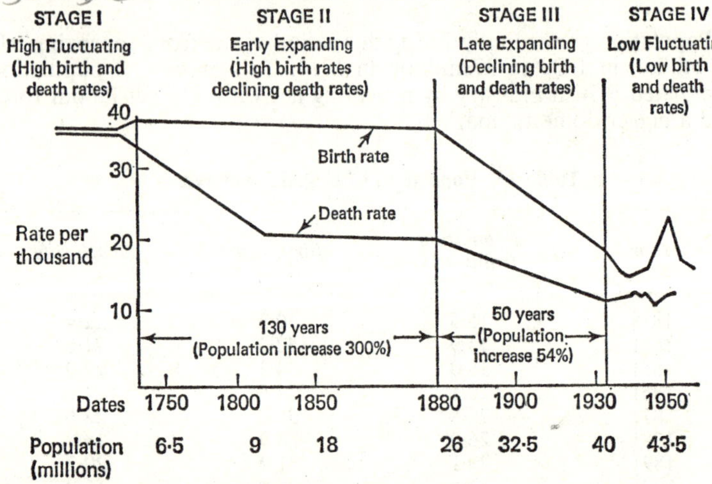

Fig. 5. The population cycle in England and Wales.

Birth Rates

The maintenance of a high birth rate of about 35 per 1,000 up to 1880 can be explained by the fact that there was an increase in the number of marriages per 1,000 of population, and the average age of marriage continued to fall still further. Earlier marriages were probably due to the continuing decline in the apprenticeship system and the tendency of farm labourers to live in their own cottages, instead of with the farmer and his family. The marriage rate per 1,000 of population in England and Wales rose from 15·4 in 1841 to 16·1 in 1861 and 17·6 in 1873.

Children were also a positive economic asset to their parents up until the 1870s since the opportunities for child employment were increasing and children could be sent out to work from an early age.

The trend began to change in the mid 1870s, and birth rates began to fall quite rapidly. This fall was probably brought about for the following reasons, though it is important to realise that the causes of falling birth rates are complex and to some extent speculative.

1. Children became increasingly an economic burden as Factory Acts restricted their employment and Education Acts insisted upon their compulsory attendance at school.

2. As people became better off so they attempted to protect their standard of comfort by limiting their family size. This applied particularly to the professional classes, whose marriages as early as the 1850s

produced fewer births than those of wage earners. This trend towards smaller families began to apply also to the wage earner when real wages increased in the last quarter of the nineteenth century.

3. There was a growing knowledge of birth control methods after the famous Bradlaugh-Besant trial of 1877 which became more widely diffused as a result of better communication made possible by improved literacy and the development of the mass media. Also, increased geographical mobility and the growth of towns helped to break down traditional ideas based on custom, leading to the evolution of new social attitudes towards the question of birth control.

4. The emigration of large numbers of young males denied many women the opportunity of marriage and the satisfaction of their maternal instincts.

5. The change in the status of women, brought about by better educational facilities and an increase in employment opportunities, probably increased the reluctance of many women to be burdened down by too large a family.

Death Rates

Death rates, which had been falling since the late eighteenth century, began to rise again during the 1820s due to the appalling conditions in the growing industrial towns. Thereafter, they stabilised at about 22 per 1,000 until the 1880s and then began to fall again. This fall was quite pronounced so that by 1914 the death rate was down to about 15 per 1,000. The main reasons for this change were:

1. Improvements in medical knowledge. The two most important advances in medical knowledge during the nineteenth century were the development of anaesthetics and antiseptics.

An American dentist, W. T. G. Morton, used ether as an anaesthetic in 1844. A short time later chloroform was adopted and extensively used in surgical operations. This lessened the need for speed in operations, thus encouraging surgeons, and probably patients to an even greater extent, to try more complicated operations. In spite of this innovation, deaths from surgical operations remained high due to post-operative complications called sepsis. This problem of the morbid inflammation of operation wounds was solved by Joseph Lister (1827–1912), who demonstrated in 1867 that the cause of the trouble lay in germs carried in unfiltered air on the surgeon's hands. By sterilising both the hands of the surgeon and his instruments in carbolic acid and by spraying the atmosphere in proximity to the operation with a carbolic acid spray, the death rate from post-operative inflammation fell immediately. This was quickly and extensively adopted, and led to the saving of countless lives.

The Medical Act of 1858, creating a General Council of medical education and registration for the United Kingdom, went a long way towards raising medical standards in the nineteenth century, by eliminating the quack doctor. The Council had powers to keep a register of qualified practitioners, to approve the bodies giving medical qualifications and to bring before the Privy Council cases where the licensing

Really just hygiene improvement

bodies were not insisting upon a proper examination or previous course of study.

2. Improvements in public health, brought about by the 1848 and 1875 Public Health Acts, considerably reduced or eliminated the health hazards arising from infectious diseases.

3. The Government accepted more responsibility for a healthier environment at work through factory and mines legislation.

4. Cheap food imports, made possible by the development of the world's railway and steamship systems and Britain's free trade policy, led to better nutritional standards. This trend towards improved diets for the masses was further helped by the increase in real wages during the last quarter of the nineteenth century.

The most striking aspect of falling death rates was to be seen in the fall after 1900 in the infantile mortality rates. In 1880 three boys in every twenty and one girl in every eight did not complete the first year of life, whereas by the 1930s this risk of death had been almost halved. This improvement was brought about by:

1. The improved health of mothers who lived in cleaner homes, and who were not burdened down by too large a family.

2. Certification of midwives, introduced by an Act passed in 1902, reduced the risks of childbearing by making sure that only properly trained and qualified individuals should 'habitually and for gain' attend women in childbirth.

These midwives, however, were independent private practitioners and it was not until 1936 that local authorities were charged with the task of making sure that their respective areas were properly catered for by an adequate number of midwives.

3. The Maternity and Child Welfare Act, 1918, made local authorities responsible for safeguarding the health of expectant mothers and children under five.

4. More babies were born in hospitals where medical care was at hand if required.

Concern for the health of schoolchildren was expressed by the report of the Interdepartmental Committee on Physical Deterioration published in 1904, which recommended the feeding of necessitous schoolchildren and school medical inspection. These recommendations were carried into effect by the Education (Provision of Meals) Act, 1906, and the Education (Administrative Provisions) Act, 1907.

Falling death rates led to a greater expectation of life, and this, together with falling birth rates, meant a bigger proportion of the growing population were in the older age group. In 1880 the average expectation of life of a newborn baby was 43; by 1940 it was 65 years, i.e. a 50 per cent improvement on the 1880 figure. The main economic implications for future generations of this trend towards an ageing population were:

1. Structural unemployment might occur if there was a decline in employment in industries making goods for the young relative to employment in industries making goods for the old.

2. Industrial inertia would increase since older people are usually much less mobile than younger people.

3. The transfer burden of taxation on the young would become greater as more and more people needed to be supported by social insurance schemes.

External Migration

External migration had the effect of slowing down the rate of population growth during the period 1830 to 1914, since the number of emigrants greatly exceeded the number of immigrants. In the period 1871 to 1911 alone there was a net outflow from Britain of 1,952,000.

In 1824 the laws prohibiting the emigration of workmen from Britain were repealed so that British labour, like British capital, was free to move to whichever country it wished. Invariably, the movement of men and capital were inextricably linked.

In the early decades after the repeal of the emigration laws a few British artisans took their skills to European countries where their influence in promoting the Industrial Revolution on the Continent was quickly felt. Later, when British capital was developing railways in such places as Europe, India and America, British labour was also used. Most of the men employed on such projects returned home after their completion, but some remained.

The size of population was affected not only because there was a net loss from external migration, but also because of the distortion in the sex balance of the remaining population, since the majority of the emigrants were young, male and unmarried.

Suggested Further Reading

Deane, P., and Cole, W. A., *British Economic Growth, 1688–1959: Trends and Structure* (2nd ed.), C.U.P., Cambridge, 1967.

Glass, D. V., and Eversley, D. E. C. (editors), *Population in History; Essays in Historical Demography*, Edward Arnold, London, 1965.

Exercises

1. In what circumstances does population growth contribute towards economic development and increased prosperity?

2. Trace and explain the main reasons for the changes in birth and death rates between 1830 and 1914.

3. What are the economic consequences of an ageing population?

4. In what ways do you think Britain benefited from being a breeding ground for overseas communities?

Summary

1. The death rate fell throughout the period whereas birth rates rose up to the 1870s and then fell.

2. Falling birth rates were probably caused by changes in the family as an economic unit, higher living standards, birth control, a growing imbalance of the sexes and the changing status of women.

3. Death rates fell due to improved medical knowledge and public health provision, and better nutritional standards.

4. The main economic effects of an ageing population are possible structural unemployment, industrial inertia and the transfer burden of taxation.

CHAPTER SEVEN

THE REVOLUTION IN TRANSPORT

At the same time as railways and steamships were being developed, many people were suffering from the structural upheavals that industrialisation had induced. Everything that was evil and ugly was being attributed by some contemporaries as being the result of the new machines which were forcing people to work in factories and to live in the squalid industrial towns.

By reducing distances and increasing trade, the development of railways and steamships demonstrated that machines could be beneficial for everyone.

Railways

The modern railway came about as a result of a union between the iron rail and the steam-driven locomotive. The iron rail came into use about 1770 and the first steam-driven locomotive used on them was developed by Richard Trevithick in 1804.

During the next few years the number of railways appreciably increased, though in 1815 they were still of much less importance than the canals in the industrial world.

It was George Stephenson (1781–1848), an engine-wright to the Killingworth colliery in Northumberland, who was responsible for the development of the locomotive in its present form.

In 1821 a group of colliery owners in the Darlington district got an Act of Parliament passed to build a railway to Stockton and George Stephenson was appointed its engineer. This line was opened in 1825 and became the first commercial locomotive route in the world.

Stephenson was then appointed engineer on the Liverpool to Manchester line, the construction of which marked the real state of large-scale public railways in this country. This line was started in 1826, and completed in 1830, after considerable engineering difficulties had been overcome. It was on this line that Stephenson's famous 'Rocket' engine was used to pull trains.

The success of this line led to many ambitious railway projects being planned and constructed during the next few years, the first period of intensive railway building taking place during 1836–7, when 1500 miles of new railway were authorised by Parliament. This boom was short-lived owing to a contraction of credit caused by a banking crisis in America. Nevertheless, in 1838 the first main line between London and Birmingham was opened by which time about 500 miles of railway were open to the public.

During the next six years little more than 250 miles of new railway were sanctioned by Parliament, although previously sanctioned line

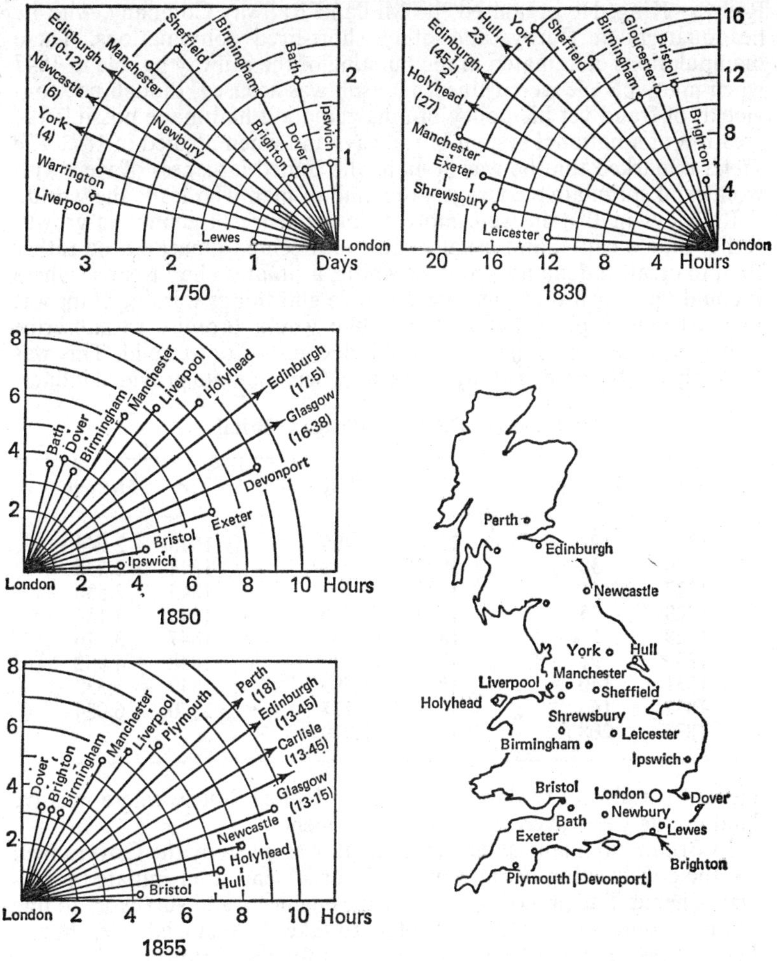

Fig. 6. Changes in times of travel within Britain.
(courtesy Penguin Books Ltd)

was completed and 1,500 miles of line were opened for traffic, bringing the total mileage of railways by the end of 1843 to more than 2,000.

A further period of intensive railway construction took place between 1844 and 1847, when the total mileage was increased to 4,000, and the main trunk routes of the modern British railway system were laid down. Table 14 shows the total railway mileage laid up to 1850.

Another feature of this period was the substantial amount of railway amalgamation which took place, amid much excitement and speculation. The leading figure in this development was the former York draper, George Hudson, who became known in the mid-1840s as the

Railway King. He organised the Midland Railway Company, with its headquarters at Derby, and other short-lived combinations. These manipulations culminated in the bursting of the railway bubble in 1847 when many people were ruined. Hudson was accused, though not convicted, of fraud yet his policy of amalgamation had made possible the creation of a national system of railways and when he died in 1871 *The Times* remarked that he was 'a man who united largeness of view with wonderful speculative courage—the kind of man who leads the world.'

Railways in Britain were more a consequence of economic growth rather than a cause, and usually came into being to meet a need rather than to create a demand. In other words, a situation had to arise where it could be shown that there were people and things wanting transport in a particular place before the public would promise to subscribe money and before Parliament would give authority to build. This was certainly not the case in many countries where the state provided induce-

Table 14. Railway Mileage in Britain

Year	*Mileage*	*Year*	*Mileage*	*Year*	*Mileage*
1825	27	1834	298	1843	2,044
1826	38	1835	338	1844	2,236
1827	41	1836	403	1845	2,530
1828	45	1837	540	1846	3,136
1829	51	1838	742	1847	3,876
1830	98	1839	970	1848	4,982
1831	140	1840	1,498	1849	5,538
1832	166	1841	1,775	1850	6,084
1833	208	1842	1,939		

ments for railways to develop, as in the United States, where massive land grants were given to railway developers.

In Britain no financial assistance at all was given by the Government for the construction of railways, and Parliament never initiated a railway scheme. The procedure was for the engineers and surveyors to find the best route and for the promoters to take the financial risk, though before they obtained legislative approval for their projected lines they had to prove that they were satisfying a public demand.

It was most unfortunate for subsequent generations that railways were not built to some kind of national plan. That does not mean to say that the Government was content to leave railway development simply to the wishes of railway companies, since as early as 1840 the Board of Trade was authorised to inspect all new railways before they were opened and two years later it was instructed to hold official enquiries into the causes of railway accidents. Perhaps the most famous of the early acts regulating railways was Gladstone's Parliamentary Trains Act of 1844. This Act aimed at providing a regular and inexpensive transport service for all classes of people by ordering all railway companies to run at least one train a day in both directions and to charge a maximum fare of one penny a mile to second-class travellers.

It also gave the Treasury the power to revise charges so that profits over a twenty-one year period should not exceed 10 per cent per annum and after that period of time the State, if it wished, had the power to take over the railways, but this option was never taken up. Another Act of 1846 settled the battle of the gauges by laying down a standard gauge of 4 ft. $8\frac{1}{2}$ in., although the Great Western Railway continued with its broad gauge until 1892.

Economic Effects of the Railways

The building of the railways was the greatest physical achievement so far carried out by the human race within such a short period of time, and their economic effects were so profound that they influenced almost every aspect of national life.

1. They led to an increase in passenger traffic, since they provided cheap, rapid and safe travel for all classes of society. The number of passenger journeys made per annum increased from 50 million in 1850 to more than 1,200 million by 1914.

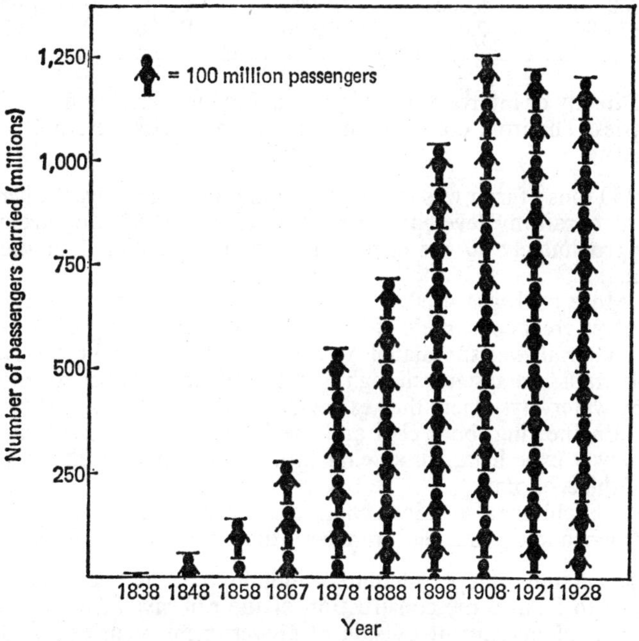

Fig. 7. Passenger traffic on Britain's railways.
(courtesy Penguin Books Ltd)

2. Railways became important transporters of freight, particularly bulky commodities such as coal and raw materials.

3. Railways stimulated employment, both in their construction and in the permanent jobs which became available when they were completed. A quarter of a million men were employed in their construction

in 1847 whilst many thousands were already permanently employed as drivers, porters, administrative staff, etc. The indirect stimulus railways gave to employment by detonating economic activity in the rest of the economy, is incalculable.

4. By uniting markets greater specialisation was facilitated, thus reducing costs and enabling British manufacturers to reach out beyond the home market to foreign markets. Also, British capital, materials and often British contractors played a crucial role in world railway construction.

Table 15. World Railway Mileage Opened (To Nearest 1,000 Miles)

Year	*U.K.*	*Europe including U.K.*	*America*	*Rest of world*
1840–50	6,000	13,000	7,000	—
1850–60	4,000	17,000	24,000	1,000
1860–70	5,000	31,000	24,000	7,000
1870–80	2,000	39,000	51,000	12,000

5. Directly or indirectly railways influenced the development of most industries. The iron, coal and engineering industries were particularly affected:

(i) 150 tons of iron was required to build one mile of track; hence at the peak of railway development between 1845 and 1847 they accounted for approximately 40 per cent of the country's entire domestic iron output.

(ii) More coal was needed to produce the iron, and railways were themselves great consumers of coal. Also, the demand for coal, being a bulky material, was stimulated by the introduction of an extensive and flexible transport system, though it still remained cheaper to transport coal by waterways where they existed.

(iii) Engineering, both civil and mechanical, was revolutionised by the railway experience, producing incalculable spin-off effects on the rest of the economy.

(iv) Agriculture also gained considerable benefits such as the marketing of perishable goods and transportation of animals to market.

6. Large sums of money had to be mobilised from impersonal lenders in order to finance the construction of the railways. This provided a new form of investment outside of Government securities, and thus influenced the attitude of opinion towards joint stock companies and the separation of ownership from management. Thus, the railway experience, by helping to modify the credit structure, promoted a further stage in the Industrial Revolution, since the raising of large sums of money was to be crucial in developing other sectors of the economy.

7. The mobility of labour was increased and movement from the countryside into towns no longer meant exile from friends and relations.

8. The railways virtually destroyed the canal system by providing a quicker and more flexible form of transport. This was a pity, since there was a place for canals in a rationalised transport system. Roads also declined in relative importance to the railways, though they were developed and extended throughout the century as feeder systems to the railways.

Social Effects of the Railways

Britain's social fabric was profoundly influenced by the coming of railways.

1. The isolation of remote country areas was broken down and extreme parochialism was transformed into provincialism as differences in speech, dress and attitude became less marked.

2. Railways encouraged the explosion of cities into suburbia so that living and working places became totally separated for many people. The tendency was for the better-off people to move further away from the towns and for solid monotonous working-class areas to establish themselves near to the city centres. The suburbs of the new towns contained numerous imitations of rich men's houses, whilst the houses in working-class areas became increasingly uniform as railways enabled heavy materials to be freely distributed at low cost all over the country. Thus, the railways abolished the cheapness of local materials, which blended into the landscape, and substituted that of national ones. The cheapest walling in the country was found to be brick and the cheapest roof covering was of North Wales slate. Thus all towns and many villages, particularly in the North of England, became contaminated by this unnatural combination.

This growth of urban working class areas increased a sense of working-class solidarity which, towards the end of the nineteenth century, was beginning to have political undertones as workers were enfranchised and large trade unions were formed.

3. The transformation of the capital market during the 'railway mania' of the 1840s led to the growth of a 'rentier' class, whose incomes were derived from interest on investments. By the end of the nineteenth century there were thousands of people who lived on the profits and savings of the previous two or three generations, in addition to those who made large sums of money by selling their land to the railway developers or property speculators. Relatively new towns, such as Bournemouth and Eastbourne, mushroomed in growth to house the comfortable families. Bournemouth's population grew from 5,600 in 1870, when the railway first reached it, to 78,700 by 1911.

4. The traditional English seaside holiday for the mass of the population was a social habit largely created by the railways. Day trips to the sea by cheap railway excursions on Sundays and Bank Holidays were introduced in 1871. Previously, seaside holidays had been reserved for the aristocracy.

5. Railways made possible a cheap and efficient postal service from the 1840s onwards and newspapers became popular and relatively cheap from the 1880s.

The Growth of State Regulation

As the nineteenth century progressed the State extended its policy of controlling the railways.

1. An Act of 1854 forbade the railway companies to give preference to particular customers for the carriage of particular types of goods.

2. The Regulation of the Railways Act (1871) laid down safety rules, required the notification of all accidents and provided for the inspection of facilities by the Board of Trade.

3. The Railway and Canal Traffic Act of 1873 established three railway and canal commissioners who were empowered to hear complaints about charging, to enforce the law prohibiting preferences to particular customers, to examine proposed railway amalgamations, because of the monopoly danger, and to sanction proposals for the railways to buy up canals.

4. The Railway and Canal Traffic Act of 1888 provided that the whole system of railway rates and fares should be revised and maximum charges set up because of the great monopoly danger of the railways. By the end of the nineteenth century the railways had virtually ceased to be competitors in the matter of fares and rates. Competition came instead in the form of improved facilities such as dining cars, sleepers, corridor trains, cheap excursions and faster speeds. The increased expenditure which this form of competition involved, together with the growing militancy of railway trade unions demanding higher wages, led to a fall in profits from the 1890s onwards.

The railways in 1914 could look back on a long period of success, though they were ill equipped, with their rigid structures and strict Government regulations, to face the imminent threat from road motor transport.

Shipping

The great expansion in world trade during the nineteenth century was made possible by the building of a large number of better designed ocean-going ships, capable of profitably transporting goods of high bulk and low unit value, such as timber, grain, coal and mineral ores.

In the early years of the nineteenth century British shipping dominated the oceans of the world, but then for a time the industry's outlook became less favourable because timber was the material from which most ships were built, and in Britain timber was becoming scarce.

The challenge to Britain's maritime supremacy at this time came from the United States, whose extensive forests and large number of skilled shipwrights gave her a great advantage in the building of wooden ships. This fierce competition from American sailing ships lasted until the Civil War when, with the sanctioning of the trans-continental railroad and the passing of the 1862 Homestead Act, Continental interests replaced Atlantic interests and America's main efforts became focused on westward expansion.

Britain's main hope in overcoming the challenge from her American rivals lay in the superiority of her technical knowledge. Important experiments in this direction took place soon after James Watt developed his rotary motive steam engine in 1769. The first marine engine was patented by William Symington, a Scot, in 1786, and in 1803 his ship, the *Charlotte Dundas*, steamed along the Firth–Clyde canal. It was another Scot, Henry Bell, who started the first regular steamboat passenger service on the Clyde.

The early steam engines were also enthusiastically adopted in America to propel boats along the great rivers. In 1807, an American, Robert Fulton, successfully launched the *Clermont* on the Hudson River, a boat powered by steam engines constructed by the British firm of Boulton and Watt.

Steamboats were then put on the sea routes. In 1816 they were used on the Irish Sea between Holyhead and Dublin, and Greenock and Belfast, and in 1818 the Dover–Calais steamboat service was started. The first steamboat to cross the Atlantic was the *Savannah* in 1819, but steam was only used as an occasional auxiliary to sail. A Canadian ship,

Table 16. Percentage of Overseas Trade of the United Kingdom, France, and the United States carried by the British Mercantile Marine, 1855–1908

Year	*United Kingdom*	*France*	*United States*
1855–9	58·8	29·4	28·7
1865–9	67·8	36·2	47·6
1875–9	68·0	40·5	51·6
1885–9	73·1	41·3	56·5
1895–9	70·8	45·3	55·3
1905–8	61·6	36·4	50·6

Source: Hoffman, *British Industry, 1700–1950.*

the *Royal William*, in 1833 was the first to cross the Atlantic using steam all the way.

Since the effect of introducing steam shipping on ocean voyages was to reduce substantially the time of voyages, the Government encouraged the development of steam shipping by giving the contract to carry the Atlantic mails to Samuel Cunard in 1839, who started a regular steamship service from Liverpool to Halifax, Nova Scotia, and later to New York. The cargoes of steamships at this time had to be of low bulk and high unit value, since the ships were small and the steam engines were inefficient, thus necessitating the carrying of large quantities of coal on long journeys. The early steamships were in a sense the equivalent of the modern passenger plane carrying low-bulk cargoes, principally passengers and mail. This disability was overcome as the century progressed and the efficiency of steam engines was improved, when it became possible for cargoes of high bulk and low unit value to be transported. This provided a further stimulus for coal exports from Britain and coal-bunkering stations were set up on British territory at many of the strategic ports throughout the world.

During the second half of the nineteenth century, Britain's mercantile marine became the largest and most powerful in the world, and thus contributed towards the unprecedented expansion of international trade. This facilitated more international specialisation and provided Britain with an important invisible export (see Table 16).

Not all the economic effects of the steamship were beneficial for Britain. Large imports of food—firstly wheat, and then with the development of the refrigerator ships, meat—brought disaster to the British farmer in the last quarter of the nineteenth century. This could have been prevented by a change in our trading policy, but the British public were against a tariff on food.

Suggested Further Reading

Aldcroft, D. H. (editor), *The Development of British Industry and Foreign Competition 1875–1914*, Allen & Unwin, London, 1968.

Lambert, R. S., *The Railway King, 1800–1871: A Study of George Hudson and the Business Morals of his Time*, Allen & Unwin, London, 1964.

Savage, C., *An Economic History of Transport*, Hutchinson, London, 1966.

Tames, R., *The Transport Revolution in the 19th Century: A Documentary Approach*, O.U.P., Oxford and London, 1971.

Exercises

1. Would you agree that in Britain railways were more a consequence of economic expansion than a cause?
2. Discuss the State's role in the development of railways in Britain in the nineteenth century.
3. What were the economic effects for Britain of the development of the steamship?
4. Assess the contribution of transport improvements to Britain's economic development in the nineteenth century.

Summary

1. The Stockton to Darlington and the Liverpool to Manchester railways, opened in 1825 and 1830 respectively, were Britain's first two commercial locomotive routes.
2. The first two periods of intensive railway building in Britain were in 1836–7 and 1844–7, after which the railway mileage totalled 4,000 and the main trunk routes of the modern railway system had been laid down.
3. Railways in Britain were a consequence of economic growth rather than a cause, and came into being to meet a need rather than to create a demand.
4. The Government did not build railways in Britain, and they were not built to any kind of plan, though Parliamentary approval was needed for the construction of new lines, and many regulations were passed laying down how they were to be run.
5. The economic and social effects of the railways were so profound that they influenced almost every aspect of national life.
6. When ships were made of wood Britain's maritime supremacy was in danger of being superseded by the United States, but with the development of iron, and later steel, steamships, Britain's maritime supremacy became assured.

CHAPTER EIGHT

AGRICULTURAL CHANGE

The changing fortunes of agriculture during the nineteenth century can be classified into quite definite periods. The prosperous Napoleonic War years, resulting from inflation and the lack of foreign competition, were followed by a period of depressed conditions, persisting until 1837. This was succeeded by a period of unprecedented prosperity lasting until 1873, when prices and demand were high and considerable improvements in productivity were made, whilst the last quarter of the century witnessed a sharp decline owing to the impact of foreign competition.

The Struggle for Repeal of the Corn Laws

By the Waterloo Corn Bill of 1815, imports of corn were prohibited when wheat rose above 80 shillings per quarter. This measure, aimed at preserving the prosperity of agriculture and passed by a Parliament dominated by the landed interest, was basically against the interests of the poorer classes. In reality, however, the law was not very effective because farm prices were very low after 1815 so that imports would not have been very important in any case. Besides, as Cobden, the great free trader, pointed out, the cost of transporting corn from Danzig to an English port was equivalent to a protective duty of 10 shillings per quarter, and there was nowhere in the world at that time where there was such a surplus of wheat as to make possible the flooding of the English market. In spite of the Corn Law being ineffective it was nevertheless modified in 1828 by replacing the absolute prohibition with a sliding scale of duties, the intention being to produce a smoother flow of trade.

Agitation against the Corn Laws began in 1815, but until the 1830s any opposition was local and sporadic. Really effective opposition to the Corn Laws dates from the founding in 1838 of the Anti-Corn Law League, which proved to be one of the most effective pressure groups of the century.

Essentially the League was a middle-class organisation based mainly in the North of England, and supported by the new manufacturing groups. As manufacturers grew in strength, so did their opposition to the Corn Laws: '. . . the owner of ten thousand spindles confronted the lord of ten thousand acres; the one grasping the steam-engine, the other the plough . . . now the time has arrived when the shadow of an injustice between such rivals could no longer be endured. . . . Trade shall no longer pay tribute to the soil. . . .' This attack by the manufacturing and commercial classes against the landed interest was reinforced by the interests of the working class, who were told that the repeal of the Corn Laws would mean cheap food.

The League embarked on a vigorous campaign involving the use of every available device of propaganda, including cheap printed posters and handbills sent by the penny post, started in 1840. The League was well led by the great free traders, Cobden and Bright, who eloquently explained its easily understood purposes to the public.

Many dissenters also opposed the Corn Laws, which for them were an attack on the parson's tithes and a wonderful opportunity to show the established Church as the thief of the poor man's bread. Cobden in a letter of 1842 wrote: 'the Church clergy are almost to a man guilty of causing the present distress by upholding the Corn Laws—they having themselves an interest in the high price of bread. . . .'

A very real and major cause of the repeal of the Corn Laws was the depression of the late 1830s and early 1840s. When Peel became Prime Minister in 1841, he attempted to solve the country's economic disorders by either removing or drastically reducing the duties on a vast number of articles of import, especially raw materials and food. Peel was at first opposed to the repeal of the Corn Laws, but was subsequently persuaded by argument and circumstances to change his mind. His decision was no doubt influenced by his background as the son of an industrialist, which probably made him realise the need for sound administrative solutions to the public necessities of an increasingly industrialised society. Peel's objectivity was well illustrated in one debate in 1845, when he admitted that he could not answer the free trade argument properly. Palmerston, who knew his House of Commons well, noted that '. . . the House of Commons is all for lowering duties and not much for raising them.'

The event which finally made up Peel's mind in favour of repeal in 1846 was the Irish potato famine, coupled with England's inability to send corn. Following the repeal, a better relationship evolved between agriculture and industry in which the landlord, who was no longer viewed so much the villain of society, joined forces with the manufacturer. The landlords' interests now became bound up with industry as agriculture profited from industrial progress and the improvements in transport facilities.

The Period of High Farming (1846–74)

The years immediately following 1815 were a period of depression for English agriculture since the industry had been overdeveloped during the war years and in the post-war years foreign competition and depressed trade resulted in the demand for food falling off. However, prosperity returned to English farming in the late 1830s and continued after the repeal of the Corn Laws despite the gloomy forecasts of those who were opposed to repeal. In fact, the repeal of the Corn Laws ushered in the most prosperous period of the century for English farmers.

In 1849 a brief pamphlet was published by a Wigtownshire farmer, James Caird, entitled *High Farming*, which recommended that the challenge of unprotected farming be taken up by the substitution of improved mixed farming for the traditional, predominantly grain, rotations. The period 1846–74 subsequently became known as the period of 'high farming', a term synonymous with the increased productivity achieved by the application of new knowledge and equipment.

The main reasons for English farming becoming more prosperous during this period were as follows:

1. Costs fell as a result of the slow readjustments of rents and wages following the prosperous period of the Napoleonic War years. By 1830 rents were down to between one third or a half on the wartime levels, and wages were down on average from 18 shillings to 10 shillings a week.

2. The population of England and Wales rose from 17 million in 1846 to 24 million in 1874, leading to higher prices for food which as yet, due to inadequate transport facilities, could not be satisfied from abroad. Prices for most agricultural products rose from between 20 to more than 50 per cent in the period.

3. Communications were greatly improved, particularly railways, which had reached Scotland and the more distant counties of England like Norfolk and Lincolnshire by the 1850s. This welding of the whole of Britain into one big agricultural market enabled remote agricultural areas to exploit the growing urban areas of London, the industrial Midlands and the North.

The transportation of animals by rail resulted in their being brought to market in better condition and with less loss of weight than if they had been driven there. The *Quarterly Review* reported in October, 1868, that 'In 1867, the total number of live beasts brought by railway was 172,300 cattle and 1,147,609 sheep. Besides these, the dead meat brought by the same lines was equivalent to 122,000 more cattle and 1,267,000 more sheep—a legion of livestock which, ranged in columns of twelve deep, would extend from London to beyond Aberdeen.'

Speedy rail travel meant that perishable goods such as milk could reach the market quickly, leading to a rapid expansion of the liquid milk market, though this sometimes adversely affected the butter and cheese sections of the dairy industry.

Bulky freight, such as fertilisers, farm implements, feed and seed could also be carried fairly cheaply, thus reducing the farmers' transport costs.

4. In England and Wales longer and better leases encouraged farmers to make long-term improvements in their farms. This was obviously an important factor since if farmers had lived under the threat of eviction without compensation for improvements, as indeed was the case in Ireland at this time, then progressive improvements in farming would not have been possible.

5. Research and study facilities were greatly improved. The Royal Agricultural Society of England was founded in 1838; there was the publication in 1840 of Justus von Liebig's *Organic Chemistry in its Applications to Agriculture and Physiology*; the establishment of the Rothamsted Experimental Station in 1842; and in 1846 a Royal College of Agriculture was opened at Cirencester. The following extract from the 1846 prospectus of the Cirencester Agricultural College illustrates the emphasis that was being placed on scientific farming at this time:

Course of Instruction

The College course extends over two years, and this is the shortest time in which any student can proceed to the final examination.

The theoretical department comprises:

(1) Oral instruction in practical agriculture by the farming superintendent.
(2) Elementary Geometry applied to surveying, levelling cubage of solids, etc.
(3) Mechanics applied to agricultural implements, to the erection of sheds, and construction of roofs, etc.
(4) Hydraulics applied to draining and irrigation.
(5) Designing and drawing plans for implements and buildings.
(6) Chemistry and General Physics.
(7) Geology and Mineralogy
(8) Botany, Vegetable Physiology and Natural History.
} in their various important relations to agriculture.
(9) Principles of the Veterinary Art.
(10) Methods of Farm Accounts.

Practical instruction. The students spend the half of each day on the farm, and take in all the manual operations of husbandry.

Knowledge about improved methods and practices was also made known to farmers through the Royal Agricultural Society's Journal and practical demonstrations could be seen at the Royal Agricultural Society shows.

6. Improved drainage, brought about by the cheapening of pipe production and Government loans, resulted in an increase in productivity since heavy waterlogged land did not provide good crops. Caird, emphasising the importance of good drainage, said that 'The first improvement, in all cases where it is required, is drainage, for until the land is freed from stagnant water, and thus rendered capable of yielding its fullest assistance to the further efforts of the agriculturalist, all other outlay is vain. There is never any difficulty in deciding upon the expediency of drainage in these islands, because wherever it is required, and is judiciously executed, it at once becomes remunerative. The under drainage of arable and good grass land, in a climate where drainage is advantageous, renders the land so much warmer and wholesome for plants and animals, everything upon it becomes so much more easy and certain in their results, that it is sure to pay.'

A series of pipe-making machines facilitating efficient drainage at reasonable cost, were developed in the 1840s, such as Reade's tile drain pipe, Scragg's pipe-making machine and Fowler's mole plough for draining. In 1851 the Royal Agricultural Society's Journal gave a report on Fowler's Draining Plough, which had attracted considerable interest at the Great Exhibition: 'Twelve years ago draining-tiles were made by hand, cumbrous arches with flat soles, costing respectively 50s. and 25s. per 1,000. Pipes have been substituted for these, made by machinery, which squeezes out clay from a box through circular holes, exactly as macaroni is made at Naples, and the cost of these pipes averages 20s. down to 12s. per 1,000. The old price was almost prohibitory of permanent drainage, excepting where stones were at hand: the new invention has reduced this permanent improvement to a rate of £4 or £3 per acre, not exceeding in cost the manure given to a single turnip crop in some high-farmed districts. This result has been obtained by a most spirited competition among machinists, as no less than 34 different tile-machines competed in 1848 at the York meeting. Since then the struggle has been practically between three only. . . . But for the American Reapers, Mr Fowler's draining plough would have formed the most remarkable feature in the agricultural department of the Exhibition. Wonderful as it is to see the standing wheat shorn levelly low by a pair of horses walking along its edge, it is hardly, if at all, less wonderful, nor did it excite less interest or surprise among the crowd of spectators when the trial was made . . . to see two horses at work by the side of the field, which the framework has quitted, you perceive that it has been dragging after it a string of pipes which, still following the plough's snout, that burrows all the while four feet below ground, twists itself like a gigantic red worm into the earth, so that in a few minutes, when the framework has reached the capstan, the string is withdrawn from the necklace, and you are assured that a drain has been invisibly formed under your feet.'

Investment by landlords in drainage also led to more investment in buildings since better drainage encouraged the expansion of mixed farming and the heavier stocking of land, which often involved the erection of additional buildings such as cattle houses, pigsties and barns. It has been estimated that £25,000,000 was invested in drainage schemes and other improvements during the quarter century following the repeal of the Corn Laws. Much of this money though—which was raised through Government loans, mortgage brokers, specialist drainage loan companies or the ploughing back of profits—was often invested without properly calculating the rate of return on capital and so much of the new investment never paid.

7. There was a growing awareness in the 1840s of the scientific value of fertilisation, and the greater use of both organic and artificial fertilisers resulted in farmers achieving increased yields. In addition to home-produced superphosphate and basic slag, guano was imported from Peru, nitrates from Chile, and from the 1860s onwards potash was imported from Germany.

8. Machinery such as the horsedrawn reaper, the seed-drill and the hay tedder came into more widespread use. Steam threshing machines and steam-ploughs were introduced, though on a limited scale. H. S. Thomson, M.P., a trustee of the Royal Agricultural Society wrote in 1864 that 'At the Newcastle Show in 1846, only one steam engine was exhibited . . . yet at Worcester (in 1863) there were 135 steam engines; and one of the successful exhibitors on that occasion has informed us that though in 1845 he made only one steam engine, and not one steam threshing machine, he has, in the four years 1859–62, turned out an average of 488 engines and 373 steam threshing machines per annum! Since 1852 he has sold enough steam engines to supply each member of the Royal Agricultural Society with one. . . . If the engines furnished by all the makers in the same time could be summed up into a grand total, it would be seen that already many thousands of steam engines have been purchased for agricultural work; showing clearly that on the farm as well as in the factory the reign of steam has commenced.'

Of much greater importance than the use of steam on the land, however, were the improvements in the traditional tools, like ploughs and hoes and the many tools that were required to deal with different types of soils.

9. More interest was also shown in pedigree cattle breeding, which by the end of the period was no longer practised only by the progressive few.

The prosperity that was introduced into English agriculture by these improved conditions, however, came to an end in the 1870s when the protection of distance was removed by improvements in transport and English farmers had to face competition from countries with a better comparative cost advantage.

Depression and Decline (1873–1914)

During the last quarter of the nineteenth century the economic climate changed and the period generally became associated with falling prices, falling profits, falling wages and fiercer competition. Despite these obvious symptoms of depression there is some controversy as to whether there was a depression of industry, but as far as agriculture was concerned it is appropriate to say that there was a depression, and this was for a number of very clear reasons.

1. There was an unusual period of bad luck with the weather, which in the past had compensated the farmer by bringing higher prices in the following year because of the resultant shortages. This, however, no longer happened since shortages were made good by increased foreign competition.

For most of the seventies the harvests were bad, especially in the years 1873, 1875, 1877 and 1879, the last experiencing the worst harvest of the century. The wet autumn of 1875 was followed by the unusually heavy rainfall of 1876–7, and in the spring of 1878 there began a period of exceptionally cold and wet weather lasting for the duration of the decade.

In addition to bad harvests, wet weather also caused liver rot in sheep, and this together with a severe outbreak of foot and mouth disease in 1881–3 inflicted heavy damage on flocks, and hit those farmers who were turning over to stockbreeding and animal husbandry because wheat growing could no longer be made to pay.

2. Wheat imports greatly increased at a time when many of the most fervent protectionists had become converted to free trade. Certainly, with respect to agriculture, any advantages of free trade became outweighed by the disadvantages.

The United States was opened up by the transcontinental railroads in the decade after the Civil War and foreign labour and capital and Government land policy helped to convert the fertile prairies into great wheat-producing areas. Wheat was grown in these regions in conditions of near perfect competition where there were many producers of a homogeneous product, and since an individual producer could not influence price by restricting output everyone produced as much as they could, thus having the aggregate effect of depressing overall prices.

Increased wheat imports also came from European countries, particularly the Crimea of Russia after the opening up of the Black Sea to Russian shipping from 1871 onwards.

The transportation of cereals by sea was cheapened by the development of large steamships, which imported wheat and other cereals on the inward journey and exported coal on the outward journey.

Thus, wheat and other cereal prices fell: in 1877, the price of wheat was 56s. 9d. a quarter; by 1886 it was down to 31s. a quarter.

3. Agricultural prices were also depressed because of the so-called 'Great Depression', which was part of a world-wide cyclical downswing of prices.

4. The development of the refrigeration ship began to damage the English meat market in the 1880s as the result of the importation of frozen and chilled meat from the Argentine, Australia and New Zealand. In the last few years of the century, English meat prices were at the lowest level for 150 years.

Arable acreages in England and Wales were reduced by about 30 per cent between 1871 and 1901, falling from $8\frac{1}{4}$ to less than 6 million acres, whilst the permanent pasture increased from $11\frac{1}{3}$ to $15\frac{1}{3}$ million acres. The size of the agricultural labour force also fell from being the largest single employer of labour in 1851, accounting for approximately a quarter of the occupied males, to hardly 12 per cent by 1901.

Agriculture remained in a depressed state until the First World War, though some improvements were made such as the adoption of the milking machine and the partial de-rating of agricultural land in 1896. What was really required was some form of protection, but since the majority of voters enfranchised in 1867 and 1884 were town dwellers for whom cheap food from abroad mattered, there was little hope that anything substantial in this respect could be done, as the Tories learnt to their cost at the 1906 General Election.

Suggested Further Reading

Jones, E. L., *The Development of English Agriculture, 1815–1873*, Macmillan, London, 1968.

Orwin, C. S., and Whetham, E. H., *History of British Agriculture, 1856–1914*, Longmans, London, 1964.

Exercises

1. Why did British agriculture continue to be prosperous after the repeal of the Corn Laws in 1846?

2. Account for the changes in the profitability of British agriculture between 1873 and 1914.

Summary

1. Agriculture experienced depressed conditions between 1815 and the late 1830s.

2. The period 1846–74 was one of prosperity brought about by increasing demand, lack of foreign competition, improved transport and better methods of production.

3. From the 1870s agriculture experienced abnormally bad times due to growing foreign competition and Britain's continuing adherence to a free trade policy.

CHAPTER NINE

THE RISE TO INDUSTRIAL MATURITY

The British economy matured in the period 1830 to 1914, when the range of modern technology was applied to the bulk of its resources. New 'leading sectors' gathered momentum as the centre of the growth process moved away from textiles towards coal, iron and steel and the capital goods industries.

Development of the Basic Industries

Cotton

The cotton industry, which had played a spectacular part in the first phase of the Industrial Revolution, began to decline in importance relative to other industries during the 1840s, though it continued to grow in absolute terms, producing an all-time record of 8 million yards of cotton cloth in 1913.

The main centres of the industry were in South Lancashire, north-east Cheshire and the West Riding of Yorkshire, these areas employing 90 per cent of the workers in cotton. By 1914 there were more than half a million workers employed in the cotton industry, a large proportion of whom were women, cotton manufacture being the most important source of female employment.

The industry did not become fully mechanised until the 1850s and 1860s, when steam power in weaving became universal. Even though factory production was the general rule by the 1870s, and increased productivity was achieved by more mechanisation, there were no major technical advances in the industry and important technological developments such as ring-spinning were ignored. Electric power was first applied to the loom in 1905, and the first electric spinning mill was opened at Pendlebury, near Manchester, later that year.

British cotton manufacture experienced a major setback during the American Civil War (1861–5) when Lancashire suffered from a cotton famine. The resulting depression and unemployment in the cotton-spinning districts led Britain to diversify her sources of supply of raw cotton, and in future increasing quantities were purchased from India and Egypt.

The industry's failure to recapitalise, and the development of cotton manufacture elsewhere, meant that by 1913 it had become an economic monstrosity that was about to be devastated by foreign competition.

Coal

The most rapid period of growth in the coal industry took place in the second half of the nineteenth century (Table 16).

Some economists, like the Manchester economist Stanley Jevons, predicted that the increase in demand for coal would have been even greater, but this did not happen because of the more efficient use of coal in industry. Better constructed boilers in steamships and locomotives, for example, used less coal, as did the big new iron blast furnaces per ton of iron produced.

An important aspect of this increase in coal production was the high rate of expansion in coal exports, rising from 3 million tons in 1850 to 94 million tons in 1914, i.e. 73 million tons actually exported and 21 million tons used by shipping engaged in foreign trade. This growth in exports resulted mainly from the industrialisation of Europe, the building of railways throughout the world, the introduction of the steel steamship, and the expansion in the tonnage of ocean-going shipping. Cardiff and some ports of the North-East grew up almost entirely on the coal export trade.

In spite of the fact that all-time production records in coal output were achieved in 1913, all was not well with the industry. Increased production was achieved mainly by increasing the size of the labour force, rather than by any fundamental improvements in the methods of

Table 16. Growth of the Coal Industry

Date	*U.K. output (million tons)*	*U.K. total value (£ million)*
1855	65	16
1870	110	28
1885	159	41
1900	225	122
1913	287	146

Source: B. R. Mitchell and P. Deane, *Abstract of British Historical Statistics.*

production. The industry's labour force grew from 200,000 in 1850 to 1,128,000 in 1913, representing a tenth of the country's male occupied labour force. This growth of manpower magnified the poor working conditions and the social problems of labour, and resulted in the spread of trade unionism amongst miners. Discontent amongst miners was also influenced to some extent by the pioneering nature of the mining communities, developing as they did on the coalfields away from the established areas of settlement. These mining villages, with their rows of dismal, indifferent houses, instilled into many miners a feeling of isolation and bitterness, particularly over the vexed questions of hours, pay and working conditions.

Whilst technical expansion continued in the nineteenth century in order to meet the needs of bulk production, it remained generally true that investment did not keep pace with the marginal efficiency of capital. Tubs and cages were substituted for the ancient corves as steam pressures and winding speeds increased; wire ropes replaced hemp ones and facilitated the hauling of heavier loads; and by 1914 improved ventilation and lighting underground had been introduced.

In contrast to these technical improvements was the extent to which machine mining had been introduced. According to Professor W. H. B. Court, the British coalmining industry down to 1914 remained 'a pick and shovel industry'. Only 8 per cent of British coal was cut mechanically in 1914 compared with 25 per cent cut mechanically in the U.S.A. in 1900, and there were only 360 mechanical conveyors for thousands of mines. Added to this were the problems created by the structure of the industry. There were some 3,000 collieries operating in the early years of the twentieth century, the largest ones of which employed up to 2,000 men and produced about three quarters of a million tons of coal per annum. The average output of mines, however, was small and the ownership of them was dispersed.

Whilst the industry had had a good record of success up to 1914, the increase in the world capacity of coal production and the development of alternative forms of power such as oil and electricity, meant that the prospects for the future of the British industry, with its fragmented structure, large labour force and lack of mechanisation, were not bright.

Iron and Steel

The development of the iron and steel industry was crucial to industrialisation since increasing quantities of iron and later steel were required for the construction of machinery, rails, ships, bridges, etc., as industrialisation spread from this country to other parts of the world.

The pattern of demand for iron varied during the nineteenth century. After the Napoleonic Wars the armament demand was replaced with orders for boilers, machine parts and gas and water piping. During the 1840s it was railways that placed the greatest demands upon the industry, whilst in the 1850s the trend towards substituting iron for wood in shipbuilding resulted in the net tonnage of iron ships built increasing from 12,800 in 1850 to 64,700 by 1860. In these circumstances, the output of pig iron rose from about 700,000 tons a year in 1830 to more than 6,500,000 tons in the boom of 1871–3, when British supremacy in the industry seemed assured.

The industry was revolutionised in the second half of the nineteenth century by a series of inventions which substituted for malleable iron the substance known as mild steel. Up to 1880 Britain had produced mainly iron, but from then onwards there was a switch to steel as the main product of the industry.

During the last quarter of the nineteenth century both railway lines and ships came to be made of steel, though there was at times a great diversity of opinion about the virtue of this. In fact, steel was a superior material for both rails and ships, steel rails being able to stand heavier traffic and steel having great advantages for shipbuilding in its relative lightness and its higher capacity to resist strain. The main reasons for the slowness in the adoption of a superior and far cheaper material were because many interests were bound up with the making of iron, such as labour, skill and capital; the change was also accompanied by an initial expense, and both ships and railways were still involved in other structural changes.

The properties of steel had been known long before the nineteenth century, but the cost of its manufacture had prohibited large-scale production. This deficiency was remedied between 1850 and 1880 when three great innovations made the large-scale production of steel possible.

1. *The Bessemer Process (1856)*. Henry Bessemer, a professional inventor, first saw the need for securing a stronger form of iron for making cannon during the Crimean War. Until then wrought-iron with a low carbon content was in common use for bridge-building, ships' hulls, boiler-plates, railway-tyres, rails and the working parts of steam engines and locomotives. Wrought-iron, which was a metal of great tenacity, though not as strong as steel, was produced by the puddling process, involving one of the most laborious and unpleasant forms of skilled labour in the world. Bessemer took great pains to point out that his process would eliminate physical drudgery for thousands of men.

This new process for making steel involved pouring molten iron into a special converter, and then, by using a powerful air blast, the chemical impurities were burnt away so that either malleable iron or steel was produced.

The resulting metal depended upon the extent to which carbon had been eliminated from the ores, since steel is a blend of iron and carbon that provides a metal far tougher and more serviceable than iron itself. Bessemer steel was more uniform in quality, more reliable, stronger and cheaper than malleable iron.

The one great disadvantage of the Bessemer process was that it could not eliminate phosphorus from the ores which it used, and steel will not form in the presence of phosphorus. Unfortunately British ores, except the haematite ores of Cumberland, North Lancashire and the Forest of Dean, contained a high phosphorus content so that it became necessary to import large quantities of non-phosphoric ores from Spain and Sweden.

2. *The Siemens Process (1867)*. William Siemens was a pioneer of heat economy and in 1856 he took out a patent for the application to furnaces of the 'regenerative' principle. In 1867 Siemens succeeded in manufacturing acid steel from pig iron melted with ore in the hearth of a shallow furnace lined with silica brick. This was a slower process than Bessemer's, but it produced a metal which was more uniform and reliable throughout. Whereas Bessemer steel was used for railway and structural use, open-hearth steel was more suitable for shipbuilding and steel sheets, where ductility as well as uniformity was important. From 1893 onwards more steel was made on the open hearth than in the converter, and by 1930 the Bessemer process had been completely superseded.

3. *The Gilchrist–Thomas Process (1878)*. Since both the Bessemer and Siemens processes could not use phosphoric iron ores there was an obvious need for a further invention. This was made in 1878 by a part-time amateur, Sidney Gilchrist-Thomas, a police court clerk, with the assistance of a chemist, his cousin Percy Gilchrist. The Gilchrist-Thomas process involved placing a lining of a basic material in the Bessemer converter or the open-hearth furnace, which would take up the phosphorus from the iron during conversion so that steel of good quality could be produced from phosphoric ores. The resulting product

was known as basic steel, as distinct from acid steel produced by the earlier processes.

This was a technique with obvious value for Britain, but a prejudice developed against basic steel in this country. This was possibly because non-phosphoric ores were easy to import, and also because the quality of basic steel was more difficult to control. Acid steel continued to maintain its reputation for reliability, and the process was preserved.

If the Gilchrist-Thomas process had value for Britain, it had even more value for foreign countries, especially the United States and Germany, each of which had rich fields of phosphoric iron ores.

Germany had acquired considerable deposits of phosphoric ores by the annexation of Lorraine from France in 1870, and consequently abandoned the acid for the basic process, whilst the United States had vast deposits of both phosphoric and non-phosphoric ores so that when the coal of Pittsburgh was joined by railways to the iron of Lake Superior she was successfully using the latest forms of all three processes.

Adaptation of the British industry to the basic process was slow, though mild steel made by the basic process gradually increased its reputation because of its cheapness and easy manipulation by presses and machine tools, so that the proportion of total output of British steel made by the basic process increased from 17 per cent in 1901 to 37 per cent in 1913. It needed the disruption of supplies of foreign ore during the First World War to bring home to British steelmakers the importance of the basic process.

Partly as a result of this British discovery, but mainly because of their extensive resources, both the United States and Germany overtook Britain in the early 1890s in steelmaking. They also produced more pig iron than Britain, the United States alone producing three times as much pig iron as Britain in 1913.

In addition to being slow in adopting new processes and techniques, the British iron and steel industry was badly organised. This was a pity, since this industry is one which lends itself well to efficient organisation and large-scale production. By 1913 some of her competitors had integrated plants with molten iron passing straight into the steelworks and rolling mills dealing immediately with the steel, whereas in Britain there were no integrated steelworks of this kind. It is not surprising therefore that whilst British iron and steel production continued to expand quantitatively up to 1914, comparatively it declined as other countries did better. In many respects Britain was suffering from the disadvantages of having been the first country to undergo rapid and sustained economic growth, since other countries learnt from her experience and mistakes. The condition of the British iron and steel industry in the quarter century before 1914 was a good example of capital, skill, plant and pride in past achievement standing in the way of new methods of production.

Engineering

Engineering as a trade came into being to meet the needs of many industries, principally textile machinery, locomotives and rolling stock, steam engines and machine tools, for which a number of specialist firms developed during the nineteenth century. The construction of steamships and marine engines became a major branch of engineering in Britain after 1850, but this will be dealt with later.

A number of important new branches of the industry were developed in the last quarter of the nineteenth century, following on the discovery of new methods of producing large quantities of cheap steel, since the connection between metallurgical discoveries and engineering progress is a very close one. The expansion of the machine-tool industry transformed many handicraft industries into machine industries and made possible the mass production by interchangeable techniques of such products as cycles and motor cars, but it is important to remember that machine tools were developed with much less vigour in Britain than amongst some of her competitors.

Cycle manufacture based on standardised parts became a prominent industry in the 1870s, and by 1879 there were about 60 firms solely in business to manufacture cycles. After the discoveries of Bell and Edison in America during the 1870s electrical engineering began to be developed, but progress in this new field of production was disappointingly slow.

The invention of the internal combustion engine around 1860 was without doubt the most significant landmark with regards to the future potential of the engineering industry, though motor-car manufacture did not become an important industry in Britain until after the First World War.

Shipbuilding

Up to the eighteenth century British shipbuilding was scattered all over the country, but by 1900 it had become concentrated on the Tyne and Clyde and to a lesser extent at Belfast and on the Mersey at Birkenhead. This change was brought about by the need for deep-water ports, since with the development of iron ships the hulls were made larger, and only a limited number of places had the necessary docking facilities.

The first iron-hulled vessel to be constructed in Britain was the *Aaron Manby*, built in 1822. There were at first serious doubts about the ocean-going capacity of iron-hulled vessels because they quickly became encrusted with barnacles; it was not until the period between 1850 and 1870, therefore, that iron replaced wood as the chief material of construction.

During the 1870s, due to the work of Bessemer and Siemens, steel began to replace iron in the construction of ship and boiler plates. This changeover resulted in a considerable reduction in the weight of the hull, and thus increased carrying capacity, as well as enabling higher pressures to be maintained in steel boilers, leading to reduced fuel consumption.

The conversion from wood to iron ships initially revitalised sailing vessels rather than steam vessels, since the early marine engines were highly inefficient and wasteful of fuel. Iron sailing ships could be made longer, thus increasing their freight carrying capacity, whereas much of the carrying capacity of the early steamships was required for coal.

An important improvement in the efficiency of the early steamship was the introduction by F. B. Smith, in 1837, of the screw propeller, thus dispensing with paddle wheels, which had proved to be unsuitable for sea journeys. Scientific calculation on the shape and speed of the revolution of propellers soon enabled maximum propulsive power to be achieved.

John Elder's invention in 1854 of the compound engine made possible considerable economies in fuel by using the same steam several times over in different cylinders.

In 1884, Sir Charles Parsons developed the steam turbine, which he demonstrated in the *Turbinia* at the Spithead Naval Review in 1897. This engine enabled larger vessels to achieve greater speeds, and was the last of the great developments in marine engineering pioneered by British shipbuilders in the nineteenth century.

Oil, as an alternative fuel for coal in raising steam, was being used before the end of the nineteenth century, and in 1912 Rudolf Diesel's heavy oil engine was adapted for marine purposes. Amongst the many advantages of oil over coal for marine purposes was that it economised on the use of space and labour, both of which were extremely important considerations to the shipowner. Even Conservative Britain, under the influence of Winston Churchill, began to bunker her battle cruisers with oil in 1906. This posed a strategic problem, since Britain was not at the time a big producer of oil, and led to the British Government becoming a major shareholder in the Anglo Persian Oil Company when it was formed in 1909. This was indeed an exceptional event since the British Government had only very rarely in the past acquired shares in a joint stock company. Investment in industrial plant and resources in Britain was invariably undertaken by private enterprise.

Amongst the other influences affecting the British mercantile marine in the nineteenth century was the Government's decision not to renew the East Indian Charter in 1833, which boosted private enterprise in the British shipping industry. This was followed by the repeal of the Navigation Acts in 1849, thereby ending State protection for British shipping. This increased the fears that already existed for the future of the British shipbuilding industry, but as events turned out these fears proved to be ill-founded, since once a ship became reduced 'to a box of machinery encased in iron', and later on steel, Britain had the technical knowledge and skills that gave her a temporary monopoly in what was virtually a new industry. This favourable position was further enhanced by the repeal in 1854 of the old Tonnage Law of 1773, under which ships had been taxed by length and breadth, thus making possible the development of more economical shallow draught designs.

Whilst the supremacy of the other staple industries was being successfully challenged in the last few decades of the nineteenth century, the British shipbuilding industry achieved its position of unquestioned superiority. This industry did not have to concern itself too much with keeping abreast of the latest techniques since, as Hobsbawm says, 'None of the advantages of modern productive technique and organisation applied to ships which were built in giant single units of largely unstandardised materials and with a vast input of the most varied and highest manual skills. They were no more mechanised than palaces.' (E. J. Hobsbawm, *Industry and Empire*).

The peak years for British shipbuilding were between 1890 and 1894, when her shipyards were producing 80 per cent of the world's ships. Output continued to increase from 3·9 million tons in 1895 to 6·0 million tons in 1915, but by then the U.K. proportion of the world total of ships built had fallen to 58·4 per cent.

The Second Industrial Revolution

Some economic historians consider that the influence of the introduction of steel, electric power, and the internal combustion engine after 1850 on economic development was no less spectacular than the impact of iron, coal and steam transport during the first Industrial Revolution. Hence, the period between 1850 and 1914 is often referred to as the 'Second Industrial Revolution'. This second phase of development was associated with new science-based inventions and the great changes which took place were a reflection of the vast increase in scientific knowledge. Whilst science and technology were still a long way apart from each other in the second half of the nineteenth century, the relationship between them was nevertheless becoming closer. This was the beginning of the movement, as we know it today, where every major industry employs its own team of professional scientists to solve any practical problems that might arise. Increasingly, industrial expansion came to depend upon the ingenuity of scientists and technologists in applying to industry the discoveries made in laboratories.

An important characteristic of this new phase of development was the increasing dependence of the industrial machine on precision, uniformity and speed. Much is owed in this respect to Henry Maudsley, who devised new tools which enabled machine parts to be made quickly, accurately and relatively cheaply, whilst Joseph Whitworth suggested the standardisation of screw threads which became common practice after 1860. The resulting increased precision of the machine-tool industry became the key to the new technology by making it possible for machines to make machines. The introduction of standardisation and interchangeability of parts revolutionised the production process. Changes in business organisation and the introduction of mass-production techniques followed as a matter of course.

Changes in Business Organisation

Until the middle of the nineteenth century most industrial expansion was undertaken by the one-man or family firm and the partnership. Businesses were usually started with quite modest sums of capital and these were frequently provided out of current earnings.

Joint Stock Enterprise

The expansion of industry would have been greatly restricted if industrialists had been tied down to their own financial resources. Hence, joint stock enterprise was devised in order to muster the savings of a number of people for industrial and commercial investment.

Unfortunately the development of joint stock enterprise was inhibited in Britain by the Bubble Act of 1720, which stipulated that any new joint stock company must first go through the lengthy and expensive process of obtaining a charter from the Crown or Parliament. Coupled with this obstacle was the insistence by the law that all the partners in the enterprise must have unlimited liability. This requirement placed in jeopardy the entire fortune of any prospective partner, thereby creating an attitude of extreme caution towards such investment. Hence joint stock enterprise was mainly confined, until the mid-nineteenth century, to a few of the older companies such as the East India and Hudson's Bay Companies.

Such restrictions on joint stock enterprise had to be removed if a further stage of the Industrial Revolution was to be promoted, and a movement for a change in the law sprang up. This movement found added strength in the difficult years after the Napoleonic Wars and in 1825 a financial crisis prompted the repeal of the Bubble Act. A further Act passed in 1844 enabled companies to incorporate by simple registration, though unlimited liability remained and even continued for three years after a partner had disposed of his interest. Parliament subsequently conceded limited liability in two Acts passed in 1856 and 1862, the later Act becoming the basis of modern company law.

The joint stock, limited liability form of company made it easier for men of limited resources to raise outside capital, as well as facilitating the quicker growth of well-established firms. Investors also benefited by being able to spread their risks over a number of companies, and by being freed from the worry of further liability.

Railways, banks, insurance companies and public utilities took advantage of the benefits of the new structure much more readily than did manufacturing industry. Most manufacturers were suspicious or indifferent to the new borrowing powers of joint stock enterprise during the 1870s and 1880s, especially since there were many failures and frauds, though many cotton manufacturers availed themselves of the facilities of joint stock enterprise between 1875 and 1885. The slow adoption of the company form was probably also influenced by finance becoming more readily available from the banks.

The steady growth of joint stock enterprise brought about a change in the human relationships in industry: 'In place of the master craftsman in close contact with his men and their work, and unaware of the dividing line between his own wages and his profits, or his business and personal expenses, control was wielded by a board, often non-expert in composition, through salaried managers, and in the interests of distant shareholders.' (M. W. Thomas, *A Survey of English Economic History*).

Industrial Combination

A natural consequence of the change in company law was the growth of giant businesses through combination, a process that proceeded much more slowly in Britain than in Germany and the United States.

An obvious incentive encouraging firms to combine were the increased opportunities that became available for firms to benefit from the economies of scale. The falling prices during the 'Great Depression' of 1873 to 1896 encouraged some businessmen to reduce costs through the economies of scale and maintain prices by gaining greater control of the market. Large concerns with large-scale planning were better able to iron out violent fluctuations in the trade cycle than were the smaller firms.

Amongst the early combinations to be set up in Britain were the Distillers Company, formed in 1877, and the Nobel Dynamite Company, formed in 1886. Several take-over bids by the sewing-thread firm of J. & P. Coats in the late 1890s made it the largest firm in British manufacturing industry, with a nominal share and loan capital of £7·5 million and a market value of £22 millions. A number of other amalgamations took place before 1914, principally in engineering, chemicals, banking and retail distribution. These mergers tended to be concentrated upon particular sectors of industry, e.g. out of the fifty-two biggest companies in Britain in 1905 seventeen were in brewing and ten in textiles.

Nevertheless, despite these amalgamations, British industry in 1914 was still composed mainly of small firms, whilst the United States and Germany were nations of large companies. This divergent development took place for several reasons:

1. In Britain the law was unfriendly towards associations in restraint of trade. In addition, a type of natural law seemed to be at work which substituted competition for monopoly, as in the case of the abolition of the Corn Laws in 1846 or the ending of the Bank of England's monopoly in joint stock banking in 1826 and 1833.
2. Many British firms were run by long-established families who had acquired a taste for control. This form of management tended to be very conservative and resistant to change.
3. Wealth was more unevenly divided in Britain than in the United States, where a mass consumer market was more developed. This resulted in the British market having a preference for articles with an individual character rather than mass-produced standardised products. This applied also to the export markets, upon which Britain was more dependent than the United States.
4. Britain's free trade policy left the home market wide open to foreign competition, whereas the big trusts in the United States and Germany were able to monopolise their home markets.
5. Industrial resources in Britain tended to be scattered, as for example coalmining, which was peculiarly competitive in its organisation, whereas in the United States and Germany the coal and iron ore resources tended to be more geographically concentrated, thus enabling them to be more easily organised on a bigger and more efficient scale.

Mass Production

The increase in the size of business units and the standardisation of parts made possible the production of commodities in continuous flows and on a very large scale. In this type of technology the pace is controlled mechanically, the work being brought to the worker and taken away on completion, usually by mechanical means. This enabled careful studies to be made of the operative in relation to the machine in order to analyse and improve the relationship, a process that was aided by the invention of the motion-picture camera. This, in turn, often led to new tools being devised and factory layout and organisation being improved.

Whilst these new production techniques were being used in Britain as early as the 1840s by some Manchester machine tool factories, the real pioneering work in mass-production methods was done in the United States where the scale of industry was generally larger. Henry Ford revolutionised the motor car industry by mass producing a cheap car which could be sold to a much wider market, thus dispelling the widely held belief that motor cars, by virtue of their cost, could only sell to a limited market. By 1913 the Americans had produced 462,000 cars compared with Britain's 25,000, partly due to America's lead in the techniques of mass production.

Assembly-line technology led to management itself becoming subdivided and much more professional and specialised in its outlook. Production engineers, personnel managers, cost accountants, buyers and sellers became specialised subdivisions of the production process as tasks and roles within industry became differentiated, and it no longer necessarily followed as a matter of course that a unit of production was managed by the man who owned it.

During the course of this second 'Industrial Revolution' more attention began to be paid to the utilisation of waste, and useful by-products were developed. Slag left behind in the making of basic steel, for example, was used as a fertiliser, whilst scrap metal was recycled and made into steel by the open-hearth process.

The Location of Industry

The coming of modern industry has led to geographical concentration so that districts, like persons, specialise in particular forms of economic activity. The most important influences on the location of industry between 1830 and 1914 were proximity to power and raw materials.

Proximity to Power

Before the eighteenth century, power-driven machinery was rarely used, with the result that manufacturing industry was widely dispersed. The woollen industry, for example, was carried on wherever there was sheep-rearing, though by the sixteenth century this industry was mainly located in South-West England, East Anglia and Yorkshire.

The coming of water power during the early days of the Industrial Revolution led to the siting of factories, mainly cotton mills, near fast-flowing streams and rivers. Many of these early power-driven factories were to be found on the western slopes of the Pennines in Lancashire.

With the development of steam power, the chief localising factor for industry became coal, since the cost of transporting coal any distance was prohibitive. Thus the big industrial areas of the country came to be centred on the coalfields where the great exporting industries of cotton, wool, engineering, shipbuilding, and iron and steel were developed.

This concentration of industry on the coalfields led to the North of England, the Midlands and South Wales becoming the most densely populated areas of the country, whilst population growth in the agricultural areas was very low.

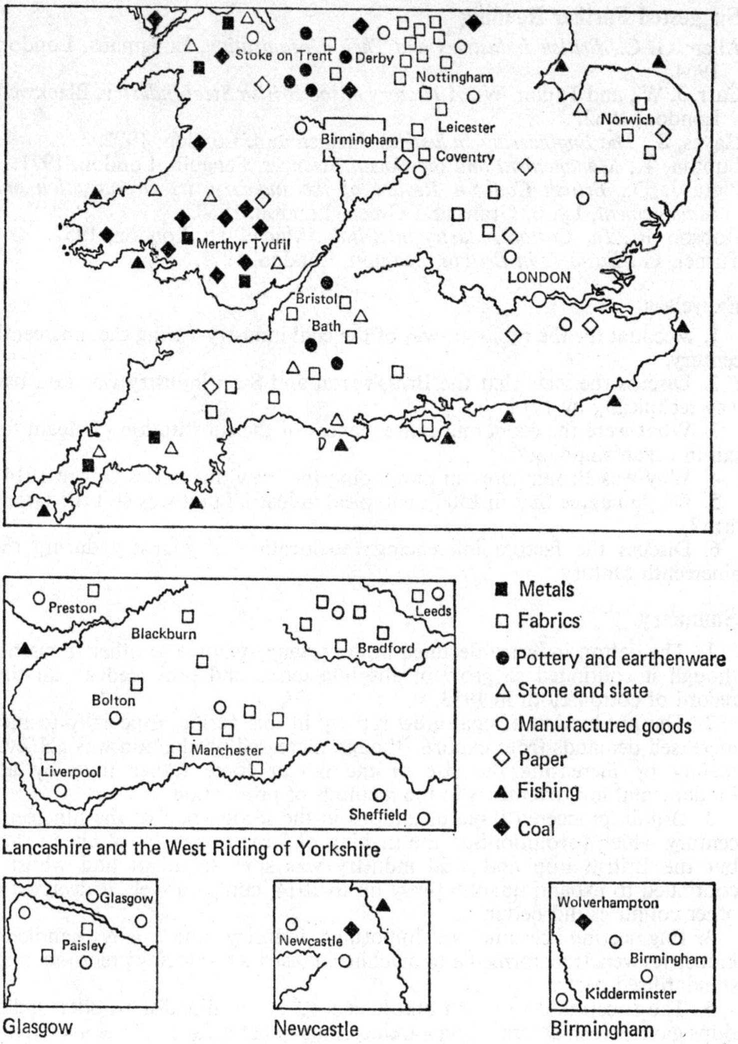

Fig. 8. The location of industry

(courtesy Penguin Books Ltd)

Proximity to Raw Materials

Nearness to raw materials very often helped to decide the actual distribution of industries among the coalfields. Proximity of iron ore and limestone to coal, for example, helped to determine the siting of the iron and steel industry. The rapid growth of Middlesbrough during the mid-nineteenth century was brought about by the exploitation of the iron ore deposits in the Cleveland Hills, which were within easy reach of coal supplies.

Suggested Further Reading

Allen, G. C., *British Industries and Their Organisation*, Longmans, London, 1964.

Carr, J. W., and Taplin, W., *A History of the British Steel Industry*, Blackwell, London, 1962.

Hayes, S., *The Engineering Industries*, Heinemann, London, 1972.

Lupton, T., *Management and the Social Sciences*, Penguin, London, 1971.

Platt, J. D., *British Coal. A Review of the Industry, its Organisation and Management*, Lyon, Grant and Green, London, 1968.

Robson, R., *The Cotton Industry in Britain*, Macmillan, London, 1957.

Turner, G., *Business in Britain*, Penguin, London, 1971.

Exercises

1. Account for the rapid growth of the coal industry during the nineteenth century.
2. Discuss the view that the British Iron and Steel industry was in a bad way technically by 1914.
3. What were the economic consequences of the substitution of steam for sail in ocean shipping?
4. Why was Britain slow in developing the 'new' industries before 1914?
5. Do you agree that in 1900 the typical industrial unit was still the family firm?
6. Discuss the factors influencing the location of industry during the nineteenth century.

Summary

1. The cotton industry declined in importance relative to other industries, though it continued to grow in absolute terms and produced an all time record of cotton cloth in 1913.
2. The production of coal grew rapidly in this period, especially to meet increased demands from exports, though increased production was achieved mainly by increasing the size of the labour force rather than by any fundamental improvements in the methods of production.
3. Britain pioneered three inventions in the second half of the nineteenth century which revolutionised the making of large quantities of cheap steel, but the British iron and steel industry was slow to adapt and whilst it continued to expand quantitatively up to 1914, comparatively it declined as other countries did better.
4. Engineering became an important industry and many handicraft industries were transformed into machine industries producing precision-made standardised parts.
5. The substitution of iron and later steel steamships for wooden sailing ships gave British shipbuilding a tremendous boost because of the availability of extensive resources and skills.
6. There was a 'Second Industrial Revolution' between 1850 and 1914 when industrial expansion came to depend more and more on new technology and improved techniques.
7. Changes in company law encouraged the growth in the size of business units, though this process was slower in Britain than in Germany and the U.S.
8. The most important influences on the location of industry between 1830 and 1914 were proximity to sources of power and raw materials.

CHAPTER TEN

THE DEVELOPMENT OF WORKING-CLASS ORGANISATION

A strong working class movement grew up in the nineteenth century, alongside the development of industry and the organisation of capital. There were many separate elements to this movement, such as the Chartists, Friendly Societies and the Mechanics Institutes, whose aims were to improve the working man's security and status. Some parts of the movement, principally the Co-operative and trade union elements, turned their attention as the century progressed towards political activity, and became the most important forces behind the establishment of the Labour Party.

The Chartists

After the conviction of the Tolpuddle Martyrs, and the collapse of the Grand National Consolidated Trades Union in 1834, there was a movement away from the utopian ideals of trade unionism and social unrest began to express itself through the political aspirations of the Chartist movement.

The London Working Men's Association, formed in 1836, issued in 1838 what became known as the People's Charter. This Charter demanded a programme of six political reforms: universal manhood suffrage, voting by secret ballot, equal electoral districts, abolition of the property qualification for M.P.'s, payment of M.P.'s and annual parliaments.

On the surface Chartism appeared to be a political movement, yet it was based largely on economic grievances, and came about for a variety of reasons.

1. It expressed disappointment in the conservative nature of the 1832 Reform Act, because it failed to bring the British parliamentary system much closer to anything resembling democracy.
2. It was a reaction from the ideals of industrial democracy following the collapse of the trade union movement.
3. It reflected the opposition of the working classes to the implementation of the 1834 Poor Law Amendment Act in the industrial areas.
4. It was a way of expressing discontent during times of cyclical depression. The movement was always strongest in the peak months of unemployment, and during the decade 1838 to 1848 three cyclical depressions occurred, causing great economic distress. As the Hammonds said: 'For some ten years the English poor found in the Chartist agitation an opportunity for protesting against the place they occupied in the raw industrial settlements spreading over the Midlands and North.'

Three mammoth petitions were organised and submitted to Parliament in 1839, 1842 and 1848, demanding the six points of the Charter.

This was done against a background of great excitement and revolutionary fervour, and certainly up to 1842 the movement gave the impression of being a real threat to the Government. Thereafter, the power of Chartism declined, and after the failure of the 1848 petition, it faded out completely for the following reasons:

1. It was mainly a reactionary movement of a politically powerless class. The backbone of support came from the old handicraft trades, such as the handloom weavers, who were suffering distress as a result of industrialisation. These people set themselves an impossible task in trying to destroy industrialism.
2. Chartism triumphed when times were bad, but by the late 1840s the benefits of industrialisation were beginning to filter through to the masses. During the third quarter of the nineteenth century unemployment fell and sections of workers such as the handloom weavers were redeployed in the expanding economy.
3. Chartism put forward the most varied aims, ranging from free trade to national education. In this respect it stood in sharp contrast to the successful Anti-Corn Law League which had a simple and easily understood message. Chartism in fact tried to do too much, and thus by the nature of things ended up by achieving nothing.
4. Chartism did not have effective leadership. There were those on the one hand who supported moderates such as William Lovett, of the London Working Men's Association, who were against revolution, and those at the other extreme who idolised Feargus O'Connor, a fiery Irishman, whose popularity amongst the rank and file derived from the Leeds newspaper, the *Northern Star*, and who made references to the ultimate use of armed force.
5. Chartism, unlike the Anti-Corn Law League, lacked middle class support, and middle class support was of considerable importance to the success of any revolution, as was demonstrated by the momentary success of the 1848 revolutions on the continent.
6. Improved communications through railways and the electric telegraph strengthened the Government's hand in controlling the threat from Chartism.

The Chartist movement itself failed but as Pauline Gregg pointed out, it marked a necessary step in working-class development, and its seemingly futile efforts were not entirely wasted. The Charter's demands may have been over-ambitious and premature at the time, but subsequently, with the exception of annual parliaments, all the demands of the Charter have been met.

The Co-operative Movement

The idea of co-operative ownership of the means of production and distribution grew up in the atmosphere of social unrest in the early nineteenth century, when vast fortunes were being made by the few at the expense of the many.

Robert Owen, the philanthropist, was one of the early advocates of co-operation, though his brand of co-operation was aimed at the establishment of communities settled on the land, consisting of groups of people working together to satisfy their collective wants.

The modern Co-operative Movement is concerned with distributive co-operation, and its beginnings generally date from the opening of the famous store of the Rochdale Pioneers in Toad Lane, Rochdale, at the end of 1844, since it was the success of this store that paved the way for the development of the whole movement, the aims of which were to sell goods at market prices for cash payments, and to distribute any surplus profit among members in proportion to the amount of their purchases.

During the next half-century, the movement spread rapidly, particularly in the industrial areas of the North. This growth was aided by the limiting of the liability of members to the amount of their shares by the Industrial and Provident Societies Acts of 1852 and 1862. In 1863 a federation of co-operative stores was formed in the North of England for the purpose of wholesale purchases and distribution to individual stores, and its interests were even extended to include the ownership of factories and steamships. The next few years were eventful in building up the movement's organisation: in 1869 a residential Co-operative College and the Scottish Wholesale Society were formed; in 1873 the Co-operative Wholesale Society, covering the whole of England, was founded; and in 1876 the Co-operative Bank was started.

By 1914 the number of members in the consumers' societies had reached 3,200,000, whilst the financial capital of these societies totalled £64,000,000.

Trade Unions

New Model Trade Unions

1850

Trade unionism underwent a revival after the demise of Chartism, though interest in trade unionism had been steadily growing during the 1840s even when Chartism had occupied the centre of working class attention. It was clear that by 1850 capitalism was much too strongly entrenched to be turned back, therefore attempts to reverse industrial progress were replaced by the efforts of certain sections of workers to improve their position within the new industrial order. There now began a long period of industrial expansion and economic growth, during which trade unionism entered a phase of steady development and consolidation, not aiming at major changes but accepting the existing pattern of society.

The unions formed during the 1850s and 1860s are often referred to as the New Model Unions. Typical of this type of union was the Amalgamated Society of Engineers, formed in 1851 from a number of unions catering for skilled workers in the metal trades. The essential features of the A.S.E. were:

1. Centralisation of control.
2. High weekly subscriptions.
3. Generous benefits to members in times of sickness, unemployment and old age.
4. Negotiation rather than strike action.

The high weekly subscriptions, as high as 1 shilling per week per member, were to belong not to the branches, but to the central body, and were not to be wastefully frittered away on strike benefits. Mainly because of the high subscriptions, this type of unionism was confined to the skilled workers, who came to be looked on as the 'aristocracy of labour'. Also the type of skilled worker began to change as the structure of industry changed. The successful unions before 1850 had been organised by the old craft trades, such as typographers and stonemasons, but with the development of machinery, the skilled mechanic, or engineer, was becoming an important figure whose skills were in great demand and who could command relatively high wages.

During the 1850s and 1860s, the carpenters and other trades began to form associations on the basis of the 'new model' of the A.S.E., and a national leadership of the trade unions emerged in the 1860s when the London-based general secretaries of these unions formed an influential group, later known as the 'Junta'. This group created a common trade union policy along moderate lines urging the avoidance of strikes and the settlement of disputes by arbitration. They also led some vigorous campaigning for various reforms such as the right of the working man to vote, and developed a common policy on a number of questions of current concern to trade unionists. When Garibaldi, the architect of Italian unification, came to London in 1864 members of the Junta were waiting to welcome him, and during the American Civil War messages of support were sent to Abraham Lincoln in his struggle against slavery.

After a period of steady development and consolidation, the unions in 1866–7 experienced some difficulties. In 1866 a series of violent incidents took place in Sheffield connected with trade unionists in the cutlery trades, as a result of which the government set up a Royal Commission to trace the 'outrages' to their source, and to examine the position of trade unions in general. These difficulties were made worse by a period of bad trade between 1866 and 1867, when trade unionists were criticised for weakening Britain's competitive position by seeking higher wages. Yet another blow was struck at trade unionists in 1867 in the Hornby versus Close case, when the Boilermakers' Society sued the treasurer of its Bradford Branch for £24 owed by him to the Society. The Society had thought that their funds were protected by the 1855 Friendly Society Act, but the Lord Chief Justice ruled against this, and added that a trade union in its aspect of restraint of trade was an illegal organisation.

The leaders of the trade unions were very anxious during these difficult years to project a more favourable image of unionism, and largely as a result of their efforts the findings of the Royal Commission Enquiry published in 1869 were favourable to trade unionism, as was reflected in subsequent trade union legislation.

The Trade Union Act of 1871 legalised the status of trade unions and gave protection to their funds, but the Criminal Law Amendment Act passed in the same year made picketing and all allied activity illegal, and thus left trade unionists as vulnerable to criminal prosecution as they had been before. The political campaign subsequently launched to get this Act repealed was successful in 1875, when Disraeli's Government legalised peaceful picketing by the Conspiracy and Protection of Property Act.

Thus, by 1875 trade unions were firmly established in law as recognised elements of a capitalist society, and were therefore in a good position to extend the scope of unionism to include the mass of unskilled workers.

New Unionism

Quite fundamental changes took place in the organisation of labour during the last quarter of the nineteenth century, the main features of which were:

1. Low rates of subscription.
2. Less interest on the Friendly Society benefits side.
3. A readiness to strike.
4. A long-term policy to improve conditions of labour by Act of Parliament.
5. A Socialist outlook advocating the acceptance by the State of more responsibility for social welfare.

This type of unionism appealed strongly to the mass of unskilled workers, whose numbers were increasing and who were beginning to feel more of a sense of working-class identity. This growth in both numbers and working-class homogeneity was brought about by the following factors:

1. The extension of the factory system lessened the dependence on skilled labour and led to a demand for large numbers of semi-skilled and unskilled workers.
2. In mining, where investment did not keep pace with the marginal efficiency of capital, expansion of output was achieved by increasing the size of the labour force; thus by 1914 upwards of one million men were employed in what were virtually pick and shovel jobs. Also, the dreary mining villages, built away from the established areas of settlement, gave the miners a feeling of isolation and encouraged a greater feeling of working-class solidarity.
3. Better transport and the expansion of towns and cities by migration from the countryside also led to a growth of working-class cohesion.
4. The provision of State education ensured a minimum of literacy, as well as giving working-class children a similar background of early experience, thus instilling into them a sense of class identity.

Typical of the unskilled workers' unions formed in this period were the General Union of Textile Workers (1882), the National Union of Gasworkers and General Workers (1889), the Dock, Wharf and Riverside Labourers' Union (1889), and the Navvies, Bricklayers', Labourers and General Labourers' Union (1890).

Successful industrial action at this time encouraged the advance of the 'New Unionism'. In 1888, the London matchgirls employed by Bryant and May, who earned a meagre living in atrocious conditions from the dangerous trade of dipping matches in phosphorus, struck for higher wages and won their case.

SOUTH SIDE
CENTRAL STRIKE COMMITTEE,
SAYES COURT, DEPTFORD.

SEPTEMBER 10, 1889.

GENERAL MANIFESTO.

Owing to the fact that the demands of the Corn Porters, Deal Porters, Granary Men, General Steam Navigation Men, Permanent Men and General Labourers on the South Side have been misrepresented, the above Committee have decided to issue this Manifesto, stating the demands of the various sections now on Strike, and pledge themselves to support each section in obtaining their demands.

DEAL PORTERS of the Surrey Commercial Docks have already placed their demands before the Directors.

LUMPERS (Outside) demand the following Rates, viz:—1. 10d. per standard for Deals. 2. 11d. per stand. for all Goods rating from 3 x 4 to 2½ x 7, or for rough boards. 3. 1s. per std. for plain boards. Working day from 7 a.m. to 5 p.m., and that no man leave the "Red Lion" corner before 6.45 a.m. Overtime at the rate of 6d. per hour extra from 5 p.m. including meal times.

STEVEDORES (Inside) demand 3d. per hour from 7 a.m. to 5 p.m. ... 1s. per hour overtime. Overtime to com...

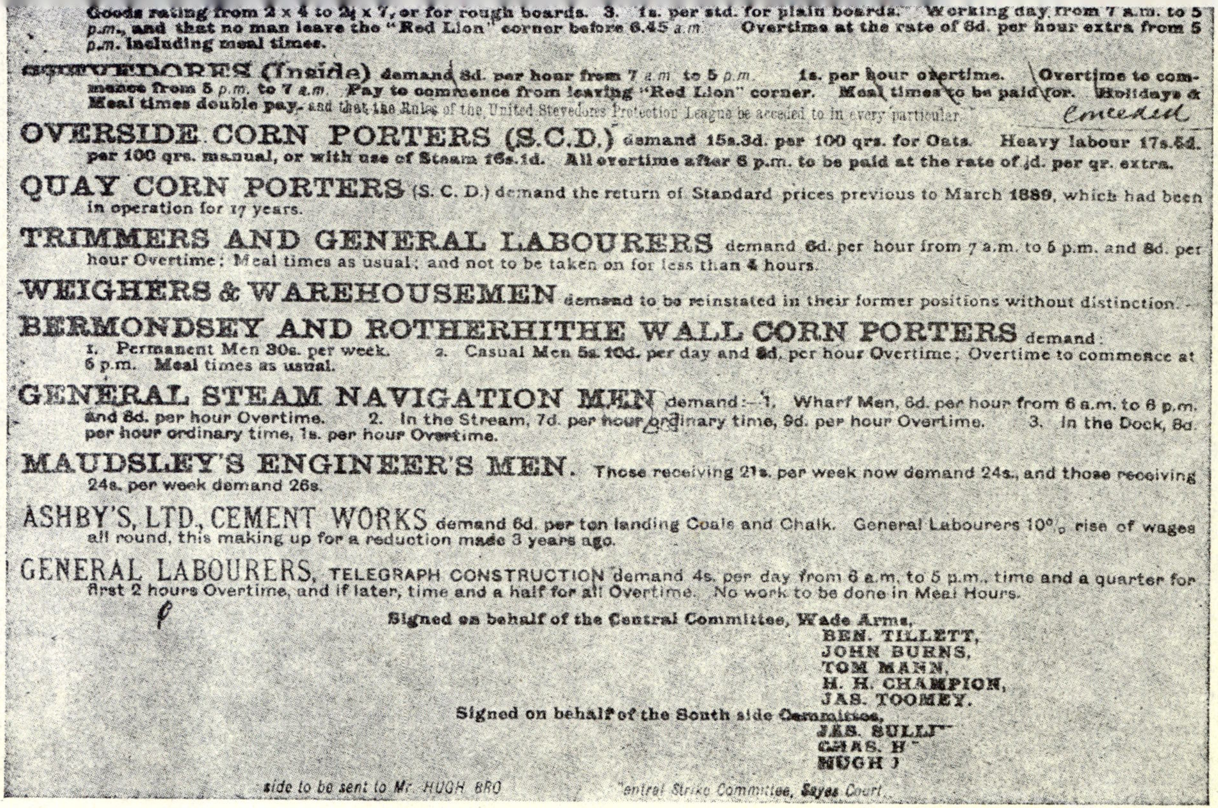
Goods rating from 2 x 4 to 2½ x 7, or for rough boards. 3. 1s. per std. for plain boards. Working day from 7 a.m. to 5 p.m., and that no man leave the "Red Lion" corner before 6.45 a.m. Overtime at the rate of 8d. per hour extra from 5 p.m. including meal times.

STEVEDORES (Inside) demand 8d. per hour from 7 a.m. to 5 p.m. 1s. per hour overtime. Overtime to commence from 5 p.m. to 7 a.m. Pay to commence from leaving "Red Lion" corner. Meal times to be paid for. Holidays & Meal times double pay, and that the Rules of the United Stevedores Protection League be acceded to in every particular. *Conceded*

OVERSIDE CORN PORTERS (S.C.D.) demand 15s.3d. per 100 qrs. for Oats. Heavy labour 17s.6d. per 100 qrs. manual, or with use of Steam 16s.1d. All overtime after 6 p.m. to be paid at the rate of ½d. per qr. extra.

QUAY CORN PORTERS (S. C. D.) demand the return of Standard prices previous to March 1889, which had been in operation for 17 years.

TRIMMERS AND GENERAL LABOURERS demand 6d. per hour from 7 a.m. to 6 p.m. and 8d. per hour Overtime; Meal times as usual; and not to be taken on for less than 4 hours.

WEIGHERS & WAREHOUSEMEN demand to be reinstated in their former positions without distinction.

BERMONDSEY AND ROTHERHITHE WALL CORN PORTERS demand:
1. Permanent Men 30s. per week. 2. Casual Men 5s. 10d. per day and 8d. per hour Overtime; Overtime to commence at 6 p.m. Meal times as usual.

GENERAL STEAM NAVIGATION MEN demand:—1. Wharf Men, 6d. per hour from 6 a.m. to 6 p.m. and 8d. per hour Overtime. 2. In the Stream, 7d. per hour ordinary time, 9d. per hour Overtime. 3. In the Dock, 8d. per hour ordinary time, 1s. per hour Overtime.

MAUDSLEY'S ENGINEER'S MEN. Those receiving 21s. per week now demand 24s., and those receiving 24s. per week demand 26s.

ASHBY'S, LTD., CEMENT WORKS demand 6d. per ton landing Coals and Chalk. General Labourers 10% rise of wages all round, this making up for a reduction made 3 years ago.

GENERAL LABOURERS, TELEGRAPH CONSTRUCTION demand 4s. per day from 6 a.m. to 5 p.m., time and a quarter for first 2 hours Overtime, and if later, time and a half for all Overtime. No work to be done in Meal Hours.

Signed on behalf of the Central Committee, Wade Arms,
BEN. TILLETT,
JOHN BURNS,
TOM MANN,
H. H. CHAMPION,
JAS. TOOMEY.

Signed on behalf of the South side Committee,
JAS. SULL[illegible]
CHAS. H[illegible]
HUGH [illegible]

side to be sent to Mr. HUGH BRO[illegible] [illegible]entral Strike Committee, Sayes Court.

Fig. 9. Dockers' Strike manifesto.

In 1889, the London gas workers, led by Will Thorne, successfully confronted the gas companies with the demand for an eight-hour day. The strike winning the greatest acclaim for its success, however, was the Dockers' Strike of 1889, skilfully led by the dockers' leaders, John Burns, Tom Mann and Ben Tillet.

Until 1889, the dockers were not guaranteed regular work, but were engaged for short periods of time to do a particular job. Ben Tillet wrote that 'to obtain employment we are driven into a shed, iron barred from end to end, outside of which a foreman or contractor walks up and down with the air of a dealer in a cattle market, picking and choosing from a crowd of men, who in their eagerness to obtain employment trample each other underfoot, and where like beasts they fight for a day's work.'

The four main demands of the striking dockers were:

1. 6d. an hour pay (the famous 'docker's tanner').
2. The abolition of contract pay.
3. Minimum engagements of four hours.
4. Extra pay for overtime.

A major feature of this campaign were the processions of dockers marching through London, and made spectacular by the banners and emblems and totem poles crowned with stinking fish-heads and rotting onions, representing current samples of the dockers' diet. The strike

Table 17. Growth of Trade Union Membership

	1888	*1889*	*1890*	*1891*
11 largest unions in shipbuilding and metal trades	115,000	130,000	145,000	155,000
10 largest building unions	57,000	63,000	80,000	94,000
Miners' Federation	36,000	96,000	147,000	200,000
Amalgamated Society of Railway Servants	12,000		26,000	30,000

was kept going by collections made on the march but as the days passed the strikers' relief funds sank lower and lower. Meanwhile, the dock owners refused to concede any of the dockers' demands, and capitulation seemed inevitable. Then came the dramatic intervention from Australia: £30,000 was collected in total from Australian trade unions and football clubs. Success was thus assured and most of the dockers' demands were conceded.

This success was a turning point in the history of trade unions since it inspired other workers—gas workers, railway men, textile workers, building workers and many others—to organise themselves into large unions. Table 17 illustrates this increase in union membership.

The period from 1889 to the First World War became very much one of direct action when strikes were frequent. Fig. 10 traces in graphic form the total magnitude of all disputes in each year from 1893 to 1912.

The years 1910 to 1914 were particularly militant, the main groups of workers involved being the miners, railwaymen and dockers. During these years trade unionism grew in strength, trade union membership increasing from 3 to 4 million between 1911 and 1913.

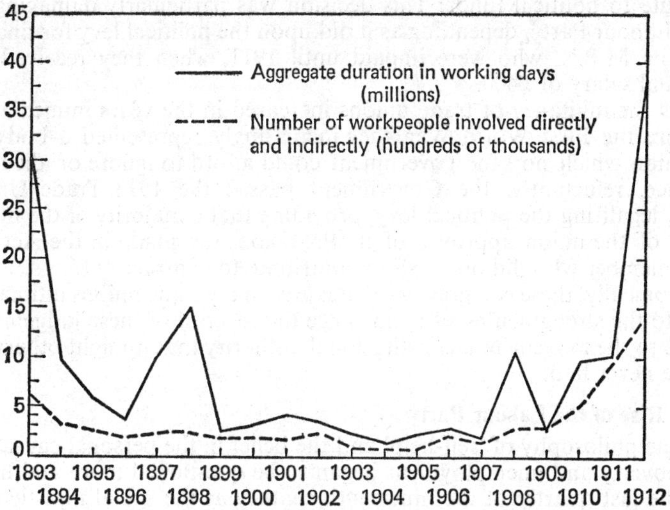

Fig. 10. Trade union disputes (1893–1912).
(source BTRSL, 1912, House of Commons Papers, 1914, Vol. XLVIII)

British trade unionism at this time became influenced by the radical philosophy of Syndicalism, developed by French trade unionists. This philosophy believed that the trade union rather than the parliamentary party was the true basis of social democracy, and that militancy was the best strategy for achieving trade union ends.

Two legal assaults made in the early years of the twentieth century significantly affected trade union development.

The Taff Vale Judgement (*1901*)

A strike took place on the Taff Vale railway in South Wales, as a result of which the railway company lost money. The company successfully sued the union for damages and they were awarded £23,000. This judgement put the whole trade union movement in jeopardy since even if a union won a strike, the costs might be ruinous.

Obviously, if the right to strike was to be preserved as an essential instrument of trade union policy, then the new principle embodied in the Taff Vale decision had to be reversed by Parliament. This was done by the Liberal Government in 1906 in the Trade Disputes Act, no doubt in return for the support to the Liberal programme of the 54 Labour candidates of various sorts who were returned to Parliament in that year.

The Osbourne Judgement (1909)

W. V. Osbourne, a member of the Amalgamated Society of Railway Servants and a Liberal in politics, brought an action to restrain the union from contributing to Labour Party funds. As a result, the Osbourne Judgement, 1909, ruled that it was unlawful for trade unions to contribute to political funds. This decision was particularly damaging to the Labour Party, depending as it did upon the political levy for financing its M.P.'s, who were unpaid until 1911, when they received an annual salary of £400.

As the militancy of trade unions increased in the years immediately before the First World War, they increasingly represented a body of opinion which no sane government could afford to ignore or alienate. Hence, reluctantly, the Government passed the 1913 Trade Union Act, legalising the political levy, providing that a majority of the members of the union approved of it. Provision was made in the Act for the member who did not wish to contribute to contract out.

Ironically, these two great legal assaults on the trade unions ultimately led to the strengthening of them, since the reversal of these judgements gave to the movement a constitutional authority that it might otherwise have never had.

The Rise of the Labour Party

The philosophy of 'self-help' and the belief in the personal causation of poverty and unemployment began to be questioned more and more in the last quarter of the nineteenth century as the social injustices in the capitalist system became more glaringly apparent. The experience of the so-called 'Great Depression' between 1873 and 1896, when the level of unemployment increased, demonstrated quite clearly that unemployment and poverty can be caused by factors outside the control of the individual, although it should be remembered that real gains were made for the majority of workers in this period. Nevertheless, in spite of the rise in living standards for the majority of those in employment, the social distance between classes became wider. This trend was accentuated by the different types of education available, thus creating class feelings from a very early and impressionable age. The growth in the size of business organisations destroyed the old personal contact between employer and worker, thus increasing class antagonism, whilst transport improvements led to the growing separation of the classes by residential area.

Against this background a Socialist ideology developed, advocating that the State should combat social injustices and accept more responsibility for social welfare. This ideology was greatly influenced by the publication in 1867 of *Das Kapital*, by Karl Marx, later to become the textbook of Communism, and *Poverty and Progress*, by the American, Henry George, published in 1879. *Das Kapital* spoke of the inevitability of working-class revolution in industrial countries, whilst *Poverty and Progress* stressed the need to have a single tax on land in order to achieve more social justice

The Reform Acts of 1867 and 1884, extending the vote to the main body of workers, made the workers more aware of their political opportunities as well as encouraging the two established political parties to compete with each other for working-class support. In 1874, the first two working-class candidates, both miners, were returned to Parliament, and by 1885 eleven working-class candidates had been returned, though all of these sat with the Liberals and were known by the term 'Lib.-Lab.'

In 1881, the Democratic Federation, a Marxist organisation later to be known as the Social Democratic Federation, or S.D.F., was founded by a London stockbroker, H. M. Hyndman. In 1884, a section of the S.D.F. broke away to form the Socialist League, and in the same year the Fabian Society was founded by a small group of intellectuals to spread Socialist ideas.

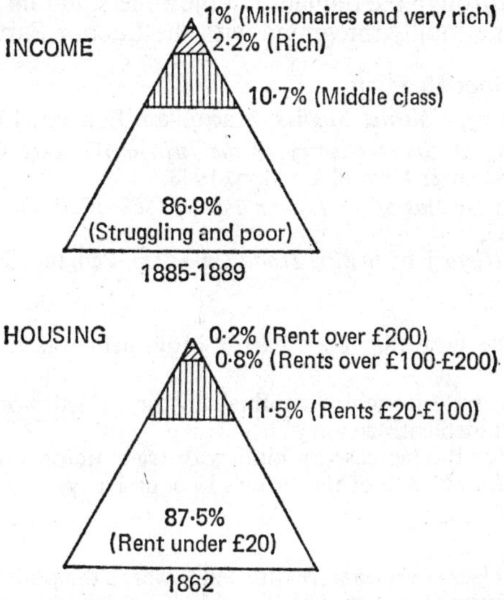

Fig. 11. Housing (1862) and income distribution (1885–9).
(courtesy Penguin Books Ltd)

The next important step was taken in 1893, when the Independent Labour Party was founded under the chairmanship of a Scottish miner, Keir Hardie, who was determined to build up a separate parliamentary Independent Labour Party. The defeat, in 1895, of all 28 I.L.P. candidates convinced Hardie that an independent labour party could only hope to be successful if it had the official support of the trade unions. This support was gained from the T.U.C. in 1899, and in the following year a conference containing representatives from the trade unions, the Fabians, the S.D.F. and the I.L.P. met and formed a Labour Representation Committee, which officially became known as the Labour Party in 1906.

Thus, in 1900, a new political party was born with a Socialist ideology. This party was to replace the old alliance between Liberals and

Labour, whose ideologies in theory were based on quite different outlooks. The Liberals, in theory, believed in private enterprise and free competition, in restricting Government interference and relying as far as possible on voluntary societies and private charity to cope with social evils. The Socialists, however, pointed out the dangers of unbridled competition and unplanned private enterprise, and welcomed State control, believing as they did in the nationalisation of the means of production, distribution and exchange. They also claimed that the poor should be helped as of right, and not be dependent on private enterprise.

The first major electoral success for the new Labour Party came in the General Election of 1906, when twenty-nine Labour candidates were elected to Parliament. This group also had the support of twenty-four other M.P.'s, including fourteen representatives from coalmining districts, elected through the influence of the miners' unions, a group which, in 1909, became totally integrated with the Labour Party.

Suggested Further Reading

Briggs, A. (editor), *Chartist Studies*, Macmillan, London, 1959.

Cole, G. D. H., *A Short History of the British Working Class Movement, 1787–1947*, Allen & Unwin, London, 1948.

Pelling, H., *The Origins of the Labour Party, 1880–1900*, O.U.P., Oxford and London, 1965.

Pelling, H., *A History of British Trade Unionism*, Penguin, London, 1963.

Exercises

1. Discuss the view that the Chartist Movement was doomed to failure from the start.
2. Why was trade unionism confined to the skilled workers in the third quarter of the nineteenth century?
3. Account for the increased militancy of trade unionism after 1889.
4. Account for the rise of the British Labour Party.

Summary

1. Working-class energies were directed towards the political aspirations of the Chartist movement between 1836 and 1848, which was a reactionary movement of a politically powerless class and therefore doomed to failure.
2. During the 1850s and 1860s trade unionism was confined mainly to the skilled artisan and emphasis was placed on friendly society benefits and negotiation rather than strike action.
3. Large unskilled workers' unions were formed from the 1870s with a socialist outlook and with a readiness to improve pay and conditions through strike action.
4. The Independent Labour Party was founded in 1893, and in 1900 a Labour Representation Committee was formed which became known as the Labour Party in 1906.

CHAPTER ELEVEN

THE CONDITION OF THE PEOPLE

There can be no doubt that there was a general rise in living standards for the great majority of the population during the nineteenth century. According to Deane and Cole, real national income per head roughly quadrupled during this period. 'In both absolute and per capita terms the growth from decade to decade seems to have been positive and continuous for the whole period.' (Deane and Cole, *British Economic Growth 1688–1959*)

Even the 'Hungry Forties' have been exposed as a myth, based on the free-trade counter-propaganda against Joseph Chamberlain's Tariff Reform campaign in the early 1900s. The hunger propaganda of the Anti-Corn Law League was probably partly responsible for the growth of the general impression that the 1840s were a period of special suffering for the working class. It is true that there were periods of cyclical depression and unemployment during the 1840s, but the fact that there was also a railway boom and a trade revival has often been ignored. Judging by the price of bread in England, the 1840s were no hungrier than the 1830s or 1850s. According to Sir John Clapham, the average price of the four-pound loaf in London in the 1820s was 10d., in the 1830s it fell to 9d., and from 1841 to 1845 it was 8$\frac{1}{4}$d. At the height of the Irish Famine in 1847 it rose to 11$\frac{1}{2}$d., but the average price for 1846–8 was only 9d.

The rise in living standards for the majority of those in employment was particularly marked between 1875 and 1895, when prices were falling and wages were reasonably stabilised. Free trade meant cheap food imports, a wider variety of which made their appearance as a result of the development of the new technical processes of refrigeration and canning. Jam and fresh fruit became available for the urban poor, whilst the first fish and chip shops were opened in the North of England during the 1870s.

As the century progressed, there was a revolution in retail distribution with such famous stores as Boots, Selfridges and Sainsbury's being established, as well as the proliferation of Co-operative stores aimed at catering for the working classes. These retail outlets were able to sell, in addition to the wider variety of food available, a bigger range of manufactured goods, such as boots and clothes made by the machine operative.

The quality of life was further improved for the masses by the introduction of new leisure facilities, the most prominent of which were the music halls, professional football and horse and dog racing, which were made more easily accessible by means of the bicycle and tram, whilst railway transport, together with the Bank Holiday, brought the seaside holiday within the scope of the middle and working classes.

NB It is very important to remember that against this background of rising living standards there were important groups, such as agricultural labourers, who benefited very little from the general improvement. Also, the vast majority of workers during the second half of the nineteenth century were manual workers who had little security of employment and who were therefore faced with the prospect of extreme poverty during periods of sickness, unemployment or old age. Unless such people had friends or family to look after them they were compelled to resort to the harsh mercies of the Poor Law. This remedy did not usually apply to skilled workers, who were invariably covered by savings or Friendly Society benefits.

At the turn of the century the findings of social surveys revealed that 10 per cent of the population did not earn sufficient money to maintain 'mere physical efficiency' (primary poverty) whilst another 20 per cent suffered similar poverty through mismanagement of their income (secondary poverty). Those in primary poverty, comprising such groups as tramps, casual labourers, dockers and workers in various 'sweated trades' such as ready-made tailoring, usually suffered the misfortunes of inhabiting the slums and drifting in and out of the workhouses.

Whilst it is true that the industrial towns of the second half of the nineteenth century were an improvement on the towns of the first half, largely because municipal reform had dealt with such horrors as bad sanitation, they were still nevertheless grim places, polluted by layers of soot and grime. Since there was no Town Planning Act until 1909, working-class houses were of the back-to-back kind, built of red brick and roofed in grey slate, and constructed in dreary monotonous rows.

A number of forces were, however, beginning to work in favour of the working classes before the close of the century, which in time brought about an improvement in the condition of the people. The extension of the franchise, in 1867 and 1884, made political parties more responsive to the needs of the working man, and hastened the introduction of important social reforms, such as old age pensions and national insurance. The introduction of public education improved communications and made the working classes more aware of the possibilities of improving the quality of their lives. Cheap newspapers read by the masses became the mouthpiece of social reformers. The organisation of large unskilled workers' unions, with emphasis on strike action, led to improved pay and conditions for some groups of workers, whilst improvements in medicine and better standards in public health resulted in a fall in the death rate.

Prominent amongst the reforms bringing about a substantial improvement in the quality of people's lives were the public health reforms, the insistence upon regulations concerning conditions of employment in factories and mines, and the introduction of compulsory education for everyone.

Public Health and Housing

There is a close connection between poor health and bad housing, particularly when a growing population was crowded into the rapidly growing industrial towns. In such conditions grave health hazards arose from epidemic diseases, the most common of which were cholera, typhus, typhoid, measles, scarlet fever and diphtheria. The following contemporary accounts give some idea of the appalling conditions that existed in the early industrial towns:

Report on the Sanitary Condition of the Labouring Population: Lords Sessional Reports, 1842.

Families were attracted from all parts for the benefit of employment, and obliged as a temporary resort to crowd together into such dwellings as the neighbourhood afforded, often two families into one house; others into cellars or very small dwellings; eventually, as the works became established, either the proprietor or some neighbour would probably see it advantageous to build a few cottages; these were often of the worst description: in such case the prevailing consideration was not how to promote the health and comfort of the occupants, but how many cottages could be built upon the smallest space of ground and at the least possible cost.

Report of the Committee on the Health of Towns 1840. Description of Conditions in Manchester by John Robertson, a Surgeon.

Manchester has no Building Act, and hence, with the exception of certain central streets, over which the Police Act gives the Commissioners power, each proprietor builds as he pleases. New cottages, with or without cellars, huddled together row behind row, may be seen springing up in many parts, but especially in the township of Manchester, where the land is higher in price than the land for cottage sites in other townships is. With such proceedings as these the authorities cannot interfere. A cottage row may be badly drained, the streets may be full of pits, brimful of stagnant water, the receptacle of dead cats and dogs, yet no one may find fault. The number of cellar residences, you have probably learned from the papers published by the Manchester Statistical Society, is very great in all quarters of the town; and even in Hulme, a large portion of which consists of cottages recently erected, the same practice is continued. That it is an evil must be obvious on the slightest consideration, for how can a hole underground of from 12 to 15 feet square admit of ventilation so as to be fit of human habitation.

J. R. Martin's Report, Parliamentary Papers, 1845.

I believe that nowhere else shall we find so large a mass of inhabitants crowded into courts, alleys and lanes, as in Nottingham, and those, too, of the worst possible construction. . . . The courts are almost always approached through a low arched tunnel of some 30 to 36 inches wide, about 8 feet high, and from 20 to 30 feet long. . . . They are noisome, narrow, unprovided with adequate means for the removal of refuse, ill-ventilated, and wretched in the extreme, with a gutter, or surface drain, running down the centre; they have no back yards, and the privies are common to the whole court; altogether they present scenes of deplorable character, and of surpassing filth and discomfort. It is just the same with lanes and alleys. . . . In all these confined quarters too, the refuse is allowed to accumulate until, by its mass and its advanced putrefaction, it shall have acquired value as manure; and thus it is sold and carted away by the 'muck majors', as the collectors of manure are called in Nottingham.

It is not surprising that in such conditions dangerous diseases were often rampant, reaching epidemic proportions from time to time, and causing great loss of life. Amongst the worst epidemics were the cholera epidemics of 1831–2, 1848–9, 1853–4 and 1866, which demonstrated quite clearly that effective action needed to be taken in the field of public health.

Edwin Chadwick, the first Secretary to the Poor Law Commissioners, was the person most responsible for bringing about the early public health reforms. Chadwick was a typical Victorian bureaucrat who was motivated more by the desire to increase overall efficiency than by any humanitarian or philanthropic motives. He was quick to recognise the close connection that existed between poverty, ill health, bad housing and a high poor rate, and reacted by publishing a report in 1842 exposing the dangers of poor living conditions, as well as emphasising the burden to the rates caused by the additional poverty resulting from ill health.

The following extract is from the conclusions to Chadwick's report published in 1842:

> That the various forms of epidemic, endemic, and other diseases caused or aggravated or propagated chiefly amongst the labouring classes by atmospheric impurities produced by decomposing animal and vegetable substances, by damp and filth, and close and overcrowded dwellings prevail amongst the population in every part of the kingdom, whether dwelling in separate houses, in rural villages, in small towns, in the larger towns—as they have been found to prevail in the lowest districts of the metropolis.
>
> That such disease, wherever its attacks are frequent, is always found in connection with the physical circumstances above specified. . . .
>
> The primary and most important measures, and at the same time the most practicable, and within the recognised province of public administration, are drainage, the removal of all refuse of habitations, streets, and roads, and the improvement of the supplies of water.
>
> The refuse when held in suspension in water may be most cheaply and innoxiously conveyed to any distance out of towns, and also in the best form for productive use, and that the loss and injury by the pollution of natural streams may be avoided. . . .
>
> That the expense of public drainage, of supplies of water laid on in houses, and of means of improved cleansing would be a pecuniary gain, by diminishing the existing charges attendant on sickness and premature mortality.
>
> . . . securities should be taken that all new local public works are devised and conducted by responsible officers qualified by the possession of the science and skill of civil engineers. . . .
>
> That for the prevention of the disease occasioned by defective ventilation, and other causes of impurity in places of work and other places where large numbers are assembled, and for the general promotion of the means necessary to prevent disease, that it would be good economy to prevent disease, that it would be good economy to appoint a district medical officer independent of private practice, and with the securities of special qualifications and responsibilities to initiate sanitary measures and reclaim the execution of the law.
>
> That by the combinations of all these arrangements, it is probable that an increase of 13 years at least, may be extended to the whole of the labouring classes.
>
> And that the removal of noxious physical circumstances, and the promotion of civic, household, and personal cleanliness, are necessary to the improvement of the moral condition of the population; for that sound morality and refinement in manners and health are not long found co-existent with filthy habits amongst any class of the community.

Chadwick's report was followed by the report of the Commission on the Health of Towns in 1844–5, which resulted in the first Public Health

Act of 1848. Under this act a General Board of Health was established with powers to set up local boards of health. These local boards of health could in turn appoint surveyors, inspectors of nuisances, and deal with such matters as the construction of sewers and drains, the provision of water, the construction of gasworks, and the disposal of refuse.

Whilst the 1848 Act was an important step towards improved public health, it was nevertheless limited in its scope by being permissive, since the Act only came into operation if 10 per cent of the ratepayers of a local authority required it, or if the death rate exceeded 23 per 1,000 per annum.

The achievement of the Board of Health was disappointing and the work of many of the local boards was frustrated by the resistance of slum landlords. As a result the Board of Health in London was wound up in 1858, and its functions were transferred to the Home Office or the Privy Council under the Local Government Act of 1858. During the next twenty years improvements in engineering and technology contributed towards a reduction in mortality rates in those areas where effective action had been taken against public health problems.

A uniform system of sanitary authorities covering the whole country was established in the 1870s, whilst the 1875 Public Health Act codified the law relating to Public Health and conferred powers on local authorities to deal with a wide range of matters. Under the 1875 Act, Local Authorities were given the responsibility for the making, paving, lighting and cleaning of streets, and for providing a proper water supply and a good system of sanitation, as well as requiring the appointment of a medical officer of health, a surveyor and a sanitary inspector.

Three important acts were passed with respect to housing before 1914. The Torrens Act of 1868 and the Artisans Dwelling Act of 1875 gave the opportunity to local authorities to remove slums and replace them with better houses, whilst the Housing and Town Planning Act of 1909 laid down minimum environmental standards by insisting upon the siting of new houses in well laid out surroundings.

Factory and Mining Reforms

In the absence of regulations, the early concentration of workpeople into factories and mines led to many abuses and social evils. Most workers, including women and children, were compelled to work long hours in appalling conditions, often with the added discomfort of harsh discipline. P. Gaskell, writing in 1833, put the case against the employment of child labour in factories:

> Factory labour is a species of work, in some respects singularly unfitted for children. Cooped up in a heated atmosphere, debarred the necessary exercise, remaining in one position for a series of hours, one set or system of muscles alone called into activity, it cannot be wondered at—that its effects are injurious to the physical growth of a child. Where the bony system is still imperfect, the vertical position it is compelled to retain, influences its direction; the spinal column bends beneath the weight of the head, bulges out laterally, or is dragged forward by the weight of the parts composing the chest, the pelvis yields beneath the opposing pressure downwards, and the resistance

given by the thigh bones; its capacity is lessened, sometimes more and sometimes less; the legs curve, and the whole body loses height, in consequence of this general yielding and bending of its parts. . . .

Persistent efforts at reform were made in the early nineteenth century, but a number of difficulties stood in the way of early factory legislation.

1. The workers lacked political power and trade unions were weak, whereas the manufacturers, who stood to gain from exploiting the working class, acquired political power by the 1832 Reform Act.

2. There was a strong tradition of resistance to centralisation in Britain which was reinforced by the teachings of economists, who maintained that interference by the state in economic matters was harmful and futile. Economists claimed that wages and conditions of work were determined by economic laws and that there should be a free market for labour. Ricardo believed that 'there are miseries in the social state which legislation cannot relieve', whilst an official report on a demand by some workers for a twelve-hour day stated: 'Such remedies as these are so contrary to the principles of political economy that I scarcely need make any further comments on them.'

3. Some people believed that better working conditions would increase the cost of production and thus price British goods out of overseas markets. This, in turn, would mean unemployment, which it was argued would be a worse detriment to the worker than long hours of labour.

4. One economist claimed that all profit was made in the last hour's work, a fallacy that was disproved by Robert Owen, the philanthropist, who reduced the hours of work at his New Lanark cotton mills and still made a profit.

5. The long wars against France were used by some as an argument for continuing to employ children since it was claimed that any restrictions on such labour would lead to reduced production.

6. It was also pointed out that parents would be unable to support children who did not work. Furthermore, too much leisure would be bad for them, since they would run wild like hooligans and receive no training or discipline.

7. Employment of children and the ill treatment and exploitation of them was no new thing, nor was it confined only to factories, since child employment had been an accepted practice for a long period of time in agriculture and the domestic industries.

In spite of all these difficulties, persistent efforts were made at factory reform, as the Acts of 1802, 1819, 1820, 1825, 1829 and 1831 bore witness to, but it was not until 1833 that the first effective Act was passed regulating the employment of children in factories. This Act was important because it provided for the appointment of salaried inspectors whose job it was to see that the law was carried out.

Subsequent Acts followed, improving the conditions of labour for children and extending the regulations on hours of labour to include women. The 1844 Factory Act reduced the hours which children could work to eight and protected women also by introducing the 'half-time' system. After 1867 the regulations concerning the employment of women and children were extended to include factories and workshops outside the textile industry.

The Sunderland Committee, set up in 1813 to investigate a series of colliery explosions, drew public attention to the terrible working and living conditions endured by miners, and eventually led to the setting up of a Select Committee in 1835, and a Royal Commission in 1840, to enquire into the whole problem. The Royal Commission disclosed that children of both sexes, some at the tender age of four, were taken down the mines to work, whilst women and young girls were employed to haul sledges of coal below ground and to carry coal in baskets up to the surface. The Mines Act of 1842 followed prohibiting entirely the employment underground of women and girls, and of boys under the age of ten.

In 1844, the first Government Inspector of Mines was appointed whose job it was to document the conditions existing in mines. These reports led to further improvements in working conditions, including better means of moving coal below ground and more efficient ventilation.

It is significant that men were noticeably excluded from any of the factory and mining reforms passed in the nineteenth century, though they did indirectly benefit from the improved working conditions secured for women and young children.

Education

Public education was slow to develop in Britain and free education for all was not provided until the end of the nineteenth century. This was a most unfortunate state of affairs, since as the leading industrial and commercial power in the world up to 1870, Britain should have diverted more of her resources towards education and thus increased her efficiency and future potential.

Educational facilities for the masses were slow to develop for the following reasons:

1. There were many doubts about the wisdom of educating the working class. Mr Davies Giddy, M.P., considered in 1807 that education would encourage the poor 'to despise their lot in life, instead of making them good servants in agriculture, and other laborious employments to which their rank in society had destined them; instead of teaching them subordination, it would render them factious and refractory, as was evident in the manufacturing counties; it would enable them to read seditious pamphlets, vicious books and publications against Christianity.'
2. Even though the economy was complex, most jobs could be learnt by doing the job, most manufacturers being proud of the skill which the working man had developed within his trade.
3. Since most businesses were small and under family ownership there was a reliance upon members of the family to occupy managerial positions rather than upon people with particular educational qualifications.
4. The laissez-faire attitudes implicit in the working of the economic system were reinforced by contemporary political discourse, the most notable being Adam Smith's *Wealth of Nations*, which advocated a policy of minimum state intervention.

The monitorial system of education, whereby the older children taught the younger children, was favoured at first because it was cheap. This system was used by the pioneers of elementary education, the National Society (Church of England) and the British and Foreign School Society (Non-Conformist), which were founded in the early nineteenth century. Joseph Lancaster, whose ideas were followed by the British and Foreign School Society, wrote in 1803:

> My school is attended by 300 scholars. The whole system of tuition is almost entirely conducted by boys. . . . The school is divided into classes, to each of these a lad is appointed as monitor: he is responsible for the morals, improvement, good order, and cleanliness of the whole class. It is his duty to make a daily, weekly, and monthly report of progress, specifying the number of lessons performed, boys present, absent, etc. As we naturally expect the boys who teach the other boys to read, to leave school when their education is complete, and do not wish that they should neglect their own improvement in other studies, they are instructed to train other lads as assistants, who, in future, may supply their place, and in the meantime leave them to improve in other branches of learning. To be a monitor is coveted by the whole school, it being an office at once honourable and productive of emolument.

A Government grant totalling £20,000 was given to the two societies in 1833 for the purpose of school buildings. This grant was extended in 1838 and a special committee of the privy council was set up to supervise it.

In 1858 a Royal Commission was appointed 'to consider the extension of sound and cheap elementary instruction to all classes of the people'. This report recommended that teachers should be paid on the basis of their pupils passing a simple examination. Robert Lowe, Vice-President of the Education Department, accepted the scheme in 1862, and it became known as the system of 'payment by results'. Speaking in the House of Commons in 1861, Lowe said: 'I cannot promise the House that this system will be an economical one, and I cannot promise that it will be an efficient one, but I can promise that it will be one or the other. If it is not cheap it shall be efficient; if it is not efficient, it shall be cheap.'

As the nineteenth century progressed so the reasons for the provision of State educational facilities became more numerous and forceful.

1. The Factory Act of 1833 required children working in factories to attend school for two hours a day.
2. Growing industrialisation demanded a certain minimum of literacy.
3. The various religious bodies, who provided most of the formal education available for the working class, believed that children should at least be able to read in order to acquire more knowledge of the Christian religion.
4. The greater competitive industrial strength of Prussia and the United States, both of which had superior educational systems to Britain, as well as the military successes of Prussia against France in 1870 and those of the North against the South in the American Civil War, helped many people in Britain to value the importance of mass education.

5. The extension of the franchise to the mass of urban workers in 1867 made it necessary to 'educate our masters'. Robert Lowe commented in 1867: 'I suppose it will be absolutely necessary to educate our masters. I was before this opposed to centralisation; I am now ready to accept centralisation. I was opposed to an education rate; I am now ready to accept one. . . . From the moment you entrust the masses with power, their education becomes an imperative necessity. . . . You have placed the government of this country in the hands of the masses and you must therefore give them an education.'

6. The rapid growth of population meant there were too many children for voluntary organisations to educate properly, with or without State aid.

Hence the Education Act of 1870 divided the country into districts, each with a School Board whose duty it was to see that suitable school accommodation was available. New schools were to be provided where the religious schools were insufficient. The Board schools were to be financed by local rates and the voluntary schools within the system were to be provided with grants.

Because of the shortage of school places, attendance did not become compulsory in England and Wales until 1880, and the minimum school leaving age was raised in stages until it was fixed in 1899 at twelve years of age.

A system of State-provided secondary education did not become available until the Education Act of 1902. Before this secondary education was provided for rich children either by a tutor or by one of the nine public schools, and for middle class children it was provided by the endowed grammar schools.

The 1902 Act abolished the School Boards and created new Local Education Authorities to be run by the County and County Borough Councils.

The new secondary schools set up under the Act charged small fees, though they did provide some free places by scholarship from the elementary schools. In practice these free places did involve some expense, which meant that the proportion of working-class children attending these schools was small.

The County Councils, created under the 1888 Local Government Act, were authorised to provide technical, evening and other advanced classes, whilst the 1902 Education Act empowered the L.E.A.'s to develop training and technical colleges and adult education. Britain, however, continued to lag behind Germany and the United States in the provision of technical and university education.

This lack of foresight, at a time when there was the rapid development of engineering, electricity and the internal combustion engine, was to have serious implications for the future.

Suggested Further Reading

Chaloner, W. H., *The Hungry Forties*, Historical Association, London, 1957.

Checkland, S. G., *The Rise of Industrial Society in England, 1815–1885*, Longmans, London, 1964.

Curtis, S. J., *The History of Education in Great Britain*, University Tutorial Press, London, 1965.
Finer, S. E., *The Life and Times of Sir Edwin Chadwick*, Methuen, London, 1952.

Exercises

1. Discuss the view that economic growth in the nineteenth century brought substantial benefits for everyone.

2. Do you consider that the term 'Hungry Forties' is an apt description of that decade?

3. Explain with reference to the nineteenth century why high standards in public health are an absolute prerequisite for civilised living.

4. Trace the development of public provision for free education before 1914.

Summary

1. Living standards rose for the majority of the population in this period and real national incomes per head roughly quadrupled.

2. The 'Hungry Forties' have been exposed as a myth arising from the controversy over tariff reform in the early 1900s.

3. The rise in living standards for the majority of those in employment was particularly marked between 1875 and 1895, when prices fell and cheap food imports led to a wider variety of food appearing in the rapidly increasing number of retail outlets.

4. Nevertheless, in spite of these gains, social surveys revealed that 30 per cent of the population in the late nineteenth century lived in dire poverty.

5. The 1848 Public Health Act was an important step towards improved public health, but it was not until the 1875 Public Health Act that local authorities were compulsorily charged with the task of dealing with a wide range of public health matters.

6. The first effective Act regulating the employment of children in factories was passed in 1833, whilst the Mines Act of 1842 prohibited entirely the employment underground of women and girls, and of boys under the age of ten.

7. Public education was slow to develop in Britain and free education for all was not provided until the last quarter of the nineteenth century.

CHAPTER TWELVE

THE POOR LAW

The treatment of the poor during the period of tumultuous change between the 1780s and 1830s was reasonably generous and humane. It was this factor, no doubt, that helped Britain to cope with the social problems arising from the rapid increase in population, the decline of the domestic system, dispossession by enclosures, war and the growth of the factory system, without having any serious rebellion among the people.

During the 1830s, however, a radical change in this policy was brought about and the treatment of the poor became harsh and severe.

Under the new system people were versed in the virtues of hard work and self-help, and spurred on by the ever-present threat of a deterrent Poor Law. The Victorian reformers in their pious zeal managed to convince themselves that too generous treatment of the poor would encourage indolence and delinquency, and that it was their Christian duty to provide discipline and correction for those who went astray. This harsh system remained intact until the early years of the twentieth century, when there evolved a more kindly attitude towards the poor.

The Poor Law Amendment Act, 1834

This Act was based upon the recommendations of a Royal Commission investigating the workings of the Poor Law between 1832 and 1834. The Royal Commission's main finding was that undeserving cases were treated with too much kindness within the workhouse and that life was made too easy for them. The Report stated that '. . . in by far the greater number of cases, it [the workhouse] is a large almshouse, in which the young are trained in ignorance and vice; the able-bodied maintained in sluggish indolence; the aged and more respectable exposed to all the misery that is incident to dwelling on such a society, without government or classification, and the whole body of inmates subsisted on food exceeding both in kind and in amount, not merely the diet of the independent labourer, but that of the majority who contribute to their support.' The Report then went on to give examples of the high cost of this generous system of poor relief, and what the implications of that high cost were:

It appears that in this parish [Cholesbury, Bucks.], the population of which has been stationary since 1801, in which, within the memory of persons now living, the rates were only £10 11s. a year, and only one person received relief, the sum raised for the relief of the poor rose from £99 4s. a year, in 1816, to £150 5s. in 1831: and in 1832, when it was proceeding at the rate of £367 a year, suddenly ceased in consequence of the impossibility to continue its collection: the landlords having given up their rents, the farmers their tenancies, and the clergyman his glebe and his tithes. The clergyman, Mr Jeston, states that in October, 1832, the parish officers threw up their books, and the poor assembled in a body before his door, while he was in bed, asking for advice and food. (1834 Poor Law Report)

The new system, set up under the 1834 Poor Law Amendment Act, projected an entirely different image of the concept of poor relief. Outdoor relief was to be prohibited for the able bodied; anyone in this category had to take the workhouse test, i.e. they had to accept any relief given in the workhouse. Also, conditions within the workhouse were not to be made 'really or apparently so eligible as the situation of the independent labourer of the lowest class'.

The reformed workhouses, with their harsh discipline, hard work and poor diet, were designed to be forbidding places acting as a deterrent to the indolent poor.

The Act also recommended that for the purposes of more efficient management the poor should be classified into four separate groups: 'The aged and really impotent; the children; the able bodied females; the able bodied males. Of whom we trust that the two latter will be the least numerous classes. It appears to us that both the requisite classification and the requisite superintendence may be better obtained in separate buildings than under a single roof. . . . Each class might thus receive an appropriate treatment; the old might enjoy their indulgencies without torment from the boisterous; the children be educated, and the able bodied subjected to such courses of labour and discipline as will repel the indolent and vicious.'

To improve and economise on the administration of the Poor Law, the existing 15,000 parishes in the country were to be formed into 640 unions, and each of these unions was to have its own workhouse with an organised body of paid officers administered by Boards of Guardians. This public welfare was to be financed from the rates, and the whole Poor Law system was to be directed from London by three full-time Poor Law Commissioners and a number of Assistant Commissioners.

The Working of the Poor Law, 1834–1909

The Commission set enthusiastically about its task of organising workhouses within the unions, and within five years the new system of unions of parishes, under Boards of Guardians elected by the ratepayers, had been extended to 95 per cent of the parishes of England and Wales, covering 85 per cent of the people.

The Commissioners were greatly helped in setting up the new Poor Law by the favourable economic conditions existing in the early years of the Act's operation, thus minimising working-class antagonism towards the new system. The exceptionally good harvest in 1834 lowered the price of bread and reduced the pressure on the poor, whilst railway construction between 1835 and 1837 provided a fresh outlook for the unemployed.

These fortunate circumstances were brought to an end in 1837 by a severe industrial depression, and when the Commissioners began to introduce the new system in the industrial areas of the North, they met with serious opposition. The implementation of the new Poor Law on a large scale quickly brought home to the working classes the implications of the Act for them, particularly in times of industrial depression, over which they had no control. In the circumstances, the Poor Law Commissioners, whilst retaining the general principle of prohibiting outdoor relief, were forced to revise the idea of prohibiting outdoor relief completely, as the General Prohibitory Order of 1844 shows.

Tenth Annual Report, Poor Law Commission, 1844
General Prohibitory Order

Article 1. Every able-bodied person, male or female, requiring relief from any parish within any of the said Unions, shall be relieved wholly in the workhouse of the Union, together with such of the family of every such able-bodied person as may be resident with him or her, and they not be in employment ... save and except in the following cases:

(1) Where such person shall require relief on account of sudden and urgent necessity.

(2) Where such person shall require relief on account of any sickness, accident, or bodily or mental infirmity ...

(3) Where such person being a widow, shall be in the first six months of widowhood ...

(4) Where such person shall be a widow, and have a legitimate child or legitimate children dependent upon her, and incapable of earning his, her, or their livelihood, and have no illegitimate child born after the commencement of her widowhood ...

(5) Where such person shall be the wife, or child, of any able bodied man who shall be in the services of her Majesty as soldier, sailor or marine.

The principle of less eligibility was fairly ruthlessly applied throughout the period covered by the 1834 Poor Law Amendment Act, the workhouses being grim institutional establishments of which poor people lived in dread.

Within the workhouse wives were separated from their husbands, and parents from their children, whilst the principle of classifying the poor was never properly applied, with the result that the deserving and less deserving inmates received much the same treatment.

Strict rules of conduct were laid down for the inmates, as the Poor Law Commission, Seventh Annual Report, 1841, illustrates:

WORKHOUSE (Rules of Conduct)

Any pauper who shall neglect to observe such of the regulations herein contained as are applicable to and binding on him:

Or who shall make any noise when silence is ordered to be kept;
Or shall use obscene or profane language;
Or shall refuse or neglect to work, after being required to do so;
Or shall play at cards or other games of chance;
Shall be deemed DISORDERLY.

Any pauper who shall within seven days, repeat any one or commit more than one of the offences specified ...

Or shall by word or deed insult or revile the master or matron, or any other officer of the workhouse, or any of the Guardians ...
Or shall be drunk ...
Or shall wilfully disturb the other inmates during prayers or divine worship;
Shall be deemed REFRACTORY.

It shall be lawful for the master of the workhouse ... to punish any disorderly pauper by substituting, during a time not greater than forty eight hours, for his or her dinner, as prescribed by the dietary, a meal consisting of eight ounces of bread, or one pound of cooked potatoes, and also by withholding from him during the same period, all butter, cheese, tea, sugar, or broth . . .

And it shall be lawful for the Board of Guardians . . . to order any refractory pauper to be punished by confinement to a separate room, with or without an alteration of the diet . . . for . . . twenty four hours. . . .

Some organisational changes in the administration of the Poor Law encouraged the better care of paupers who were unable to care for themselves. In 1847 the original Poor Law Commission had its powers transferred to a new Poor Law Board, having a minister at its head, who was responsible for the actions of the Board to Parliament; this Board was later succeeded by the Local Government Board in 1871.

Towards the end of the nineteenth century there were some indications that the treatment of the poor was being improved upon, such as better medical care and the provision of education for children in the workhouse school, though during the period of the 'Great Depression', 1873–96, outdoor relief was more effectively prohibited, as Table 18 shows.

Table 18. Paupers of All Ages in Britain, 1849–92

	Number of 'indoor' poor	*Number of 'outdoor' poor*	*Total*	*Number per 1,000 of the population*
1849	133,513	955,146	1,088,659	62·7
1852	111,323	804,352	915,675	50·9
1862	132,236	784,906	917,142	45·6
1872	149,200	828,000	977,200	42·9
1882	183,374	604,915	788,289	30·3
1892	186,607	558,150	744,757	25·6

Source: Report of the Royal Commission on the Aged Poor, 1895.

The Break-up of the Victorian Poor Law

A number of circumstances contributed towards the evolution of a more humane attitude towards the poor in the last quarter of the nineteenth century, leading to a series of social reforms in the early years of the present century, which laid the basis of the modern welfare state.

1. The extension of the franchise to the working class in 1867 and 1884 made governments of all parties more sensitive to the wishes of the workers. Political parties began to vie with each other in offering bigger and better reforms in order to increase their electoral popularity.

2. There was the impact of a Socialist ideology advocating more involvement by the state in caring for people's welfare.

3. The experience of the 'Great Depression', 1873–96, demonstrated that unemployment can be caused by factors outside the control of the individual.

4. More knowledge became available on the subject of poverty, thus eradicating ignorance as an excuse for doing nothing:

(i) Social surveys helped to reveal the extent of the problem. Charles Booth published the first of his seventeen volumes surveying *The Life and Labour of the People of London* in 1889, and Seebohn Rowntree published his detailed investigation of York, *Poverty, a Study of Town Life* in 1901. The findings of these two investigations were strikingly similar. In London 30·7 per cent, in York, 'a typical provincial town', 27·84 per cent of the population were in poverty, and so 'we are faced by the startling probability that from 25 to 30 per cent of the town populations of the United Kingdom are living in poverty'. Lloyd George, the Liberal politician, said during his campaign for social reform that Booth and Rowntree had 'revealed a state of things, especially in the towns, which it would be difficult even for the orators of discontent to exaggerate. There are ten millions in this country enduring year after year the torture of living while lacking a sufficiency of the bare essentials of life.'

(ii) Concern was also expressed by the revelation of the poor physical condition of many of the recruits who volunteered for service in the South African War of 1899–1902. This led to the Report in 1904 of the Committee on Physical Deterioration which recommended school meals for underfed children and school medical inspection.

(iii) In 1906 the *Daily News* organised the Sweated Industries Exhibition, displaying particulars about the hours of work, the earnings, the products produced and the conditions of work of the sweated workers.

These revelations of the extent and causes of poverty deeply disturbed the political thinking in some quarters, and left their mark on the programmes of the political parties.

6. Between 1905 and 1909 a Royal Commission enquired into the problem of the aged, poor and unemployed; both a majority and minority report were produced.

The majority report recommended that the administration of the poor would be more efficient if it was put into the hands of the 180 Counties and County Boroughs rather than being spread over 640 Poor Law Unions. The Report also wanted to see the mixed workhouse abolished and a proper classification of the poor made. They further recommended a system of unemployment and sickness insurance, public work schemes for the unemployed, and employment exchanges to put workers and employers in touch with each other.

It was the Minority Report, however, which captured the public's imagination by recommending the breaking up of the Poor Law into the separate problems it involved, such as education, pensions and a public medical service. This Report considered that low income was a product of social conditions rather than personal failure and that the State should concern itself with discovering and eliminating the causes of poverty.

The first major onslaught on poverty was begun when the Liberals were returned to office in 1906 in a landslide victory. During the next few years they put through a radical programme of social reforms.

1. The Trade Disputes Act 1906 reversed the Taff Vale decision of

1901 by which it was held that trade union funds were liable for acts committed by individual members of a union; trade union funds were thus safeguarded in the event of a strike.

2. The Workman's Compensation Act (1906) compelled employers to compensate a worker for injuries received at work.

3. School meals, medical inspection and juvenile courts were provided by Acts of 1906, 1907 and 1908.

4. An eight-hour working day Act was introduced for miners in 1908.

5. Old age pensions were introduced in 1908 for those people over 70 years of age and in receipt of not more than £21 a year or 8 shillings a week. These people were to receive a maximum pension of 5 shillings weekly, whilst those with higher incomes not exceeding £31 a year received pensions scaled down proportionately to 1 shilling per week.

6. The three most important social reforms of 1909 were:

(i) A Housing and Town Planning Act to deal with the problem of slums by laying down certain minimum environmental standards; back-to-back housing became illegal under the provisions of this Act.

(ii) Labour Exchanges were set up throughout the country for the purpose of putting employers and employees in touch with each other.

(iii) The Trade Board Act fixed minimum wages in some of the worst paid 'sweated' industries such as ready-made tailoring.

7. The highlight of the Liberals' programme of social reform was the National Insurance Act of 1911, which provided for health and unemployment insurance in the building, engineering, shipbuilding, ironfounding and a limited number of other trades. This Act set up a State run insurance fund to which employers contributed 3d. per week, employees 4d. and the state 2d. From the fund workmen could then draw benefit in times of sickness and unemployment through their approved Friendly Societies. Later the scheme was extended to cover all workers.

Thus, by 1914 the old Victorian Poor Law was in the process of breaking up, and whilst there was still a long way to go before a basic minimum security could be demanded by everyone as of right, the basis for future development had been laid.

Suggested Further Reading

Bruce, M., *The Rise of the Welfare State: English Social Policy 1601–1971*, Batsford, London, 1973.

Cole, G. D. H., and Postgate, R., *The Common People, 1746–1946*, Methuen, London, 1962.

Williams, G., *The Coming of the Welfare State*, Allen & Unwin, London, 1967.

The Long Debate on Poverty, published by the Institute of Economic Affairs, London, 1972.

Exercises

1. Why was the Poor Law Amendment Act passed in 1834?

2. Comment on the view, with reference to the period 1834–1909, that a deterrent Poor Law makes a country more efficient.

3. Why was Britain being forced along the path towards more social welfare in the late nineteenth century?

4. The Liberal Governments between 1906 and 1914 laid the basis of the modern welfare state. Discuss.

Summary

1. The 1834 Poor Law Amendment Act put an end to outdoor relief for the able-bodied and insisted on their presence in the workhouse where the harsh discipline, hard work and poor diet were designed to act as deterrents to the indolent poor.

2. The 1834 Poor Law Amendment Act recommended that the poor should be classified into four separate groups and that the existing 15,000 parishes in the country should be formed into 640 unions, each with its own workhouse and organised body of paid officers administered by boards of guardians.

3. The workhouses became grim institutional establishments and the principle of classifying the poor was never properly applied with the result that the deserving and less deserving inmates received much the same treatment.

4. The evolution of a more humane attitude towards the poor in the last quarter of the nineteenth century was influenced by the extension of the franchise, the impact of a socialist ideology, the experience of the 'Great Depression' and a growing awareness of the extent of poverty.

5. The Royal Commission Minority Report inquiring into the problem of the aged, poor and unemployed, recommended in 1909 that the Poor Law should be broken up into the separate problems which it involved, such as education, pensions, and a public medical service.

6. The Liberal Governments between 1906 and 1914 took the first major steps towards breaking up the old Victorian Poor Law, the two most important reforms being the introduction of old age pensions in 1909 and national insurance in 1911.

CHAPTER THIRTEEN

COMMERCIAL AND FINANCIAL DEVELOPMENTS

By the third quarter of the nineteenth century, Britain had become the greatest industrial nation in the world, producing more than half of the world's coal and pig iron, and nearly half of the world's cotton cloth and steel. Her free trade policy stimulated the growth of trade and encouraged the international movement of labour and capital to the areas where they could be best employed. This, together with the development of the world's railway and steamship systems and the investments made by other European countries in the rest of the world, led to the emergence of an international economy of which Britain, with her strong balance of payments and relatively advanced banking system, became the centre.

The Emergence of an International Economy

Countries find it profitable to trade because of the different advantages they have in relation to each other either in terms of skills or resources. Coal, for example, is chiefly mined in the United States, Great Britain, Germany and Russia, whilst iron comes mainly from the United States, France, Sweden and Russia. This, of course, means that these countries are best able to trade in these particular resources and the products made from them. Certain products depend upon climatic conditions or particular types of soils; most rubber, for example, comes from Malaya and the East Indies, whilst most of the world's coffee comes from Brazil. On the other hand, a special skill may be the operative factor in the determination of a region's speciality; for example, the Scots in the production of whisky.

International trade is very important in raising living standards because by increasing the exchange of primary products and manufactured goods, countries are able to utilise a much wider range of commodities than would otherwise be possible. The nature and scope of the international economy was considerably transformed in the century before 1914, for the following reasons, thus making possible the enjoyment of higher living standards for millions of people.

1. The spreading of personal freedom promoted economic development. With the abolition of serfdom and slavery, men became free to move and choose their own occupation, resulting in a complete reconstruction of agricultural life in Europe. The late L. C. A. Knowles pointed out 'that everywhere the law had to be recast to fit the new conditions of ownership designed for persons who were free to buy and sell, free to move, free to acquire land, free to leave it by will, free to marry and free to emigrate, all of which things were new for the bulk of the population in the nineteenth century.'

2. This new freedom of movement applied not only to movement within a person's country of birth, but also to movement between nations. Thus an expanding world population provided potential immigrants for several vast areas, which were rich in natural resources and yet had too small a population to utilise them effectively. According to Ashworth, the Americas in 1850 contained about one twentieth of the world's population in one third of its land area, whereas in Europe and Asia, where population was rapidly rising, there were more than four fifths of the world's population in two fifths of its land area. Obviously, a more equitable distribution of the world's factors of production would lead to more efficiency and increased output, which could in turn lead to more international trade.

The increased international mobility of labour in the nineteenth century was a major factor contributing towards this end. Between 1820 and 1930 the number of people in the world who emigrated and who did not return home was about 62 million, of which

The United States received	61·4 per cent
Canada	11·5 per cent
Argentina	10·1 per cent
Brazil	7·3 per cent
Australia	4·5 per cent
New Zealand	3·0 per cent
South Africa	2·2 per cent

It is significant that in all the chief receiving areas of immigrants, the average levels of incomes tended to be higher than elsewhere, and international trade played an important part in their economic lives.

3. The accumulation of capital in the developed countries and its increased international mobility provided the finance for new areas to develop. This growth in capital accumulation was stimulated by the evolution of banking and credit facilities, and by gold discoveries in California (1849), Australia (1851), New Zealand (1861), South Africa (1886), and the Klondike (1897). The four main exporters of capital before 1914 were Britain, France, Germany, and from the 1890s onwards, the U.S.A.

4. International trade was encouraged from the 1870s onwards by world currency stability brought about by most countries being on the Gold Standard. Under this system a country was compelled to deflate when it was losing gold, and inflate when its stock of gold was increasing, thus automatically bringing about a balance of payments, as Fig. 13 shows.

5. There was an increase in the physical product of agriculture and industry as new techniques became more widely diffused, thus making more goods available for international trade. Increased industrial production was particularly marked after 1850, when the extended use of the recently invented machine tools and the increase in the numbers of skilled engineers made possible a greater amount of mechanisation in industry.

Britain, for example, experienced at this time a second 'Industrial Revolution' when power was extensively applied to manufacturing

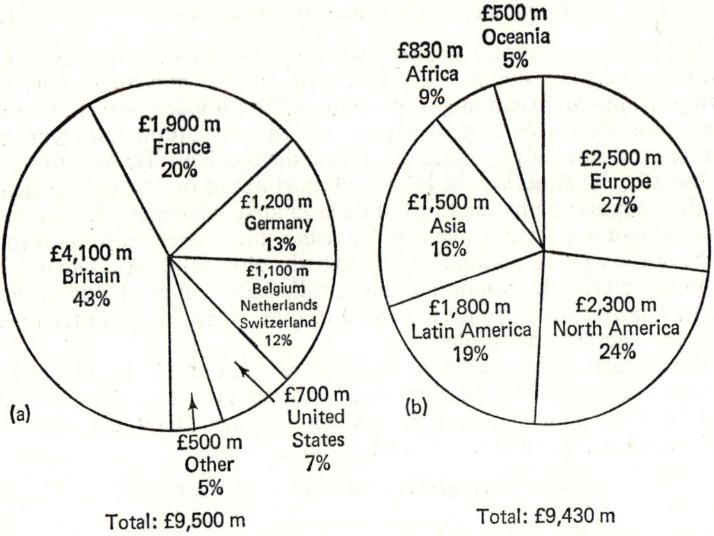

Fig. 12. Distribution of foreign investments in 1914 (a) by investing regions and (b) by recipient regions.
(courtesy Kenwood and Lougheed, *Growth of the International Economy*, Allen & Unwin

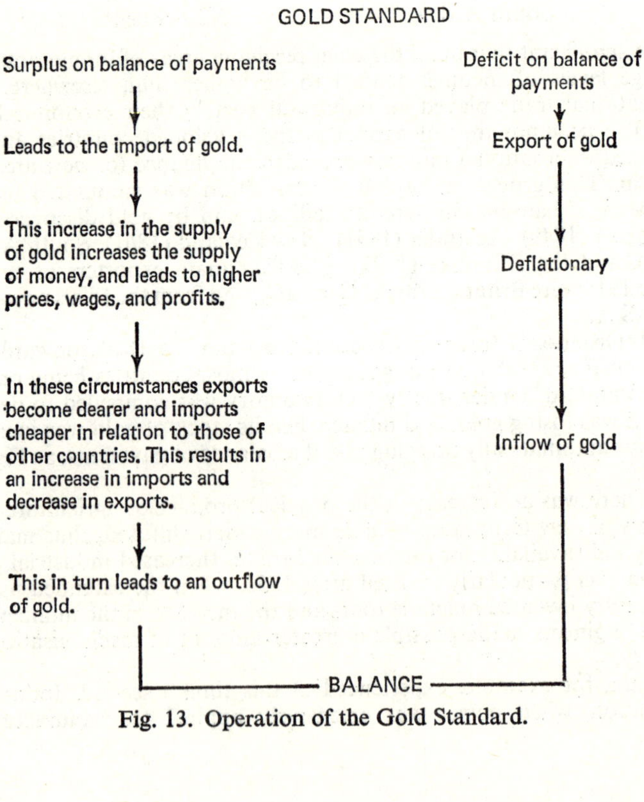

Fig. 13. Operation of the Gold Standard.

industry; business organisation and production techniques were improved upon; and the factory rather than the small workshop became the typical unit of production. The same was true for the primary producing countries, where increased mechanisation led to big increases in agricultural production.

Increasingly, as the century progressed, more goods entered into international trade, not only because of the increased product of agriculture and industry, but also because countries were trading in a larger proportion of their product. In Britain, for example, the output of approximately one worker in every five in 1880 was being sold abroad.

6. The area of international trade was immensely widened by improvements in transportation. The development of the world railway and steamship systems, coupled with the opening of the Suez and Panama Canals, opened up previously inaccessible territories. In this way the relatively new areas, such as the Americas, Australia, New Zealand and South Africa, were able to provide industrial countries with increasing quantities of foodstuffs and raw materials, whilst taking in return increasing quantities of manufactured goods.

The Content and Direction of British Trade

During the nineteenth century, Britain came to rely on imports of food and raw materials and exported manufactured goods. From 1823 onwards, Britain had a trade deficit which became quite marked in the quarter century before 1914.

Table 19. Britain's Balance of Trade

	Imports	*Exports*	*Surplus*	*Deficit*
		FOOD		
1890–4	£169,985,000	£10,233,000		£159,752,000
1910–13	£263,104,000	£31,647,000		£231,457,000
		RAW MATERIALS		
1890–4	£110,209,000	£23,316,000		£86,893,000
1910–13	£195,400,000	£55,862,000		£139,538,000
		MANUFACTURES		
1890–4	£75,850,000	£199,649,000	£123,799,000	
1910–13	£150,322,000	£368,932,000	£218,600,000	

Source: The Balfour Report, *A Survey of Overseas Markets.*

This trade deficit of visible imports over visible exports was, however, more than counterbalanced by the growth of invisible exports, i.e. trade consisting of services, such as shipping, banking and insurance services, rather than of goods (see Table 20).

Thus it was possible for Britain to keep a strong balance of payments position, in spite of her trade deficit, so long as she maintained her invisible exports.

Table 20. Britain's Invisible Trade

	1907	*1913*
	(in £ million)	
Trade deficit on visible account	142	158
Income from shipping services	85	94
Income from financial services	35	35
Interest on overseas investments	160	210
	280	339
Surplus on overall balance of payments	138	181

Source: The Balfour Report, *A Survey of Overseas Markets.*

Imports

The cotton industry purchased all its raw cotton from abroad, whilst imports of raw wool, mainly from Australia and New Zealand, became increasingly significant from the 1850s onwards, so that by 1914 over four fifths of the woollen industry's requirements were being imported. Other important raw materials imported were timber, rubber, oil and non-phosphoric iron ore for steelmaking.

Britain also became progressively more dependent on food imports in the nineteenth century—principally sugar, tea, wheat and meat—as the population increased and free trade enabled cheaper food to be purchased from abroad.

On the outbreak of war in 1914, Britain found herself in an extremely vulnerable position, being dependent on overseas supplies for seven eighths of her raw materials—excluding coal—and over half of her food requirements.

Exports

The stable exports until 1914 were textiles, iron and steel products, machinery and coal. Textiles, mainly cotton goods, accounted for approximately 60 per cent of home produced goods sold abroad in 1850; iron, and later on steel exports, became of immense importance with the development of the world railway systems; whilst coal exports, which made a valuable contribution both in terms of the utilisation of shipping space as well as currency earned, rose from 3 million tons in 1850 to 94 million tons in 1914.

Direction of British Trade

After 1870 there was a tendency for British trade to move towards more distant regions in the Empire and towards areas with low incomes and large populations, such as South America and the Far East, due mainly to the growth of foreign competition and the imposition of high protective tariffs in the wealthier markets of the world.

As can be seen from Table 21, there was a marked tailing off during the last quarter of the nineteenth century in the rate of increase in trade with the United States. Until the Civil War, the Atlantic economy had rested on a profitable trade between two complementary economies, Britain and the United States. Between 1820 and 1850, 50 per cent of U.S. exports went to Britain; while between 1820 and 1860, 40 per cent of U.S. imports came from Britain. According to Frank Thistlethwaite in the *Economic History Review* (1954), Britain provided the United States frontier with 'more axes, knives, clothing, more ploughs, more

Table 21. Destinations of U.K. Exports (£ million)

Destinations	*1846*	*1880*	*1914*
Western Europe	7·5	30·6	50·4
U.S.A.	6·8	30·9	34·0
British North America	3·3	7·7	17·9
Central and South America	5·6	17·4	32·7
India	5·8	30·5	62·9

Source: Mitchell and Deane, *Abstract of British Historical Statistics.*

machinery and hardware, more canals and railways, better breeds of cattle and sheep, cheaper credits than the Americans themselves could command', whilst for Great Britain, North America was an outlet of importance for her 'internal adjustment to the conditions of modern industrial society'. However, the Republican policy of protection during and after the Civil War meant that Continental replaced Atlantic interests in the United States, and American industries, safe behind tariff walls, were able to capture traditional British markets, thus forcing British industrialists to expand their markets elsewhere.

British Trading Policy

The most important development in British trading policy during this period was the move towards free trade, the beginnings of which were Peel's budgets between 1842 and 1845, when duties were either removed or drastically reduced on a vast number of articles of import, especially on raw materials and food. These measures were then followed by the repeal of the Corn Laws in 1846, and of the Navigation Acts in 1849.

Gladstone's two budgets of 1853 and 1859, and the subsequent Cobden Chevalier trade treaty of 1860, completed the transition to free trade. The 1853 budget abolished the duties on 123 articles and reduced the rates on 133 others, whilst the 1859 budget abolished almost all of the remaining duties. The loss of revenue proposed in the budget changes of 1853 was to be made good by increasing the duty on whisky, extending the legacy duty to real and personal property passing by will, and renewing the income tax (reintroduced in 1842) for seven years on incomes exceeding £100. In fact, income from customs and excise duties following these measures actually increased.

In the Cobden Chevalier trade treaty of 1860 France abolished all prohibitions on British imports and agreed that the maximum rate of duties on all British imports would be 30 per cent ad valorem for four years, and then 25 per cent. In return, Britain lowered the customs duty on French wines and brandy, and abolished all duties on manufactured goods, including silk.

The British concessions made to France applied to all countries, whereas the French concessions applied only to Britain. However, various other countries signed similar commercial agreements with France, thus producing in Western Europe a network of low tariff agreements which greatly facilitated the expansion of international trade.

During the next twenty years, when Britain enjoyed unprecedented economic growth and development, free trade really did seem to pay, and many of those who had opposed free trade changed their minds. Disraeli, for example, who had strongly opposed Peel's Government on the issue of repealing the Corn Laws, expressed the view that 'protection was both dead and damned'.

In the last quarter of the nineteenth century, however, circumstances changed, and there arose fresh demands for at least some form of protection, on the following grounds:

1. Whilst British industry continued to grow absolutely, doubling its output between 1870 and 1913, comparatively it declined, and industrial rivals, particularly Germany and the United States, began successfully to challenge her economic supremacy. In 1870 Britain was producing almost a third of the world's manufactured goods, but by 1913 the proportion was only about one seventh.

Foreign manufactured goods not only threatened Britain's overseas markets, but also, on account of her free trade policy, the home market was threatened, resulting in growing demands from manufacturers for a protective tariff. Some idea of the growing threat from German industrial expansion at home can be acquired by a glance at the following passage deploring the growth of German competition. This passage illustrates the literature of the movement for tariff reform, and is taken from a best selling pamphlet published in 1896 entitled *Made in Germany*, by E. E. Williams.

The phrase is fluent in the mouth: how universally appropriate it is, probably no one who has not made a study of the matter is aware. Take observations, Gentle Reader, in your own surroundings: the mental exercise is recommended as an antidote to that form of self sufficiency which our candid friends regard as indigenous to the British climate. Your investigations will work out somewhat in this fashion. You will find that the material of some of your own clothes was probably woven in Germany. Still more probable is it that some of your wife's garments are German importations; while it is practically beyond a doubt that the magnificent mantles and jackets wherein her maids array themselves on their Sundays out are German made and German sold, for only so could they be done at that figure. Your governess's fiancé is a clerk in the City; but he also was made in Germany. The toys, and the dolls, and the fairy books which your children maltreat in the nursery are made in Germany; nay the material of your favourite (patriotic) newspaper had the same birthplace as like as not. Roam the house over, and the fateful mark will greet you at every turn, from the piano in your drawing room to the mug on your kitchen dresser; blazoned though it be with the legend 'A Present from Margate'. Descend to your domestic depths, and you shall find your very drain pipes German made. You pick out of the grate the paper wrappings from a book consignment, and they also are 'Made in Germany'. You stuff them into the fire, and reflect that the poker in your hand was forged in Germany. As you rise from your hearthrug you knock over an ornament on your mantelpiece; picking up the pieces you read, on the bit that formed the base, 'Manufactured in Germany'. And you jot your dismal reflections down with a pencil that was made in Germany. At midnight your wife comes home from an opera that was made in Germany, has been enacted by singers and conductor and players made in Germany, with the aid of instruments and sheets of music made in Germany. You go to bed, and glare wrathfully at a text on the wall; it is illuminated with an English village church, and it was 'Printed in Germany'. If you are imaginative and dyspeptic, you drop off to sleep only to dream that St Peter (with a duly stamped halo round his head and a bunch of keys from the Rhineland) has refused you admission into Paradise, because you bear not the mark of the Beast upon your forehead, and are not of German make. But you console yourself with the thought that it was only a Bierhaus Paradise any way; and you are awakened in the morning by the sonorous brass of a German band.

It must of course be remembered that whilst this type of evidence was looked on by British manufacturers and tariff reformers in general with great disfavour, it was also looked on by others as being evidence of an improvement in the quality of people's lives.

2. Large imports of grain and meat following the opening up of new lands and the development of the world's railway and steamship systems led to a depression in British agriculture in the early 1870s. Whilst it is true that Britain had a poor comparative cost advantage to produce primary products, and cheap food imports did lead to a rise in living standards for the masses, there were nevertheless those who were concerned from an aesthetic point of view, irrespective of maximising the country's productive efficiency, of the growing imbalance between agriculture and industry, as well as those who were concerned about the strategic implications of being dependent on food imports.

3. By the end of the nineteenth century Britain stood alone amongst the large nations as a free trade country, as other countries for varying reasons increased their tariffs. The United States protected its infant industries after the Civil War with tariffs; France, after reluctantly going along with Napoleon III's liberal tariff policies in the 1860s, seized the opportunity after his demise to return to their traditional policy of protection; whilst Germany also introduced a tariff in 1879 as part of its policy of fostering internal economic development.

Great Britain was thus alone amongst the Great Powers in pursuing a policy of free trade, and as such she was unable to use the tariff as a means of gaining concessions in foreign markets. Many people argued that whilst cooperative and mutual free trade by all was a worthwhile policy, to pursue such a policy alone was folly.

4. As the size of the Empire increased, and the direction of trade moved towards it, so the idea of a system of Imperial Preference became more attractive. Between 1880 and 1900 the surface area of the British Empire was increased from 7·7 million square miles to 13 million square miles, whilst its population grew from 268 millions to 370 millions. Britain could thus, it was argued, conduct a policy of preferential trade

within this area, without suffering the disadvantages of free trade with the rest of the world.

5. The experience of the so-called 'Great Depression' between 1873 and 1896, with its adverse effects on profits, helped to convince many businessmen of the need for a protective tariff.

6. A protective tariff would also have provided an additional source of revenue to help meet the growing Government expenditure on welfare and armaments.

The most influential and eloquent advocate of tariff reform was Joseph Chamberlain who in 1903 formed the Tariff Reform Movement. Chamberlain managed to win over the support of the Conservative Party for the cause of protection, and this became the most important issue in the 1906 election, when the Conservatives suffered a stunning defeat. This election proved that whilst tariff reform may have been a prudent policy in the overall national interest, the masses felt that it was against their individual short-term interests, since they associated a protective tariff with expensive food on which they spent a large proportion of their income.

Thus Britain continued dogmatically to pursue a free trade policy, even though the nation's overall advantages were rapidly becoming outweighed by the disadvantages, and little more was heard about tariff reform until the inter-war years, when depressed conditions brought the issue to the fore again.

Foreign Investment

Britain was a net importer of capital in the eighteenth century, mainly from Holland, but during the Napoleonic Wars, when Britain's wealth and capacity for capital accumulation was increasing in relation to the wealth of other countries, London replaced Amsterdam as the centre of the international money market. The vast outflow of money from Britain to all corners of the world in the century before 1914 was an important invisible export as well as stimulating industry by opening up new markets for British products.

A host of European countries resorted to the international loan market in the aftermath of the Napoleonic Wars in an effort to get back on their feet; Prussia borrowed £5 million in 1818, Russia £2 million in 1822, and Austria £1 million in 1822. France borrowed £10 million in Britain after the war through the Baring Brothers; this enabled her to pay the war indemnity imposed on her as a consequence of peace, thus enabling her to get rid of the foreign troops stationed on her soil.

The main areas of British overseas investments up to the 1850s were in Europe and the United States; the bulk of this investment was in Government stocks, railways, industrial enterprises, and public utilities, such as gas works. Investment was particularly popular in the United States during the 1830s, until many investors lost a great deal of money in the American banking crisis of 1837. It must be remembered that poor communications greatly increased the risks involved in overseas investment since trading news was often based on rumour and was slow to circulate.

Investors were extremely nervous and cautious after this crisis, so that

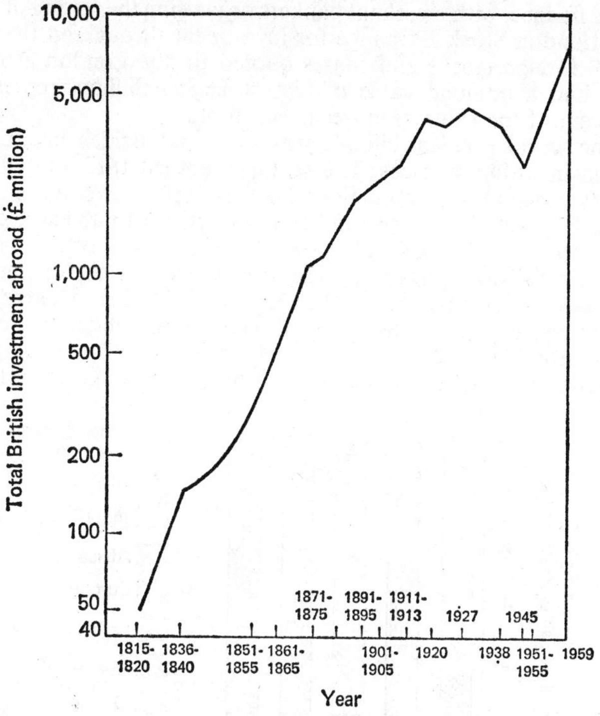

Fig. 14. British foreign investment.
(courtesy Penguin Books Ltd)

there was little foreign investment in the decade following the American crisis; British capital was instead directed towards railway investment at home, particularly between 1844 and 1847. Foreign investment was vigorously resumed again after the collapse of the railway boom in 1847, rising from £200 million in 1850 to the immense total of £4,000 million in 1914. This colossal growth of foreign investment was encouraged by several factors.

1. A healthy balance of payments during most of the period, achieved in spite of a trade deficit, due to the growth of extensive invisible exports, such as banking and shipping services.
2. The level of profit in many British industries tended to be low in comparison with the earnings on many foreign investments.
3. The linking up of countries by telegraphic cable facilitated the speedy exchange of trading news, thus reducing the risks involved in overseas investment; Britain and France were joined by cable in 1850, and by the 1870s India was linked to Washington by cable.
4. Investment in the East, particularly in Indian railways, was encouraged by the opening of the Suez Canal in 1867.
5. The City of London gained a reputation as the centre of inter-

national finance, with merchant bankers organising the raising of capital on the London Stock Exchange for investment throughout the world. In 1913, foreign stocks and shares quoted on the London Stock Exchange had a nominal value of almost £6,800 million, representing 60 per cent of the value of all securities quoted.

6. The world political climate was such that British investors felt secure in investing overseas. The century between 1815 and 1914 was relatively peaceful, with no major wars taking place over a long period of time. Furthermore, British military strength and influence, particularly up to the 1870s, helped to secure the safety of British property overseas. This was a power that the British Government was prepared to use, as was demonstrated in the Don Pacifico affair, where a Portuguese moneylender, who claimed British citizenship on account of being born in Gibraltar, had his house raided in Athens. The Greek government refused to give him compensation, whereupon Don Pacifico

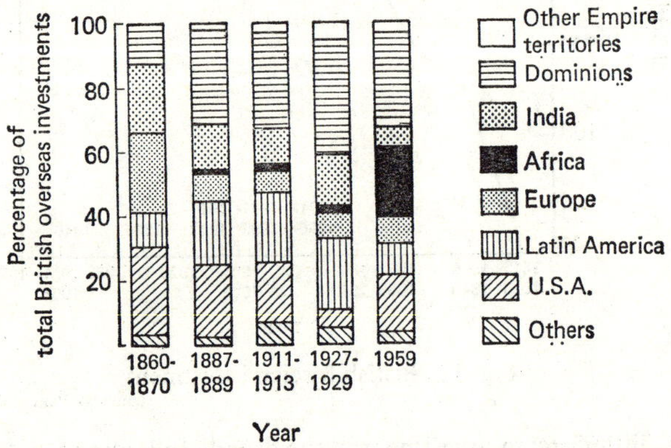

Fig. 15. Geographical distribution of British foreign investment.
(courtesy Penguin Books Ltd)

Table 22. British Foreign Investment, 1830–1914

		1830 (%)	*1854* (%)	*1870* (%)	*1914* (%)
Europe		66	55	25	5
United States		9	25	27	21
Latin America		23	15	11	18
British Empire:	India			22	9
	Dominions	2	5	12	37
Other regions				3	9
Total		100	100	100	100
Total investment	(£m)	110	260	770	4,107
	($m)	536	1,266	3,750	20,000

Source: A. G. Kenwood and A. L. Lougheed, *The Growth of the International Economy.*

appealed for help from the British Government. In response, Lord Palmerston, the British Foreign Secretary, ordered a blockade of the Greek coast, thus provoking an international incident for which he was strongly criticised. Palmerston, in perhaps the most famous speech of his life, defended his action in Parliament by claiming the same security for all British subjects, no matter how obscure their claim to British nationality might be, that had once been enjoyed by the Roman citizen, who could say '*Civis Romanus sum*' (I am a Roman citizen).

This type of security, together with the fact that there had been no major international incident, such as the Bolshevik Revolution of 1917, wherein large sums of foreign money had been confiscated, encouraged British investors unhesitatingly to invest their money where they could get the highest returns.

7. The marginal propensity to save was high in Britain, thus creating a high marginal propensity to invest. This was brought about by the inequality in the distribution of the national income and the low level of taxation, which was never more than 1s. 2d. in the pound up to 1914.

As the century progressed investment tended to move away from Europe and the United States towards the Empire and underdeveloped countries (see Fig. 15 and Table 22).

Roughly 30 per cent of this investment was in foreign government stocks, whilst another 40 per cent was invested in foreign railways. The rest was invested in industrial enterprises, and public utilities, such as gas works and electric light and railway companies (Fig. 16).

The bulk of this foreign investment was undertaken by individuals and companies rather than by Government agencies; the only two investments of any importance undertaken by the British Government before 1914 were the acquisition of Suez Canal shares in 1875 on the

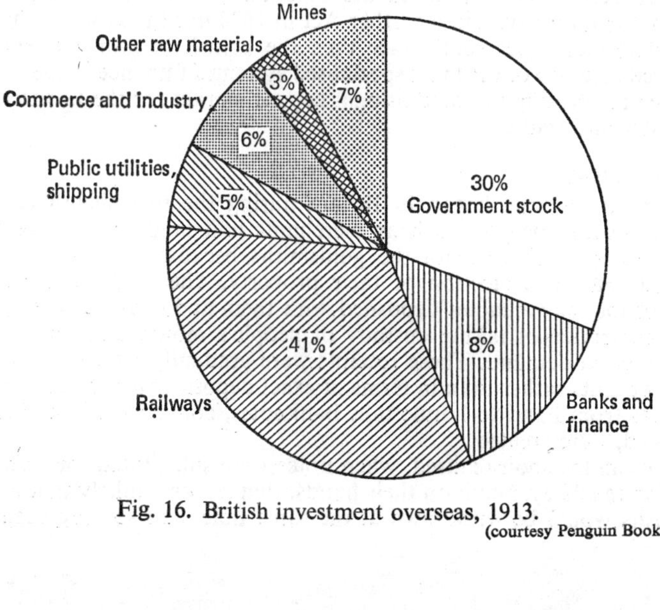

Fig. 16. British investment overseas, 1913.
(courtesy Penguin Books Ltd)

initiative of Disraeli in order to secure the route to India, and the purchase of a majority interest in the Anglo Persian Oil company in 1909, in order to safeguard against the strategic threat posed by the conversion of naval ships from coal- to oil-fired bunkering.

No Government restrictions were imposed on foreign investments, so that individuals were free to invest their money where they got the highest returns. Thus, 40 per cent of British investment was undertaken abroad between 1870 and 1913, whilst in the peak period of foreign investment between 1911 and 1913 Britain was investing twice as much abroad as at home. This had serious implications for British industry, which was beginning to look archaic in comparison with some of her competitors. Major industries, such as coal and iron and steel, were in a bad way technically in 1914, whilst investment in the newer industries, such as the chemical and electrical industries, was sadly lacking.

According to Graham Turner (*Business in Britain*), the contrast between Britain and her major Continental competitor, Germany, in this respect is most striking: 'In the years 1901–5 and 1911–13 only 5·7 per cent of total German investment went abroad; between 1905 and 1914 the figure for Britain was 52·9 per cent.' Whilst it is true that the income from foreign investment was a major contribution to Britain's balance of payments, as well as helping to foster international trade and world economic growth, it would nevertheless have been more prudent in the long run if a larger proportion of British savings had been invested in the restructuring of British industry.

The Development of Banking

The development of banking in Britain was inhibited in earlier times due to the medieval distrust of usury, i.e. the lending of money at excessive rates of interest. Gradually opinion on this matter changed, and an Act of 1545 legalised the exaction of reasonable interest, as distinct from usury, and a further Act in 1624 fixed the maximum rate of interest at 8 per cent. Since then the British banking system has evolved into one of the most specialised systems of finance in the world, as well as creating an international capital market for the financing of industry and trade.

Early Banking

Deposit banking began in Britain during the seventeenth century when wealthy people, such as merchants and landowners, began to leave their valuables with the goldsmiths because of the safes they owned for the protection of their property. The goldsmiths gave a receipt for the valuables deposited with them and charged a small fee for the service of taking custody of people's money and paying out amounts on demand. These receipts were gradually made out in convenient units rather than in terms of exact deposit amounts, and began to pass from hand to hand; thus banknotes, convertible into coin on demand, were created.

Goldsmiths soon realised, when notes were substituted for coin and they were left with coin on their hands, that it was unlikely that all the deposits would be withdrawn at the same time, and so they began to lend out the surplus for a rate of interest. This led to a system whereby notes were created in excess of the coin available; thus credit was being created. Obviously the bankers had to be very careful in their issuing of notes over and above the coin held by them since the slightest suspicion by depositors of poor bank management could result in a run on a bank and consequent failure.

The Founding of the Bank of England

The Bank of England was founded during the war of the Grand Alliance against France (1689–97), when it was realised that the war was too costly to be financed wholly out of the proceeds of taxation.

William Paterson, a Scot, produced a scheme in 1691 for the foundation of the Bank, and his suggestions were subsequently accepted in 1694. In return for a Royal Charter of Incorporation the Bank agreed to subscribe £1·2 million of the money required for the war at a rate of interest of 8 per cent. Under the terms of the Charter, the Bank's main business was to receive deposits, discount approved bills of exchange, and make loans on approved security.

In 1708 an Act of Parliament decreed that no other bank with more than six partners should be established with the right of issuing notes. This provision gave a monopoly of joint stock banking to the Bank of England, since the issuing of notes was essential to profits. This was an extremely harmful measure to Britain's economic development, since when industrialisation spread the only competitors of the Bank of England were the private banks, which were either small family businesses or private partnerships, and since they were often excessively tied to local conditions they were not very safe.

In 1750 most of the banking business was concentrated in London, but during the second half of the eighteenth century, under the stimulus of the Industrial Revolution, there was a proliferation of banks throughout the country. The number of London banks increased from between twenty and thirty in 1760 to about seventy in 1800, whilst the number of country banks increased from 12 in 1750 to almost 700 in 1815. This proliferation of provincial banks was a response to an increase in trade, especially in the growing industrial areas of the Midlands, the North, and South Wales. Banks were needed in the industrial towns to provide short-term credit to hard-pressed manufacturers, whilst surpluses of cash in the rural areas were lent via the country banks to the growing industrial areas.

Most of the country banks were small unit banks which had a high rate of mortality during times of crisis. This was because when there was any doubt about a small banker's solvency there would be a run on the bank resulting in bankruptcy; between 1815 and 1830 there were no fewer than 206 bank failures. Hence a strong movement developed for the legalisation of joint stock banking. The first positive move in this direction was an Act of 1826 legalising the establishment of joint stock banks with unlimited liability, but they were only allowed to issue notes provided they operated at least 65 miles from London. A further Act passed in 1833 permitted the establishment of joint stock banks in London, though these banks were not given the right to issue notes.

From then onwards the number of joint stock banks increased, 99 having been established by 1836, of which twenty were in Yorkshire and two in London. Hence banks with more adequate resources were created which stood a better chance of supplying the country with a more secure paper currency, whilst the number of private banks declined from 781 in 1821 to 321 in 1841.

The Bank Charter Act, 1844

This Act settled a controversy concerning the unlimited circulation of paper money, which had been raging for many years.

In 1797, when there were fears of an invasion from France, and a threat to the Bank of England's gold reserves, the Government authorised the Bank of England to suspend gold payments on its notes; in other words Bank of England notes were no longer convertible into gold. As a result of subsequent inflation gold began to appreciate in terms of currency and the value of British currency fell on the foreign exchanges. This led to the setting up of a Bullion Committee by the House of Commons in 1810, which recommended the resumption of gold payments on notes in order to check the inflationary spiral. The purpose of this recommendation was to deflate the economy by progressively reducing the issue of Bank of England notes so that the price of gold bullion could be brought back to the mint level, thus enabling cash payments to be resumed. The immediate adoption of such a course of action would have impaired Britain's ability to bring the war with France to a successful conclusion; therefore the decision was deferred and gold payments on notes were not resumed again until 1821—the date from which Britain could be said to be 'on the Gold Standard'.

As a result of the various commercial crises which followed, notably those in 1825, 1836, and 1839, when many banks failed to honour their obligations, there arose the famous controversy between the Currency and the Banking schools of thought. The Currency school of thought believed that the issuing of notes should be restricted by being tied down to gold, whilst the Banking school of thought believed that the bankers were the best judges of their own interests, and should therefore be given greater latitude. The Prime Minister, Sir Robert Peel, became converted to the Currency school of thought, the philosophy of which was embodied in the Bank Charter Act of 1844.

The Act had two main objectives:

1. To make Bank of England notes more secure. This was to be done by dividing the Issuing Department of the Bank from the Banking Department, and by decreeing that notes could only be issued if backed by gold, plus a legal fiduciary issue of £14 million, which was to be backed by Government securities. Provision was also made for the fiduciary issue to be increased when a private bank note issue lapsed by two thirds of the lapsed issue. The Act also required the Issue Department to publish the Bank's accounts in the form of a weekly statement.

2. The second main objective was to restrict the note issue of all other banks in England and Wales. This was done by restricting their note

circulation to the 1844 circulation, and by building in a provision that banks lost their right to issue notes if they opened a London office, amalgamated, or went bankrupt. Also new banks were not to be given the right to issue notes.

As a result of these measures the Bank of England gradually became the sole note-issuing authority in England and Wales. This was finally achieved in 1921 when Fox, Fowler and Company of Taunton lost their issue rights as the result of an amalgamation with Lloyd's Bank. Thus the paper currency up to 1914 was 'as good as gold', since the Bank of England undertook to convert notes into gold, and gold coins were used as currency.

This restricting of the supply of notes to the amount of gold held by the Bank of England could have had a very damaging effect on Britain at a time when she was poised for rapid economic development, since an increasing supply of money was necessary for an expanding economy. In practice, however, the money supply was expanded in two ways. Firstly, there was an increase in the world supply of gold as a result of big gold discoveries in California and Australia in 1849 and 1850, and much of this gold found its way into Britain because of Britain's surplus on her balance of payments. Secondly, the country's supply of money was increased by the commercial banks creating credit through the profitable cheque and overdraft systems.

The Bank Charter Act was suspended during four periods of crisis in 1847, 1857, 1866 and 1914. This permitted an increase in the fiduciary issue, although the power to over-issue notes was only used twice, in 1857 and 1914, since confidence was restored on the other occasions without recourse to such action. During the crisis of 1866 the Bank of England accepted the responsibility of acting as lender of last resort.

As the nineteenth century progressed the Bank of England, partly as a result of the experience of these crises, slowly learnt the essential techniques of central banking and before the end of the century was controlling the credit policy of the commercial banks through a sensitive use of bank rate and open market operations.

Commercial Banking 1844–1914

The extension of the principle of limited liability to banks in 1862 removed the last important barrier to the growth of the large joint stock banks, though it was not until after the failure of the City of Glasgow Bank in 1878 that many banks took advantage of the privilege. This development encouraged the growth of larger banking concerns amongst the joint stock banks.

On the face of it the Bank Charter Act, by limiting the note issue, fundamentally changed the position of the commercial banks, which previously had extended their notes beyond their gold reserves. In practice, however, the banks continued in exactly the same way by using Bank of England notes as their credit base, and instead of lending in notes, loans were granted by 'creating deposits' which served as money, since bankers knew that in a system in which deposits were transferred from person to person by cheque they would rarely be required to repay any major part of their deposits in Bank of England notes or gold coin. Hence, the increased use of cheques reduced the importance of the restriction on the note issue, and the commercial banks created credit by use of the profitable cheque and overdraft system.

This period was characterised by the development of large-scale banking either by individual banks opening branches or by amalgamation of banks. This development culminated in the formation of the 'Big Five', viz. Barclays, Lloyds, Midland, National Provincial and Westminster Banks, which among them had 3,200 branches in 1914.

The Advantages of Branch Banking

1. Reserves could be centralised to meet sudden local needs, thus eliminating the need to maintain large reserves at each individual branch.

2. Risks could be diffused over the whole country rather than being centred on a particular industry or locality. This was particularly relevant in Britain, where industry was highly localised. It is significant that during the world economic blizzard of 1929–33 not one bank failed in Britain, whereas in the United States during the same period, where there was not the equivalent of the 'Big Five', thousands of banks failed.

Hence by 1914 there had evolved in Britain a sophisticated and safe system of commercial banking, the monetary operations of which were being responsibly controlled by the Bank of England. This banking system played a critical part in making London the most important commercial and financial centre in the world.

Suggested Further Reading

Ashworth, W., *A Short History of the International Economy Since 1850*, Longmans, London, 1962.

Cairncross, A. K., *Home and Foreign Investment, 1870–1913: Studies in Capital Accumulation*, C.U.P., Cambridge, 1953.

Hall, A. R. (editor), *The Export of Capital from Britain 1870–1914*, Methuen, London, 1968.

Imlah, A. H., *Pax Britannica: Studies in British Foreign Trade in the Nineteenth Century*, Harvard, 1958.

Kenwood, A. G., and Lougheed, A. L., *The Growth of the International Economy, 1820–1960: An Introductory Text*, Allen & Unwin, London, 1971.

Pressnell, L. S., *Country Banking in the Industrial Revolution*, O.U.P., Oxford and London, 1956.

Saul, S. B., *Studies in British Overseas Trade, 1870–1914*, Liverpool University Press, Liverpool, 1960.

Schlote, W., *British Overseas Trade from 1700 to 1930s*, Blackwell, London, 1952.

Exercises

1. Discuss the view that Britain's prosperity in the nineteenth century was based on the export trade.

2. Describe the main factors influencing the growth of the international economy in the nineteenth century.

3. Trace and account for the changing direction of British trade in the nineteenth century.

4. By the 1870s the disadvantages of free trade were beginning to outweigh the advantages. Discuss.

5. In what ways did British foreign investment help, and in what ways did it hinder Britain's economic development in the century before 1914?

6. By the 1870s the Bank of England was effectively operating as the first central bank in the world. How did this come about?

7. What factors were responsible for stabilising the banking system in the late nineteenth century?

8. In the period 1844 to 1914, British money was 'as good as gold'. What did this mean, and what were the advantages and disadvantages of such a system?

Summary

1. The increased international mobility of labour and capital in the second half of the nineteenth century, together with the development of the world's railway and steamships systems, led to the emergence of an international economy of which Britain, with her strong balance of payments and relatively advanced banking system, became the centre.

2. Britain came to rely on imports of food and raw materials in the nineteenth century and exported manufactured goods.

3. After 1870 Britain's trade tended to move towards the Empire and to areas with low incomes and large populations in South America and the Far East.

4. Between 1846 to 1860 Britain completed the transition to free trade and during the next twenty years free trade really did seem to pay.

5. The advantages of free trade became outweighed by the disadvantages in the last quarter of the nineteenth century but the movement for tariff reform was unsuccessful in its attempts to reintroduce protection.

6. Britain invested £4,000 million abroad before 1914, mainly in Government stocks and railways. Most of this investment was undertaken by individuals though the Government did invest in Suez Canal shares in 1875, and purchased a majority interest in the Anglo-Persian Oil Company in 1909.

7. By the 1870s the Bank of England had learnt the essential techniques of central banking, whilst changes in company law encouraged the development of large-scale banking which resulted in the formation of the 'Big Five'.

CHAPTER FOURTEEN

THE PERIOD REVIEWED

It is important to realise that the successful and worthwhile study of economic history does not involve the learning of a welter of facts on the growth and development of trade, industry and commerce; indeed, such an approach is likely to be destructive of any interest in the subject, as well as being onerous and wearing. Instead, the student of economic history should be more concerned with identifying the common qualities of apparently disparate situations than with the uniqueness, concreteness or particularity of historic events. That is not to say that unique cases are not important, since obviously an analysis of individual cases is necessary in order to discover whether they have features in common, as for example in rapid growth phases or slumps. If this approach of identifying the uniformities of particular situations is adopted, then 'the feel' for a period will be acquired.

Economic History lends itself well to this approach, since it is possible easily to identify quite definite periods and trends; this is mainly because industrialisation inevitably involves exposure to the trade cycle, which is characterised by booms and depressions occurring at regular intervals. During the nineteenth and early twentieth centuries the interval between one depression and another was never less than five years and never more than eleven years; and superimposed upon these short-term price fluctuations were quite clearly defined periods of medium-term fluctuations. It is these medium-term trends in prices which are important, since through these a basic understanding of the period will be acquired. These trends affected national production, and hence the standard of living that could be enjoyed, as well as influencing employment, thus having a direct bearing on the levels of poverty and unhappiness in the community.

Four main periods of medium-term fluctuations in prices can be identified in the century between 1815 and 1914.

Post-War Depression and the Railway Boom, 1815–47

This was a period of falling prices, when, according to the various price indices, prices fell by just over 40 per cent. This was not a uniform fall in prices, since there were periods—for example, during the railway boom of 1844–7—when the general trend was arrested; indeed, one of the major characteristics of this period was that good times all too frequently alternated with bad.

Different people were affected in different ways by this deflation. The working classes, for example, were particularly affected by the fact that food prices did not fall as much as industrial prices, mainly on account of the pre-1846 policy of agricultural protection. The ill effects of this on the working classes were, however, to some extent offset by the rise in real wages for the town workman, since wages in general did not fall as much as prices.

An important reason for the fall in prices during this period was that the supply of money did not increase as rapidly as the volume of trade. The use of private bank notes fell off after the banking failures of 1825, and the passing of the Bank Charter Act of 1844 restricted the amount of notes unbacked by gold.

In spite of falling prices, however, there was a growth in real wealth during the 1820s and 1830s, and there is plenty of evidence of businessmen showing energy and enterprise in the promotion of trade and industry. The development of the locomotive steam engine is the classic example of the enterprise shown during this period.

The High Water Mark of Victorian Prosperity, 1847–73

This was a period of rising prices, when profits and wages rose and when the level of employment was high. This rise in prices was partly brought about by the increase in the supply of money following the gold discoveries in California (1849) and Australia (1850) and the trend towards the modern banking techniques of creating credit through the use of the cheque and overdraft systems.

Both agriculture and industry prospered during these years. Agriculture, in spite of the gloomy forecasts made at the time of the repeal of the Corn Laws in 1846, entered the period of High Farming and remained prosperous until the early 1870s. Industry was stimulated both by the growth of home demand, as the population rose from 21 million in 1851 to 26 million in 1871, and by the growth of the international economy, which stimulated Britain's export industries and gave her the reputation of being the 'workshop of the world'. Visible exports rose from £97 million in 1854 to £256 million in 1872, whilst visible imports grew from £133 million to £297 million.

This atmosphere of growth and prosperity encouraged both optimism and confidence about the future, as well as fostering attributes of complacency and pride in past achievement, which later were to inflict considerable damage on the economy.

The 'Great Depression', 1873–96

This period of deflation is often referred to as 'the Great Depression', and was characterised by falling prices, falling profits, and fiercer competition. This general trend of falling prices was, with the exception of the years 1880–5, part of a world-wide phenomenon, and occurred for the following reasons:

1. It was the inevitable consequence to the good years of 1847–73, representing the down-swing of the trade cycle.
2. Improved efficiency reduced costs, and hence prices.
3. The growth of competition, both at home and abroad, forced down prices.
4. Prices tended to depreciate in terms of gold, since the increase in the world supply of gold did not keep pace with the increase in the demand for it. This increased demand for gold was brought about both by the expansion of industrial output in Europe and North America,

and by more and more countries going onto the Gold Standard (Table 23).

The use of the term 'Great Depression' to describe the period 1873–96 is something of a misnomer, since the period was definitely not one of unrelieved economic adversity. Whilst the classic symptoms of depression were present—viz. deflation and unemployment—there were also many signs of prosperity. The aggregate of commodities produced by British capital and labour increased; 50 per cent more coal, for example, was mined in the early 1880s, and during the same period the production of pig iron was doubled. There was also a steady increase in imports, contributing towards rising living standards, as well as an expansion in the volume of exports, even though there was a decline in their value. The terms of trade moved in Britain's favour, which meant that there was a bigger drop in the prices of commodities customarily bought by Britain in relation to the prices of the commodities she customarily sold, i.e. Britain was able to obtain an increasing quantity of imports for a given quantity of exports. Furthermore, real wages for the mass of the

Table 23. Changes in the World's Monetary Stock of Gold

Year	*World's stock of gold available for money (in million £)*	*Percentage increase in preceding decade*
1851	144	—
1861	376	161
1871	544	45
1881	650	19
1891	714	10
1901	1,000	40
1911	1,532	53

population rose, since money wages steadily increased whilst prices and profits fell; most money wage rates rose by between 15 to 20 per cent in the period 1873–96.

On the other hand, it is possible to list a number of quite definite features in the economy which indicate depression:

1. As far as the agricultural sector of the economy was concerned, there is no doubt that the term 'Great Depression' is an appropriate description, due to the growth of foreign competition in primary products. Wheat prices, taking the base 100 as the average of prices in 1867–77, fell to 88 in 1875–9, 58 in 1885–9, 54 in 1890–4, and to 50 in 1900–4; and by the mid 1890s, following the development of refrigerated freight cars and ships, meat prices were at their lowest level for 150 years.

2. Whilst the British economy continued to grow, the rate of growth began to slow down.

3. Britain's industrial supremacy was also being successfully challenged by the United States and Germany. This point will be dealt with more fully at the end of this chapter.

4. The level of unemployment increased, since businessmen, whose

profits were diminished as a result of the change in the economic climate, were less inclined to invest in marginal prospects of profitability. Also attempts to combat the 'depression', such as rationalisation and the introduction of labour-saving inventions, usually led to unemployment rather than cuts in wages. Unemployment at this time of course meant that more people were exposed to the horrors of the Victorian workhouse; so that one can conclude quite categorically that for these people there was justification in describing the period as the 'Great Depression'.

It seems that the people who suffered the most, apart from the unemployed, were those whose incomes were directly related to profits, such as businessmen; and it was these people of course, being the more articulate members of society, and having access to the media of communication, who projected a feeling of depression out of all proportion to the true state of affairs for the mass of the people. The quality of life improved for the majority of people as real wages went up and a wide variety of food and manufactured goods made their appearance in an increasing number of retail outlets, whilst industrial output continued to rise and trade continued to expand. The Royal Commission appointed in 1886 to enquire into the depressed state of trade and industry, summed up the situation by saying that there was a depression of a certain kind, and defined it as 'a diminution, and in some cases, an absence of profit, with a corresponding diminution of employment for the labouring classes'.

The End of an Era, 1896–1914

After 1896 British and world prices began to rise, partly as a reaction to the preceding twenty-three years of falling prices, and partly as a result of substantial gold discoveries in South Africa during the 1890s. However, wages in Britain did not rise as fast as prices and profits, with the result that a larger proportion of the national income went to the better off sections of the community, thus making even more pronounced the unequal distribution of wealth. This in turn increased a sense of social injustice, which manifested itself in industrial strife, particularly in the four years before the outbreak of the First World War.

The Challenge to Britain's Economic Supremacy

It was inevitable that sooner or later Britain's economic supremacy would be successfully challenged as other countries with more extensive natural resources set about the process of industrialisation.

Britain reached a position of economic pre-eminence in the international economy during the 1860s and early 1870s and, whilst she continued to grow quantitatively after this time, comparatively she declined as industrial giants such as the United States and Germany stepped up their production of manufactured goods, and took up the challenge.

The United States

The Civil War proved to be a major turning point in American economic development, and brought about fundamental changes in the relationships within the Atlantic community, the most important being an informal partnership within this community between the British and American peoples. Before the 1860s, the United States, comprising a group of states on the eastern seaboard, looked towards a wider Atlantic community for its livelihood and sold the greater part of its most important export, cotton, on the British market, receiving in return, mainly from Britain, large amounts of manufactured goods as well as capital and labour.

The half century following the Civil War may be regarded as the Industrial Revolution period in American history, when industry replaced agriculture as the main economic pursuit and continental interests replaced Atlantic interests. In 1865 the United States ranked fourth as an industrial power in the world: thirty years later she had jumped to first place. By 1890 the value of the manufactured product was greater than that of the agricultural product. This remarkable development was achieved as a result of a number of factors:

1. The building of the trans-continental railroads, the first of which was sanctioned in 1862, welded the country together into one huge domestic market, thus making possible the efficient exploitation of the country's rich natural resources. The railways, whose interests were intimately bound up with the settlement of the country, also acted as colonising agents, as well as attracting large amounts of foreign capital: by 1914, $3,000 million of foreign money had been invested in U.S. railways, most of the money having come from Great Britain.

2. The Federal Government encouraged the settlement of the West by its cheap land policy, embodied in several Homestead Acts, the most far-reaching of which was the 1862 Homestead Act. Under this Act settlers could acquire 160 acres of virgin land for a nominal sum provided they cultivated it for a minimum period of five years. This led to the putting of thousands of acres of virgin prairie soil under the plough.

3. High tariffs and large distances protected American industries from their European competitors.

4. Large-scale industry, stemming mainly from industrial amalgamations, flourished in the United States in spite of anti-trust laws. Large groupings were formed, starting in 1872 with John Rockefeller's Standard Oil Company, all aimed at cutting costs and controlling prices. In this way industry became more tightly structured, thus facilitating large-scale production.

5. The population of the United States was bigger than Britain's and was growing at a faster rate, thus giving her both a larger labour force and a bigger home market. Britain's population rose from 31·8 million in 1870 to 45·3 million in 1911, an increase of 42·4 per cent, whereas the United States population in the same period rose from 38·5 million to 91·7 million, an increase of 138 per cent.

6. It was in the United States rather than in Britain that modern management techniques were developed. Henry Ford perfected the use of the assembly line and propagated the idea that the way to make money was to reduce prices and reach out to the mass markets. The idea also became widespread in the United States that business should

not be confined to satisfying familiar wants, but could create new wants by advertising.

7. Thrift became old-fashioned in the United States, and people were persuaded to spend not only what they had, but also to anticipate future earnings by borrowing on the hire purchase system. In this way effective demand was influenced, thus creating more economic buoyancy.

8. The Americans also went in for large-scale cooperative research organised by the big corporations and universities, and assisted and encouraged by organised philanthropy in the form of the Carnegie Endowment and the Rockefeller Foundation.

Germany

Germany, where similar events were taking place, was also well equipped from the 1870s onwards to embark on a vigorous course of industrialisation, for the following reasons.

1. The new national pride stemming from the unification of Germany after the Franco-Prussian War of 1870 became a powerful factor in her economic development.

2. Germany annexed Alsace-Lorraine from France in 1870, and received an indemnity of £300 million. Lorraine, with its vast deposits of phosphoric iron ore, became of particular importance to Germany after the development in 1878 of the Gilchrist-Thomas process of steelmaking.

3. The proliferation of cartels and combinations led to the growth of large-scale industry. The electrical, steel and chemical industries were organised into huge industrial combines which were able to produce standardised products and reap the economies of scale.

3. The State took an active role in industrialisation—for example in the establishment of museums, fairs and shows for the promotion of industry. It also encouraged the development of the canal and river system, railways and shipping, thus providing Germany with an excellent communications system.

4. A close liaison was maintained between banks and industry. Banks often represented their clients at company meetings, as well as becoming instruments for the promotion of new companies and for the promulgation of rationalisation schemes. In fact, German banks were basically a combination of commercial bank, investment bank and investment trust, and as such they played an important part in Germany's economic development.

5. Both German industry and agriculture were given the protection of tariff walls.

6. Population growth was rapid. Between 1871 and 1911, German population grew from 41 million to 64·9 million, an increase of 58·2 per cent.

By 1914 it was clear that the United States was a greater economic power than Great Britain, and that Germany was at least its equal. Furthermore, other countries, such as France and Japan, were beginning to embark upon the road of industrialisation. Meanwhile Britain continued to rely on the staple export industries, all of which continued

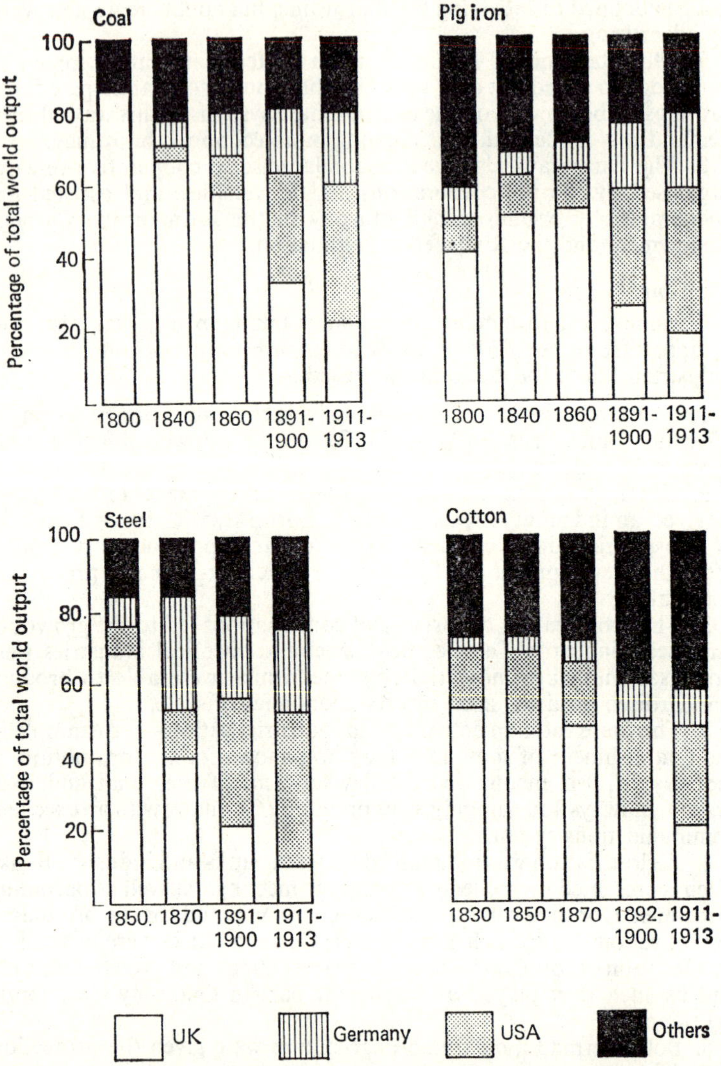

Fig. 17. Britain's share of world industry.
(courtesy **Penguin Books Ltd**)

to expand quantitatively up to 1914, though comparatively they declined in relation to the increased output of some countries (Fig. 17). Record outputs were being reported from all quarters on the eve of the First World War; coal reached 287 million tons in 1913; 8 million yards of cotton cloth were produced in 1913; and shipbuilding had a record production between 1911 and 1912. The British economy, however, in spite of these achievements, was becoming sluggish and conservative compared with its competitors. Basically the trouble was due to the failure of management to keep abreast with the changing times, and this was linked to several factors.

1. Past achievements bred an attitude of complacency. This was well illustrated by the failure of British industry to respond to the changing structure of the international economy. When, for example, foreign competition and protection pushed British products out of traditional markets, British industry continued to specialise in the same lines by extending her markets to the Empire and beyond, and thus avoided restructuring the economy towards future needs. Events were later to prove that distant markets were far from secure, particularly with respect to traditional products, such as cotton textiles.

2. The recruitment of management was generally based on hereditary principles rather than on seeking out the best man for the job.

Since the typical type of industrial unit was the family firm or partnership, management was usually recruited from family dynasties, the quality of which tended to deteriorate with the second or third generation of owners as the taste for a more genteel style of life evolved. There were many other disadvantages of relying upon family ownership to produce the best results in the national interest. For example, families who had already made their fortunes were often inclined to repair and replace existing machines rather than to scrap and innovate for the benefit of posterity. Also many firms may well have resisted growth in order to avoid the loss of family control.

Management selection in the United States, however, tended to be very different where it was chosen more for its competence rather than for family connections. Also, in spite of the fact that British trade unionism was more developed than in the United States, the American employer and employee seemed to have a closer relationship than their counterparts in England, where class differences abounded.

3. Britain was slow in developing a good educational system, whereas both the United States and Germany were relatively more progressive in this respect, particularly in the provision of technical education. The tradition of an enlightened system of technical education in Prussia dates back to the 1820s, so it is not surprising that by the last quarter of the nineteenth century German industry had available an adequate supply of academically trained scientists. Scientific expertise was, of course, absolutely essential in the new growth industries, such as the chemical and electrical industries, which were based entirely on scientific knowledge; and these were the areas where British industry was sadly lacking in comparison with German industry.

Whilst there were many advantages in being the first country to industrialise, there were also many disadvantages. Other countries, for example, were able to benefit from Britain's experience and mistakes; they were able to develop their industries on the basis of the latest knowledge and equipment, unhampered by vested interests and old fashioned plant. Britain would have profited in the long run if she had directed more of her capital in the twenty-five years before 1914 towards newer industries instead of depending upon the continuing success of the staple industries; she would also have profited if the State had taken a more positive role in directing economic development instead of relying upon private enterprise to do the right thing. Increasingly, after 1914, however, the laissez-faire attitudes of Government towards the economy were eroded away, as Britain became beset by the exigencies of war and by the need for major changes in the aftermath of war.

Suggested Further Reading

Deane, P., and Cole, W. A., *British Economic Growth, 1688–1959*, C.U.P., Cambridge, 1967.

Hobsbawm, E. J., *Industry and Empire*, Pelican, London, 1969.

Mathias, P., *The First Industrial Nation: An Economic History of Britain, 1700–1914*, Methuen, London, 1969.

Saul, S. B., *The Myth of the Great Depression, 1873–1896*, Macmillan, London, 1969.

Sayers, R. S., *A History of Economic Change in England, 1880–1939*, O.U.P., Oxford and London, 1967.

Exercises

1. Discuss the view that the third quarter of the nineteenth century was the high water mark of Victorian prosperity.
2. Do you consider that the term 'Great Depression' is a suitable description of the period 1873–96?
3. Why was the Edwardian era a period of growing discontent?
4. Discuss the challenge to Britain's economic supremacy in the last quarter of the nineteenth century.
5. Trace the main economic periods between 1830 and 1914.

Summary

1. The movement of the trade cycle makes it possible for economic historians to identify quite definite periods and trends.
2. In spite of the general trend for prices to fall between 1815 and 1847 there was a growth in real wealth and evidence of businessmen showing energy and enterprise in the promotion of trade and industry.
3. Both agriculture and industry prospered during the third quarter of the nineteenth century when prices, profits and wages rose and the level of employment was high.
4. The use of the term 'Great Depression' to describe the period of deflation between 1873 and 1896 is misleading since the aggregate of commodities produced by British capital and labour increased and real wages rose for the majority of those in employment.
5. The period between 1896 and 1914 was one of rising prices, wages and profits, though wages did not rise as rapidly as profits, with the result that a larger proportion of the National Income went to the better-off sections of the community.
6. Whilst Britain continued to grow quantitatively up to 1914, comparatively she declined as industrial giants such as the United States and Germany stepped up their production.
7. The British economy tended to become sluggish and conservative in the last quarter of the nineteenth century and past achievements bred an attitude of complacency.

SECTION THREE

WAR, DEPRESSION AND RECOVERY 1914–39

The coming of the First World War marked the ending of an era, though many important economic and social developments that were to have a profound influence in shaping the future had already made their appearance.

In the last few decades before 1914 there had been a gradual retreat from the policy of undiluted laissez faire and a move towards collectivism. The need for social reform had become recognised by both the main political parties, and a third political party had emerged, committed to a policy of evolutionary Socialism and destined to replace the Liberal party as the party of 'the workers by hand and brain'. Even in the sphere of industry, where State interference was almost unknown, Acts were being passed restricting the hours of labour and providing for improved measures of health and safety. This trend towards the organisation of British life on a collectivist basis, inevitable as it might have been, was greatly accelerated by the coming of the First World War, when people increasingly found that they were required to serve the State, rather than to pursue exclusively their own affairs. The dislocating effects of the War, and the subsequent changes brought about in Britain's position in the world economy, provided the right background for collectivism finally to triumph over individualism. Thus, between the wars the nation's social security apparatus was extended, free trade gave way to protection, and the State became concerned with such matters as the rate of investment, technical innovation, the distribution of income and wealth, and the aggregate level of demand.

This growth of State intervention led inevitably to a big increase in the Government's revenues and expenditures. In 1914, income from property and income tax amounted to £43·9 million and death duties were £27·4 million; the figures for 1939 were £335·9 million and £77·4 million respectively. Increasing amounts of money were required during these years for expenditure on unemployment benefits, road-building, house-building, and by the late 1930s large sums of money were needed for rearmament.

Contrary to expectations a slump did not immediately follow the War, but instead there was a brief boom lasting until the summer of 1920. This was followed by a slump lasting until 1922, after which Britain's staple export industries of coal, iron and steel, textiles and shipbuilding sank into a long period of stagnation and decline, and the economy became characterised by a large amount of involuntary unemployment.

Some increased buoyancy in the economy was experienced between 1925 and 1929, but with the onset of the world liquidity crisis following the Wall Street crash of 1929 an intense depression set in, lasting until

1933. Considerable efforts at recovery were made from 1931 onwards, and a slow recovery did take place.

Many people looked back nostalgically after the First World War to the pre-war days, and readily supported President Harding's slogan of 'back to normalcy'. It was naive, however, to ignore the fundamental changes affecting the British economy since the outbreak of war, and any serious attempt at returning to pre-war standards and conditions was to ignore reality. The dislocation of the international economy, for example, and the changed structure of international demand meant that even in the best years the volume of exports was never more than 80 per cent of the 1913 level. The trend after the war should have been away from internationalism and towards the domestic market. The development of new sources of power in the twentieth century, such as oil and electricity, constituted a new Industrial Revolution, and led to the creation of important new industries, geared more towards satisfying consumer wants on the home market than towards the production of capital goods for the export markets.

It is wrong to assume, however, that because the inter-war years are renowned as a period of high unemployment and depression that there was no improvement in the quality of life for the ordinary British people. It is true that there were periods of intense depression, and advances in industrial efficiency and technology were unevenly spread, but taking the period as a whole the growth record of the British economy was better than before 1914, and there was a marked increase in industrial production and in real income per head. The war had arrested the growth of real national income per head, which in 1924 was approximately the same as it had been in 1911, and for the duration of the 1920s very little improvement was made, but by 1937 industrial production was about 80 per cent more than it had been in 1907, and real income per head had increased by about 30 per cent. The reason why Britain failed to share fully in the general world prosperity in the period between 1925 and 1929 was the relative stagnation of her old staple industries, but with the collapse of the international economy around 1930, growth in Britain became more domestically based, and the so-called 'new industries' gave the economy a new dynamism.

In addition to the increase in real income per head, the quality of life for the average working man was further improved by a shorter working week, whilst the trend towards smaller families meant that there were fewer dependants for him to support. In spite of these gains though the working man's standard of living was considerably below that of the lower middle class salaried worker, who according to Mark Abrams 'ate twice as much fresh milk, fish, vegetables and fruit; spent twice as much on clothes and fuel, and nearly three times as much on entertainment, and nearly four times as much on household furnishing and equipment'. (M. Abrams, *The Condition of the British People 1911–1945*).

CHAPTER FIFTEEN

THE IMPACT OF WAR

The century before 1914 was relatively peaceful, and episodes such as the Crimean and Boer Wars had been mere skirmishes in contrast with the holocaust of the First World War, requiring no fundamental readjustments to the economy. In such circumstances few people had any conception of the economic readjustments which would have to be made or the suffering that would be involved in waging a modern full-scale war. People were also naive in thinking that the war would be short in a situation where the combatants preferred to engage all their modern technology and resources rather than to admit defeat.

A short-lived financial crisis occurred in July, 1914, and panic buying in the shops pushed up prices. Also, the loss of overseas markets pushed up the level of unemployment, but this proved to be only temporary and the economy quickly recovered from the initial shock of war. Winston Churchill coined the slogan 'business as usual', and it was not until 1916 that people began to realise that the war was going to be a long and bitter struggle with irreparable damage being done on all sides.

War Finance

Britain had been on the Gold Standard since 1821, and by 1914 it had become the norm almost everywhere, the major exception being China, which was on a Silver Standard. This system gave stability to world currencies and by 1914 the world had become used to stable exchanges. The lack of exchange controls in 1914 enabled people to exchange their money without restriction or limit. British currency at this time consisted of Bank of England notes in denominations from £5 upwards, and the silver token coins and gold coins were maintained by the fact that the mint was willing to stand the loss of wear and tear by exchanging old gold coin for new gold coin.

The Gold Standard was not legally abandoned until April 30, 1919, but circumstances during the war rendered it for all practical purposes inoperable. A necessary prerequisite of being on the Gold Standard was the importing and exporting of gold, and this was suspended due to the submarine hazard with the result that gold coins practically disappeared from circulation as more notes were printed and gold coins appreciated in terms of paper money. The Currency and Bank Notes Act of 1914 authorised the issuing by the Treasury of £1 and 10-shilling currency notes in order to meet an expected shortage of cash. The Government backed these notes with Treasury Bills, and managed the issue by creating the Currency Note Account held with the Bank of England. This paper money, however, did not contribute much to inflation even though the note circulation rose from £34 million in 1914 to £299 million in

1918, because the notes were mainly replacing the gold in circulation, the greater part of which was returned to the Bank of England.

The financial cost of waging a modern full-scale war proved to be immense since large sums of money had to be found to pay for the upkeep of the armed forces and to provide them with expensive equipment and munitions. Previously wars had been financed by borrowing rather than out of current revenue, so the Government prepared to borrow heavily. This resulted in the National Debt rising from £650 million to £7,000 million, thus jeopardising future prosperity by creating a burden of interest that had to be paid later.

The Government made practically no attempt during the war to use the Budget as an instrument of economic and social policy. Taxation was increased, but this source of revenue covered only 30 per cent of Government expenditure on the war. The yield from direct taxes was raised from £94 million in 1914, when income tax was 1s. 2d. in the pound, to £508 million in 1918, when income tax stood at 6 shillings in the pound. An excess profits duty of 50 per cent on the standard rate of pre-war profits was introduced in 1915, which in spite of much evasion yielded 25 per cent of the total Government revenue between 1915 and 1921. Britain slightly deviated from her free trade policy in 1915 when the McKenna Duties were introduced on imported cars, motorcycles, cinematographic films, clocks, watches and a few other luxury items. These duties became a valuable source of revenue and were therefore retained, amidst much free trade opposition, when the war was over. Britain also sold 25 per cent of her overseas investments, representing a sum of £1,000 million, in order to help pay for the war. This measure had serious implications for the future since this important invisible export had helped to finance Britain's trading deficit before the war.

Considerable concern was expressed both during and after the war over the increased burden of the National Debt. Feeling ran high about who was to pay for the war, particularly since some people had made large profits as a direct result of the war. When compulsory conscription of men into the armed forces was introduced in 1916, the T.U.C. suggested that there should also be conscription of wealth, and thus the suggestion was made that a capital levy should be introduced in order to ensure that the burden of financing the war should fall on the broadest backs. This controversy was continued after the war, and one notable instance of this was Stanley Baldwin's famous letter to *The Times* in 1919 declaring his decision to make a voluntary levy of 20 per cent against his own wealth, amounting to £150,000 for cancellation against the War Debts, no doubt hoping that others would follow suit. However, the controversy died down when the post-war deflation started towards the end of 1920, though it remained on the Labour Party programme until as late as July, 1927.

The Effects of War on British Industry

In the early days of the war the Government was content to intervene only at a few selected points of the economy, and to allow the market mechanism to distribute resources in response to the needs of war. This approach was not surprising really since Asquith's Government was a

Liberal Government, having behind it a long tradition of free trade and ideological opposition to extensive and detailed State control.

One of the first measures taken to secure more economic control was the requisitioning of the railways authorised by an Act of 1871. Under this Act the railways were guaranteed their 1913 dividends, and were to be run as one complete unit by a Railway Executive Committee consisting of the General Managers of the ten leading railway companies under the direction of the Board of Trade. Concern about sugar supplies and dyestuffs was also immediately shown since two thirds of Britain's sugar and four fifths of her dyestuffs had come from Central Europe before the war. Consequently, the Government imported supplies of sugar from the West Indies, and bought half the share capital of a new company called British Dyes Ltd in order to encourage the development of a British dyestuffs industry. The Government also undertook the purchase of a wide variety of foodstuffs and raw materials.

As the war progressed it soon became obvious that the market mechanism was not capable of distributing resources in response to the needs of war. There was soon a shortage of shells and equipment, partly due to the recruitment into the armed forces of experienced engineering workers. Exemption badges were thus issued to discourage further recruitment from labour employed on essential war work. Agreement was also reached with the unions on the 'dilution' of labour, whereby the unions allowed the employment of unskilled labour and women in the engineering establishments in return for certain safeguards, the most important of which was the promise that there would be a return to the status quo after the war and that profits would be limited.

The Defence of the Realm Act (D.O.R.A.) was passed in March, 1915, empowering the Government to take over any existing factory or workshop making munitions, whilst two months later, in response to the 'Great Shell Scandal', the Ministry of Munitions was created under the leadership of Lloyd George and given wide powers to muster the necessary resources to fulfil the armament demands of war. The political scandal associated with the shortage of shells eventually led to the downfall of Asquith and the creation in December, 1916, of a new government with Lloyd George as Prime Minister. This event led to a great proliferation of Government controls in the economy and opened up a new phase in the conduct of the war. The need for increased food supplies led to the setting up in 1916 of County War Agricultural Executive Committees with wide powers of direction and eviction, whilst the Corn Production Act of 1917 encouraged increased production by guaranteeing minimum prices and fixing minimum wages. In 1917, the coal industry, flour mills, iron mines, and nearly all the country's canals were taken over by the State. This policy of State control was later extended to include merchant shipping and shipbuilding, docks and harbours. The Government continued also to undertake the bulk purchase and distribution of food and raw materials and fixed many of their prices.

The Economic Consequences of the War

Britain emerged from the First World War in a fundamentally changed position, with respect both to the structure of the international economy and to her own internal economic structure. Some of the changes proved to be only temporary, but some were to have a lasting effect on Britain's economic development. Many of the changes, however, were inevitable and had been merely accelerated by the war.

The successful challenge to Britain's economic supremacy started before 1914, was extended still further during the war by the acceleration of the trend towards economic nationalism, which was encouraged by the following factors.

1. Technical changes reduced the need for rigid international specialisation in many cases. For example, new forms of power, such as oil or hydroelectric power, meant that industry no longer needed to be in close proximity to coal. Nor did a country necessarily need to have special skills in order to be a successful industrial power, since machines could be run by unskilled or semi-skilled operatives, as was the case in the early phases of Japanese industrial development.

2. The Versailles Treaty led to the changing of state boundaries and whilst this may have settled problems relating to nationalities, it paid little attention to preserving the pattern of established commerce. The changing of state boundaries intensified a feeling of national consciousness and invariably led to protection. Tariffs were of course also a convenient form of revenue for a newly created state. Amongst the new states created were Poland, Czechoslovakia, Yugoslavia, Estonia, Lithuania and Latvia.

3. The international economy was further distorted by the removal of Russia from the international scene in 1917, and the virtual extinction of Germany as a great trading nation due to the loss of her colonies and mercantile marine, as well as much of her industrial capacity.

4. The reversal of the trend towards international specialisation was intensified further by the continuation of high tariffs in the United States and Europe.

5. International trade was also adversely affected by the confusion created in world finance. The period of the Gold Standard up to 1914 had been one of unique monetary stability with paper currencies in Europe maintaining their relative values, and funds being allowed to move freely under the influence of market forces and without restriction, except in very exceptional circumstances of crisis. Under this system, if the demand for a currency increased, then there would be a slight movement in the rate of exchange, whilst any excessive movement in the rate of exchange would make it cheaper to move gold rather than to purchase the currency concerned. This was an extremely inconvenient and expensive method of payment, and the loss of gold by a country led to deflation and credit restrictions, thereby encouraging countries to take great care in balancing their books.

The coming of the First World War put an end to the nineteenth-century system of payments and countries left the Gold Standard and inflated their currencies. Inflation also flared in many countries once the fiscal expediencies of war, such as rationing or price controls, were removed. This led to a depreciation of European currencies at varying rates, thus bringing about changes in their respective exchange values.

This was particularly true in Central and Eastern Europe, where considerable programmes of reconstruction were needed and where the situation was aggravated by the imposition of reparation payments, as was the case in Germany, Austria, Hungary and Bulgaria. In Germany the mark fell from 8·5 to the dollar in mid-1919, to 4,200 milliard to the dollar by November, 1923, when it was withdrawn and replaced by a new rentenmark at the rate of one for every 1,000 milliard old marks. Currency instability was also common amongst the currencies issued by the many 'new' countries created under the Versailles settlement.

Part of the cost of the war was met in some countries, such as Britain and France, by the sale of overseas assets and by borrowing. Britain lent £1,741 million to her allies and borrowed £1,365 million, most of which came from the United States. These transactions led to a new structure of international debts, with the United States ceasing to be a debtor and becoming a net creditor, whilst Germany, formerly a creditor country, was at the other extreme burdened down with reparation demands and owing money to eleven countries. The introduction of war debts and reparation payments, which had nothing at all to do with the ordinary market forces of supply and demand, together with the changes in world trade, completely altered the international payments position, thus causing considerable confusion and acting as a formidable dislocating force. This dislocation was concealed for most of the 1920s when Europe lived beyond her means on short-term loans, mainly from the United States who preferred to re-lend the money owed to her, and more besides, rather than having vested interests threatened by the repayment of the colossal sums owed to her in the form of goods. This linking of European economies to the American trade cycle through short-term loans created a very dangerous situation indeed. Everything was all right so long as the American economy flourished, but should a liquidity crisis occur, as it did at the time of the Wall Street crash, then this international structure of debt would collapse and cause the liquidity crisis to spread to Europe.

The financial instability following the First World War forced many governments to protect their currencies by exchange controls and to restrict international trade by tariff barriers. The fluctuations in the value of currencies also encouraged exchange speculation, thus making the situation worse.

Some countries greatly benefited from the war by being provided with an opportunity to build up new industries, either to supply their own needs or to produce exports. Japan, for example, which had been imitating the West in industrial and commercial activities since the introduction of the Meiji reforms from 1867 onwards, was able to invade traditional British markets in the Far East with manufactured textile goods. In fact, the Japanese, with their low level of wages, had before 1914 been increasingly obliged to look for markets overseas rather than relying upon the demand of the home market. Japanese industrial production, geared mainly to the export markets, increased by 75 per cent during the period 1914–20.

In addition to the loss of visible trade, Britain's invisible trade was undermined, and London as a financial centre was weakened. This meant that increasingly during the inter-war years Britain was less able to finance a trade deficit by the money earned from interest on overseas investments, banking, insurance, shipping and other services.

At home it was difficult to estimate the cost of the war in terms of capital depreciation. There was the wear and tear on machines and equipment that took place when normal renewals and repairs had not been carried out; stocks in warehouses and shops were depleted; private house-building was stopped, and many existing houses and public buildings fell out of repair; many inefficient firms were kept in being as a result of the exigencies of war; and many people's personal possessions, such as clothes and furniture, were in need of repair and replacement. In addition to these losses 40 per cent of the merchant fleet had been destroyed by enemy action.

It is important to remember, however, when calculating the cost of the war, that there was a credit side to the balance sheet, and industry benefited in many ways.

1. The war stimulated scientific research, which had been badly neglected in Britain compared with Germany and the United States. Both the universities and industry began to undertake research during the war, often under the sponsorship of the Department of Scientific and Industrial Research set up by the Government in 1916.

2. Certain industries neglected before the war were developed, such as sections of the chemical and the scientific instrument industries.

3. Business organisation was favourably influenced in some firms due to the need for more efficiency and increased output. Rationalisation was encouraged, as in the steel industry and banking, resulting in economies of scale.

4. The war encouraged the further growth of trade associations which could be used for allocating raw materials, price control or organising common research projects.

A natural corollary to the increase in State control was an increase in the size of the Civil Service, with existing Government departments growing in size and function, and the new Ministries of Munitions, Blockade, Shipping and Food being set up as temporary expedients. This proliferation of Government officials helped to educate the public towards the idea of more State intervention, as well as providing a wealth of experience for the permanent extension of State activities in the future.

Agriculture, industrial relations and welfare were also significantly influenced by the war, but these aspects will be dealt with later.

Post-War Boom and Slump

Britain enjoyed a boom from the Spring of 1919 to the early Summer of 1920, when wages and prices rose sharply. The main causes of this boom were:

1. The necessity of replenishing run-down stocks in shops, factories and warehouses. After the war shortages of all kinds existed, and the demand for goods in general was high.

2. There was the need to replace many worn-out machines, and to maintain and repair much of the existing capital equipment.

3. Prices were forced up by speculation in important industries such as textiles, shipping, shipbuilding and engineering. The flames of this speculation were fanned by the wartime memories of large profits, thus perpetuating the trend towards amalgamation often when the situation did not warrant it.

4. The immediate aftermath of the war was looked on by many businessmen as an opportunity to have a last fling, and this was often done by the inflation of capital through the issuing of bonus shares.

5. The Government made the inflationary situation worse by maintaining expenditure at high levels and selling surplus war supplies, such as motor vehicles, on the domestic market.

The boom did have some beneficial short-term effects. It facilitated a smooth switch-over from war to peace and the high level of employment speeded up demobilisation, but as with most feverish periods of inflation the advantages were outweighed by the disadvantages. In this atmosphere of boom conditions many companies had made unwise decisions and thus put their future prosperity in jeopardy, whilst for the individual the post-war inflation meant a fall in real wages, since wage increases did not keep pace with rising prices, and this in turn increased the sense of grievance already existing between labour and capital.

By the middle of 1920 most of the short-term post-war replacement demands had been met, and this together with a raising of the Bank Rate from 6 to 7 per cent had the effect of damping down the boom. During the course of the next year there was a marked fall in prices, and the number of people out of work began to rise. *The Economist* summed up the situation by saying: 'In April 1920 all was right with the world. In April 1921 all was wrong.' Although few people realised it at the time, Britain's economic supremacy as an industrial nation was over, and she was embarking on a long period of stagnation and decline. For the remainder of the 1920s, unemployment was never to fall below the one million mark. 'The Intractable Million', as a contemporary Cambridge don Professor Pigou dubbed it, became looked on as the norm, and many people settled down to years on the dole. This was a far cry from 'the homes fit for heroes' promise that Lloyd George had made during the war. The prospects of long periods of unemployment for thousands of demobilised soldiers and sailors stood in marked contrast to the position of those who had made large profits during the war and its immediate aftermath. It was a situation that created a legacy of bitterness and hatred which was to manifest itself during the ensuing years in industrial strife and confrontation.

De-Control

During the war numerous Government controls had been introduced to secure for the Government the great quantities of specialised goods and services required for the war effort. In the industrial sphere Government permission was required to start new firms or extend old ones, and the Government controlled the supply and use of most raw materials. New Ministries had also been created and the Government had taken control over railways, shipping and the coalmines.

In a country with a long tradition of laissez faire, controls were initially introduced with great reluctance, but this new experience gave the country the opportunity to look at its national equipment in a new light.

The Labour Party, having greatly grown in strength during the war, wanted to see the wartime controls translated into outright nationalisation when the war was over, a view that was shared by large numbers of workers who had seen their position improve during the period of Government controls. Many of the reports produced for the Ministry of Reconstruction set up in 1917 were also against the return to a laissez faire policy towards industry of the type existing before the war, and favoured instead a continuation of the wartime controls into peacetime. Management and owners, on the other hand, successfully pressed for the abolition of controls, and by 1921 most of the wartime controls had been dismantled.

Suggested Further Reading

Milward, A. S., *The Economic Effects of the Two World Wars on Britain*, Macmillan, London, 1970.

Pollard, S., *The Development of the British Economy, 1914–1950*, Edward Arnold, London, 1962.

Exercises

1. 'Business as usual.' Is this an appropriate description of the British economy during the first half of the Great War?
2. How did Britain pay for the First World War?
3. Account for the growth of world economic nationalism between 1914 and 1920.
4. Discuss the economic consequences for Britain of the First World War.
5. 'In April, 1920, all was right with the world. In April, 1921, all was wrong.' Discuss with reference to Great Britain.

Summary

1. Few people realised the full implications of a modern war.
2. The war rendered the gold standard inoperable and required the raising of huge sums of money through taxation, the imposition of selected import duties and the selling of foreign investments.
3. At first the Government intervened at only a few selected points in the economy, but after 1916 there was considerably increased Government intervention.
4. The dislocation of the international economy caused by the war, and the selling of overseas investments, had profound implications for Britain as a trading nation.
5. The war was followed by a boom lasting until 1920 after which there was a depression of considerable duration.

CHAPTER SIXTEEN

BRITISH INDUSTRY AND ITS ORGANISATION

After 1914, Britain underwent a relative decline as an industrial nation, and emerged from the war with her capital seriously depleted. Much of her export trade was lost, some of it irrecoverably, with the result that she produced a smaller proportion of the world's exports (Table 24).

Table 24. Britain's Proportion of World Exports

	Exports	*Percentage reduced to 1913 price level*		*Percentage share of World exports 1913*	*1929*
1913	£525,000,000	100	United Kingdom	14	10·8
1921	£703,000,000	50	Germany	13	9·2
1927	£709,000,000	79	France	7	6·0
1929	£730,000,000	82	U.S.A.	13	15·8

Source: A. Birnie, *An Economic History of the British Isles.*

This damage to Britain's export trade had serious implications for the nineteenth-century giants of British industry, viz. the textile, coal, shipbuilding and iron and steel industries. Britain's prosperity up to 1914 had been narrowly based upon these few great export industries, and once the favourable conditions conducive towards them in the world economy had been removed, then Britain suffered from a distorted industrial structure resulting in heavy unemployment amongst industrial workers in certain districts. Britain did, however, benefit from the twentieth-century technological revolution and after the war capital investment was heaviest and technical advance most rapid in the new industries, such as electrical manufacturing, motor engineering, chemicals and the artificial fibres industry. These expanding industries tended to cater for the home market, whilst the contracting industries were geared more towards the export markets. By the early 1930s, the trade balance had become so bad that the invisible exports, themselves depleted by the events of the previous two decades, were no longer sufficient to pay for the excess.

Decline of the Staple Export Industries

The staple export industries of coal, iron and steel, shipbuilding and textiles had been slow to adjust to change before the war, and even though they had expanded absolutely and achieved all time records in 1913, they were, generally speaking, in a bad way technically.

The changes brought about during the war to the structure of the international economy, and the failure of the staple industries to regain their pre-war export markets, led to their suffering from a chronic depression following the collapse of the postwar boom in 1921.

Coal

The British coal industry in 1913 was very important in terms of the number of men employed, but it was a badly organised and under-mechanised industry. Coal undertakings were numerous and ownership dispersed, whilst the average output per mine was small. Lack of investment was to some extent due to the geological structure of the mines, which did not lend themselves so readily to mechanisation as did some of the mines of Britain's competitors, but also it was due to the neglect of the owners, who found that they could invest their money on better terms elsewhere, whilst at the same time being able to step up coal production by utilising the large pool of cheap unskilled labour that was available. Geological circumstances were also responsible for the coal industry lacking some of the uniformity existing in many branches of manufacture, thus making many of the industry's problems highly regional in character. Labour was the one great unifying factor, amongst both the declining and the developing coalfields, and the plight of the mining communities became the most important element in industrial relations in the period between the wars.

Table 25. The Coal Industry

Year	*Output (million tons)*	*Exports (million tons)*	*Numbers employed (thousands)*	*Annual output per person employed (tons)*
1913	287	73	1,105	260
1923	276	79	1,203	229
1929	258	60	957	270
1932	209	39	819	255
1936	229	35	767	298
1937	240	40	778	308
1938	227	36	782	290

The industry suffered during the war from the loss of overseas markets and also from the decline in its labour force as miners joined the armed forces. A quarter of a million miners had joined up during the first year of the war, causing an eventual drop in coal production by about 10 per cent. Profits and prices, however, continued to rise more than wages. In the five years 1914–18, profits and royalties amounted to £160 million, representing £25 million more than the whole of the pre-war capital of the industry.

Government control was extended to the coalmines in February, 1917, but whilst this measure succeeded in stimulating production and controlling prices and profits it did not result in any significant improvements in the methods or organisation of production. Output per man fell heavily mainly because of the lack of capital investment due to the limitation of profits under the control agreements.

After the war, the miners hoped that the industry would be nationalised, whereas the coal owners wanted the industry to be de-controlled and run on the same basis as it had been before the war. The miners also wanted a 30 per cent increase in wages and a six-hour day, since they saw no prospects for miners who had been in the armed forces finding work unless hours of work were reduced.

The Government reacted by setting up in 1919 a Royal Commission under the chairmanship of Mr Justice Sankey to enquire into the future of the industry. The evidence made known to the Royal Commission concerning the large wartime profits made by the coal owners stood in marked contrast to the evidence relating to the atrocious housing conditions in the mining villages, and in due course three interim reports were presented: one by the mine owners, one by the miners' representatives and one by Sir John Sankey and the three independent industrial leaders. The recommendations of these reports covered a wide area. The miners' representatives wanted complete nationalisation, in addition to the reduction in hours and the full increase in wages demanded, whilst the coal owners urged a speedy return to private ownership, with no strings attached. The Government, for its part, ignored most of the proposals made by the Royal Commission, using as an excuse the lack of a clear majority report. In these circumstances, the miners kept their existing wages and all that came of the high hopes of the Sankey Commission was the imposition of the seven-hour day by Act of Parliament in 1919, and Government control was prolonged. These results greatly disappointed the miners who felt that they had been let down, whilst the coal owners were horrified that the question of nationalisation had been discussed so seriously, and therefore became determined to hang on to whatever they had at all costs. Thus, the 'two nations' referred to by Disraeli were now clearly identifiable and preparing to make war with each other.

Basically, the main troubles facing the industry after the war were as follows:

1. Coal was becoming more difficult to reach as the coalmines became older. By the mid 1920s the average age of all coalmines employing more than 500 persons was about 50 years.

2. In many instances the better quality seams of coal had been exploited, leaving only the thinner seams to be worked. In these circumstances output per miner fell from the record of 400 tons in the 1880s to 229 by 1923.

3. Coal had to face increasing competition from other forms of fuel, such as electricity and oil.

4. Whilst it is true that the demands for coal from the gas and electricity industries increased, the amount of gas produced and electricity generated increased in greater proportion than the additional amount of coal used, and electricity and gas were of course alternative forms of power to coal.

5. Foreign coalfields were rapidly developed during the 1920s, with

Poland particularly becoming a keen competitor for British markets. Continental production increased after 1913 by about the same amount represented by the fall in British production, and during the later part of the 1920s, when Continental coal production rose sharply, British production declined. Further damage was also inflicted on the British industry by the reparation agreements, which forced Germany to provide coal to former British customers.

6. The coalmines were under-mechanised, with only 14 per cent of coal being cut mechanically in 1921, and only a small proportion of the mines were equipped with mechanical conveyors. Coal was thus mined at the expense of maximum human effort with one and a quarter million men employed in the industry in 1924 comprising approximately one in ten of the country's insured workforce.

7. Selling arrangements were on a small scale, and the majority of coal undertakings themselves were small. According to Professor W. H. B. Court, in the *Economic History Review* (1945), there were 2,481 mines in 1924 belonging to about 1,400 separate colliery undertakings, and of these 323 produced over 84 per cent of the output.

The first major crisis for the coal industry after the war coincided with the onset of the trade depression in 1921, when the Government quickly de-controlled the industry. Naturally, the coal owners were compelled to run the coalmines as viable concerns, and so they were forced in the economic climate of the time to make reductions in miners' wages, which were imposed after a bitter strike lasting thirteen weeks. This was followed by a number of circumstances, bringing back to the industry a moderate degree of prosperity.

1. The French and Belgian coalfields had been badly affected by the war and took several years to re-equip.

2. The three months' strike of 1921 created arrears of orders that had to be cleared.

3. In 1922 there was a four months' long coal strike in the United States, creating an unexpected demand for British coal from there.

4. In 1923 the Germans defaulted on their reparation payments. Britain looked on this as being a technical default due to Germany's difficult circumstances at the time, but France, with its long tradition of hostility towards Germany, looked on it as being a wilful default, and occupied the Ruhr in accordance with the provisions of the Versailles Treaty. This led to a temporary decline in German coal output, and provided yet another opportunity for the British coal industry.

By the mid 1920s the influence of these short-term demands was over, and it became possible to see the future prospects of the industry in perspective; and these prospects were far from bright. The situation was further aggravated by Britain's decision to return to the Gold Standard in 1925 at the pre-war parity of $4·86 to the pound, thus overvaluing Sterling by about 10 per cent and making it even more difficult to sell coal abroad. This decision, together with the prospect of further wage cuts, brought about the threat of a General Strike in 1925. The threat was, however, averted for nine months by the Government providing a

1938 > 1/2 coal cut + conveyed mechanically

subsidy of £10 million to the industry in order to delay the wage cuts, whilst a Royal Commission under the chairmanship of Sir Herbert Samuel enquired into the industry. In 1926 this Royal Commission recommended the speedy reorganisation of pits, selling arrangements on a larger scale, the ending of the subsidy, and the nationalisation of royalties. However, the miners were disappointed with these recommendations, and the threatened strike took place.

Unfortunately there was to be no quick and easy solution to the miners' problems, and the path towards improvements was to be long and arduous. Nevertheless, the General Strike proved in many ways to be a turning point, because it marked the beginning of new efforts to rationalise the industry. The initial efforts to speed up amalgamations under the Mining Industry Act of 1926 were disappointing, but further efforts to promote amalgamations were made, and in the eight years from 1926 to 1933, 38 amalgamations took place, involving 369 mines and 240,000 workers. Progress was also made in the mechanisation of the pits, so that by 1938 over half the coal was conveyed and cut mechanically. This facilitated a reduction in the industry's labour force from 1·2 million men in 1923 to 780,000 men in 1938, and led to a 26 per cent increase in the average output of coal per miner employed.

Iron and Steel

The iron and steel industry was pioneered by Britain in the nineteenth century, but by the 1890s both the United States and Germany had overtaken Britain in the production of iron and steel. In 1913, Britain was a very poor third in the league tables of steel producers, producing only 7·6 million tons of steel as against Germany's 17 million tons, and the United States' 31 million tons.

The British industry at this time was managed more on the basis of past achievements than on the needs of technical efficiency, and was technically backward compared with its counterparts in Germany and the United States. The impact of the First World War, however, with its huge demand for armaments, and the re-stocking boom that followed it, brought important changes to the industry.

1. There was a greater dependence on home ores due to the difficulties involved in importing foreign ores; and since most of Britain's ores were phosphoric, more use was made of the basic open-hearth process of steel manufacture, which was a suitable process for phosphoric ores. This, in turn, enabled the amount of scrap used in steelmaking to be raised from 14 per cent in 1914 to 50 per cent in 1918.
2. The Government provided financial help for the expansion of the steel industry, and instigated the construction of twenty new blast furnaces so that by 1920 blast furnace capacity had been increased by 50 per cent.
3. The war created a demand for special types of steel for use in the manufacture of shells, and led to collective research in the production of alloys for the manufacture of tanks and aircraft. In spite of this research, however, British fuel consumption remained high, mainly because of old-fashioned equipment.

4. Basic slag from the furnaces was converted into fertiliser on a large scale, thus producing a very useful and marketable product.

These developments did of course improve the efficiency of the industry, but it would be wrong to conclude that there was any radical reorganisation of plant, since the industry was kept going mainly by patching up existing plant. This had serious implications for the industry's future prospects because the iron and steel industry is an industry that lends itself well to efficient organisation and large-scale production, so that when the world demand for iron and steel collapsed in 1921, the British industry fared badly. Furthermore, the iron and steel industry was particularly vulnerable to changes in the economic climate, largely on account of the large capital outlay involved. During periods of depression, steel producers invariably endeavour to keep as much of their expensive plant operational as possible, even if it means selling at rock bottom prices. This may involve producers selling at one price on the home market and a lower price on the foreign market, so that domestic consumers in some countries subsidise exports to other countries. Britain with her free trade policy was a suitable victim for this practice of 'dumping', from which the iron and steel industry suffered severely during the 1920s. Not surprisingly, therefore, the British iron and steel producers were amongst the most ardent supporters of a protective tariff. When this was finally granted in 1932, the industry was struggling against a mass of cut-price imports resulting from a huge excess in world capacity.

The granting of a 33⅓ per cent ad valorem duty on imported iron and steel was made conditional upon a certain amount of reorganisation within the industry. With this purpose in mind, an official watchdog committee was appointed in the shape of the Import Duties Advisory Committee. This Committee acted for producers through the British Iron and Steel Federation, formed in 1934, whose job it was to fix prices and to negotiate with foreign cartels the quantitative restrictions to be imposed on imports.

By 1937 the industry had substantially recovered and produced a tonnage 46 per cent above the 1913 level. There was also a certain amount of rationalisation, but the policy of reducing competition by tariffs weakened the pressure on firms to modernise their plants, and whilst some mergers did take place in the 1930s, leading to a reduction of costs through the economies of scale, the old habit of patching up plant continued.

The recovery experienced by the industry after 1933 was brought about for the following reasons.

1. The depreciation of Sterling in 1931, following the abandonment of the Gold Standard, made imports dearer and exports cheaper.

2. The 33⅓ per cent ad valorem duty imposed in 1932, and later raised to 50 per cent in 1936, enabled the British iron and steel industry to take full advantage of the home market, which more than made up for the failure of exports to recover in the 1930s.

3. Home demand was stimulated by: (a) the development of the motor industry; (b) the moderate recovery in shipbuilding and engineer-

ing; (c) the partial substitution of steel supports for timber in coal mining; and (d) the growing rearmament demands of the late 1930s.

Shipbuilding

In the second half of the nineteenth century, Britain, with her technical know-how, plus the head start she had over other nations in the industrialisation process, acquired the largest shipping fleet and shipbuilding industry in the world. In 1913, British shipyards were building more than 60 per cent of the gross merchant tonnage launched annually, and her ships carried about half of the entire seaborne trade of the world, but as was the case in other spheres of the economy this pre-eminent position was inevitably eroded away as the other countries caught up in the industrialisation process (see Table 26).

Table 26. World Shipping Tonnage (Million Gross Tons), 1914–38

Country	*1914*	*1938*	*Percentage change*
Great Britain and Ireland	18·9	17·8	−5·8
British Dominions	1·6	3·1	93·7
Denmark	0·7	1·1	52·1
France	1·9	2·9	52·7
Germany	5·1	4·2	−17·6
Greece	0·8	1·8	125·0
Holland	1·5	2·9	93·3
Italy	1·4	3·3	135·7
Japan	1·7	5·0	194·1
Norway	1·9	4·6	142·1
Sweden	1·0	1·6	60·0
Spain	0·8	0·9	12·5
United States			
Sea	2·0	8·9	345·0
Lakes	2·2	2·5	13·6
Others	4·0	6·4	60·0
World total	45·5	66·9	46·0

Source: L. Jones, *Shipbuilding in Britain.*

Because of its strategic importance, Government control was extended to the shipbuilding industry during the war. This proved fairly successful when both the construction of naval and merchant vessels were stimulated by wartime conditions. Unfortunately, however, the war also provided an opportunity for shipbuilding capacity to be enlarged elsewhere—for example in Japan and the United States—with the result that whilst shipbuilding capacity in Britain increased by about 25 per cent between 1914 and 1918, world capacity was approximately doubled. A further vigorous expansion of British shipbuilding capacity took place in the two-year boom after the war, due mainly to the following circumstances.

1. Replacement demands were created by the loss of 15 million tons of shipping through enemy action, 8¾ million tons of which were British.
2. Long-delayed ships repairs had to be made good. At one point in 1918, 12 per cent of the British mercantile marine was in dry dock for repairs.
3. Congestion at the ports, caused through the accumulation of merchandise in warehouses during the war, created a temporary shortage of shipping space.
4. More berths for building ships were required because ships were taking longer to build as a result of the shorter hours of work in the shipbuilding industry. The average length of time taken to build a ship had increased from one year in 1913 to twenty months by 1920.

Shipbuilding capacity was still in the process of expansion in 1920, when a record two million tons of shipping was launched. By 1921 the immediate post-war demands had been met, and when prices fell in the general depression later in the year prospects in the shipbuilding industry also fell. Shipbuilding capacity had been over-extended, and the industry was suffering from excess capacity. Further damage was done to the industry by Britain accepting 2·5 million tons of shipping from the confiscated German mercantile fleet as part of the reparations settlement. Thus for the remainder of the 1920s the fortunes of the British shipbuilding industry fluctuated, and even in a good year, such as 1925, capacity was seriously underemployed.

Basically, the main trouble in the shipbuilding industry was excess capacity, and changes in world trade had not justified the increase in the world's capacity for building ships. The world demand for new ships fell from the average of 6 per cent per annum in the period 1900 to 1914, to 1·5 per cent per annum between 1914 and 1939. 'Since the end of 1921, the shipyards of the United Kingdom could have produced the whole of the new tonnage constructed in each year in the world, and still not have exhausted their capacity.' (Balfour Committee, 1928)

Attempts to deal with this problem of surplus capacity were made by the industry, particularly during the Great Depression of 1929–32, when the industry suffered from a major slump. Discussions between the major shipbuilders led to the setting up in 1930 of a private company called National Shipbuilders' Security Limited. This company was supported by nearly all the shipbuilding firms in the country and its object was to buy up and dismantle obsolete shipyards in order to concentrate production in the more efficient yards. This was to be paid for by imposing a levy of 1 per cent of the contract price on vessels above a certain size.

The N.S.S. Ltd was busy up until the end of 1934, by which time one million tons of shipbuilding capacity had been scrapped. After this date, the activities of the Company petered out as the demand for new-ships increased.

Meanwhile, the Government was also attempting to help the industry. In 1934 the Government provided financial help for the completion of the *Queen Mary*, begun in 1930, and for the construction of a sister ship. In 1935, the British Shipping Act provided financial help to British owners who were prepared to scrap two tons of shipping for every one built, the idea being to utilise unemployed resources whilst at the same time modernising the existing fleet. The scheme had, however, only a limited success.

After 1934, under the stimulus of trade recovery, and later through rearmament, there was a steady increase in shipbuilding, leading to a more extensive utilisation of the industry's resources.

Cotton

The century before 1914 was one of almost uninterrupted expansion for the cotton industry, particularly in the last twenty years when the output of yarn rose by twenty-five per cent. Cotton at this time was Britain's most important manufacturing industry, and a large proportion of the cotton goods produced were exported.

In 1830, cotton exports represented half of the total exports from the U.K.; in the 1890s one third, and in 1914 one quarter. More than 80 per cent of the record production in 1913 of 8,000 million square yards was exported, representing more in volume than all the cotton exported in the rest of the world put together. Furthermore, Britain was the world's most important producer and exporter of textile machinery, which was the biggest section of the British engineering industry.

The cotton industry reached its peak in 1914, and subsequently underwent a decline, due mainly to the growth of foreign competition (Table 27).

Table 27. Britain's Cotton Industry

Year	*Production of yarn (million lb.)*	*Production of piece goods (million sq. yd.)*	*Exports of yarn (million lb.)*	*Exports of piece goods (million sq. yd.)*
1924	1,395	6,026	163	4,444
1930	1,047	3,320	137	2,407
1935	1,228	3,386	142	1,948
1937	1,375	4,288	159	2,000

Source: G. P. Jones and A. G. Pool, *A Hundred Years of Economic Development.*

During the First World War the industry was not considered to be of importance to the war effort, and therefore did not receive any special privileges. After 1916 output and exports fell and supplies of raw cotton from the United States dried up, leading to some short-time working and higher prices. In these circumstances more attention was paid to the production of higher-quality cottons, which required less shipping space and could be sold more easily to the richer countries of North America and Europe. Meanwhile, Britain was losing its grip on many traditional markets in the East, particularly in India, which before the war had been Britain's most important market. Exports of cotton cloth to India fell from 3,000 million yards in 1913, to 900 million yards in

1918, and to 292 million yards in 1938. Britain's most formidable competitor in the East was Japan, who was provided by the war with a golden opportunity.

At first, in the immediate aftermath of the war, it looked as though the industry was going to assume its old dominance, when it experienced a short boom between 1918 and 1920 in response to a backlog of home and world demand. This boom encouraged considerable speculation, causing 42 per cent of the capacity of the cotton spinning industry to change hands; large combines were floated, and many firms bought new machinery and equipment in the hope of returning to the type of prosperity that the industry had experienced before the war. This optimism was ill founded, however, and by 1921 the boom was over. For the remainder of the inter-war years, the industry was faced with the problem of surplus capacity and growing foreign competition. During this time exports slumped, whereas home demand actually increased, so that in 1938 exports constituted one half of total output, compared with seven eighths in 1913.

Some attempts at rationalisation were made to encourage amalgamations and to scrap redundant machinery, but the industry remained depressed and was characterised by much short-time working and unemployment. The labour force, consisting of a large proportion of female labour, fell from 620,000 in 1913 to 378,000 in 1939.

Agriculture

In 1914, Britain was heavily dependent on imported food, importing four fifths of her wheat supplies and two fifths of her meat. The First World War was expected to be of short duration, and the Government completely underestimated the danger from submarine warfare; therefore the only measures taken in the early stages of the war to increase agricultural production were to provide more allotments and to encourage farmers to grow more wheat.

By December 1916 the successful German U-boat campaign was beginning to create serious food shortages in Britain, thus forcing the Government to adopt a more positive approach towards agricultural production. The two most important measures taken were the setting up in 1916 of County War Agricultural Executive Committees, to instruct farmers what crops to grow and how best to grow them, and the Corn Production Act of 1917, which gave farmers and farm workers more security by fixing guaranteed minimum prices for corn and oats, and by the fixing for the first time of minimum wages for farm workers by an Agricultural Wages Board.

After the war it was hoped that Britain would be able to maintain a permanently expanded agricultural sector in her economy, both for aesthetic and strategic reasons. It was with this aim in mind that the Government passed the Agricultural Act of 1920, guaranteeing farmers minimum prices for cereal crops. In return farmers were expected to observe minimum standards of husbandry and to pay wages laid down by the Agricultural Wages Board. Within the year, however, world grain prices had crashed, and the 1920 Agricultural Act was repealed by the Corn Production (Repeal) Act, 1921, on the grounds that the cost of the subsidy in the changed circumstances was too high. Wage fixing by the Agricultural Wages Board was also abolished, resulting in farm labourers' wages falling from 42 shillings for a 48-hour week to 36 shillings for a 50-hour week. Thus, British agriculture reverted for the remainder of the 1920s to its pre-war trends of reducing arable

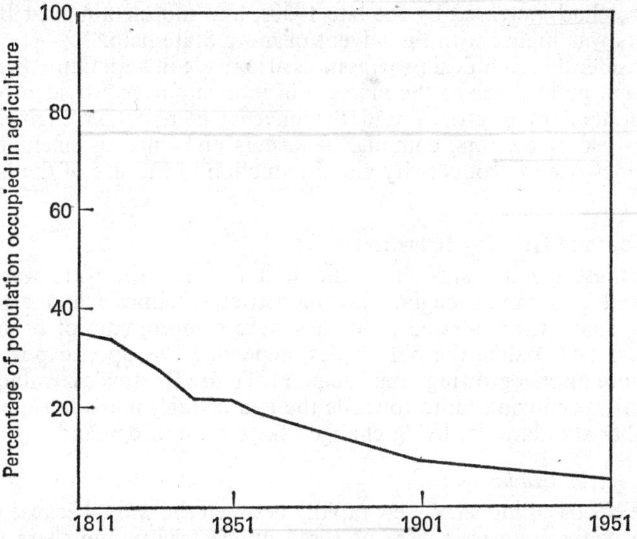

Fig. 18. Decline of the agricultural population in Britain (1811–1951).
(courtesy Penguin Books Ltd)

acreages and concentrating on the production of dairy produce, fruit and vegetables.

Prices fell throughout the 1920s, and slumped during the world economic depression of 1929–33. Many farmers went bankrupt, particularly those tenant farmers who had borrowed money to buy their farms at the high prices of 1919–20, from landlords faced with increased death duties. State regulation of agricultural wages, however, was restored by the Agricultural Wages (Regulation) Act of 1924, and this, together with increased productivity, led to an improvement in agricultural wages, though they were still low compared with industrial wages.

Government Policy Towards Agriculture

Whilst the general policy of governments towards farming in the 1920s was mainly one of non-interference, some help was given.

1. The Agricultural Holdings Act of 1923 gave the tenant farmer greater security of tenure.
2. The Wheat Act of 1932 guaranteed farmers a standard price of 45 shillings a quarter.
3. The introduction of general protection by the Import Duties Act

of 1932 paved the way for agriculture to be turned into a highly protected and subsidised sector of the economy.

By 1938, about one third of all farm produce was raised and sold under official marketing schemes, and the State was spending £14 million a year in direct subsidies to raise output. It is true that Government policy did not result in any appreciable increase in prices, but wheat acreages had increased by the late 1930s, and morale amongst British farmers was higher with the advent of more State help.

Considerable technical progress was also made in agriculture between the wars, mainly due to the increase in motive power provided by the development of electricity and the internal combustion engine. The greater use of tractors, combine harvesters and milking machines led to an increase in productivity and a reduction in the size of the labour force.

The New and Growing Industries

Amongst the industries that did well between the wars were the electrical and motor engineering industries, chemicals and artificial fibres. These science-based industries were symptomatic of economic progress and, unlike the old staples, depended less upon export sales and more upon a growing home demand. To use Rostow's terminology, Britain was moving more towards the age of high mass consumption as higher standards of living changed the nature of demand.

The Electrical Industry

The electrical industry grew rapidly between the wars, because many of the newer industries were powered by electricity, and there was a substantial growth in the use of domestic electrical equipment and appliances. Prominent among the new domestic electrical equipment were vacuum cleaners, wireless sets, floor polishers, as well as appliances for lighting, heating and cooking.

The rapid increase in the demand for electricity generation and distribution in the early 1920s led to the setting up in 1926 of a Central Electricity Board to promote a national distribution system by means of the grid. Thereafter, the demand for electricity grew in leaps and bounds, electricity production rising from 4,275 million kilowatt-hours in 1920 to 20,409 million in 1939. Some idea of the growth in the electrical engineering industry can be gained by a glance at the increase in its labour force, which grew from 70,000 in 1911 to 300,000 in 1937.

The Motor Industry

The motor industry in England was developed around Coventry and Birmingham in 1896, when the English Daimler Motor Company was formed. It was above all other industries to affect profoundly both the economic structure of the country and the style of people's lives. Business organisation, based on mass-production methods using standardised parts, was adopted by British motorcar manufacturers on the American style, the idea being to make the motorcar something more than a rich man's toy by reducing prices and reaching out to mass markets. The average factory price of a motorcar in the United Kingdom fell from £308 in 1912 to £130 in 1936, by which time there were 2·1 million cars on the road.

Amongst the many industries whose fortunes became linked to the development of the motorcar were the mechanical and electrical engineering industries, machine tools, leather, rubber, metallurgy and the oil refining industry. The growth of the industry can be seen by the increase in the annual output of cars, which rose from 32,000 in 1920 to 342,000 by 1938. During the same period, amalgamations, leading to more efficient production methods, led to the number of firms engaged in the industry falling from 90 to 33.

The Chemical Industry

The modern chemical industry dates from the mid-eighteenth century, when scientific laws were being discovered and various substances isolated. Rapid expansion of the industry took place during the nineteenth century, particularly in Germany, in response to the growing demands for chemicals from industry, particularly from textiles and agriculture.

The British chemical industry lagged behind its more progressive rivals before 1914, but from then onwards a period of immense and rapid growth took place, the number of workers employed rising from 155,000 in 1911 to 276,000 in 1938. During and after the First World War, Britain caught up with Germany in the production of nitrogen, used for the manufacture of explosives and fertilisers, and made rapid progress in the production of industrial gases, fine chemicals and plastics. The growth of the oil refining industry in Britain between the wars led to the founding of a petrochemical industry; petroleum chemicals were later used for the manufacture of plastics, synthetic detergents, synthetic fibres, paint solvents, fertilisers and insecticides.

In 1926, the merger of four chemical companies—namely, Bruner Monds Ltd, United Alkali, Nobel Industries and British Dyestuffs, to form the Imperial Chemical Industries—led to the creation of Britain's largest industrial undertaking.

The Artificial Fibres Industry

The rayon or artificial silk industry was a science-based industry, and its development therefore depended upon the successful organisation of research. This encouraged the concentration of production in a few, large and highly mechanised plants, the biggest and most well-known being Courtaulds.

Unlike the cotton industry, this branch of textiles was to a very large extent a home market product, and its success was due in large measure to the fall in the price of rayon in relation to that of natural fibres. In 1920, rayon yarn cost as much as raw silk, but by 1933 it was selling at half the price. This led to the rapid world development of the industry, so that by 1939 rayon comprised 20 per cent of world textiles, compared with only 3 per cent in 1931. In Britain, the artificial fibres industry, unhampered by a past and geared mainly to the home market, stood in marked contrast to the depressed cotton industry, dependent as it was on the world export market.

The Changing Location of Industry

The regional distribution of employment changed with the decline of the staple industries of coalmining, textiles, iron and steel, shipbuilding and engineering. These industries had been attracted during the nineteenth century to the coalfields, and were located in such areas as Tyneside, Teesside, Merseyside, parts of the Midlands, South Wales, Scotland, Yorkshire, Lancashire and West Cumberland. If the new and expanding industries had established themselves in the older industrial areas, then the employment opportunities presented by them would simply have absorbed the unemployed resources of the ailing industrial giants. Instead, there was a tendency for the newer industries to establish themselves in London, South-East England, and to a lesser extent in the Midlands, leading to a drift of population from Northern England and South Wales to the Midlands and the South-East.

Table 28. Geographical Distribution of the Employed Population

Region	*Percentage of employed (aged 16–64) in each region*			
	June 1923	*June 1929*	*June 1932*	*June 1935*
London	18·9	20·7	22·3	22·4
South-Eastern	5·9	6·8	7·5	8·4
South-Western	6·8	7·2	7·8	7·5
Midlands	15·0	15·1	15·1	15·6
North-Eastern	11·2	10·7	10·3	10·4
Northern	6·6	5·9	5·1	5·5
Scotland	11·0	10·5	10·0	10·0
Wales	5·8	4·4	3·9	3·9
Northern Ireland	2·1	2·1	2·0	1·8
Total	100	100	100	100

Source: P.E.P., *Report on the Location of Industry in Great Britain.*

This shift of the population in pursuit of economic opportunity took place for the following reasons.

1. Most of the new industries were light industries requiring only relatively small amounts of power, such as those producing radios and electrical equipment or those manufacturing branded and patented foodstuffs, whose power requirements could be provided quite satisfactorily by gas, oil or electricity, upon which there were few geographical restrictions. New forms of power, therefore, encouraged the dispersal of industry, whereas steam power had encouraged the concentration of industry on the coalfields. It is possible that the small workshop type of production prevalent in Britain in the first half of the nineteenth century might well have survived if electrical power had been developed before steam power.

2. After 1919, nearness to a large centre of population became an attraction to new industry, because it provided both a source of labour

supply and a market for an industry's product. London and the Home Counties, comprising 20 per cent of the home market, became the most popular location for the new industries, whilst the depressed areas situated amongst the most densely populated parts of the country did not attract new industries for the following reasons:

(i) Until the de-rating act was passed in 1929 there were wide disparities in the cost of the local rates between the more and less prosperous areas of the country. This was because the cost of welfare services was much higher in areas suffering from prolonged unemployment.

(ii) With the increasing mechanisation of industry, special skills became of less importance, particularly if they were located in areas with a tradition for strong trade union organisation. Also, areas suffering from long periods of unemployment very often left a legacy of hatred and bitterness between employer and employee that could well develop into future industrial strife and confrontation. Employers preferred instead to set up their new factories in pleasant environments where there was plenty of semi-skilled labour.

(iii) The development of road motor transport between the wars broke the railway's monopoly of inland transportation, and lessened the need for the rigid localisation of industry, mainly because motor transport was both cheaper and more flexible than the railways, thus enabling industry to be set up in the remotest parts of the Kingdom if so required.

(iv) The Government attempted through its Special Areas Legislation of 1934 and 1936 to influence the location of industry, either by helping people to move from distressed areas to development areas, or else by offering inducements to firms who were willing to set up in business in the distressed areas. However, these early attempts by the Government to influence the location of industry met with only limited success.

The southward shift between 1921 and 1931 of the country's industrial centre of gravity involved the migration of half a million new workers, mainly in the younger age groups, from the depressed areas to London and the Home Counties, and gave rise to fears that the old centres of industry on the coalfields might become derelict areas. This eventuality was to be avoided at all costs since there was much social capital invested in the old industrial centres in the form of roads, schools, hospitals, libraries, etc. An effective Government policy towards the location of industry did not come, however, until resources were more fully employed during the Second World War and post-war periods. Whilst there was still unemployment between the wars the Government preferred a firm to set up in business almost anywhere if the alternative was for it not to be set up at all, and Government policy therefore had few teeth and was largely ineffective.

Business Organisation

Business in Britain was slow to organise itself into trusts and corporations before 1914, since considerable faith was placed in the old individualistic form of enterprise upon which Britain's nineteenth-century economic growth had been based. The economic controls introduced during the war, however, together with the need for more efficient production, led to the weakening of nineteenth-century habits of individual economic freedom and encouraged the growth of corporate capitalism. The war did much to dispel people's faith in free competition, and helped to bring about the realisation that trends towards monopoly could have a beneficial side in the form of increased production by eliminating the wastes associated with severe internal competition. On the other hand many fears were expressed concerning the dangers of monopolistic competition, and in 1918 a Committee on Trusts was set up to consider what action should be taken to safeguard the public interest. The suggestions made by the Committee, however, were very moderate indeed, and the Government failed to implement any of them.

The growth of industrial combination took several forms, ranging from loose agreements at one end of the spectrum, to outright amalgamation at the other.

Trade Associations

Adam Smith noted in the eighteenth century that 'people of the same trade seldom meet together even for merriment and diversion, but the conversation ends in a conspiracy against the public, or in some contrivance to raise prices.'

Before 1914, there were only a few trade associations in existence, but from then onwards they greatly increased in number. In 1916, the Federation of British Industries was formed out of 50 such affiliations, whilst by the late 1930s the number in existence was in excess of 2,000. Their main aims were to maintain prices and restrict output, whilst cooperation on common research projects and the exchange of information on business techniques and advertising were amongst their more benevolent activities.

Cartels

A cartel fixes prices, or allots quotas, and establishes a central selling agency through which it undertakes the business of marketing. Cartels were sometimes sponsored by the Government in an attempt to revitalise an industry; for example, the Coal Mines Act of 1930 ordered the formation of regional cartels in the coal industry to restrict output, allot quotas and fix minimum prices. Marketing schemes were also sponsored by the Government for agriculture and iron and steel, whilst many other cartels were privately formed.

Amalgamations

Horizontal combinations were fashionable during this period, i.e. combination between competing firms at the same stage of production, with the object of restricting competition and, if possible, establishing a monopoly. A spate of mergers in banking between 1917 to 1920 led to the emergence of the 'Big Five' (Barclays, Lloyds, National Provincial, Westminster and the Midland).

Extensive horizontal combinations also took place in railways, coal, iron and steel and textiles.

Amongst the important *vertical* combinations during this period, i.e. the amalgamation of firms at different stages of production, were

Imperial Chemical Industries in 1926 and the combination of soap and margarine interests (to form Unilever) in 1929.

Government Involvement

The experience of Government control over some sectors of industry during the First World War led to considerable discussion over the future role of Government in the economy. The question was, should industry return to its pre-war dress, or should there be some form of State capitalism? The main undertaking operated by the State before 1914 had been the Post Office, and there were many who believed that this form of enterprise should be extended. The 1918 Constitution of the Labour Party promised 'to secure for the workers, by hand or by brain, the most equitable distribution thereof that may be possible upon the basis of the common ownership of the means of production, distribution and exchange'. The Sankey Royal Commission enquiry into the Coal Industry in 1919 recommended nationalisation of the industry, though the proposal was not implemented.

Nationalisation of the railways was seriously considered after the war, but what emerged instead was a system of grouping. It soon became clear that Parliament was not favourably disposed at this stage to a policy of full State ownership of private enterprise, and what in fact did appear in those cases where it was felt that an undertaking should not be left entirely to private enterprise, was a new type of business unit called the Public Corporation.

Certain sectors of the economy have within them a degree of natural monopoly, in which there are serious disadvantages in the operation of even a limited profit motive. Transport, both land and air, broadcasting and electricity supply fall into this category. Obviously railways, airlines, broadcasting stations, electric supply lines, docks, etc., must be limited, which means that private competition must be limited too. This, in turn, provides an opportunity for private enterprise to make large profits, and often it is impossible to relate profits to either the efficiency or adequacy of what are in essence public services. How can Parliament, for example, entrust to private interests decisions about where there should be electricity supply lines since this will influence amongst other things important national considerations such as the location of industry and the growth of towns? The answer meeting with widespread approval amongst all political parties between the wars was the Public Corporations, which were public bodies charged with general statutory obligations to provide a service. Even though these public bodies were ultimately answerable to Parliament, they were nevertheless vested with complete autonomy within the statutory limits laid down for them.

The Public Corporations set up between the wars were the Forestry Commission (1919), the British Broadcasting Corporation (1926), the Central Electricity Board (1926), the London Passenger Transport Board (1933), and the British Overseas Airways Corporation (1939).

Labour Organisation

The coming of the First World War marked the beginning of a big increase in the power, status and size of trade unions. Trade union membership doubled during the war, and in spite of wartime regulations there were outbursts of militancy in the engineering industry, and a major strike on the South Wales coalfield. The war also led to the development of a radical shop stewards' movement, which for a time was looked on by the more militant trade unionists as a permanent alternative leadership.

In 1917, the Trade Union Amalgamation Act, secured by Labour as a consequence of the Government's wartime reliance upon the cooperation of the trade unions, made the amalgamation of unions easier, and led to the establishment of a few very large unions, prominent amongst which were the Amalgamated Engineering Union, formed in 1920 from several societies in the engineering trades, and the General and Municipal Workers founded in 1922, claimed to be the largest trade union in the world at that time. The prestige of the labour movement was further enhanced by the fact that a number of its leaders had for the first time served in the Government. Hence, the labour movement emerged from the war not only with a greater determination to get a better deal for its members, but also with a greater capability to make its influence felt.

Immediately after the war a wave of industrial unrest swept through Britain, and the period up to 1926 was one of unprecedented militancy. The employers on the one hand wanted to eliminate all traces of Socialism from the economy and get wages back on the private enterprise basis of supply and demand, whilst the trade unionists were determined to consolidate the gains made during the war, in order to build up a fairer society. In 1919 there was a successful rail strike, but it was clear that if the strike had gone on much longer the Government would have won. This strike demonstrated that some form of central executive of the labour movement was required; therefore in 1920, the General Council of the T.U.C. was formed, consisting of 32 members, which was to become a kind of Cabinet of the movement. The General Council of the T.U.C. grew in strength as the old Triple Alliance, formed in 1913 to increase cooperation between the transport workers, miners and railwaymen, faded out on account of the lack of cooperation between the miners' and the railwaymen's unions. The Government, in turn, attempted to strengthen its hand by passing the Emergency Powers Act of 1920, which could be used against strikes, or threatened strikes, concerned with the distribution of water, fuel, light and transport.

The main area of strife between employers and labour in the early 1920s was to be found in the coal industry, which in 1924 employed 10 per cent of the insured work force. The miners, already embittered by the failure of the Government to implement the recommendations of the Royal Commission enquiry into the industry in 1919, had to accept reductions in wages after a bitter three months' strike in 1921, though they did secure an agreement with the Mining Federation, which regulated miners' wages with certain minimum rates.

This agreement remained in force until 1924, when it was replaced by a further agreement raising minimum rates, but owing to the exhaustion of several windfall demands in the coal industry, the coal owners gave notice to terminate the agreements of 1921 and 1924 as from July 31, 1925, and the minimum wage was to be abolished. It was this event which precipitated the General Strike, though the threatened wage cuts and the strike were delayed until the following year pending a Royal Commission enquiry under the chairmanship of Sir Herbert Samuel. The recommendations made by the Royal Commission in March, 1926, for improving the coal industry did not appease the miners, and the strike began in early May, having been sparked off by the refusal of the workers at the *Daily Mail* to print an editorial branding the threatened strike as revolutionary.

The General Strike lasted only nine days, whilst the miners stayed out several months longer. The Government maintained an intractable position throughout the strike, and refused to parley until the strike was called off unconditionally. The T.U.C. and the rank and file of the labour movement had no wish for their part to bring the country to its knees, and therefore the strike was called off without any tangible concessions being made by the Government. The miners felt betrayed, and many workers considered that the General Strike had been an exercise in futility, and yet, taking a broader point of view, only by a head-on collision of forces so fundamentally opposed could there have been any hope of reconciliation. There is no doubt that after the General Strike the air was cleared somewhat and the period between 1926 and 1939 was one of comparative industrial peace. Trade union membership fell up until 1933, when it stood at 4·4 million, after which it recovered again, reaching 6·3 million in 1939. Many trade unionists were embittered by the Trade Disputes Act of 1927, making illegal sympathetic strikes and any strike designed to coerce the Government by inflicting hardship on the people.

The Act also required the Civil Service unions to dissociate themselves entirely from the T.U.C., and enforced a contracting-in system, instead of a contracting-out system, for contributing towards political funds. Many workers were also penalised and victimised by their employers for participating in the strike, though by and large the Prime Minister, Stanley Baldwin, adopted a moderate approach, and restrained the more right-wing elements in his party from taking revenge on the trade unionists.

Better relations between employers and employees emanated from the Mond-Turner talks of 1928; Ben Turner being the leader of the wool textile workers, and chairman of the General Council of the T.U.C. in 1928, whilst Sir Alfred Mond was chairman of I.C.I. The idea behind the talks was that there should be some machinery for joint consultation about the more general problems of industry, between the representative employers' organisations and the representatives of the trade unions. There can be no doubt, however, that the labour movement as an influence on Government had been weakened by the events of 1926, and trade union leaders did not easily recover the privileged position they had achieved during the war and immediately after it.

Suggested Further Reading

Allen, G. C., *British Industries and Their Organisation*, Longmans, London, 1959.
Bullock, A., *The Life and Times of Ernest Bevin*, Vol. 1, Heinemann, London, 1960.

Carr, J. C., and Taplin, W. A., *History of the British Steel Industry*, Blackwell, London, 1962.
Court, W. H. B., Problems of the British Coal Industry Between the Wars, *Economic History Review*, 15 (1945).
Jones, L., *Shipbuilding in Britain*, University of Wales Press, Cardiff, 1957.
Pelling, H., *A History of British Trade Unionism*, Penguin, London, 1963.
Robson, R., *The Cotton Industry in Britain*, Macmillan, London, 1957.
Sayers, R. S., *A History of Economic Change in England, 1880–1939*, O.U.P., Oxford and London, 1967.
Turner, G., *Business in Britain*, Penguin, London, 1969.

Exercises

1. Discuss the view that Britain's main economic difficulties between the wars were caused by the depressed state of the staple export industries.
2. Trace the changes in Government policy towards agriculture between 1914 and 1939.
3. Discuss the growth of one of the following industries between the wars: (a) chemical, (b) motor car, (c) electrical, or (d) artificial fibres.
4. What were the most important influences bringing about a change in the location of industry between the wars?
5. Identify the main causes of the growth in industrial combination after 1914.
6. Do you agree that the General Strike of 1926 was an exercise in futility?

Summary

1. The coal industry was badly in need of reorganisation and nationalisation after the war.
2. The iron and steel industry was technically backward after the war and therefore fared badly during the period of intense foreign competition in the 1920s, though the introduction of protection in 1932 and the stimulation of home demand led to some recovery by 1937.
3. The supremacy of both the textile and shipbuilding industries was successfully challenged between the wars due to intense foreign competition.
4. Government help to agriculture was discontinued in the 1920s but was restored again in the 1930s.
5. Amongst the industries that prospered between the wars were the electrical and engineering industries, chemicals and artificial fibres.
6. The new industries tended to establish themselves in London, S.E. England and the Midlands.
7. Industrial relations were marked by strife and confrontation up to 1926 after which there was a period of comparative industrial peace.

CHAPTER SEVENTEEN

TRANSPORT, COMMERCIAL AND FINANCIAL DEVELOPMENTS

Railways and Road Motor Transport

Railways

Up to 1914 the railways in Britain had had a virtual monopoly of inland transportation, though since they consisted of 120 separate undertakings they were often in competition with each other. As soon as the First World War broke out they were taken over by the Government and administered by a Railway Executive Committee which was designed to ensure that all military needs were properly catered for. However, control became much less specific and according to the Royal Commission on Transport, Final Report, 1930, 'developed into a comprehensive financial transaction entirely divorced from military considerations and covering the whole area of railway administration'. During this period of control, shareholders were guaranteed a net revenue equal to what they had earned in 1913, and competition between the various undertakings was removed.

This, together with the lack of manpower and investment, resulted in the standard of service declining and the depreciation of railway property.

After the war, there was much discussion and speculation about what was to be done with the railways. Amongst the alternatives considered were:

1. To operate the railways on the same basis as before the war, i.e. having twelve large railway companies and many smaller ones run on a private enterprise basis.
2. To continue wartime control.
3. To organise the railways into a large privately owned railway trust.
4. To nationalise them.

The Ministry of Transport, created in 1919, was charged with the task of working out a new railway policy. After two years of political debate a compromise solution of grouping was decided upon. Under the Railway Act of 1921, the railways were amalgamated into four large groups, i.e. the London Midland and Scottish Railway, the London and North Eastern Railway, the Great Western and the Southern Railway. These groups remained in existence until the railways were nationalised in 1948. Under this system competition was preserved between London and the South West, and between London and many of the main industrial areas in the country.

The 1921 Act also set up a Railway Rates Tribunal to fix standard charges which were due to come into operation in 1928, as well as providing the owners of the railways with £160 million compensation in order to make good the wear and tear suffered by the railways during the war. Unfortunately, this compensation, by and large, was not used in the way it was intended, and was frittered away by giving the shareholders a last fling.

The two outstanding reasons for the stagnation of British railways between the wars were the depression in the staple trades, particularly industries like coal and steel, and the growth of road motor transport, which meant that railways were never able to earn the standard net revenue that their charges were supposed to yield under the 1921 schedules. Consequently, railway property depreciated and by 1939 the railways were generally in a bad way.

Road Motor Transport

Road motor transport provided a new convenient, flexible and relatively cheap alternative to rail transport. The evolution and growth of road motor transport followed the development of the internal combustion engine in the 1890s, and after the legal recognition in 1903 of the motor as distinct from the light locomotive, the number of vehicles rapidly increased.

The growth of the road motor industry was stimulated after the First World War by the following factors:

1. Technical improvements in engine and vehicle construction were made during the war.
2. There was increased demand for motor transport on account of:

(a) Much railway having been closed down during the war.
(b) People were better off than in 1914.
(c) Suburban development created new traffic.
(d) The railway strikes of 1919 and 1926 diverted traffic to the road, some of which remained after the strikes were over.

The decade following the war were boom years for the motorbus business and the road haulier, both of whom competed against the railways with unfair advantages, since the railways were tied down by their nineteenth-century monopoly restrictions. Road hauliers were in the happy position of being able to pick and choose both their freight and their routes, whereas railways were obliged to provide a service over uneconomic routes, as well as having to accept any load, however inconvenient. The railways, who were directly responsible for maintaining an expensive permanent way, were compelled to charge set rates, whereas the road hauliers, who did not have an expensive permanent way to maintain, could choose which freight they carried and charge whatever rate the market would bear. In addition, road transport had the advantage of speed and reliability, and was able to serve the whole country.

A Royal Commission on Transport was appointed in 1928, partly in response to the opposition of the railways to unfair competition, and partly because of the haphazard way in which motor transport had developed. Its recommendations of a system of licensing for public road motor transport were embodied in the Road Traffic Acts of 1930 and 1933.

Air Transport

The development of civil aviation in the 1920s was a slow and uncertain process. This was a time when aircraft technology was in its infancy and therefore air travel was unreliable and somewhat dangerous.

In 1924 Imperial Airways was formed for the purpose of encouraging air travel between Empire countries, and within a few years air services had been started to the Far East, South Africa and Australia. Numerous companies operating domestic air routes were also started, though these proved to be uncompetitive with traditional means of transport.

In 1935, when many British trains were averaging more than 60 m.p.h. on their journeys, F. C. Shemerdine estimated that the travelling time spent on a 100-mile journey by air was as follows:

Road journey to and from airports	40 minutes
On and off loading aircraft	10 minutes
Aircraft manoeuvres—approximately	15 minutes
100 miles by air at 160 m.p.h.	37 minutes
	1 hour 42 minutes
	Average speed 58·8 m.p.h.

A rapid expansion in civil aviation did nevertheless take place in the 1930s and between 1930 and 1938 the number of passenger miles flown increased from 6 million to 53 million. The record year was in 1935, when 121,559 passengers were carried by nineteen separate companies. In the same year British Airways was formed by the amalgamation of the three leading companies in the business. This was later merged in 1939 with Imperial Airways to form the British Overseas Airways Corporation.

The Content and Direction of British Trade

Britain's trading position deteriorated between the wars, with the volume of exports decreasing and the volume of imports increasing, thus bringing about the decline and eventual disappearance of a surplus

Table 29. United Kingdom and World Exports and Imports

Year	*U.K. volume indexes*		*U.K. as a percentage of world*	
	Net exports	*Net imports*	*Exports*	*Imports*
1913	100·0	100·0	13·11	15·24
1924	80·0	106·4	12·94	17·62
1927	81·8	118·3	11·10	15·92
1929	86·6	121·3	10·86	15·40
1932	54·5	106·9	9·92	16·30
1936	65·4	124·6	10·30	17·60
1937	71·6	132·5	9·87	17·03

Source: A. E. Kahn, *Great Britain in the World Economy.*

for overseas investment. Britain's relative decline as a trading nation is illustrated by her percentage share of world imports increasing, whilst her percentage share of world exports fell (Table 29).

The main reasons for Britain's poor export performance between the wars were the growth of foreign competition and the spreading of economic nationalism; and the main declining sectors in exports were textiles, coal and basic engineering products. Cotton exports were badly hit by former customers producing more for themselves, and by their buying more from sources other than Britain, particularly from Japan. Exports of textile machinery also fell heavily. Coal exports suffered the biggest fall, dropping from 94 million tons in 1913 to 53 million tons in 1934; even in the best coal export year (1929) exports were only 80 per cent of the 1913 figure.

Three things, however, prevented the decline in Britain's staple exports from having a disastrous effect on the balance of payments.

1. The terms of trade moved in Britain's favour, i.e. the price of primary products fell relatively to the price of manufactured goods. Professor Pollard considers that 'the improvement in Britain's terms of trade was one of the outstanding characteristics of the whole period' and that this improvement 'permitted, and in part caused the rising standard of living in Britain, while condemning the export industries to unemployment and decline. If labour and other resources could have been transferred quickly enough from export goods to new and expanding industries, these remarkably favourable terms could have given Britain a splendid opportunity to raise living standards at a quite exceptional rate. As it was, part of it was wasted by unemployment in the export sectors.' (S. Pollard, *Development of the British Economy*)

It must, of course, also be remembered that the fall in the price of primary products had an adverse effect on Britain, since it reduced the capacity of primary producers to buy manufactured goods from Britain.

2. Britain's invisible exports remained in surplus, i.e. income from shipping, banking, insurance and other financial services.

3. New industries, such as the chemical, electrical and motor industries, began to contribute to exports.

On the import side, Britain continued to buy large quantities of food and raw materials from abroad; in 1924 for example, four fifths of her wheat and flour, three fifths of her meat, all of her raw cotton requirements, nine tenths of her wool and timber, and over one third of her iron ore. Amongst the important new raw material imports were crude petroleum and rubber, whilst motorcars and cinematographic films were amongst the relatively new manufactured imports.

The main change in the direction of trade between the wars was away from Western Europe and the non-Sterling bloc, towards Empire regions, particularly after the signing of the Ottawa Agreements in 1932.

British Trading Policy

The great nineteenth-century politico-economic issue of free trade or protection was finally settled in 1932, when Britain, in the depths of the World Depression, returned to protection. This long-delayed decision came about only after considerable controversy and much compromise, since both the Liberal and Labour parties supported free trade until the bitter end, believing that free trade meant cheap food and thus worked for the benefit of the poorer classes. This rather narrow point of view failed to take into account the overall interests of the nation, as well as ignoring the fundamental changes that had taken place in Britain's position in the world economy.

The central feature of the mechanism of Britain's free trade system before 1914 was the international Gold Standard, associated with an expanding export trade, and a progressive foreign investment policy. The export trade provided the funds for the foreign investment, and the foreign investment made openings for further exports, thus bringing about increased trade and prosperity.

The disadvantages of foreign competition before the war were already beginning to outweigh the advantages of free trade, but with the growth of economic nationalism during and after the war in both monetary policy and trade, the case for a return to protection became irrefutable. It was lunacy for Britain alone amongst the great economic powers to pursue a policy of free trade since there were no incentives for other powers to cooperate with Great Britain so long as her market and financial facilities continued to be freely available to all traders.

A number of breaches were made in the policy of free trade before the introduction of a general tariff, but the proportion of protected British trade by the late 1920s was very small; by 1928, the safeguarded industries were only employing between 50,000 and 60,000 people, constituting one third of 1 per cent of the labour force. The following measures were the main exceptions to Britain's free trade policy:

1. The McKenna duties were introduced in 1915 as a temporary wartime measure to restrict the use of shipping space and to conserve foreign exchange. Under this measure duties were imposed on imported cars, watches, clocks, musical instruments and cinematographic films; the duty was to be 33⅓ per cent ad valorem, and 1d. a foot on film. These duties were continued after the war, with the exception of a short period between 1924 and 1925, in spite of the efforts of many free traders to have them repealed.

2. The Dyestuffs (Import Regulation) Act was passed in 1920, with the object of encouraging the growth of a British dyestuffs industry, since Britain was at that time the greatest textile manufacturer in the world and had in the past imported most of her dyestuffs. At the same time the British Dyestuffs Corporation was set up, and within a decade Britain was supplying 80 per cent of her dyestuff requirements. This Act did not introduce duties, but instituted a system of licensing operated by the Board of Trade.

3. The Safeguarding of Industries Act, 1921, imposed three sets of duties, viz.

(i) Key products, such as scientific, optical and precision instruments, which had a 33⅓ per cent ad valorem duty imposed on them. The main consideration here was strategic, since Germany had been the chief producer of these instruments before the war.

(ii) Duties were imposed on products coming from a country where the currency was depreciated in relation to Sterling; these duties were applied during the course of the 1920s to gloves, gas-mantles and glassware.

(iii) Dumping duties could be imposed on any goods, with the exception of food and drink, when such goods were being sold in this country at below cost of production, though in practice no use was made of this provision.

4. The German Reparation (Recovery) Act of 1921 attempted to use the tariff to collect reparations from Germany. Under the provisions of this Act, which lasted only three years, duties of up to 50 per cent ad valorem were imposed on German imports in part payment of reparations.

5. In 1925 the Conservatives extended the duties under the Safeguarding of Industries Act to several more commodities. This followed from the lessons that Stanley Baldwin had learnt from his decision in 1923 to go to the country on the issue of introducing general protection. The defeat of the Conservatives in the ensuing election convinced Baldwin that any further protection would have to be dealt with through the Safeguarding of Industries Act. Amongst the duties imposed in 1925 were the silk, hops and sugar duties.

6. The Merchandise Marks Act of 1926 laid down that imported goods bearing a British manufacturer's name could not be sold without an indication of origin. For example, if a British manufacturer bought a supply of pencils from abroad, and then stamped his name on them, he also had to stamp on the country of origin.

7. The Cinematographic Films Act of 1927 introduced a quota system in order to safeguard the infant British film industry from extinction due to the heavy competition from the American film industry.

In spite of these measures, Britain was still almost wholly a free trade country. In 1930 only between 2 and 3 per cent of imports had protective duties on them; and during the course of the following year several more safeguarding duties were allowed to lapse. This period proved to be the high water mark of free trade in post-war Britain, since with the onset of the 'Economic Blizzard' in 1931, and a turn for the worst in Britain's balance of payments, free trade was doomed. In February, 1932, the Government passed the Import Duties Act, providing initially for a general 10 per cent ad valorem tariff on most imports, including many raw materials and foodstuffs; and provision was made for the Import Duties Advisory Committee to recommend higher duties, which could then be imposed by the Government. Empire goods were exempted from the provisions of the Act, and negotiations were begun between Britain and the Dominions culminating in the setting up of a system of Imperial Preference, embodied in the Ottawa Agreements of 1932, and later extended to the Crown Colonies in 1933.

On and Off the Gold Standard

Britain officially left the Gold Standard on March 31, 1919, though in practice it had been inoperable since 1914, when the Currency and

Bank Notes Act permitted the printing of notes unbacked by gold. The war effort was in fact largely financed by inflation, with the result that wholesale prices during the war rose by 140 per cent, and the cost of living by 125 per cent. In these circumstances the pound Sterling depreciated in relation to the American dollar, with British wholesale prices being a third higher than American wholesale prices in 1918 compared with 1914. During the war the pound was artificially pegged at a value of $4·76, but from March, 1919, onwards it was allowed to slide, and plummeted to $3·40 by February, 1920.

Considerable concern was felt in some quarters about these changes in the currency, particularly amongst those who were anxious to return to 'normalcy', i.e. to the conditions existing before the war. With this question in mind the Government, in January, 1918, set up a committee under the chairmanship of Lord Cunliffe, Governor of the Bank of England, to consider 'the various problems which will arise in connection with currency and the foreign exchanges during the period of reconstruction'. The main recommendation of this committee was that 'the conditions necessary to the maintenance of an effective gold standard . . . should be restored without delay'. (Cmd. 9182.) The report went on to recommend that 'the actual maximum fiduciary circulation in any year should become the legal maximum for the following year'. This recommendation was accepted by the Government and embodied in the Treasury Minute of December 15, 1919.

The acceptance by the Government of a ceiling on the fiduciary issue of currency notes, and the damping down of credit by a high Bank Rate, helped to induce the severe deflation starting in April, 1920. This policy of working towards the restoration of the gold standard at the 1914 parity of $4·86 to the pound poured cold water on any liberal credit recovery policies that might have been suggested in the early 1920s, and helped to bring about a soaring level of unemployment.

By 1922, the pound sterling had become more or less stabilised around $4·40, where it was to stay. The Cambridge economist, John Maynard Keynes, was later to argue that this was the parity at which Britain should have gone back to gold, but even this rate was probably too high, considering the high level of unemployment at the time. As it was, favourable conditions in 1925 helped the exchange towards par, and with Winston Churchill as Chancellor of the Exchequer, Britain took the decision to return to the Gold Standard at the 1914 parity of $4·86 to the pound.

Much criticism has since been levelled at this decision, since many people considered that the interests of industry were sacrificed to the interests of the City, and that returning to gold was the prime cause of the relative stagnation of the British economy throughout the second half of the 1920s. Some critics went so far as to assert that the resulting weakness of Sterling was a major cause of the international currency collapse of 1931, but as with most decisions it is easy to be wise after the event. Treasury papers now available at the Public Records Office show that at the time few people spoke against it. In fact, it is now clear that the decision to go back to gold was an extremely well considered one, taken only after the consideration of much expert advice. Typical of the advice given at the time was that of Montagu Norman, a Governor of the Bank of England, who was by nature a gloomy man. He wrote that 'the Gold Standard is the best "Governor" that can be devised for a world that is still human, rather than divine'. It is now apparent that Winston Churchill, who as Chancellor of the Exchequer had to take the brunt of the subsequent criticisms for returning to gold, was quite unimpressed by the importance attached to gold and the Gold Standard: 'Survivals of rudimentary and transitional stages in the evolution of finance,' as he called them. He looked forward to the day when gold could be 'left to the fine arts'. Nevertheless, the main body of advice was for a return to the Gold Standard, and Churchill went along with that advice.

One of the most outspoken critics of returning to the Gold Standard was Keynes, who wrote a pamphlet entitled *The Economic Consequences of Mr Churchill*. In this pamphlet he spoke of the miners, and others to follow, as being 'the victims of the economic juggernaut. They represent in the flesh the fundamental adjustments engineered by the Treasury and the Bank of England to bridge the moderate gap between \$4·40 and \$4·86. They are the moderate sacrifice still necessary to ensure the stability of the Gold Standard.'

Professor Sayers has more recently argued that going back on the Gold Standard was essentially an employment policy, since by helping to restore stability to world finance, one of the principal causes of trade depression and unemployment was eradicated. According to Sayers it was not fantastic to argue that by 1929 the restoration of international currency stability had promoted the growth of world trade, and this was of particular help to Great Britain where the bulk of unemployment was in the staple export industries.

Essentially, the main trouble in going back on the Gold Standard was the over-valuation of Sterling by about 10 per cent, which priced British exports out of overseas markets. The only way open for Britain to compete on world markets was to lower production costs, which meant reducing wages, and this in turn created unemployment and much social friction. The obvious remedy of abandoning the Gold Standard was avoided until Britain was forced off in 1931, when she was no longer able to meet her obligations due to balance of payments difficulties.

Immediately the situation improved, since as soon as the pound was free to find its own level it fell by more than a quarter on the foreign exchange, falling from \$4·86 to \$3·80, later to \$3·23, and then fluctuating around \$3·40. This of course meant a corresponding reduction in the price of British goods, thus boosting the export trade. The hyperinflation expected by some did not materialise, and Britain on the whole, particularly in the short run, benefited from abandoning the Gold Standard.

The Economic Blizzard, 1929–33

The origins of the world financial crisis between 1929 and 1933 were to be found in the United States, where in the Autumn of 1929 the stock market collapsed, bringing about an almost complete breakdown in the American economy. This came at the end of a decade of unprecedented growth and prosperity for the American people, who saw nothing ahead but constant material progress.

President Coolidge, in his annual message to Congress in 1928, said: 'No Congress of the United States ever assembled, on surveying the state of the Union, has met with a more pleasing prospect than that which appears at the present time.' Later in the same year, the successful Republican candidate for the Presidency, Herbert Hoover, stated: 'We are nearer today to the ideal of the abolition of poverty and fear from the lives of men and women than ever before in any land.' These statements proved to be tragic in the light of subsequent events, but at the time there was much truth in them. The American people had come nearer to the final triumph over poverty than ever before in the history of any other land, and yet the prosperity had been laid on an insecure foundation.

The wealth that was generated was unfairly spread, with the eventual result that too few people could afford to buy the increasing number of goods pouring onto the market. Furthermore, America restricted world trade by imposing high tariffs at home whilst at the same time encouraging trade by investing large sums of money abroad. By the late 1920s the Americans were investing abroad more than $1,500 million annually, the most important area of investment being in Europe. Thus, the world economy settled down into a quasi-equilibrium, and from 1925 to 1929 world trade improved, and most countries enjoyed a period of moderate recovery. This prosperity, however, depended upon the American trade cycle, and when the liquidity crisis broke in the United States during the Autumn of 1929, it gradually spread and became a world crisis, since most European economies were geared to the United States through an elaborate system of debt.

The immediate effect of the Wall Street crash on Britain was to ease her monetary problems by curbing the uncomfortable flow of short-term funds across the Atlantic in response to the high interest rates prevailing in America before the crash began. Furthermore, the collapse of agricultural prices caused through the world over-production of primary products and aggravated by the Wall Street crash, resulted in a marked improvement in Britain's terms of trade, though this development had the disadvantage of impairing the effective demand of primary producers for manufactured goods.

By 1931, the international liquidity crisis had spread to Central Europe, causing a collapse of credit in Austria and Germany, which resulted in a large outflow of gold from London to Germany. Meanwhile, the May Committee, appointed by Ramsay MacDonald's Labour Government of 1929–31 to enquire into national expenditure, recommended new taxes and huge cuts in expenditure. These recommendations for economies in public expenditure included cuts in unemployment relief and reductions in the salaries and wages of all public employees. It was a combination of the loss of gold through the spreading liquidity crisis, and the distrust by financiers of a Labour Government, together with the gloomy report of the May Committee, that forced Britain off the Gold Standard in September, 1931.

Recovery, 1931–9

The desire by Britain in the 1920s to get back to the internationalism of the pre-war situation was replaced in the 1930s by a more inward approach aimed at solving the internal problems causing mass unemployment. This involved resorting to a restrictive commercial policy, and the acceptance by the Government of more responsibility for the management of the economy. The main features of this recovery were as follows.

Devaluation

Devaluation was brought about in 1931 by detaching the pound from gold, thus allowing the pound Sterling to find its own level at a point considerably below its Gold Standard level. The short-term advantages of this move were the cheapening of exports, the restriction of imports, and the stimulation of employment, whilst the long-term advantages stemmed from techniques of deliberate monetary management, made possible by the insulation of the internal price structure from outside influences through the Exchange Equalisation Account. Britain now had more control over her own destiny, and was thus able to move away from the deflationary pressures which had plagued her during the previous decade.

Cheap Money

The favourable effects on the economy of abandoning the Gold Standard paved the way for lower interest rates, and by June, 1932, Bank Rate had been brought down to 2 per cent, where it stayed more or less intact until 1951.

This was followed shortly afterwards by the conversion of War Loan stock, representing some 27 per cent of the National Debt, from a 5 per cent basis to a 3½ per cent basis, thus forcing down interest rates on long-term securities and reducing Government expenditure by lowering interest payments on the National Debt. This had the effect of lowering interest rates generally, thus making credit cheaper for potential borrowers.

One of the outstanding features of recovery in Britain during the 1930s was the building boom, which had detonating effects on the rest of the economy through the multiplier process. This was made possible by larger mortgages becoming more easily obtainable through building societies at lower rates of interest, whilst building firms found it easier and cheaper to finance new building projects. It is significant that a large proportion of the new building constructions undertaken in the 1930s was in the private sector. More than two thirds of the houses built at this time were for private owners, and many of the new owners were amongst the better paid sections of the working class, such as skilled artisans and clerical workers. This extension of ownership to the lower-paid members of the community represented a social revolution, since the new houses were a great improvement on anything that had previously been available for anybody below the upper middle class.

Environmentally, too, this period of house building left its indelible mark on Britain, with its housing estates sprawling far beyond the previous boundaries of towns and cities. Often houses in this period were of the ribbon development type, straggling along the main roads, far into the countryside, thus evoking much criticism from later generations of more environmentally conscious planners.

Protection

There were many obvious advantages of introducing a protective tariff. A tariff could be used to curb foreign competition and build up preferential markets, and Britain so used these advantages after 1932 to build up a system of Empire Preference. However, some reservations have been expressed in recent years questioning the commonly held view that protection played a big part in promoting recovery during the 1930s. Pollard, for example, 'doubted whether protection helped greatly to pull Britain out of her exchange difficulties, still more out of the slump', since Britain's new trading relations with her foreign neighbours resulted in both retaliatory action and the diversion of trade, rather than the creation of new trade. On the other hand, Pollard found it difficult to identify any ill effects of protection. 'Apart from the special case of agriculture, it would be hard to point to a single industry fostered in Britain by the tariff which was obviously uneconomic or inappropriate for this country.' (S. B. Pollard, *The Development of the British Economy 1914–1950*)

The Ban on Foreign Lending

British foreign investment almost ceased after 1931, partly due to Government policy on account of the balance of payments situation, and partly due to the risks involved in investing in a world that was for the most part worse hit by the Economic Blizzard than Britain. What little foreign investment did take place in the remainder of the 1930s was directed towards Empire regions or into those projects where British foreign trade would directly benefit. This trend away from indiscriminate investment abroad freed whatever investible funds were available for use in the recovery programme at home.

In addition to these measures, Government assistance was given in various forms to the depressed industries, and attempts were made at rationalising industry and curing unemployment, all of which are dealt with elsewhere in this book.

Two striking aspects emerge when taking an overview of the British recovery programme: firstly, its orthodoxy, and secondly, its fragmentation. Certainly the measures taken in Germany and the United States to overcome economic depression were far more inspired and novel than those taken in Britain. Arndt makes the point that 'the Great Depression did not lead to any marked increase in State interference in, or control of, the economic system. It was left to private enterprise, aided only by protection from foreign competition, cheap money and minor internal measures of assistance to lift the British economy from the depression.' (H. W. Arndt, *Economic Lessons of the Nineteen-Thirties*)

Britain, unlike Germany and the United States, did not attempt to reflate the economy by Budget deficits, but preferred instead to balance the Budget by the deflationary method of cutting back expenditure and raising taxes, thus slowing down the rate of recovery. It was relatively easy from 1932 onwards, however, for Britain to maintain a balanced budget without taking further deflationary measures. Britain also failed to take advantage of cheap money to devise a full-blooded public works programme; here was the opportunity to modernise cheaply the nation's social overhead capital, such as roads and public buildings, yet the public works programme that was devised was planned and executed on a totally inadequate scale.

By the 1930s economic growth had become much more dependent upon the domestic market, and could therefore be more effectively influenced by British economic policy making. Nevertheless, there were a number of fortuitous circumstances, outside the Government's influence, which contributed towards Britain's recovery. Prominent amongst these were the favourable movement in her terms of trade, the upswing of the trade cycle from 1932–3 onwards, the temporary revival of world trade in the mid-1930s, and the rearmament boom beginning in 1937.

Suggested Further Reading

Alford, B. W. E., *Depression and Recovery: British Economic Growth, 1918–1939*, Macmillan, London, 1972.

Arndt, H. W., *The Economic Lessons of the Nineteen-Thirties*, Cass, London, 1963.

Lewis, W. A., *Economic Survey, 1919–1939*, Allen & Unwin, London, 1949.

Pollard, S., *The Development of the British Economy, 1914–1967*, Edward Arnold, London, 1968.

Sayers, R. S., The Return to Gold, 1925, Chapter XII, in L. S. Pressnell (ed.), *Studies in the Industrial Revolution*, Athlone Press, London, 1960.

Exercises

1. Why did railways decline between the wars?
2. Discuss the view that it was 'pure lunacy' for Britain to retain free trade until 1932.
3. Was it a mistake for Britain to go back on the Gold Standard in 1925?
4. How did the Wall Street crash affect the British economy?
5. Do you agree that Britain's recovery programme in the 1930s was orthodox and unimaginative?

Summary

1. Railways declined between the wars due to economic depression and the growth of road transport.
2. Britain's trading position deteriorated between the wars; therefore protection and a system of Imperial Preference were introduced in 1932.
3. Britain returned to the Gold Standard between 1925 and 1931 with an exchange rate of \$4.86 to the £.
4. Britain's recovery from the world economic depression of the early 1930s involved a restrictive commercial policy and measures designed to assist industry and revive employment.

CHAPTER EIGHTEEN

SOCIAL CONDITIONS

By 1914, the basis of the modern welfare state had been laid, though it took two World Wars and an intervening period of economic depression and high unemployment before a system was provided which guaranteed everyone a basic minimum of social security as of right. The period between the two World Wars saw the extension to more people of the measures already passed in the great era of Liberal reforms between 1906 to 1914. Between 1911 and 1939, 'with the exception of widows' and orphans' pensions, the changes were merely those of expansion. The numbers covered by health insurance grew from 13,000,000 in 1914 to 20,000,000 in 1938; old age pensioners from 800,000 to 2,500,000, and those covered by unemployment insurance from 2,250,000 to 15,000,000. In 1914 the benefits paid under these three schemes amounted to approximately £30,000,000; in 1938 they had reached £200,000,000.

'In spite of this growth, in 1938, 3 per cent of the population of England and Wales, and 4 per cent of the population of Scotland were in receipt of Poor Relief, and at least another 6 to 7 per cent of the population was living in poverty. In their ranks were many of the new beneficiaries of old age pensions, unemployment and health insurance. The improvement since the pre-1906 days of Booth was considerable, but not complete.' (Mark Abrams, *The Condition of the British People, 1911–1945*)

Both the World Wars in the twentieth century have had a profound influence on the development of the social services. Unemployed resources were mopped up, the health services were improved; housing shortages were created, either by destruction, or by diverting resources away from their construction. Modern full-scale wars require sacrifices from everyone, and in such circumstances class boundaries become less marked. Class differences, of course, do not disappear overnight, but the hierarchical structure of British society, of the type evident in the Edwardian era, was never to be the same again. The introduction of conscription into the armed forces in 1916 encouraged the view that equality of sacrifice called for equality of opportunity. This philosophy was, of course, the basis of Socialist ideology, which was growing in strength throughout the world. The Russian Revolution of 1917 demonstrated to the world that the workers could, in theory at least, seize power by force. Lloyd George, who became Prime Minister in 1916 and who did not himself come from the traditional privileged background of British Prime Ministers, sympathised with the cause of the underdog, and promised the returning soldiers a 'home fit for heroes'. Thus, at the end of the war the less privileged classes were more conscious of the need for more social justice, and many people were prepared to do something about it.

The onset of economic depression in 1921, and the prevalence of mass unemployment for the remainder of the 1920s and most of the 1930s, forced an expansion of the social services as much by economic necessity as by political conviction, since the existing social security apparatus was insufficient to cope with the problem.

Population Trends

The continued fall in both birth and death rates after 1914 led some observers to conclude that Britain's population was actually entering a period of decline. This was the view held by the contemporary demographer, Professor A. M. Carr Saunders, who wrote: 'The population of this country has now almost reached its peak; decline will shortly set

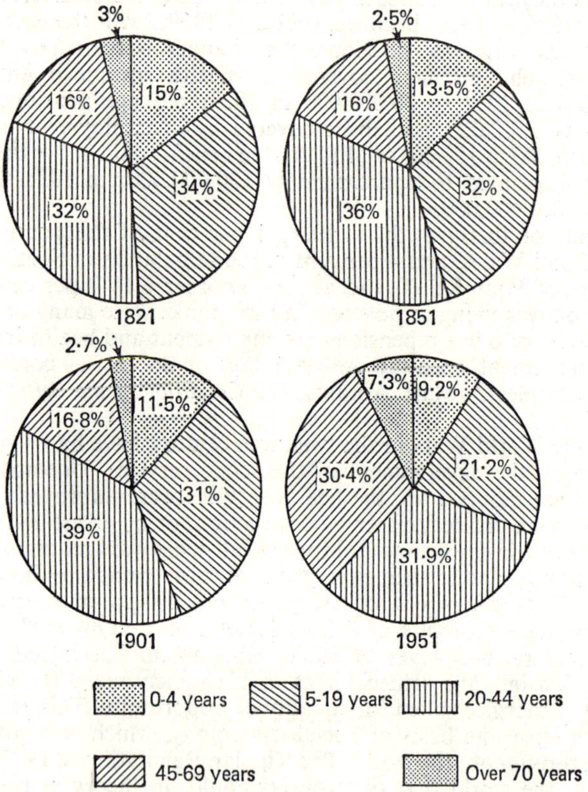

Fig. 19. Age distribution of the population of Britain.

in, and even if fertility remains at its present level, that decline will soon become rapid.' Another view expressed was that unless massive immigration took place then the population within a century would be down to 5 million.

Population did not in fact decline, but continued to grow, though at a slower pace and with a higher proportion in the older age groups. The population of England and Wales rose from 37 million in 1914 to 41·5 million in 1939.

Table 30. Birth and Death Rates for England and Wales (per 1,000 Population)

Year	*Birth rate*	*Death rate*	*Rate of natural increase*
1914	23·8	14·0	9·8
1919	18·5	14·0	4·5
1924	18·8	12·2	6·6
1929	16·3	13·4	2·9
1933	14·4	12·3	2·1
1938	15·1	11·6	3·5

The fears concerning the slowing down in the rate of population growth were prevalent elsewhere, particularly in Europe, where it was estimated that the population was 22 million smaller in 1920 than it would have been if the First World War had not taken place. France's population actually declined between the wars, giving rise to much concern within France about her future prospects as an economic power.

Birth Rates

By the 1930s the typical family consisted of one or two children, and the 'crocodile', once the family out for its Sunday walk, became relegated to the family photograph album. This fall in the birth rate was brought about by the following factors.

1. Birth rates fell during the war on account of the absence of large numbers of men, and future birth rates were affected by the loss due to enemy action of three quarters of a million men and the wounding or mutilation of 1·6 million more.

2. The status of women continued to improve largely on account of the contribution they made to the war effort. In 1918, the Representation of the People Act gave women over the age of thirty the right to vote, and in 1928 women were given the vote on equal terms with men. More opportunities for women in higher education and the professions also became available, but these spheres were still mainly the preserve of the middle class. Such advances as these towards female equality led to a changing role for women within the family, and frequently resulted in a fall in family size.

3. Social Surveys revealed that when an average working man was in employment, he was only capable of maintaining the minimum human needs standards for two adults and three children. This insecure state of affairs for the working man was made even worse by the high level of unemployment at the time, and by the serious housing shortage. Such economic pressures may well have encouraged many poor people to lighten their burdens by restricting the size of their families.

4. There was also a connection between smaller families and those

people who were becoming better off since there seemed to be a correlation between rising living standards and smaller families as people attempted to consolidate their gains. Many people preferred 'Baby Austins' to real babies.

5. With the raising of the school leaving age to fourteen and the abolition of part-time employment by the Fisher Education Act of 1918, children became more of a financial liability to their parents.

6. There was a further change in attitudes towards birth control and the development of new methods of contraception.

Death Rates

Death rates continued to fall, and kept slightly ahead of the fall in the birth rate. Further improvements in medicine and better environmental standards resulted in people living longer so that the expectation of life of a newborn baby increased from fifty-three years in 1911 to sixty years by 1931. The greatest gains were to be found amongst the

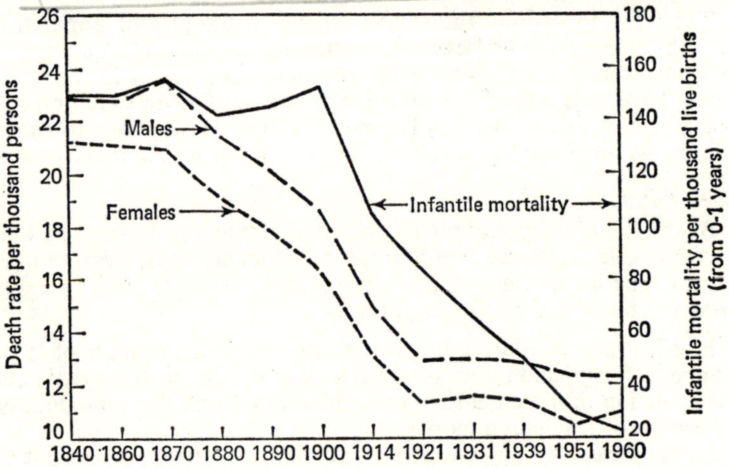

Fig 20. Death rates, England and Wales.

(courtesy Penguin Books Ltd)

young where infant mortality fell rapidly in the first few decades of the twentieth century, and fewer young adults died.

Death rates among people over sixty-five years of age changed little so that population growth was not due to people living longer, but rather to the fact that more people were surviving into older age groups.

The death rate from tuberculosis was more than halved during the period and the incidence of infectious diseases, such as scarlet fever and diphtheria, was reduced.

Migration

The nineteenth century trend of a net outflow of migrants continued up to 1929, and was then followed by the unusual phenomenon of a net inflow (Table 31).

Table 31. Migration in Britain

Period	*Net loss or gain*
1911–21	−860,000
1921–31	−565,000
1931–9	+525,000
Net loss 1911–39	−900,000

The majority of the emigrants from Britain between 1911 and 1931 went to Empire countries with very few going to the United States, where strict immigration restrictions had been imposed. With the onset of the World Economic Blizzard in 1931, however, and the collapse of prices, the primary-producing countries fared worse than the industrial countries, so that many emigrants were attracted back to the home country where conditions were not so bad. In addition Britain became during the 1930s the refuge for many political émigrés from Nazi persecution.

Unemployment and Insurance

The unemployment rate never fell much below 10 per cent between the wars, and at one point in 1932 it stood at 22 per cent. The number out of work shot up from 691,000 at the end of 1920 to 1,355,000 in June, 1921. After that unemployment fluctuated between 1·2 million and 1·5 million for the remainder of the 1920s, and never fell below 1 million.

The intractable million, as the Cambridge economist Professor Pigan called it, became a part of British social life, and many people settled down to years on 'the dole'. Some areas were much more seriously affected by the problem than others; the areas suffering most being South Wales, Central Scotland, Northern and North-Western England. The level of unemployment was highest in the depressed staple export industries, particularly in shipbuilding, where in the worst year, 1932, 63 per cent of the industry's workforce was unemployed.

Gradually, the 1911 Insurance scheme was extended to cover all workers. The first major extension of the scheme came in 1916, when all munitions workers and those in the metal, chemical and other industries were included, making a total insured workforce of four million. The Unemployment Insurance Act, 1920, repealed earlier legislation and extended the scheme to cover all industrial and commercial workers, except agricultural and domestic workers, who were not included until 1936.

In the following year, 1921, a further Insurance Act introduced uncovenanted benefits beyond what the working man was entitled to by his contributions, which were paid during the period from the 16th to 32nd weeks of unemployment. The idea behind the Unemployment Insurance Fund set up under the Acts was for it to accumulate a surplus in times of low unemployment and to borrow from the Treasury in bad times. However, since the level of unemployment was consistently high, the Unemployment Fund became hopelessly insolvent, and by 1931 it owed the Treasury £110 million. This meant that the idea that unemployment relief could be given from an Unemployment Insurance Fund had to be scrapped, and the State had to assume more financial responsibility for the unemployed.

Meanwhile, the Poor Law Guardians had become increasingly incapable of handling the high level of unemployment, and gradually became concerned with little more than the aged poor. The Local Government Act of 1929 transferred to the County and County Borough Councils the duties of the Guardians, whilst the State provided more and more assistance to the unemployed workers. In 1930, the Government introduced transitional benefits for those who had exhausted their claims, though in 1931, on the recommendations of the May Committee, unemployment relief was cut and limited to 26 weeks, after which the unemployed had to apply for relief, based on a means test, from Public Assistance Committees run by the local authorities. In 1932, the Royal Commission Report enquiring into Unemployment Insurance was produced, and this led to the passing of the Unemployment Assistance Act in 1934. Under the provisions of this Act, those who had lost their entitlement to insurance benefits were placed under the care of an Unemployment Assistance Board whose job it was to make relief payments, based on a means test, to unemployed persons who had exhausted or were ineligible for unemployment insurance payments.

Attempts to deal with the problems relating to particular areas were made in two Special Areas Acts passed in 1934 and 1936, which recognised particular unemployment problems in Scotland, South Wales, West Cumberland and Tyneside. These Acts were aimed at reviving economic activity in these areas and relieving unemployment by encouraging the transfer of labour to areas where it was required. However, the schemes met with only limited success, and after 1937 the level of unemployment began to rise again. It was only with the coming of the Second World War that the problem of a high level of unemployment was solved.

Housing

Most houses were provided on a rental basis before the First World War, since mortgages were difficult to obtain and the cost of a house was much more than an average family could afford. Consequently, in the absence of housing regulations, poor-quality housing was built by private enterprise to meet the growing demand, at rents that people could afford.

During the First World War, the construction of new houses was ended, and this, together with growing demand, led to an estimated shortage of 800,000 houses when the war was over. This provided a dilemma, since wartime inflation had pushed up wages and the cost of building materials with the result that private enterprise was unable to provide the houses needed at rents which people could afford. This situation was further complicated by the existence of legislation insisting upon the maintenance of minimum environmental standards. Housing could no longer be built with complete disregard to planning, and adequate space and lighting had to be provided. Hence the State compelled local authorities, through the Addison Housing Act of 1919, to survey the housing needs of their areas and to provide the necessary houses with the aid of a Government subsidy. Further Housing Acts were passed, and by 1931, 585,000 houses had been built by local authorities, and 1,075,000 by private enterprise.

Rapid progress was made in house-building during the 1930s, when about 2,700,000 houses were built, thus making a total of 4½ million new dwellings built in Great Britain between the wars, two thirds of which were constructed by private enterprise. More attention was paid by local authorities during the 1930s to slum clearance, and after 1933 only dwellings to replace slums qualified for a Government grant. Meanwhile, the building boom of the 1930s brought about by the Government's cheap money policy, the fall in building costs and the provision by building societies of more loans repayable over a longer period of time, became the most important aspect of Britain's internal recovery programme.

Education

Many social reformers believed that the best way of eradicating social differences in the long run was by providing a better system of free education for all. It is not surprising, therefore, that plans were worked out during the First World War, when there was much talk of more social justice for the future, to improve the education of the country, and in 1918 the Fisher Education Act was passed. The main provisions of the Act were to raise the school leaving age to 14, and to provide for compulsory part-time education until the age of 18, though the latter recommendation was not implemented due to the economy cuts made following from the Geddes Report on national expenditure in 1921.

More emphasis began to be placed between the wars on psychology within the school, which involved recognising definite stages of mental development, ranging from the nursery school stage to the turbulent period of adolescence. No doubt it was this outlook that prompted the setting up of the Hadow Committee in 1924 to consider the 'Education of the Adolescent'. Many people, particularly in the Labour Party, recognised that the grammar schools were providing secondary education mainly for the middle classes, and they wanted to see a type of secondary 'modern' school education available for all. The report, published in 1926, declared that everybody should stay at school until the age of 15, and should receive secondary education between the ages of 11 and 15. By the time the report was published the Labour Party was out of office, though when back in power again in 1929 the Labour Party introduced a Bill to implement the recommendations of the Hadow Report. Unfortunately, the onset of the World Economic Blizzard in 1929 led to further economy cuts which prevented the school building programme necessary for the school leaving age to be raised to 15, though by 1938, 63·5 per cent of all children over 11 years of age were in reorganised 'modern' schools.

Suggested Further Reading

Abrams, M., *The Condition of the British People, 1911–1945*, Cedric Chivers, London, 1946.

Bruce, M., *The Coming of the Welfare State*, Batsford, London, 1961.

Carr-Saunders, A. M., Jones, D. C., and Moser, C. A., *A Survey of Social Conditions in England and Wales*, Clarendon Press, Oxford, 1958.

Curtis, S. J., *A History of Education in Great Britain*, University Tutorial Press, London, 1967.

Glass, D. V., and Eversley, D. E. C. (editors), *Population in History; Essays in Historical Demography*, Edward Arnold, London, 1965.

Orwell, G., *The Road to Wigan Pier*, Secker & Warburg, London, 1937.

Exercises

1. The First World War speeded up the process of social change. Discuss.
2. Trace the development of the social services between the wars.
3. Discuss the important influences affecting population change during this period.
4. What measures did the authorities take to combat the problem of mass unemployment between the wars?
5. How did the State influence the development of housing after 1918?
6. In what ways, if any, do you think that better educational facilities would have helped Britain to overcome her economic difficulties between the wars?

Summary

1. The war encouraged the view that equality of sacrifice called for equality of opportunity and after the war there was a growing consciousness of the need for more social justice.
2. Population continued to grow, though at a slower pace and with a higher proportion in the older age groups.
3. The 1911 National Insurance scheme was gradually extended to cover all workers, though by the early 1930s the Unemployment Fund had become hopelessly insolvent because of the consistently high level of unemployment and the Government had to assume more financial responsibility for the unemployed.
4. The Special Areas Acts of 1934 and 1936 attempted to deal with the problems relating to special areas, but the schemes met with only limited success.
5. Local Authorities were compelled by legislation to survey the housing needs of their areas, and to provide houses with the aid of Government subsidies, whilst the Government's cheap money policy in the 1930s stimulated house building in the private sector.
6. Attempts to improve educational facilities and opportunities between the wars were frustrated by Government economy measures.

SECTION FOUR

BRITAIN'S ECONOMIC AND SOCIAL DEVELOPMENT SINCE 1939

The coming of the Second World War was yet another important turning point in Britain's economic and social development. Much had been learnt during the long years of depression and recovery between the wars, and in many respects the onset of the war provided the nation with the opportunity to purge itself of many of the economic and social ills from which it had been plagued for so long.

In 1945, people in general did not look back to the pre-war days as being normal times as they had done in 1918, and there was no general desire to return to the pre-war standards. Instead the majority of people in all political parties looked forward to building a new Britain which would provide the populace with full employment and more social justice. There was much justification for this change in attitudes. The industries developed most during the war were the newer ones such as chemicals, oil refining, aircraft production and the manufacture of motor vehicles. These industries had good future prospects and were capable of being competitive in the world export markets. The old staple export industries on the other hand continued to decline, with the result that Britain's future no longer depended upon the production of cotton, coal and ships which had so bedevilled her prospects in the period between the wars.

After an initial period of post-war austerity Britain moved quite definitely during the 1950s and 1960s into Rostow's fifth period of growth, i.e. the period of high mass consumption. More and more durable consumer goods, such as motor cars, television sets and washing machines, became readily available to the British public, whose quality of life correspondingly improved. The State also did away with the last vestiges of the old Poor Law, and increasingly sought to provide better welfare facilities. In this 'never had it so good' atmosphere, however, new problems began to appear. Britain's growth performance, for example, was poor in relation to that of her competitors, whilst inflation and balance of payments problems became increasingly a threat to the British people's standard of living and economic prospects.

CHAPTER NINETEEN

THE SECOND WORLD WAR AND ITS CONSEQUENCES

The effects of the Second World War on the economy were similar in nature to those of the First, though the transference of resources from a peace-time to a war-time basis was done on a much bigger scale and at a time when Britain was a weaker economic force in the world than in 1914. Some of the effects were favourable and many economic problems of the 1930s disappeared. Unemployment, for example, was reduced to acceptable levels, and shortages of all kinds existed instead of the problem of overproduction. Many of the long-term effects, however, were unfavourable for Britain, as for example the selling of investments, capital depreciation and the reduction of exports.

The War Economy

No expense was spared by the Government in maximising the country's war effort so that during the war public expenditure on goods and services represented over three fifths of the net national income, compared with only one fifth in 1938. Large sections of the labour force were mobilised and redeployed for the war effort.

The new Ministries of Supply, Home Security, Economic Welfare, Information, Aircraft Production, Shipping and Food were formed in the first two years of war. When the end of the war was in sight the additional Ministries of Civil Aviation, Town and Country Planning, Reconstruction, Production and Education were set up for the purpose of dealing with some of the problems that were likely to arise when the war ended.

The pre-war trend of developing the lighter consumer goods industries was replaced by the expansion of the engineering and iron and steel industries. This led to the manufacture of tanks, aircraft and ships becoming the most important branches of war production. Agriculture was also expanded, partly because of the memories of the First World War blockade, and also because of the necessity of conserving shipping space. County War Agricultural Committees of the type set up in the First World War were re-established, and farmers were given generous subsidies and encouraged to concentrate on arable rather than animal husbandry. By the end of the war the agricultural labour force had risen from 711,000 in 1939 to 887,000, whilst more mechanisation led to the output per man increasing from between 10 to 15 per cent. This improved level of efficiency, together with the lack of foreign competition, increased home demand, and higher prices made farming much more profitable so that by 1945 the industry was in a much healthier state than before the war. Meanwhile, as much finance as possible to pay for the war was raised through increased direct and indirect taxation rather than relying too heavily on borrowing. People were also encouraged to invest any spare capital they had in National Savings Certificates and Defence Bonds, whilst Treasury Bills were used to transfer any available funds from the money market to the Government.

Britain also obtained credit by accepting post-war claims against herself and by the sale of overseas investments in order to finance the widening trade gap caused through the rise in imports and the fall in exports.

The Economic Consequences

From an economic point of view the consequences of the war were more serious than those following the First World War.

1. Whilst fewer British lives were lost in the Second World War, the physical destruction was much greater. Aerial attack resulted in damage to the main centres of production throughout the country and an estimated one house in three suffered some degree of damage. Furthermore, Britain was adversely affected by the physical damage abroad which extended beyond Europe to the Far East. This damage brought about distortions to the international economy and increased the dependence of the world economy on the United States, leading to a serious dollar shortage.

2. A number of circumstances combined to bring about a serious deterioration in Britain's balance of payments position, viz.

(i) Britain's income from overseas investments fell from £248 million in 1938 to £120 million in 1946 due to the sale of more than £1,100 million of overseas assets.
(ii) Britain's overseas financial and insurance business declined.
(iii) Income from shipping services fell following the loss of 30 per cent of the British Mercantile Marine.
(iv) Most serious of all was the adverse movement in Britain's terms of trade brought about by the steep rise in food and raw material prices. This was indeed a reversal of the situation following the First World War when overproduction of the primary producing countries led to a fall in the price of food and raw materials, thus improving Britain's terms of trade.
(v) Britain's commitments abroad became heavier mainly because of the need to maintain a larger contingent of troops in occupied territory.
(vi) The political division of the world into communist and non-communist countries affected trade because it was also a commercial division.
(vii) The growing dependence on the United States to provide essential supplies created a serious dollar shortage.

These circumstances necessitated a substantial increase in exports if Britain was to pay her way in the world, and yet her capacity to achieve such an aim was impaired by the war. The railways, iron and steel, and electricity generating plant had been badly run down; many houses and factories had been damaged or destroyed in the blitz; and the mercantile marine had suffered heavy damages. Furthermore, not all of Britain's efforts could be directed towards increased exports since the British people had endured considerable suffering and deprivation during the war, thus necessitating the allocation of some of the nation's resources in peace time towards the construction of new homes and better living standards.

Fortunately there was also a credit side to the balance sheet and in many ways Britain's prospects of promoting a successful recovery were much better than after the First World War. Attitudes were very different following the lessons learnt during the bitter years of depression between the wars. The Keynesian Revolution provided the means to combat mass unemployment and the White Paper on Employment Policy published in 1944 pledged that one of the primary aims and responsibilities of Government in the future would be the maintenance of a high and stable level of employment.

The Social Consequences

Britain's system of social services in 1939 was good compared with the provision of social services elsewhere. Basic reforms such as old age pensions and national insurance had been gradually extended and built upon since the early years of the century and a more humane outlook towards the treatment of the poor had been steadily evolving. Nevertheless, the system was not comprehensive, and it contained many inadequacies. Some people were still living in poverty and some of the vestiges of the old Poor Law still remained.

The Second World War considerably speeded up the move towards a fairer society as people of all classes strove together in a united effort to achieve victory. The community spirit was heightened by the sacrifice that was demanded from everyone, and the intermingling of people from different backgrounds in such circumstances as mass evacuation and aerial bombardment, brought the different classes closer together. Many of the inadequacies and lack of uniformities in the existing social services were also revealed by the exigencies of war.

On an international scale the Second World War highlighted the conflict between the three major political ideologies existing in the world, i.e. the ideologies of capitalism, communism and fascism. Each of these different systems sought through propaganda to convince people that their beliefs were the best basis on which to build the future. Dr Goebbels, the German propaganda chief, took great pains to impress upon the world the superiority of the so-called 1,000-year Reich, whilst the communists also went to great lengths to sell the virtues of their system.

Britain also needed a good plan upon which the new-model Britain could be built when the war was over. This plan was provided by the Beveridge Report of 1942, which proposed a national minimum of social security for everyone. The Report considered that everyone should have enough money to live on, as well as State provision of adequate health, housing and educational facilities. Two important steps were taken by the wartime coalition towards implementing these proposals, viz.

1. The Education Act, 1944, provided for free secondary education for all, the raising of the school leaving age to 15, and later 16, with

compulsory part-time education up to the age of 18, the abolition of fees in State secondary schools and better facilities for the support of university students. The main feature of this Act was the organisation of secondary education into three types of school: secondary modern, secondary grammar and secondary technical, with selection usually decided by the eleven plus examination. Lack of resources, however, prevented the full implementation of the Act. The school leaving age was not raised to 16 until 1971, and compulsory part-time education has still not been adopted.

2. The White Paper on Employment published in 1944 pledged the commitment of Government in the future to the maintenance of a high and stable level of employment.

International Preparations to Meet Post-War Difficulties

Many of the world's economic, political and social problems between the wars could have been avoided if nations had cooperated with each other both politically and economically instead of pursuing policies of economic nationalism and political isolationism. Bearing this in mind, a number of nations endeavoured during the Second World War to learn from their previous mistakes by making preparations to meet expected difficulties when the war was over. The following institutions were thus established for the purpose of facilitating the transition of the international economy from a wartime to a peace-time basis. Such institutions it was felt would help to establish a sound international economy based on peaceful cooperation.

1. The United Nations Relief and Rehabilitation Administration was established in 1943 to deal with the problem of displaced persons. Its main function was to care for, and repatriate, the victims of war.

2. The International Bank for Reconstruction and Development and the International Monetary Fund were established in 1944 to deal with the financial phases of reconstruction and the threat of inflation. These institutions were invaluable in restoring the necessary basis for international trade in a world ravaged by war.

3. The United Nations Organisation was established in 1945 to prevent international conflict and to settle international disputes.

Much of the initiative in setting up these institutions, as well as a large proportion of the capital needed to finance them, came from the United States. This represented a fundamental change in America's position in the world economy. Instead of withdrawing into isolation as after the First World War, the United States realised that as one of the two superpowers, she was no longer able to extricate herself from the world's economic and political problems. Indeed, with the world divided between the two distinct ideologies of capitalism and communism, the United States accepted a role of deep political and economic involvement in the non-communist world, accepting as she did that it was no longer in her interest to remain isolationist. Hence, since 1945 there has been unprecedented economic, political and military cooperation between the countries of Western Europe and the United States.

The Organisation for European Economic Cooperation was set up in 1948 as a direct consequence of this policy. The purpose of this organisation was to develop economic cooperation between member countries and to assist the United States Government in carrying out its programme of aid to Europe. Such cooperation brought about a relatively speedy recovery in Europe and paved the way for Britain to embark on a programme of reconstruction and reform.

Suggested Further Reading

Hancock, W. K., and Gowing, M., *The British War Economy*, H.M.S.O., London, 1949.

Milward, A. S., *The Economic Effects of the Two World Wars on Britain*, Macmillan, London, 1970.

Pollard, S., *The Development of the British Economy, 1914–1950*, Arnold, London, 1969.

Youngson, A. J., *Britain's Economic Growth, 1920–1966*, Allen & Unwin, London, 1967.

Exercises

1. What were the economic implications for Britain of 'total war' between 1939 and 1945?
2. Discuss the economic consequences for Britain of the Second World War.
3. Identify and discuss any short- or long-term benefits which Britain derived from the war.
4. In what ways, if any, did the Second World War influence Britain's position in the world economy?

Summary

1. During the war the Government involved itself in the management of the economy on an unprecedented scale.
2. Aerial attack resulted in damage to the main centres of production in Britain and many homes were damaged.
3. Britain's trading position was undermined by the war and there was a serious deterioration in Britain's balance of payments position.
4. The war speeded up the move towards a fairer society, and the Beveridge Report of 1942 provided the blueprint upon which the new-model Britain could be built when the war was over.
5. Plans were worked out during the war for more international economic and political cooperation in the future.

1950-79 Pop. 50.2m → 55.9m
1951-71 increased by 1/10th
Pop now stationary

CHAPTER TWENTY

POST-WAR SOCIAL POLICY

Population Trends Since 1945

Population trends since the war have been quite different from those of previous generations. Because of the low birth rates between the wars, the adult population after 1945 grew fairly slowly until the mid-1960s. However, fears of a declining population which were prevalent in the inter-war years (see p. 190) proved to be unfounded since during the Second World War the birth rate increased quite markedly from 14·7 per thousand in 1940 to 16·3 per thousand in 1945. After a drop in the birth rate during the early 1950s it revived again as the decade progressed, the upward trend lasting until 1965 when it reached 18·4 per 1,000, after which it fell again to 14·9 per 1,000 in 1972 and then down to 12·3 per 1,000 in 1978. Thus in the years between 1950 and 1979 population grew from 50·2 million to 55·9 million, the increase being due almost entirely to an excess of births over deaths. After increasing by about one tenth between 1951 and 1971, the population of the United Kingdom has now become almost stationary. It rose by only 0·6 per cent between 1971 and 1974, and has fallen by 0·2 per cent from then until 1978.

Because of the tendency over the past few decades for death rates to fall the structure of population has also changed, resulting in a larger proportion of the total population being in the older age groups.

This trend towards an ageing population in Britain since the war has had profound economic and social implications, namely:

1. The size of the actual working population has been affected but the contraction in the number of adult males entering the labour market has been offset by the growing tendency of married women to seek employment. In the early post-war years, when there was evidence of a manpower shortage, this influence could have had adverse effects on Britain's economic growth performance, but during the 1970s, with increasing unemployment, the trend probably helped alleviate the problem somewhat.

2. The pattern of demand can be expected to change since people in different age groups demand different types of things.

3. Older people tend to be less mobile than younger people; therefore an older working force can contribute towards industrial inertia and thus have a retarding effect on economic change.

4. An ageing population, together with the extension of full-time education amongst young people and the rise in birth rates over part of the period, has had the effect of increasing the proportion of the dependent population in relation to the working population. This means a bigger transfer burden of wealth in the form of taxation from the working population to the non-working proportion. This problem has

of course been made worse because of the disproportionate rise in the age groups which make the heaviest demands on the social services—namely, the young people and the elderly.

The Setting up of the Post-War Welfare State

Since 1945 the Welfare State has become an accepted part of the British way of life. The name itself is of quite recent origin and was probably first used by Archbishop William Temple, in his pamphlet *Citizen and Churchman*, published in 1941, in which he wrote: 'In place of the concept of the Power State we are led to that of the Welfare State'. The philosophy of the Welfare State had in fact been spelled out by Beatrice Webb in her famous Minority Report on the Poor Laws in 1909, when she spoke about the need for a basic minimum of social security for everyone as of right, but its realisation did not come about until all the political parties accepted the Beveridge plan of 1942 outlining a basic minimum of social security for everyone.

It was the Labour Party above all that identified itself with social reform because it had been committed for a long time to building a fairer society with more social justice embodying one nation and not two, as Disraeli had depicted in the second half of the nineteenth century. It was not surprising therefore that the success of the Labour Party in the 1945 General Election, which inaugurated the first ever majority Labour Government, was followed by a series of social reforms which swept away the last vestiges of the old Poor Law and provided the framework within which the better Britain was to be built. Now the State was not merely to be a policeman that kept law and order and intervened only with great reluctance in economic and social matters, in line with the laissez-faire philosophy that the best Government was the Government that governed least, but its role now was to promote positively the welfare of its citizens. This involved the Government in providing not only basic social security and equality of opportunity as far as was feasible in health, housing and education, but also an obligation on the part of the Government to steer the working of the market economy in the directions considered to be socially desirable.

The basic security for everyone, and not just those sections of the population who were considered to be most at risk, was provided by the Family Allowances Act, 1945, the National Insurance Act, 1946, the Industrial Injuries Act, 1946, and the National Assistance Act, 1948. The National Health Service Act, 1946, set up a comprehensive National Health Service available to everyone whatever their means, whilst the Children Act, 1948, provided for greater care and a better chance in life for the child deprived of a normal home life. Attention was also directed through the New Towns Act, 1946, and the Town and Country Planning Act, 1947, towards the improvement of general environmental standards.

These basic measures have since been extended and improved upon by numerous Acts of Parliament. Social security benefits, for example, have been increased several times and in 1966 a new system of Supplementary Benefits was introduced to replace National Assistance.

This was done because National Assistance had some of the stigma of the old Poor Law attached to it, and many people who were eligible for such assistance did not apply for it. Since 1968 these services have been administered by the Department of Health and Social Security and a Secretary of State for the Social Services has been appointed.

Basically there are two main elements in the services provided within the Welfare State: (i) there are those services providing cash benefits, which together form the system of social security, i.e. National Insurance (General and Industrial Injuries), National Assistance (now Supplementary Benefit), Family Allowances and War Pensions; (ii) there are the main services providing benefits in kind, i.e. Education, Housing and the National Health Service.

The Social Security System

Beveridge's plan for social security was intended to ensure that no one in the population would fall below a subsistence level. This was to be done by a comprehensive system of insurance, with flat-rate contributions linked closely to employment, and flat-rate benefits at subsistence level. Considerable emphasis was also to be placed on family allowances because of the strong correlation in the past between poverty and large families. Also, people were encouraged to supplement any benefits they might receive by undertaking additional private insurance. The National Assistance Scheme was devised as a 'safety net' for those who by one means or another fell outside the scope of the National Insurance scheme and it was thought that it would become increasingly obsolescent as the State Insurance Scheme became fully operational.

When the post-war Labour Government under the premiership of Clement Attlee embarked on setting up a system of Social Security they followed the Beveridge Report plan of 1942 very closely, and despite many changes the British social security system remains essentially the same as that set up by the Attlee Government.

The system basically consists of four main sectors:

1. The National Insurance Scheme. The main benefits are:

   retirement pensions,
   widows benefits,
   sickness, industrial injury and unemployment benefits,
   maternity grants and benefits,
   the death grant,
   invalidity pensions and allowances.

2. The supplementary benefits system.
3. Family allowances.
4. A variety of tax relief schemes (offering tax exemptions, e.g. to people contributing to private pension schemes).

The principal legislation now covering the National Insurance Scheme is the Social Security Act, 1975, which consolidated earlier legislation dating effectively from 1946. Under this Act, which became operational from April 1978 and which affects practically every employer and employee in Britain, the level of contribution must be reviewed annually with reference to changes in the general level of earnings. Contributions under the Act may also be changed according to the state of the national insurance fund.

Note: Details of the current level of insurance contributions and benefits may be obtained from the DHSS leaflet on Family Benefits and Pensions, which is published annually.

Private Occupational Schemes

Occupational pensions have been in existence long before the state scheme. However, the 1975 Social Security Pensions Act has accelerated the steady spread of private sector occupational pension schemes. The Government recognised that occupational schemes, to quote from the 1974 White Paper on pensions, 'are socially valuable and economically important', and was anxious to see the continued development of good occupational schemes.

The number of private pension schemes has in fact roughly doubled over the last 25 years and at least half the total of all employees are now covered by such schemes.

Table 32. Occupational Pension Schemes, 1975

	% whose employer has a scheme	*% who are members of a scheme*	*Coverage of schemes*					
			Men		*Women*		*Total*	
Private sector	80	48	52%	5·0m	17%	1·1m	39%	6.1m
Public sector	100	75	84%	3·7m	59%	1·7m	75%	5·4m
All employees	77	65	63%	8·7m	31%	2·8m	50%	11·5m

Source: *Department of Employment Gazette*, May 1977.

In 1975, when a full survey was made, there were 11½ million employees in occupational pension schemes, and 4 million retired employees getting pensions from these schemes. Whilst more and more private pension schemes are being developed in the private sector of industry the public sector pension schemes (i.e. for civil servants, employees of nationalised industries, etc.) do offer fuller coverage. However, whilst Government experts estimate that though there will be some further expansion of the occupational pension sector, nevertheless the limitations on this expansion are such that even by the end of the century fully one third of all retirement pensioner households will have no occupational pension of any sort. Therefore if poverty in old age is to be avoided in the future there will be great need for the reliance of old people on the State social security system.

Housing

Many lessons were learnt from the experience of the inter-war years with respect to the provision of housing. The two most important lessons of all were, first, that now there was a developed system of house purchase through mortgages extending over a long period—say twenty or thirty years—more and more people would become owner occupiers, including the better-off skilled manual workers; and, secondly, the supply of newer housing to let which before 1914 had been such a sound investment for the speculative landlord, would become almost the sole responsibility of local authorities. Thus the private rented sector has been declining rapidly since the end of the war, as Fig. 21 shows, due to the uneconomic forms of rent control imposed over the years, combined with subsidised competition from council housing and owner occupation.

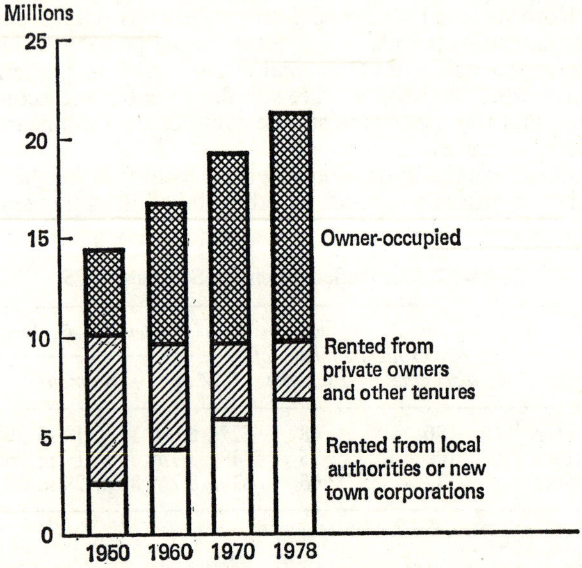

Fig. 21. United Kingdom stock of dwellings, by tenure.
(Source: *Housing and Construction Statistics*, Department of the Environment)

In 1939 a rough balance between the number of houses and families had been achieved as a result of vigorous housebuilding in both the public and private sectors during the 1920s and 1930s. However, by 1945 there was once again a serious housing shortage resulting from the cessation of housebuilding during the war and war damage, as well as increasing demand through changing demographic structure resulting in smaller family units.

The post-war Labour Government adopted the view that housebuilding should be confined largely to the public sector and that council housing should now cater for the whole community and not just the poor. Thus the Housing Act of 1946 changed the scope of the existing law by enacting that Local Authorities were under a duty to provide houses for all sections of the community and not just the working classes. Meanwhile rents of privately owned properties were pegged at the 1939 level, which made it increasingly difficult for landlords to undertake necessary repairs when repair costs rose.

During the Conservative period of office between 1951 and 1964 a free market in housing was restored and attempts were made to confine Local Authority building to slum clearance and the relief of overcrowding. In the meantime the 1957 Rent Act attempted to bring about a big increase in the supply of privately rented houses by introducing a large-scale measure of de-control. All houses became de-controlled that had a rateable value of £30 or more (with the exception of London and Scotland where the rateable value was to be £40 or more) and other rent controls ceased with a change of tenant. The hoped-for effects, however, on the supply of rented houses did not take place since private letting still was not an economic proposition. Hence landlords simply waited to gain vacant possession of their properties and then sold, with the result that between 1957 and 1962 about 1·8 million dwellings switched from private renting to owner occupation.

Thus the majority of people have shown that, given the choice, they would prefer to own their own houses rather than rent them. Home ownership has of course proved to be the best investment that most people make in their lives and has been responsible for considerable redistribution of the national wealth over the past few years. Home owners do in fact buy an appreciating asset with depreciating money and have an added bonus of tax allowances which have made actual repayments negligible in real terms. Home ownership amongst the less well paid has meanwhile been helped by the 1967 Option Mortgage Scheme which gives borrowers the option of either claiming their income tax relief on the interest payment on their loan, or of forgoing tax relief and having the rate of interest they pay reduced by up to 2 per cent, whilst Mrs Thatcher's Conservative Government in 1980 introduced provisions making council houses available for purchase by sitting tenants at bargain prices.

Policies towards the letting of private accommodation have changed considerably from time to time depending to some extent upon which political party was in power. When the Labour Party was returned to office between 1964 and 1970 policy was switched by the Rent Act, 1965, towards favouring the tenant more by introducing rent regulation based on so-called 'fair rents' in respect of houses with a rateable value of up to £200. This policy was subsequently changed by the Conservatives in 1972 by their Housing Finance Act which sought to create a 'fair deal for housing' by raising all rents whilst at the same time providing rent aid or remission for those who were eligible. Policy once again was switched back towards favouring the tenant as opposed to the landlord when Labour were returned to office and in 1975 they introduced measures which gave tenants in privately rented furnished accommodation security of tenure. Meanwhile, in the public sector the Housing Rents and Subsidies Act, 1975, introduced a new housing subsidy system which required local authorities to charge their tenants reasonable rents without making a profit, whilst at the same time attempting to keep a balance between the interests of tenants and ratepayers. Supplementary subsidies were also made available to assist local authorities throughout Britain with slum clearance and a national system of rent rebates and allowances covering most tenants was introduced.

Another important aspect of housing policy over the years has been the availability of grants to improve properties in need of repairs or modernisation. The Conservatives in their Housing Act of 1962 introduced improvement grants with the aim of encouraging landlords to increase the stock of privately rented accommodation available, but the grants tended to be used much more by owner-occupiers than by landlords, many of whom looked on their properties as a burden to be got rid of as soon as possible. However, in 1968 the Labour Government introduced a White Paper entitled 'Old Houses into New Homes', which increased grant levels for housing improvements, and introduced the concept of a General Improvement Area. Thus the total number of dwellings in Great Britain for which improvement grants were approved increased from 124,000 in 1969 to 453,000 in 1973, and the amount of grant-aided improvement work approved increased from about £70 million to £460 million in the same period.

A glance at housing statistics since the war are really quite impressive. Between 1945 and 1975 some 8½ million houses were built in Great Britain and in addition to the new stock 3 million homes have been improved. Now more than half the homes in the country have been built since 1945 or have been modernised. Thus statistically compared with international standards the country is now relatively well housed, having in 1978 an estimated 20·1 million households with 2·8 inhabitants per household. Thus it is important to realise that there is no longer a national housing problem; rather there are different problems in different parts of the country. London and some of the big conurbations do have housing shortages but in contrast to this there are now areas of housing surplus—for example, in South Wales and North Lancashire—where population decline results in low demand for housing, particularly older housing, and to some dereliction, whilst in some towns there is evidence that overbuilding of council housing has taken place during the 1970s.

In 1978, of new building erected, 43 per cent was for the public sector, and 57 per cent for the private sector. The public sector's proportion has tended to decline in recent years, particularly in the period up to 1980 due to pressure to cut public expenditure. All the signs are now that housebuilding is beginning to slow down. In 1968 there were 220,000 private sector and 192,000 public sector dwellings completed, whereas in 1979 only about 234,000 houses were built, 133,000 for the private and 101,000 for the public sector. The stock of dwellings net of demolitions was rising at the rate of about 1½ per cent a year in the 1950s but had now slowed down to less than 1 per cent. By the end of the 1970s the proportion of housing occupied by owners had risen steadily to 54 per cent; 32 per cent being rented from local authorities and other public bodies, and 14 per cent being privately rented.

Thus, whilst in theory we ought by the 1980s to be within sight of an end to the housing problem, in practice by concentrating on particular subgroups like the homeless, of which in 1978 there were 26,000 families, or immigrants, or on the outworn parts of our large cities, we can still say that we have a long way to go.

Education

One of the biggest landmarks in educational reform this century has been the 1944 Education Act, which introduced a system of universal and free secondary education for all (see p. 202). This Act has been described as the greatest Education Act ever, and it provides the basis of our present education system.

What the Act did was to set up a tripartite system of secondary education—namely, secondary grammar, secondary technical and secondary modern, with selection decided by the eleven plus examination. Thus the former county and county borough secondary schools were transformed into grammar schools for the more academic pupils while the few existing junior technical schools became the secondary technical schools for pupils with academic ability but with a technical bias. These schools were far outnumbered by the secondary grammar schools. The secondary modern schools for the less academic majority were formed from the existing senior elementary schools.

Thus over the years, Great Britain, in common with most other advanced industrial countries, has developed a complex system of educational services run by the State or by institutions closely associated with it. This has been achieved at enormous public cost. Public expenditure on education in the United Kingdom in 1978 amounted to £8,756 million. This expenditure has more than doubled its share of the Gross National Product since 1951, as Table 33 shows.

Table 33. Growth of United Kingdom Public Expenditure on Education at Current Prices

Year	*Public education expenditure* (£m)	*Gross national product* (£m)	*Public education expenditure as a proportion of GNP* (%)
1951	401	12,926	3·10
1956	637	18,499	3·44
1961	1,173	24,491	4·79
1966	1,768	33,492	5·28
1970	2,640	44,045	6·00
1971	3,023	49,571	6·10
1972	3,559	55,519	6·41
1973	4,083	64,830	6·30
1974	4,746	74,903	6·34
1975	6,840	94,095	7·27

Source: *National Income and Expenditure Accounts.*

Thus education has undoubtedly been a growth industry from 1951 onwards due to the big increase in demand for education. This increase in demand has been brought about by wider age groups within the span of compulsory education, more children going on to the senior forms of secondary education, and many of these young people then going on to further and higher education.

By the 1960s secondary education was once again going through a period of change since there was a growing feeling that the secondary education system set up under the 1944 Education Act was too discriminatory and too wasteful of the nation's talent. The idea of a 'comprehensive school' had been gaining support in some quarters during the 1950s and the Labour election programme of 1964 included strong support for such a system. Once elected, the Labour Government in 1965 requested that all local education authorities should plan the organisation of secondary education on comprehensive lines. With a few exceptions most local authorities complied with this request and those that did not became 'threatened' by the Education Act 1976, which required local education authorities to go comprehensive.

The numbers of students in full-time further and higher education has also increased rapidly since the war. Higher education received a big boost in 1963 with the Robbins Report on Higher Education, which proposed a programme of vast expansion, and which was at once accepted in principle by the Government. The 1960s were therefore boom years for higher education and in 1965 the polytechnics were established through the amalgamation of some of the country's main colleges of commerce, art and technology. The student population in higher education thus rose from less than 200,000 in the early 1960s to around half a million full-time students by the late 1970s. This has led to a big increase in the 'qualification' density of the British population. In 1966 there were about 780,000 economically active people who possessed a degree or an equivalent professional qualification. By the early 1980s the figure was well over a million.

Much criticism has been levelled over the years at the British educational system. The system of a high degree of selectivity in the past, both with respect to income and levels of intelligence, has probably contributed towards a 'them and us' attitude between workers and management which has resulted in inadequate communication and a failure to recognise mutual self-interest and interdependence. Also the 'non-vocational' character of many courses has led some people to question the value of such courses to the nation, particularly during times of economic stringency and when there are high levels of unemployment amongst graduates. There is no doubt that in the past there has been a bias towards the arts and social science subjects, and away from the applied scientific, engineering and business studies which can be related to a country's potential economic efficiency. It could therefore be argued that the educational system in the United Kingdom has contributed towards Britain's poor productive performance which is undoubtedly at the root of Britain's economic ills.

Since public expenditure on education has grown so rapidly since 1945 and represents such a large proportion of the gross national product it is not surprising that attempts have been made to use the resources available as efficiently as possible to secure more educational equality. It was with this aim in mind that the 'Plowden Report' of 1967 advocated the establishment of 'Educational Priority Areas' to which scarce resources could be channelled in order to redress the imbalance in socially deprived areas. Also, after 1979, education became a prime area for expenditure cuts, when Government economic policy was directed towards cutting the Public Sector Borrowing Requirement as one of its prime objectives.

Health

Since the Second World War Britain has developed a comprehensive Health Service in line with the ideas put forward in the Beveridge Report of 1942, which envisaged a comprehensive health service, covering all the necessary services from general practitioner to hospital consultant, and free to all. The legislation upon which the system is based was passed in 1946, and came into force in 1948.

Health services up to the Second World War had grown up in a piecemeal fashion and consisted basically of three parts:

1. There were the general practitioner services which had grown out of Lloyd George's National Insurance Scheme of 1911. Under this scheme insurance against sickness was introduced for workers earning less than £250 per year. At first the scheme was limited in scope but between the two world wars it was extended to cover most workers so that by 1939 more than half the population was covered by a basic family doctor scheme.
2. There was the hospital service, which in some cases had grown out of the sick-bays of the workhouses, whilst in others they had been set up by the Local Authorities or depended largely on charity, as did the voluntary hospitals, some of which stretched back into the distant past, such as St Bartholomews which was founded in the Middle Ages.
3. Local Authority services had evolved largely from the public health and education reforms of the previous seventy years. Since 1875 Local Authorities had had Medical Officers of Health and the better ones provided extensive services for mother and child care, whilst a school medical service had been run by the Local Authorities since 1907.

Thus when the National Health Service was set up under the guidance of the Minister of Health, Mr Aneurin Bevan, there were many vested interests to cater for, and it is not surprising that there arose a tripartite structure:

1. The general practitioner service, which comprised the family doctors, dentists, opticians and chemists. These were to be administered by over 160 local executive councils on which doctors, dentists and pharmacists were to be represented. Private practitioners were not compelled to join the service but almost all of them did.
2. The hospital and specialist services, which were to be administered through 20 regional hospital boards and nearly 500 hospital management committees, all of which were to be under the authority of the Minister of Health.
3. The Local Authority services, consisting of maternity and child welfare, services for the prevention of illness, home visiting, health visiting, home nursing, domestic help, ambulance services, etc., which were to be administered by the larger local authorities.

Since the setting up of the National Health Service it has been subject to much criticism and experienced many problems. Doctors no doubt found it difficult to work within a framework of regulations and red tape whilst hospitals found it difficult to fit their organisation into a larger national scheme. Also, the system has been open to much abuse by patients, many of whom no doubt have demanded an undue amount of attention for minor troubles. The structure of the Health Service itself caused many problems in the early years of its operation because of the separation of separate forms of medical care which should be operated in close conjunction—for example, in maternity and child welfare cases all three branches of the medical service were involved: the mother and baby would be under the care of their family doctor as well as the hospital in which the baby was born, and in addition the mother and baby would be involved with Local Authority clinics and health visitors. It was with this problem in mind that the Health Service was restructured in 1974.

Under the new structure the three branches of the Health Service, i.e. the hospital services, the family practitioner services and the Local Authorities' services, have been unified and three operating levels were set up: (i) the Region; (ii) the Area; and (iii) the District (see Fig. 22).

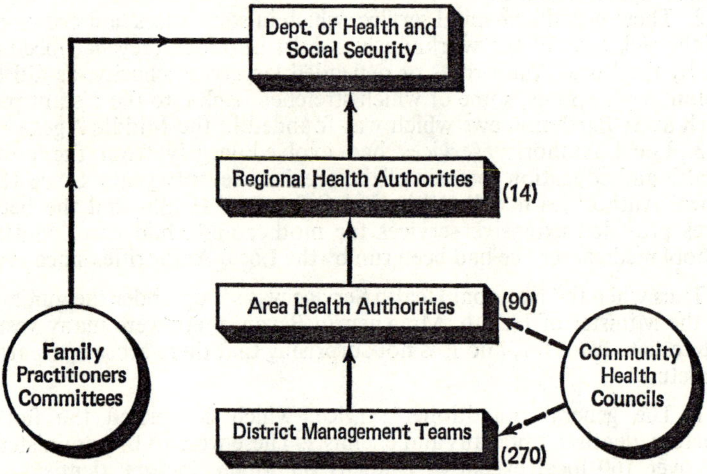

Fig. 22. Structure of the National Health Service from 1974.

Since 1974, the new structure which was designed to overcome the divisions of the tripartite structure and present a unified and closely coordinated system, has itself been the subject of much criticism. The main criticism has been that of too much red tape and bureaucracy which has slowed down decision-making and absorbed scarce resources, which has led some people to think that reorganisation was unnecessary and all that was wrong previously was lack of resources.

This question of lack of resources has been a constant problem for the National Health Service since its inception in 1948. At first the problem was dealing with the large backlog of unsatisfied demand from those who previously could not afford the treatment, especially with respect to dental and ophthalmic services. This was one of the factors leading to the introduction of prescription and other charges in 1952, thus destroying the Beveridge ideal of a Health Service free of charge for everyone. The problem in recent years has been that of inflation, made particularly worse in the Health Service due to its labour-intensive nature, plus the fact that more sophisticated and expensive forms of treatment have been developed. This problem has also been aggravated by other factors. For example, in a steadily evolving, more sophisticated and better educated society, people have rising expectations, are better informed about treatment and therefore expect their doctors to keep them healthier. In addition, the growth of the elderly, dependent population has put great strains and stresses on the Health Service.

Increasingly during the 1970s, largely because of lack of funds and the labour-intensive nature of the Service, health care workers have become amongst the poorest paid in the community. This has led to strained industrial relations which, together with the other problems facing the National Health Service, has led some observers to fear that the Service was in the process of breaking down.

Meanwhile, a long-standing controversial debate has been going on about the place of private medicine within the Health Service since many doctors work both privately and for the N.H.S.—for example, about half of hospital consultants undertake some part-time private work. Government attitudes towards this practice vary according to which party is in power, with the Conservatives generally favouring more private practice and Labour sticking to the principle of a public Health Service. In 1976, the Labour Government passed the National Health Service Act which was designed to phase out the 'pay beds' in National Health Service hospitals, except for overseas patients, and introduced licences for private nursing homes and hospitals.

Suggested Further Reading

Byrne, A., and Padfield, C., *Social Services Made Simple*, Heinemann, London, 1978.

Cooper, M. H. (Editor), *Social Policy, A Survey of Recent Developments*, Blackwell, Oxford, 1973.

Sleeman, J. F., *The Welfare State. Its Aims and Benefits*, Allen and Unwin, London, 1973.

Exercises

1. Critically assess the aims and achievement of the Welfare State set up after 1945.
2. How successful has the system of social security based on the Beveridge Report recommendations been in eradicating poverty in Britain?
3. Assess the extent to which educational reforms after the Second World War have been successful in providing equality of educational opportunity for all.
4. Account for the crisis in the British National Health Service during the 1970s.

Summary

1. The population of the United Kingdom grew from 50·2 million to 55·9 million between 1950 and 1979 and has now become almost stationary. The trend has been towards an ageing population and this has caused profound economic and social implications.

2. In the immediate post-war years a series of measures were introduced which established a 'Welfare State', which promised to provide everyone with a basic minimum of social security as of right.

3. Social security was to be provided through a comprehensive system of insurance, and people were encouraged to supplement any benefits they might receive by undertaking additional private insurance.

4. Since the war more people have become owner occupiers of housing and the supply of newer housing to let has become almost the sole responsibility of local authorities.

5. Statistically there is now no longer a national housing problem but rather there are different problems in different parts of the country.

6. In common with many other advanced countries Britain has developed at enormous public cost a complex system of educational services run by the State or by institutions closely associated with it.

7. Britain set up a comprehensive National Health Service providing free treatment to everyone as of right, but rising costs and industrial troubles have brought it to the verge of breakdown during the 1970s.

CHAPTER TWENTY-ONE

POST-WAR ECONOMIC POLICY

Government Management of the Economy

The main aims of macro-economic policy are the achievement of full employment, an adequate rate of economic growth, price stability and a balance of payments surplus. Governments in the post-war period have been much more conscious than their predecessors of their responsibilities with respect to the achievement of these aims though experience has shown that the attainment of any one of them may be incompatible with the complete attainment of the others. Economic growth, for example, may create problems for the balance of payments, whilst full employment may affect the level of prices.

It was John Maynard Keynes in the 1930s who started the process of changing the way of thinking about economic problems. He considered that mass unemployment was due to the lack of effective demand and that governments ought to influence the level of effective demand through the use of monetary and fiscal policy. Monetary policy involves the Government in manipulating the money supply by such measures as enforcing the reserve assets ratio of the banks, fixing lending ceilings, calling for special deposits, selling bonds in order to mop up excess liquidity, changing interest rates or directing the banks to lend only for approved purposes. Fiscal policy, however, is concerned with raising revenue through taxation and working towards budget deficits or surpluses, which is of prime concern for the Government because this influences the level of demand in the economy.

A government which follows the Keynesian school of thought on economic management would use fiscal policy as its main tool with the aim of bringing about changes in the size of the national income and consequently altering the level of employment and production.

A second school of thought on economic management which has become the vogue in the Conservative administration of the early 1980s is the monetarist school of thought. One of its major proponents is Milton Friedman, and it believes that the money supply is the most effective lever bearing on employment and production.

Whilst both fiscal and monetary policy are both important tools of economic management most economists tend to emphasise the efficacy of either one or the other, and governments tend to favour one school of thought or the other. For a long time after the war the Keynesian school of thought was favoured, though this did not mean to say that monetary policy was considered unimportant. Following the period of 'cheap' money policy in the immediate post-war period, when interest rates were deliberately held low, monetary policy in the 1950s and 1960s was used in conjunction with fiscal policy as a tool of demand management. In particular, with a fixed exchange rate, monetary policy was frequently dictated by external developments, with a balance of payments deficit and pressure on sterling leading to restrictive monetary and fiscal measures. At other times when fiscal policy was expansionary and there was no immediate external balance problem, monetary policy was usually accommodating. The main focus of attention for monetary policy was interest rates, with the timing of changes in short-term rates being determined mostly by leading rate changes acting as a signal. There was also quite frequent variation of hire-purchase terms and, particularly in the latter part of the 1960s, directives on bank lending to control the volume and allocation of credit.

Between 1945 and the early 1970s, successive governments steered the economy in a jerky fashion through using the tools of fiscal and monetary policies and experience showed that during times of inflation the level of unemployment was high, thus showing a fairly stable inverse relationship between the rate of unemployment and the rate of inflation. By the mid-1970s, however, the combination of these problems failed to occur in the usual way, and inflation and unemployment began to advance hand in hand so that by 1975 inflation had reached 25 per cent per annum and unemployment was over a million. The name 'stagflation' has been given by economists to this relatively new phenomenon of high inflation and high unemployment, which was a situation so different from that of the 1930s when high unemployment could be alleviated by increasing public spending—which now simply causes prices to rise even further, thus causing even more unemployment. It was becoming obvious by the mid-1970s that no combination of monetary and fiscal policies of the orthodox kind could deal with the situation, so emphasis began to be placed on a third kind of policy directly controlling prices and incomes, which had first been introduced in the United Kingdom in the mid-1960s and has subsequently been used for a number of purposes on and off by different governments. Experience showed in the second half of the 1970s that prices and incomes policies only appeared to work successfully over a short period of time. In 1979 policy was switched towards putting great emphasis on monetary policy as a means to cure the nation's economic ills, in line with Professor Friedman's ideas and theories.

Thus post-war governments have been aware of what the main economic problems are and have developed the means to cure them, but whilst they may have learnt how to achieve one or more of the main economic aims at any particular time through the use of the Government's tools of economic management—namely, fiscal, monetary and prices and incomes policies—the achievement of fulfilling all the aims at the same time has proved to be more difficult.

Full Employment

There was widespread support during the 1940s for the view that there should not be a return to the type of mass unemployment experienced between the wars when there had been more than a million men, and during the World Economic Blizzard in the early 1930s more than two and a half million men, looking for work and unable to find it. This level of unemployment had caused untold misery and suffering and had created a considerable amount of class antagonism and bitterness. It was also wasteful of the nation's resources because it prevented the economy from achieving its highest and most efficient level of output. Thus the White Paper on Employment Policy, 1944, stated quite categorically that 'the Government accept as one of their primary aims and responsibilities the maintenance of a high and stable level of employment after the war'. Such a pledge had been made practicable following the publication in 1936 of J. M. Keynes's *General Theory of Employment, Interest and Money*, which demonstrated how governments could achieve full employment through the management of aggregate monetary demand.

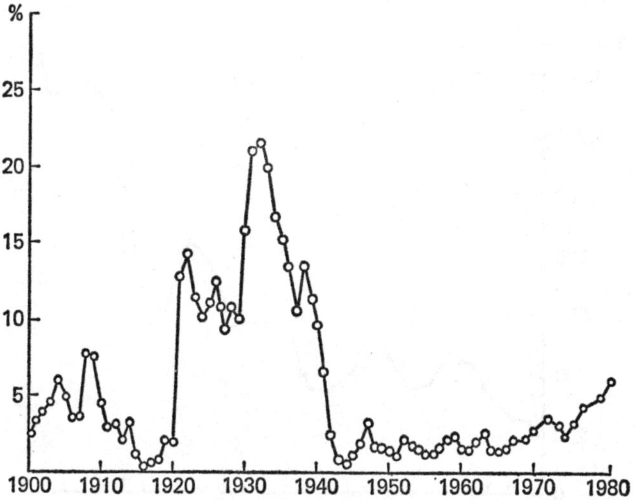

Fig. 23. Unemployment in the United Kingdom in the twentieth century.

As can be seen from Fig. 23, unemployment after 1945 was considerably below the percentage levels achieved during the inter-war period. In fact, in the early post-war years full employment as a policy aim was a prime economic objective because of the bitter memories amongst the workforce of the mass unemployment experienced between the wars. In the early post-war years unemployment was kept below 2 per cent, a level many economists might consider to be too low since the aim of having more vacancies than there are unemployed workers to fill can result in over-full employment which can contribute towards inflation, balance of payments difficulties, a high labour turnover, and a shortage of skilled workers.

An important factor that should be borne in mind when considering post-war unemployment levels is the changing demographic structure which meant that since the 1930s a decreasing proportion of the population was of working age, resulting in the working population not keeping pace with the growth in total population. This, together with the rising school leaving age and more young people going on into further and higher education, has restricted the supply of labour onto the labour market. However, account must also be taken, as a counter-balancing factor, of the growing numbers of women who work, particularly married women, since the proportion of women in the total working population increased from 32 per cent in 1951 to 36 per cent by 1971. In spite of this factor, however, the working population has still been a declining proportion of the total population, a factor which has no doubt influenced the levels of unemployment over the years.

Thus unemployment, which was rarely less than 10 per cent throughout the inter-war years, was below 3 per cent between 1945 and the early 1970s. However, unemployment has been on a rising trend since the mid-1960s.

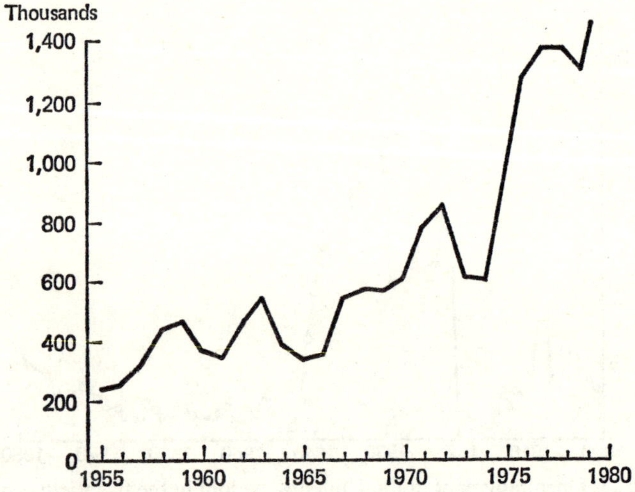

Fig. 24. United Kingdom unemployment, excluding school leavers (annual averages).

(Source: *Economic Progress Report*, September 1980)

During the 1970s the trend has been positively upwards and rose above 4 per cent for the first time in mid-1975. Since 1975 the unemployment rate has soared, reaching 1,696,000 by August 1980, which represents over 6 per cent of the total working population. It is important to note, however, that this phenomenon has been experienced by many other industrialised countries, as Fig. 25 shows.

The unemployment rate is by no means universal throughout the country and regional unemployment problems continue to persist. London and the South-East is still the most prosperous area of the United Kingdom with unemployment levels below the national average, whilst other areas, such as Scotland, Wales and Northern Ireland, have unemployment levels above the national average.

The regional disparities which exist have been partly due to the decline of the basic staple industries of shipbuilding, mining, textiles

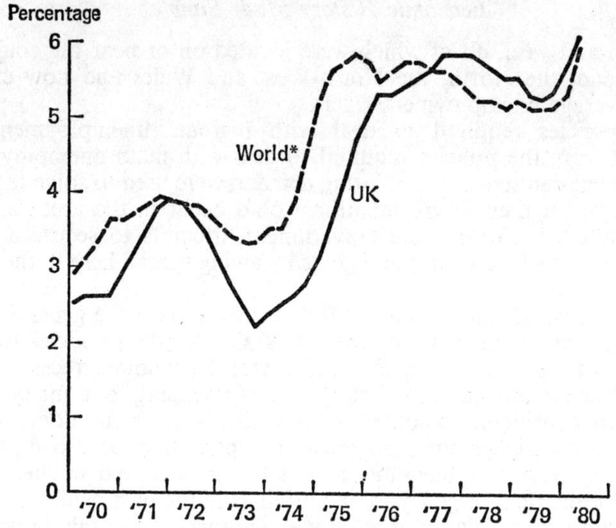

Fig. 25. World and United Kingdom unemployment (seasonally adjusted).

*For some countries seasonally adjusted data were not available and unadjusted rates have been used.

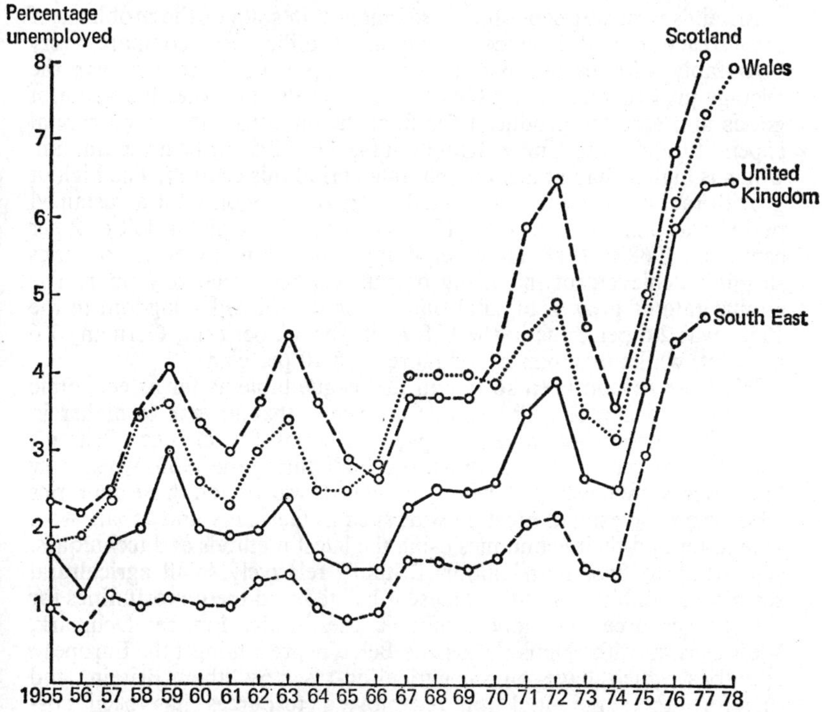

Fig. 26. Unemployment in Britain by region.

and iron and steel, all of which were located on or near the coalfields in Scotland, the North, the North-West and Wales and now exhibit above average unemployment levels.

The policies required to deal with regional unemployment are different from the policies required to deal with mass unemployment. If the Keynesian remedy of reflating demand were used to solve regional unemployment then severe inflation would occur in the areas already fully employed. Instead, the Government attempts to secure a more equitable balance between the regions by giving special help to the areas in need.

Various reasons have been put forward to explain the general rising level of unemployment during the 1970s. Government policies to curb inflation as well as the effects of the world economic recession are amongst the main causes of rising unemployment, but many other factors are considered to contribute towards the problem. Some people consider that higher unemployment compensation and compulsory redundancy payments have meant that the unemployed worker is not faced with the same urgency to find a job as in the past, whilst employment protection legislation discourages employers from taking on staff who might at some later date be difficult to get rid of.

Economic Growth

Britain's post-war economic performance, in spite of the problems of reconstruction and balance of payments difficulties, compares very favourably with earlier periods of development. Since the war the average growth rate of the Gross Domestic Product (i.e. the value of goods and services produced for final use in consumption or capital expenditure) for the United Kingdom has been 2·5 per cent per annum, which is higher than at any comparable period this century. The highest growth rate achieved by the United Kingdom economy for a sustained period was 3·25 per cent from 1958 to 1968, after which it fell to 2 per cent from 1968 to 1978. However, compared with many other countries Britain's achievement in raising output has been relatively poor. The annual rate of growth of total output for the United Kingdom in the 1950s was 2·6 per cent; in the U.S.A. it was 3·2 per cent, Germany 7·6 per cent, whilst in Japan it was more than 10 per cent.

Why has Britain been so low in the league table as far as economic growth is concerned? The simple answer is that growth is higher in those countries that have a bigger potential for change. Britain's potential for growth, for example, was high during the 1930s when 'new industries' were developed, whilst in the post-war period those countries which were devastated most by war, such as Germany and Japan, were able to rebuild their economies using the latest methods and techniques. According to Professor Kaldor, Britain's relatively small agricultural sector has inhibited growth because it has reduced the opportunities for shifting resources to more profitable uses. Italy, France, Denmark, West Germany, the Netherlands and Belgium are amongst the European countries which have bigger agricultural sectors than Britain, and therefore their potential for redeploying resources has been correspondingly greater.

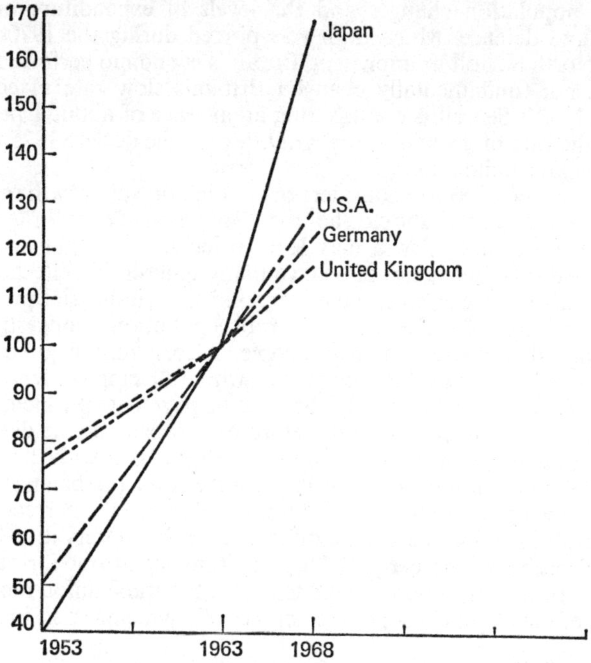

Fig. 27. Comparative growth rates.

Economic growth in a trading country such as that of Britain must derive from growth in exports, as well as growth in domestic demand, which inevitably leads to higher imports. But export performance and import penetration of the domestic market depend on the competitiveness of British goods and services in overseas markets. Insufficient international competitiveness has been a recurring problem through much of the post-war period, when the temporary attainment of an average growth rate of more than 4 per cent per year over a two-year period has invariably produced a current account deficit on the Balance of Payments. This has focused attention on better export performance as an important objective in a strategy to improve economic growth, and this in turn has led to concentration on manufacturing industry's performance as a crucial factor in determining overall growth potential. This is because of the overwhelming importance of manufactures in British exports. The trend has been in the post-war years for Britain's share of world trade in manufactures to decline and this together with an increase in the imports of manufactured goods has led many economists and politicians to conclude that a major factor in Britain's poor economic growth rate has been a general lack of competitiveness of her manufacturing industry. Theories and explanations for this phenomenon abound, not least of which are lack of investment and the attitude of trade unionists and management to change.

There are of course other factors which influence economic growth, such as population changes and the levels of expenditure on social welfare and defence. Much faith was pinned during the 1970s on the role of North Sea oil in improving Britain's economic performance but this has not fundamentally changed Britain's slow rate of economic growth. North Sea oil is contributing an average of about ½ per cent a year to the rate of growth of real G.D.P. over the decade 1975 to 1985, as production builds up.

Not everyone of course considers that a high rate of growth regardless of the consequences should be the Government's main economic objective. Economic growth may lead to increased output and higher living standards, but it can also have many undesirable effects as well. The Japanese, for example, have increased their industrial production at the expense of inflicting intolerable pollution, congestion and psychological pressures on their people. Also, whilst a good rate of economic growth may be compatible with full employment, it may contribute towards inflation and balance of payments problems.

Post-war governments have therefore had to balance the desirability of having full employment and rising living standards with the problem of controlling inflation and securing a surplus on the balance of payments, knowing full well that any failure to achieve the correct balance could result in serious economic difficulties. The Conservative Government's decision in the early 1970s, for example, to opt for economic growth with the full support and backing of the trade union movement, was one of the major causes of the balance of payments crisis in 1973/4.

Price Stability

Inflation, or the fall in the value of money due to rising prices, has increasingly become a serious problem in Britain. In 1969, earnings were up 240 per cent on their 1947 level, and retail prices were up 138 per cent. During the 1970s, however, when there was a considerable rise in important prices such as those of oil, raw materials and foodstuffs, and when many wage settlements were difficult to justify in terms of productivity, and public expenditure was running at a high level, the rate of inflation shot up reaching a peak level of 24·2 per cent in 1975, after which it dropped to 8·3 per cent in 1978, then rose to 18·0 per cent in 1980 and then began to fall again. Britain's average rate of inflation between 1969 and 1979, as measured by the rise in retail prices, was 12·5 per cent per year, which was slightly greater than that of Italy (12·3 per cent) and considerably more than that of Japan (9 per cent), the United States (7·1 per cent), France (8·8 per cent) or Germany (4·9 per cent). The fact that the Retail Price Index has tended to rise faster in Britain than in other major countries has had profound economic implications for Britain, since it has made it more difficult for Britain to sell goods abroad whilst manufactured imports have tended to increase in volume due to their relative cheapness. This in turn has posed a threat to the maintenance of full employment and the attainment of a reasonable level of growth since British governments have found that it is virtually impossible to achieve full employment and price stability at the same time, whilst price stability also seems to be incompatible with the achievement of an acceptable level of growth.

The traditional methods of solving this inflation have been to deflate the economy using the Keynesian tools of monetary and fiscal policies. Thus on the monetary side, throughout the 1950s and 1960s, credit squeezes were regularly introduced by raising the bank lending rate, imposing restrictions on bank lending and making the borrowing of money through hire purchase agreements more difficult. Each of these measures was designed to reduce the amount of credit available to individuals and companies and thus to reduce the pressure of demand. Money was also withdrawn from the economy from time to time through increased taxation, though this in itself tended to be inflationary as increased indirect taxes led to higher prices and increased direct taxes led to bigger wage demands. Thus a reduction in the rate of inflation was achieved only at the expense of rising unemployment, as Fig. 28 shows.

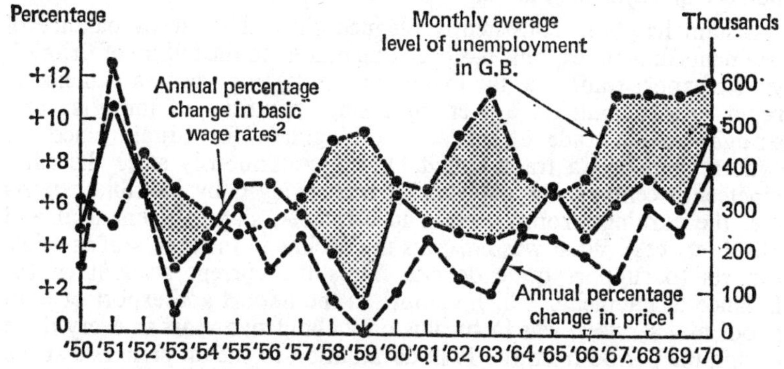

Fig. 28. Level of unemployment and annual change in prices and wages, 1950–70.

(Source: *Barclay's Bank Review*)

Notes

1. Retail prices, mid-Dec. to mid-Dec.
2. Hourly rates from 1956, weekly rates before 1956; 1956 figure for 11 months expressed at annual rate.
3. Figures for period to July expressed as annual rates in case of wages and prices.

These traditional policies for deflating the economy proved to be inadequate on occasions, and were therefore reinforced by more drastic measures. In 1948, the Attlee Government introduced a temporary wage and price freeze, and in 1961 the Conservative Chancellor of the Exchequer, Selwyn Lloyd, introduced a pay pause. By the mid-1960s, the balance of payments problem had become so serious that Harold Wilson's Labour Government set up in 1965 a National Board for Prices and Incomes, and in 1966 a pay and prices freeze was introduced for six months—to be followed by a period of severe restraint during which increases were to be paid to the poorly paid and those showing increases in productivity. Government efforts to contain inflationary pressures through pay policy guidelines continued into the 1970s but emphasis shifted towards achieving an atmosphere of moderation through the voluntary observance of non-statutory guidelines, rather than statutory limits.

The rapid acceleration of inflation during the 1970s led to counter-inflation objectives assuming a greater importance than before and considerable discussion turned towards the role of monetary policy. Before the late 1970s there had never been a prolonged tight monetary squeeze in the United Kingdom and therefore there was considerable speculation as to whether or not such a policy would work in bringing down inflation. The post-1979 Conservative Government considered that a prolonged, tight monetary squeeze would bring down the rate of inflation and therefore monetary policy became central to the Government's economic strategy.

Balance of Payments Surplus

Britain has been consistently plagued since the war by balance of payments difficulties. This has been due mainly to the failure of Britain's visible export trade (i.e. the export of goods) to grow at a sufficiently rapid rate to match the ever increasing quantities of imports. This straight visible trade deficit was nothing new for Britain since the country had had a trade deficit almost continuously since the early nineteenth century, the gap having been bridged by invisible exports (i.e. the earnings from overseas investments, shipping, financial and other services). What was new was the decline in the ability of invisible exports to support trade deficits. Thus the current account of the Balance of Payments, which comprised the import and export of both goods and services, was in surplus only about two years in every three during the period from the 1949 devaluation to the oil price rise at the end of 1973.

This current account deficit on the balance of payments over the years has usually meant downward pressure on the sterling exchange rate and an outflow of reserves. When this happened, deflationary fiscal and monetary measures were introduced in order (i) to bring about an improvement in the current account of the Balance of Payments, (ii) to discourage speculation against the exchange rate and (iii) to prevent short-term capital inflow as a result of higher interest rates, thus insulating the internal credit structure from outside influences.

For most of the period Britain was on a fixed exchange rate, and it was largely because of the outflow of reserves for supporting the exchange rate during periods of selling pressure that governments took deflationary action when they ran into current account deficits in their Balance of Payments. If this deflationary action had not been taken it would have been necessary to devalue the currency, as happened in 1949 and 1967.

In the post-war period balance of payments problems have placed great constraints on British governments in their economic policy-making since attempts to secure fuller employment or faster economic growth have caused prices to rise, which in turn has led to external deficits in the trade balance. When this happened governments imposed restraints on domestic activity, thus producing a jerky pattern of growth, commonly referred to as the 'stop-go' cycle (see Fig. 29).

The period between 1952 and 1964, for example, falls into three distinct cycles, i.e. 1952–5, 1956–60 and 1961–4. Each of these periods begins with a trade surplus and rising unemployment. As soon as deficits occurred unemployment tended to fall and prices tended to rise more rapidly, causing a higher level of demand and a rise in imports. Monetary and fiscal measures were then introduced to dampen down the boom and secure a surplus on the balance of payments. Devaluation

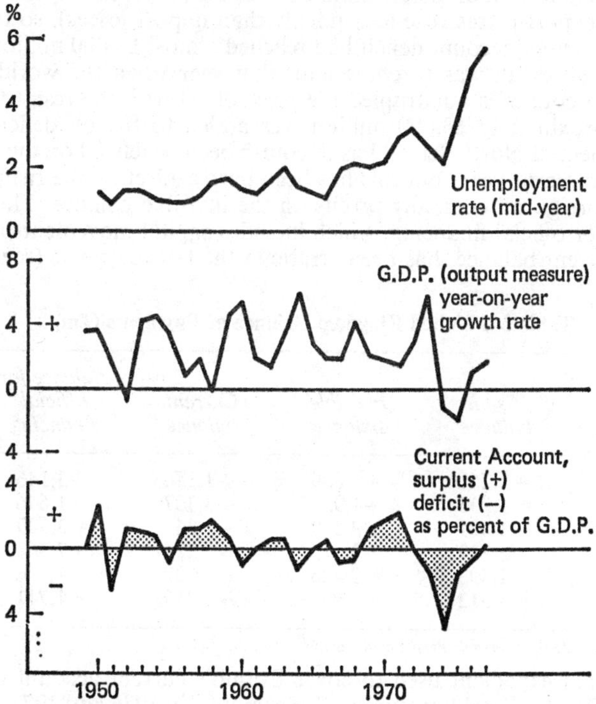

Fig. 29. Unemployment, G.D.P. growth and the Current Account.
(Source: *Economic Progress Report*, July 1978)

as a cure for balance of payments problems was reserved as a last resort, though poor trade figures and heavy speculation forced the Government in 1967 to resort to this remedy. This brought about an improvement in the balance of payments position and between 1969 and 1972 a surplus was earned on the current balance. It was these favourable circumstances that tempted Edward Heath's Conservative Government to opt for a higher rate of economic growth in the early 1970s and this, together with Britain's accelerating inflation rate, caused the balance of payments position to deteriorate rapidly.

Meanwhile, in the early 1970s the Bretton Woods system of fixed exchange rates collapsed and from June 1972 the pound was no longer tied to any fixed parity against the U.S. dollar or any other currencies. By going on to a floating exchange rate in 1972, the Government hoped that it would solve its growing balance of payments problem because, according to economic theory, as the current account of the balance of payments moved into deficit so the resulting depreciation in the exchange rate would restore equilibrium by making exports more competitive and imports less attractive. Unfortunately for Britain, other countries such as the U.S., Japan and Western European nations were experiencing a boom too, which pushed up world commodity prices causing a substantial deterioration in Britain's terms of trade (i.e. Britain's export prices rose less quickly than import prices), so that by 1973 the current account deficit had reached almost £1,000 million. The worst shock of all was to come later that year when the world's oil-producing countries quadrupled the price of oil with the result that in 1974 approximately £3,000 million was added to the oil deficit. The development of North Sea oil has of course been beneficial on the visible balance in recent years but this has been partly offset by the rising outflow of foreign oil company profits on the invisible balance. Thus, the balance for official financing, which includes capital movements as well as the current balance, has been erratic in the last few years (see Table 34).

Table 34. United Kingdom Balance of Payments (£m)

	Visible balance	*Invisible balance*	*Current balance*	*Balance for official financing*
1971	+ 261	+ 889	+1,150	+3,146
1974	−5,235	+1,928	−3,307	−1,646
1976	−3,601	+2,579	− 842	−3,629
1977	−2,239	+2,015	− 224	+7,361
1978	−1,493	+2,425	+ 932	−1,126
1979	−3,312	+ 993	−2,319	+1,711

Source: Lloyds Bank, *Economic Profile of Britain.*

The main expedient used to cover Britain's current account deficits after 1972 was official borrowing—for example, in 1976 and 1977 official financing drew from the International Monetary Fund, on the strength of Britain's North Sea oil assets, a total of £2,131 million. This led some people to fear that Government, rather than using the North Sea oil assets for regenerating British industry and providing a sound basis for future prosperity, was instead using this important asset as a mortgage to bale Britain out of its economic difficulties.

The balance of payments difficulties after 1972, together with a generally faster inflation rate in the United Kingdom than the average for industrialised countries, caused sterling to depreciate against most other currencies, reaching a record low point of $1·57 at the end of October 1976. After this date sterling tended to rise, particularly after the steep rise in interest rates between 1979 and 1980, reaching $2·37 in May 1980. This in turn has made it more difficult for British manufacturers to sell their products abroad and has cheapened the cost of imports. The official reserves, which are mainly in dollars, rose sharply from $4,000 million at the end of 1976 to more than $20,000 million at the end of 1977, and stood at $28,200 million at the end of June 1980.

Economic Planning

Economic planning became the vogue during the 1960s in an attempt to maintain a steady rate of investment and to improve the rate of Britain's economic growth which compared so badly with some of her competitors. The rationale behind this was that without some form of planning, production in an advanced industrial economy would operate on a hit and miss basis because the plans of different industries would not harmonise.

It was a Conservative Government in 1962 that set up the National Economic Development Council with a brief to study the country's economic performance in order to suggest how improvements could be made. There were already in existence a number of advisory bodies, but the NEDC, with a permanent secretariat in the form of a National Economic Development Office was envisaged as a rather more powerful body, specifically designed to identify the reasons for the poor growth rate and to point the way to a better performance. The first important task they set themselves was an industrial survey to explore the implications of an annual growth rate of 4 per cent between 1961 and 1966. Many people looked on this 'target' with extreme scepticism, pointing out that the British economy had hardly ever achieved a 4 per cent growth rate, except for very short periods of time. Events were to prove that this was indeed an unrealistic forecast and by 1964 it had become clear that the economy was not going to grow at this rate.

In 1964, when Harold Wilson's Labour Government came into office, planning assumed a new role of importance. The Department of Economic Affairs was set up in 1964, and a National Plan was published in 1965. This document set out its purposes as follows: 'The projections of the Plan are essentially attempts by Government and industry, working in cooperation, to break down the general objectives of a higher growth rate into the implications for particular industries. These projections should help firms and industries to take more informed decisions than if they were left in the dark about other people's intentions and beliefs.' The National Plan set a growth rate target of 3·8 per cent per annum, which though less than the NEDC target had been, was nevertheless unrealistic given the constraints of the balance of payments at the time. In the event, the National Plan had to be abandoned only ten months after its inception when economic circumstances necessitated the imposition of an economic freeze.

Since then planning has been confined to key sectors of the economy as part of the industrial strategy.

Britain and the European Economic Community

The E.E.C. grew out of the need after the war among some Western European countries to have closer cooperation with each other. They wanted to replace their economic rivalry with more constructive cooperation and by binding themselves together through common economic interests they wanted to prevent the possibility of war in the future.

With these aims in mind, three European Communities have evolved, which all share the same institutions:

1. The European Coal and Steel Community (E.C.S.C.), set up by the Paris Treaty in 1951. It began work on August 10, 1952, and paved the way for economic unity by placing its six founder members' coal and steel in a single 'common market'.
2. The European Atomic Energy Community (Euratom), set up by the Rome Treaty in 1957, to promote the peaceful uses of nuclear energy within the Community.
3. The European Economic Community (the Common Market), set up by a second Treaty of Rome in 1957, which together with Euratom began work on January 1, 1958.

Since setting up the E.E.C. in 1957, the six founder members—Belgium, France, Germany, Italy, Luxembourg, and the Netherlands—were joined by Britain, Denmark and Ireland on January 1, 1973, and by Greece on January 1, 1981. Britain's membership was confirmed in a referendum in 1975, when 67·2 per cent of the votes cast were in favour of membership. The last remaining customs tariffs between the original six members of the European Community and the three member states that joined in 1973 were removed on July 1, 1977, at the same time as Britain, Denmark and Ireland adopted the common external tariff, thus in effect giving Britain a four-year transition period. It was not until 1979, however, that the British, together with other Community citizens, voted for their first directly elected representatives to the European market.

The main economic argument in favour of Britain joining the Common Market was to achieve a higher rate of economic growth and raise material living standards. Between 1963 and 1973 the combined Gross Domestic Product of the six rose by approximately 5·0 per cent per year while that of Britain grew by only 2·9 per cent per year. Membership of the Community, it was argued, would enable British manufacturers to benefit from the economies of large-scale production through having access to a home market five times larger. This would enable British industry to spread its overhead costs more widely, and exposure to more competition would encourage efficient firms to grow and inefficient firms to contract or close. Furthermore, there would be more opportunity for cooperative research and participation in joint projects such as Concorde or space technology.

However, many people have expressed disappointment with Britain's achievements whilst in the Common Market and the feeling has developed into the 1980s among some sections of public opinion that Britain's membership is somehow temporary, negotiable or even revocable. To a large extent these feelings have been fostered by the problems incurred by Britain through the Common Agricultural Policy (C.A.P.) and Britain's Budget contributions.

Under the C.A.P. farmers are supported by intervention buying, which maintains the price and hence farmers' incomes. The procedure under this system is that the Council of Ministers set common target prices, which are considered to give a fair return to farmers, and if the free market price threatens to fall below an intervention price, the Community, through the guarantee section of the European Guidance and Guarantee Fund, can buy in and store the surplus to maintain the price. The system Britain operated before joining the Community was to import food at low world prices. The Ministry of Agriculture then negotiated guaranteed prices with the farmers' union and the Government paid deficiency payments designed to bridge the gap between guaranteed prices and import prices.

The C.A.P. is an extremely favourable arrangement for countries that have large agricultural sectors such as France, the Netherlands and Denmark, but Britain with a relatively small agricultural sector has lost the cheap food from the Commonwealth due to the Community imposing levies for agricultural imports, and has to import more expensive European products. In 1977 it was estimated that Britain would save £200 million a year by importing food from outside the Community, and an additional £430 million by not having to pay into the C.A.P. funds. Thus a system has been established within the Community which has created butter and beef mountains and wine lakes, with farmers in the exporting countries with large agricultural sectors being supported partly by the consumers and taxpayers of the importing countries rather than by their own consumers and taxpayers. This means that major food-producing and exporting countries like France, the Netherlands and Denmark receive funds from the Common Market budget to buy up surplus production to maintain prices, and then they receive subsidies to enable them to export their higher-priced food to third countries where prices are lower.

The result of this policy is that two of the three poorest countries in

Table 35. Transfers under the E.E.C. Budget and Common Agricultural Policy, 1978–79

	Total net cash receipts (£m)	*Ditto per capita* (£)	*National income per capita* (% *of average*)
UK	−1125	−20	69
Germany	−675	−11	130
Italy	−650	−12	55
Belgium/Lux.	+150	+16	129
Ireland	+475	+158	48
Holland	+625	+45	120
Denmark	+625	+124	136
France	+725	+14	113

Source: *New Society*, April 26, 1979.

per capita terms, Britain and Italy, were two of the largest three net contributors to the C.A.P. in 1978–9, while Denmark, the richest, was the second largest net recipient (see Table 35).

During the 1970s, therefore, Britain found that the system of Community finance developed increasingly into an unfair burden, since over 70 per cent of the Community budget was spent on agriculture, even though Community funds were also to be used for regional policy, social policy, industrial policy, energy policy and overseas aid for underdeveloped countries, as well as providing the administrative costs for running the Community. Thus Britain, like all other members, was turning over its customs duties and farm levies to Brussels (plus a slice of its VAT which was required to top up the total) and getting very little back because she was neither in surplus nor an inefficient agricultural producer. Between 1973 and 1978 Britain's net budget contributions were as shown in Table 36.

Table 36. Britain's Net Contribution to the E.E.C. Budget

1973	£102 million
1974	£ 31 million
1975	–£56 million
1976	£167 million
1977	£369 million
1978	£730 million
Total	£1343 million

This situation produced a long, bitter debilitating dispute between Britain and her E.E.C. partners and threatened the Community with disintegration. The problem was temporarily resolved in May 1980 at the Dublin Summit Conference when Britain's net contribution was reduced until the end of 1981, by which time, if the imbalance in the budget had not been eliminated, similar proposals would be adopted to solve the problem.

Table 37. Net Receipts/Payments to E.E.C. Budget—Average 1980 and 1981 (estimated) (£m)

	Before Brussels agreement	*After Brussels agreement*
W. Germany	–752	–1,061
U.K.	–1,184	–404
France	14	–220
Luxembourg	183	181
Netherlands	297	240
Denmark	297	272
Belgium	327	284
Ireland	361	353
Italy	486	383

Source: *European Trends*, August, 1980.

Britain's trade with the Community was consistently in deficit throughout the 1970s, though the proportion of her exports to the E.E.C. had risen from less than 30 per cent in 1972 to 42 per cent in 1980. In 1979, visible exports to the E.E.C. rose by 30 per cent whereas imports increased by 25 per cent, thus raising the hope that Britain's trade with the E.E.C. might run into surplus during the 1980s.

Table 38. British Trade with the Rest of the E.E.C. (£1,000m)

Year	*Exports*	*Imports*	*Percentage of imports covered by exports*
1973	3·7	5·1	73
1974	5·4	7·6	71
1975	6·1	8·7	70
1976	8·8	11·1	79
1977	11·4	13·5	85
1978	13·1	15·8	83
1979	17·0	19·8	86
1980	12·4	13·0	95

Source: *Facts*, 1980.

Britain, along with other members of the Community, benefits from the E.E.C. regional fund. Thus bigger redundancy payments have been made available for Britain's steelworkers and jobs in high unemployment areas have been financed from the E.E.C. regional fund. Part of Britain's rebate to the Community budget agreed in 1980 is to be made available in the form of regional help for the North West and Wales, as Table 39 shows.

Table 39. Community Contributions in Respect of U.K. Public Expenditure Programmes, 1980–81

	North-West		*Wales*	
	£m	%	*£m*	%
Roads	15·9	30	24·6	30
Rail	12·0	30	6·0	30
Water and sewerage	15·6	30	9·3	30
Advance factories	0·8	20	14·2	20
Telecommunications	48·6	30	30·3	30
Total	92·9		84·4	

Suggested Further Reading

Lewis, D.E.S., *Britain and the European Economic Community*, Heinemann, London, 1978.

Lobley, D., *Applied Economics Made Simple*, Heinemann, London, 1980.

Morris, D. (Ed.), *The Economic System in the U.K.*, O.U.P., London, 1979.

Maunder, P. (Ed.), *The British Economy in the* 1970s, Heinemann, London, 1980.

Exercises

1. Examine the view that low productivity is the root cause of Britain's economic ills.
2. Why has Britain had such a poor growth performance in recent years compared with her major competitors?
3. Explain why inflation has become the main macro-economic policy concern of Governments in Britain during the 1970s.
4. Account for the phenomenon during the 1970s of both a high rate of unemployment and a high rate of inflation.
5. Explain why Britain's attempts at economic planning failed in the 1960s. How has Government policy towards planning changed since then?
6. Assess the advantages and disadvantages of Britain's membership of the E.E.C. since 1973.

Summary

1. Since the war governments have been much more conscious than their predecessors of their responsibilities with regard to the achievement of full employment, an adequate rate of economic growth, price stability and a balance of payments surplus.
2. For a long time monetary and fiscal policies were the main tools of economic management but later these policies were supplemented by prices and incomes policies, which only appeared to work successfully over a short period of time.
3. Low levels of unemployment were achieved between 1945 and the mid-1970s but since then unemployment has risen dramatically.
4. Britain's growth rate since the war compares favourably with previous growth rates in her history, but compared with many other countries Britain's achievement in raising output has been relatively poor.
5. The rate of inflation has rapidly increased in Britain since 1972 and this has threatened Britain's balance of payments position, employment prospects and rate of economic growth.
6. The Balance of Payments problem in Britain has imposed constraints on economic policy from time to time and led to a jerky pattern of growth during the 1950s and 1960s.
7. The attempts at indicative planning during the second half of the 1960s failed, probably due to the unrealistic targets set. Since then planning has been confined to key sectors of the economy rather than being applied to the economy as a whole.
8. Britain has been a member of the European Economic Community since 1973 but in spite of the benefits problems have been experienced with the Common Agricultural Policy and Community budget contributions.

CHAPTER TWENTY-TWO

POST-WAR INDUSTRIAL POLICY

The basic objective of governments in developing an industrial policy is to make Britain more efficient and to arrest the relative decline of Britain's industrial performance since the war. Compared with other countries the industrial output per head of the labour force has been at a low level and has been growing less quickly too, which means that people's material living standards have not been rising as rapidly as elsewhere.

Basically the problem is that of low productivity, which results in low wages, low profits and high prices. Compared with other countries Britain has been getting less out of its investment and manpower and therefore the costs of production have been relatively higher than production costs in more efficient countries (see Fig. 30).

In a highly unionised country such as Great Britain, wages can be a major cause of inflation, since over the years there have been many

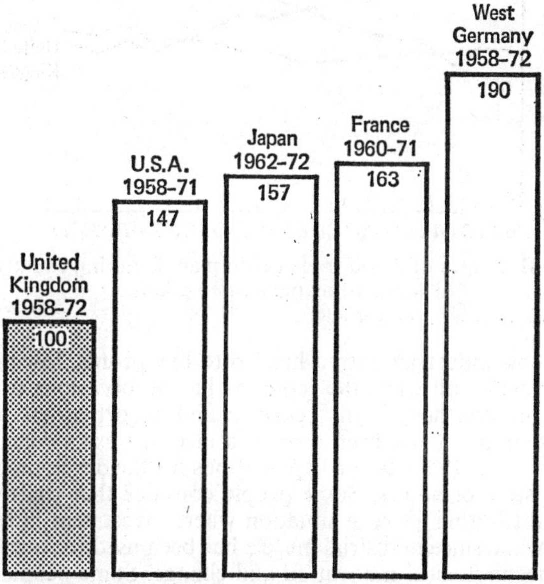

Note: The period of comparison for each country has been chosen to eliminate distortions due to cyclical influences.

Fig. 30. Measuring efficiency (increase in net output per unit of investment—United Kingdom=100).

(Source: *Economic Progress Report*, March 1979)

instances of trade unions obtaining higher wage increases for their members than can be absorbed through higher productivity. This results in higher prices, which makes it more difficult for British exporters to sell in international markets, and leads to a falling share of world trade (see Fig. 31) and balance of payments problems.

This decline in export competitiveness caused sterling to weaken from time to time, thus requiring governments to deflate in order to defend sterling. This had the effect of dampening down investment and thus impairing industrial productivity, resulting in a vicious circle of low growth leading to low growth so that many of Britain's competitors have been in the process of becoming more prosperous than the British.

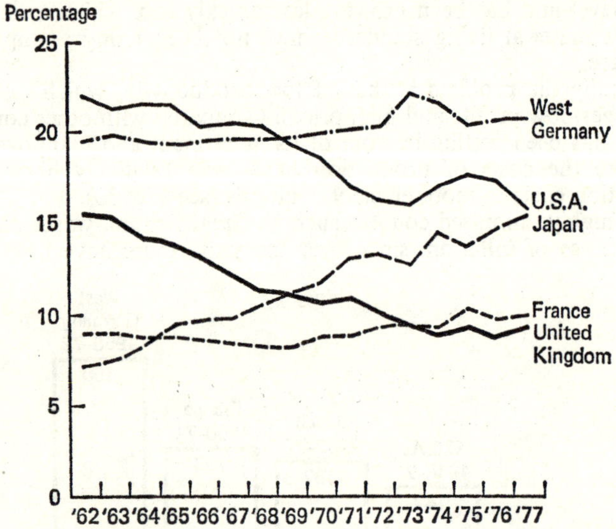

Fig. 31. Shares of world trade (main manufacturing countries' exports of manufactured goods).

(Source: *Economic Progress Report*, March 1979)

Therefore, low industrial output has led to low profits, low investment and low growth, and when the economy has on occasions temporarily picked up imports have been sucked in and export orders have been lost because industry has been unable to meet the extra demand.

There are many theories and explanations for the development of this deplorable state of affairs. Some people consider that trade unionists have helped to bring about a situation where investment in industry is not worth while since industrial muscle has been used to squeeze profits and resist technological innovation and change. Some people attribute blame to successive governments for not providing the right economic climate for industry to prosper and spending too much of the nation's wealth on services that we cannot afford. Yet other people blame private businessmen for not investing in industry in spite of tax and other inducements provided by the central authorities from time to time.

Governments have over the years attempted to improve industrial performance through various policy measures, and several strands of policy measures can be identified.

Competition Policy

Competition policy is concerned with controlling monopolies, mergers and restrictive business practices and its primary objective is to increase economic efficiency.

Policy towards controlling competition in the U.K. was not developed until after the Second World War. Indeed, during the inter-war years governments encouraged industries to concentrate and rationalise, thereby ensuring their survival in times of low demand and inadequate profits. During the depressed 1920s and 1930s, when unemployment had stuck obstinately at levels of over 10 per cent of the workforce, there had arisen numerous agreements between firms, collectively known as restrictive trade practices, which kept many inefficient firms in being. Governments between the wars, therefore, had turned a blind eye towards 'live and let live' policies, which took the form of collusion between firms about such practices as fixing prices and sharing out the market, which under normal economic conditions would be considered contrary to the public interest.

Throughout the twentieth century there has been a trend towards the concentration of business into large units, a trend which was accentuated after 1945 by nationalisation and the emergence of large companies through take-over bids and mergers. Table 40 illustrates the growth of the merger movement between 1935 and 1958 amongst private sector enterprises employing 5,000 persons or more.

Table 40. Analysis by Total Employment Size

Size of enterprise	*Number of enterprises*		*Employment (thousands)*	
	1935	*1958*	*1935*	*1958*
50,000 and over	—	8	—	547
20,000–49,999	9	24	273	750
10,000–19,999	21	42	308	566
5,000–9,999	58	106	413	709
Total–5,000 and over	88	180	994	2,572

Source: *Census of Production Reports.*

There are arguments both for and against the growth in the size of business units. The main arguments in favour of large firms are that they lead to economies of scale and strengthen competitiveness in export markets, whilst the main arguments against are that they may lead to an undesirable reduction in competition and limit choice. Monopoly thus confers power without responsibility and can be used for good or evil. There is an obvious need for control to ensure that public interests are not abused, and monopolies in Britain are therefore regulated rather than prohibited, with the benefits of monopoly in each individual case weighed against the possible economic and social disadvantages.British competition policy is therefore aimed at getting the best of all worlds, which is very difficult to achieve due to the obvious difficulties of measuring exactly the public benefits and disadvantages resulting from a monopoly situation.

Over the past thirty years competition policy has been directed towards the investigation and control of restrictive practices and monopoly, and in more recent years towards consumer protection. The following legislative enactments are the main measures of control:

1. *The Monopolies and Restrictive Practices (Inquiry and Control) Act, 1948*

This act established a Monopolies Commission with responsibility for investigating and reporting on monopoly situations, defined as markets or industries in which one third of a class of goods (the proportion is now one quarter) was supplied in the U.K. by a single firm or a group of firms acting together so as to restrict competition. The Commission did not have the power to initiate its own enquiries nor could it implement its recommendations; the Government alone reserved the right to take any action which it thought necessary. Such a procedure was slow and cumbersome and it would have taken many years for the Commission to deal effectively with the abuses of monopolies and restrictive practices throughout British industry. Thus the Commission produced only twenty reports before 1956, though it did valuable work in revealing the extent to which restrictive practices existed. The Commission found evidence that collective restrictive practices, involving agreements between two or more firms restricting competition, were widespread in British industry and the need to reduce the incidence of such practices emerged as the most important aspect of competition policy at that time. This revelation paved the way for the passing of the 1956 Restrictive Trade Practices Act.

2. *The Restrictive Trade Practices Act, 1956*

This Act transferred the Monopoly Commission's responsibilities for restrictive trade practices to a newly created Restrictive Trade Practices Court. A restrictive agreement was defined as any agreement between two or more persons carrying on business in the production or supply of goods, under which restrictions are accepted by the parties in respect of the prices to be charged, the terms or conditions of sale, quantities or types to be produced, the process of manufacture, the persons or areas to be supplied or the persons or areas from which goods are to be acquired. Under the Act, a Restrictive Practices Registrar was appointed to register such practices and bring before the Court any which seemed to be against the public interest.

The Act did not make restrictive trade practices illegal as such, since some agreements might be considered to be in the public interest. For an agreement to survive the parties involved have to convince the Court that it meets one or more of seven gateways, stipulated in the Act as constituting the public interest. These are:

(*a*) That the restriction is reasonably necessary to protect the public against injury.

(*b*) That the removal of the restriction would deny to the public, as purchasers, consumers or users of any goods, specific and substantial benefits.

(*c*) That the restriction is reasonably necessary to counteract measures taken by a person, not party to the agreement, with a view to restricting competition.

(*d*) That the restriction is reasonably necessary to enable fair terms to be negotiated with a large supplier or purchaser.

(*e*) That the removal of the restriction would be likely to have a serious and persistent adverse effect on unemployment in areas in which the industry is concentrated.

(*f*) That the removal of the restriction would be likely to cause a substantial reduction in export business.

(*g*) That the restriction is reasonably required for the purpose of supporting other restrictions in the agreement which are in the public interest.

The Restrictive Trade Practices Act, 1968, added a further 'gateway' —namely, that the restriction does not directly or indirectly restrict or discourage competition to any material degree in any relevant trade or industry and is not likely to do so.

Experience over the years has shown that the most important gateways used in cases brought before the Restrictive Trade Practices Court have been (*b*), (*e*) and (*f*).

Since the passing of the 1956 Act a large number of firms dropped their restrictive practices voluntarily rather than face the publicity and expense of a court hearing, but approximately 3,000 agreements have been registered. By comparison the number of actual Court cases has been small, so that by 1976 only 37 agreements became Court cases, and of these only 11 were considered by the Court to be in the public interest.

3. *The Resale Prices Act, 1964*

The Resale Prices Act, 1964, declared illegal all resale price maintenance clauses designed to keep prices at prescribed levels, unless these were registered with the Registrar of Restrictive Trade Practices and the Restrictive Trade Practices Court deemed them to be in the public interest. The rationale behind this Act was that the 1956 Act had made it extremely difficult for firms to engage in collective price agreements; therefore manufacturers attempted to maintain prices by specifying the prices at which distributors could sell their products. This measure particularly inhibited large retailers, who were growing in numbers, from reducing prices in order to achieve a higher volume of turnover.

Table 41. Retail Outlets (1957–70)

	1957 Number	1957 Turnover (£000's)	1961 Number	1961 Turnover (£000's)
Total	577,405	7,587,154	577,307	8,918,860
Co-operative societies	28,945	904,796	29,396	959,339
Multiple retailers	59,105	1,883,809	63,299	2,580,073
Independent retailers	489,355	4,798,548	480,612	5,379,448

	1966 Number	1966 Turnover (£000's)	1971 Number	1971 Turnover (£000's)
Total	504,412	11,131,816	485,346	15,217,963
Co-operative societies	26,684	1,015,938	15,343	1,117,463
Multiple retailers	73,852	3,837,244	67,479	6,061,363
Independent retailers	403,876	6,278,634	402,524	8,039,137

Source: *Annual Abstract of Statistics.*

Convincing arguments both for and against resale price maintenance were readily forthcoming. Amongst the arguments in favour was that fixed prices are not necessarily high prices but fair prices. Also, some consumers may prefer fixed prices rather than prices that might be fluctuating daily, weekly or monthly. And the fact that prices were fixed did not mean no competition at the retail level since retailers could compete with each other through offering better service. The opponents of resale price maintenance, however, argued that fixed prices resulted in too many retail outlets with the least efficient retailer being subsidised by the most efficient ones. This resulted in an inefficient use of resources and higher prices and inhibited the development of new trading techniques which relied on low profit margins and high turnover trading, such as supermarkets and mail order firms.

The result of the 1964 Act has been that the vast majority of resale price clauses restricting competition have now been either abandoned voluntarily or else declared illegal by the courts. The Act did, however, lay down certain circumstances in which resale price maintenance was to be allowed when the resulting benefits to consumers outweighed any detriments. The number of manufacturers who have successfully established resale price maintenance in their products, however, have been few in number. Only the manufacturers of books, maps and certain medicaments have proved their case before the Restrictive Trade Practices Court.

4. *The Monopolies and Mergers Act, 1965*

Prior to 1965 legislation had established a framework for dealing with monopoly situations once they had developed but the Government had no powers to prevent industrial concentration which might lead to monopoly. The Monopolies and Mergers Act of 1965 attempted to fill this gap.

The frequency of merger activity increased after the 1956 Restrictive Trade Practices Act, probably because it was no longer feasible for firms to collude with each other on prices and they therefore sought to maintain prices by reducing the number of their rivals through merger activity.

Under the 1965 Act, the Board of Trade (and, after 1973, the Department of Prices and Consumer Protection) may refer any proposed merger which is likely to result in one third (later reduced to one quarter) of the market being in the hands of a single supplier or if the assets acquired exceeded £5 million. In spite of all these measures, however, concentration of economic activity throughout the economy continued with increasing momentum, as Table 42 shows.

Table 42. Acquisition of Independent Companies

	Number acquiring	*Number acquired*	*Value* (£m)
1969	593	742	961
1970	484	608	954
1971	498	620	745
1972	710	931	2,337
1973	722	949	1,055
1974	306	366	451

Source: Department of Trade and Industry.

It is interesting to note that of the 110 mergers notified to the Government in 1969, only four were referred to the Commission. In fact, about 97 per cent of proposed mergers have been allowed to proceed without reference to the Commission, but of those mergers which were referred to the Commission only about 30 per cent were allowed to go ahead with the merger.

5. *The Fair Trading Act, 1973*

This Act established a Director-General of Fair Trading who was responsible for the regulation of monopolies, mergers and restrictive practices, and a new emphasis was placed on consumer protection. An entirely new concept was introduced by the Act since previous competition policy had been primarily concerned with monopolies and the public interest whereas the new Act redefined the public interest to include as one of its elements the desirability of maintaining and promoting competition. Thus the brief of the renamed Monopolies and Mergers Commission was considerably extended by giving it discretion to interpret the public interest in 'all matters which appear to . . . be relevant'. The Fair Trading Office has become a new central source of information and advice for Ministers on consumer protection, monopoly, mergers, and restrictive practices.

Regional Policy

Regional difficulties are created whenever there is an imbalance of resources between different parts of the country, e.g. when there are differences in regional levels of income, poverty and unemployment, or differences in rates of growth and migration. In Britain economic imbalance between the regions has been brought about largely by the decline of the old staple industries between the wars, such as coalmining, shipbuilding and textiles, and the growth of newer and expanding industries which have tended to develop mainly in the Midlands and the South-East. Meanwhile, unemployment since the war has remained a persistent problem in Scotland, Wales, Northern Ireland and some parts of England, particularly in the North and on Merseyside.

The ending of regional imbalance has been an objective of successive Governments ever since the 1930s. The attempts by Governments between the wars, however, to arrest the movement of industry away from the depressed areas towards the Midlands and the South-East met with only limited success and it was not until a situation of near full employment had been achieved that Government policy stood much chance of success in influencing a balanced distribution of industry and a reduction of regional unemployment, since in the economic climate of the 1930s a Government would have preferred a factory to be set up almost anywhere if the alternative was for it not to be set up at all.

During the war, the Government's capacity for influencing the location of industry was greatly strengthened and it established more than one hundred new factories in the pre-war Special Areas. Much thought was also given to the question of industrial location and the maintenance of full employment when the war was over, particularly as there were fears in some quarters that the ending of the war might bring a return of massive unemployment to the Special Areas.

Thus many attempts have been made since the war to secure a more equitable balance of resources between the regions.

Government Policy, 1945–60

The Distribution of Industry Acts, 1945 and 1948, extended the number of pre-war Special Areas and renamed them Development Areas. By 1953 there were 11 such areas to which special help was to be given and new industries established. Under the Acts the Board of Trade was given powers to control industrial building through the issuing of Industrial Development Certificates which were required before a new industrial development of more than 5,000 square feet could take place. The initial results were excellent—for example, between 1945 and 1947 half of the new industrial building in the country was in the Development Areas, which contained only one fifth of the population.

Provision was also made in the New Towns Act, 1946, for the construction of completely new towns. Twenty-seven new towns have since been built under the provisions of the Act to reduce the pressure on overcrowded cities and to encourage development in certain areas.

Government Policy in the 1960s and 1970s

This can best been seen through the following key years:

(*a*) *The Local Employment Act, 1960.* This Act consolidated all the post-war legislation and abolished the large Development Areas, replacing them by smaller Development Districts. These qualified for assistance by having an unemployment rate of more than 4·5 per cent. The Act also tightened control on new industrial development by requiring I.D.C.'s for new developments exceeding 3,000 square feet.

(*b*) *The Local Employment Act, 1963.* This Act amended and greatly strengthened the 1960 Act, making assistance available on a massive scale.

(*c*) *The Industrial Development Act, 1966.* This Act abolished the Development Districts and replaced them with the geographically wider Development Areas, comprising more than 40 per cent of the land area of Britain and 20 per cent of the population. The Act also introduced a system of capital grants to induce firms to set up in areas of high unemployment.

(*d*) *The Special Development Areas and the Regional Employment Premium, 1967.* The Special Development Areas were set up in 1967 within the Development Areas, in districts affected by colliery closures because of the imminence there of high and persistent unemployment. They were later extended to other areas.

The Regional Employment Premium was introduced as a direct subsidy to all firms in Development Areas per employee, per week, with different rates for men, women, and minors.

(*e*) *The Local Employment Act, 1970.* This Act introduced the 'Intermediate (grey) Areas' and 'Derelict Land Clearance Areas'. It was based on the recommendations of the Hunt Committee, which had been established in 1967 to enquire into areas outside the development areas that were nevertheless suffering problems similar in kind if not in acuteness, and likely to decline relative to areas which either had natural advantages or were already receiving assistance. Thus the Intermediate Areas were areas that had no immediate pressing problems, but if left alone might degenerate and become the problem areas of the future.

(*f*) *The Industry Act, 1972.* This Act contained provisions designed to encourage investment and the modernisation of industry throughout Great Britain in order to maintain a higher rate of economic growth. As well as providing national and regional investment incentives, the Act extended the Assisted Areas and made provision for more retraining and greater mobility of labour.

Thus, by the early 1970s there were three different categories of Assisted Area—namely, Special Development Areas, where the need for jobs was the strongest, Development Areas and Intermediate Areas—and help was given to them according to the category of need they were in. After Britain joined the Common Market this help was supplemented by the E.E.C.'s European Regional Development Fund set up in 1975, and loans became available on favourable terms from the European Investment Bank and the European Coal and Steel Community.

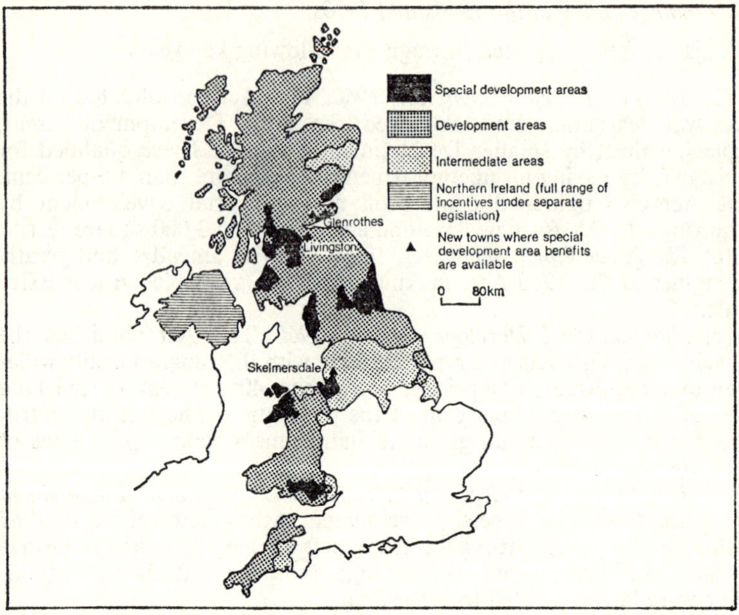

Fig. 32. The Assisted Areas, 1979.

Government Policies for Industry

Both Labour Governments and Conservative Governments have over the years intervened in industry in an attempt to promote industrial efficiency. This was particularly the case during the 1970s when the term 'industrial strategy' was much bandied about by both the main political parties. Generally speaking, Conservative Governments in theory dislike industrial intervention and warn industries and firms not to count on them to rescue them from their difficulties, whilst Labour Governments tend to be more favourably inclined towards intervention. However, circumstances over the years have drawn whichever party was in power increasingly into the industrial arena, and a number of acts have appeared on the statute book specifically referring to industry.

The Industrial Reorganisation Act, 1967

This Act established the Industrial Reorganisation Corporation to promote industrial restructuring, and was a good example of the policy of increased intervention in industry adopted by the Labour Government which came into office in 1964. The White Paper preceding the formation of the I.R.C. pointed out the need to improve Britain's industrial performance through the 'concentration and rationalisation' of industry, which would make possible economies of scale and facilitate more research and development.

The idea that size in industrial organisation was synonymous with efficiency was nothing new in Britain. Many critics of Britain's comparative economic decline as far back as the late nineteenth century had attributed blame to the failure of British industry to organise itself on a sufficient scale to benefit from the economies of increased dimensions. Of course people realised that large firms have the potential power to oppress customers by restricting output and charging higher prices, but little attention seemed to be paid in the mid-1960s to the possibility that mergers might lead to less efficient firms being created.

Between 1967 and its disbandonment in 1971 by the Heath Conservative Government, the I.R.C. made loans available to motorcar manufacturing, aircraft, the computer industry and engineering. The largest loans went to the motorcar industry and the I.R.C. sponsored the merger activity which led to the setting up of British Leyland Ltd. Events later on were to prove this merger extremely controversial and an on-going debate developed as to whether a successful producer of buses and lorries should have become involved with the accumulated problems of a different type of business.

The Industrial Expansion Act, 1968

This Act was designed to provide Government support for schemes which would improve economic efficiency, expand productive capacity and promote technical improvements. Amongst the projects to benefit from this Act was Concorde which received loans and credit guarantees.

The Industry Act, 1972

This Act introduced broad measures for the provision of public money to improve investment. Discretionary funds were made available to create, maintain, or safeguard employment in development areas and more general assistance anywhere and for any purpose was to be provided if it was considered to be in the public interest.

The sums originally spent under the Act were reasonably modest due to the incumbence of a Conservative Government which had declared itself to be less interventionist than its predecessor, but when Labour returned to office in 1974 more money was readily forthcoming so that by 1978 nearly £300 million had been offered to assist projects under the general assistance provisions of the Act.

The Industry Act, 1975

This Act set up the National Enterprise Board as a publicly owned industrial holding company. The functions of the Board were:

(i) To control and manage existing Government shareholdings. Thus it took over assets that the Government had acquired in British Leyland, Rolls-Royce and Ferranti, which had been acquired mainly as a result of rescue operations.

(ii) To extend public ownership into profitable manufacturing industry by the acquisition of shares. This was a controversial aspect of the Act because it gave the N.E.B. the power to extend public ownership not only to companies asking for help, such as Rolls-Royce or British Leyland, but also into profitable companies.

(iii) To act as a source of advice for companies in difficulties.

The N.E.B. was given initial finance of up to £1,000 million to assist firms, but it was required to earn an 'adequate' return on its capital, and any acquisitions exceeding £10 million in a company or 30 per cent of a company's shares had to have the consent of the Secretary of State for Industry.

Speculation was rife at the time of the setting up of the N.E.B. as to whether or not it would lead to a major extension of public ownership. In fact this did not happen, and in the period up to the 1979 election its influence was limited. After the election, the Conservatives reduced the role of the N.E.B. and declared its intention to sell off the greater part of its portfolio and to restrict its future powers of acquisition and investment.

Subsidy Policy and 'Lame Ducks'

Successive governments since the 1960s have intervened in the market and baled out industrial undertakings that have been in difficulties. Amongst the most notable examples of this have been Government help given to the Upper Clyde Shipbuilders, the Concorde project, Rolls-Royce, and last, but not least, British Leyland. This type of intervention to secure an improvement in market performance has been extremely controversial, because some people believe that it encourages workers in certain industries to adopt restrictive practices and strike for higher wages, in the belief that in the last resort, however high they push their employers' costs, they are so large and vital to the national interest that the Government will always succumb and foot the bill to keep them in business.

Upper Clyde Shipbuilders. When shipbuilding ran into difficulties on the Clyde in the late 1960s, the Upper Clyde Shipbuilders' Group was formed out of five independent shipyards in February 1968, with financial help from Harold Wilson's Labour Government. In many ways the venture was doomed from the start because the industry was overmanned and there was strong union resistance to the slimming down of the workforce. Furthermore, the Clydeside shipyards had a strong reputation for union militancy and a long tradition of work avoidance with the result that productivity was low and ships were delivered late. For over three years the U.C.S. staggered from one financial crisis to another, consuming £20 million of public funds in the process. Both the Labour Government and the subsequent Conservative Government insisted that no more public funds were available, and in June 1971 a receiver was called in. After some employees had staged a communist-led 'work in', Mr Heath's Conservative Government changed its mind and injected £35 million of public funds to form a new company out of four U.C.S. yards called Govan Shipbuilders. Later the Government provided a further £12 million as an inducement to Marathon Manufacturing of Texas to take over the fifth U.C.S. yard for oil-rig building.

Such Government help might well have been justified if it had been a long-term solution rather than a short-term expedient, but events were to show that the new company failed to achieve financial success largely because of its failure to improve productivity sufficiently.

The Concorde Project. This was a joint project by Britain and France to develop a supersonic passenger aircraft. It was argued that as well as being a prestige project it would also provide technological 'fall-out' which would benefit industry generally, and that in the long term it would help the balance of payments.

When the project was started in 1962 it was estimated that the total cost of developing the Concorde up to production stage was between £150 million and £170 million. This estimate had risen to £280 million by 1964, and by 1965 the Labour Government seriously considered abandoning the project, but decided not to in case it had to pay the French Government £100 million in compensation. By the early 1970s the estimated cost had risen into the region of £1,000 million, and both the British and French Governments were beginning to despair at the apparently open-ended subsidy they were making to the project. U.K. evidence has subsequently shown that there are sectors other than aircraft, such as the chemical industry and mechanical engineering, which make greater contributions to technology and the balance of payments.

Rolls-Royce. The Rolls-Royce crisis (1971) was brought about by technical difficulties in the development of the RB211 engine within the constraint of a fixed-price contract in highly inflationary times. Substantial help had been given to the company since 1969 when the Labour Government had given £47 million towards the development of the engine. Additional help was provided by the Industrial Reorganisation Corporation (£10 million) to overcome the firm's cash flow problems, and in 1970 the Government made available a further £60 million to help the company. In 1971 the firm's financial problems led to the nationalisation of the company's aero-engine division.

British Leyland. British Leyland was created in May 1968 when the two largest British-controlled motor manufacturers, British Motor Holdings (BMH) and Leyland Motors, were merged together. (BMH had come into being in 1966 through the merger of the British Motor Corporation, Jaguar and the car body-producing firm Pressed Steel. Leyland Motors was the product of a merger in 1962 between Leyland and Standard-Triumph, followed by the absorption of Rover and Alvis in 1967.) The rationale for the 1968 merger was provided by all the old cliches—economies of scale, improved efficiency, rationalisation, greater competitive power and greater availability of capital for future investment. All of these ingredients were supposed to provide an exciting prospect, which unfortunately has not yet been realised.

During the 1970s the labour troubles at Leyland and the corporation's poor production record compared with that of overseas competitors, became a symbol of Britain's abysmal industrial performance. In 1973, for example, British Leyland produced 5·9 vehicles per man, Ford U.K. produced 8·3, Ford Germany produced 10·1, Volkswagen Germany produced 11·6 and the French Renault workers produced 14·6 vehicles per man, two and a half times as many vehicles as the Leyland worker.

The time lost in industrial disputes more than doubled between 1970 and 1974. Amongst the most prominent explanations for this terrible record were inadequate investment, bad management, inadequate communications, militant shop stewards and poor industrial relations.

Thus by the mid-1970s British Leyland faced formidable problems, and in 1975 the Government produced the Ryder Report, entitled 'British Leyland: the next decade'. This Report recognised that State help was needed in order to put right some of the problems caused by mismanagement in the past. In fact, large sums of money were needed both to provide working capital and to modernise the company extensively.

Since the Ryder Report large amounts of taxpayers' money have been ploughed into the company both for new equipment and, particularly during the economic recession of the late 1970s, to provide working capital to keep the company afloat. In spite of the post-1979 Conservative Government's commitment to reduce public expenditure and withdraw from costly industrial intervention, it has nevertheless been forced into providing huge sums of public money to tide the company over whilst new and more promising models start rolling off the production lines. Mrs Thatcher's Government, however, is anxious that there should be no automatic assumption that there will be a 'no strings' pledging of the £1,000 million of taxpayers' money between 1981 and 1984.

The New Industrial Strategy

This term has become popular since the publication in 1975 of the Government White Paper, 'An Approach to Industrial Strategy' (Cmnd. 6315), which was an attempt by Government to point out industry's shortcomings and lead the way into a new and more successful direction. The basic objective of the strategy was for Britain to become 'a high-output, high-wage economy . . . by improving our industrial performance and raising the growth of productive potential'.

With this aim in mind the National Economic Development Council brought together leaders of Government, unions and management to discuss Britain's economic and industrial problems and ways of overcoming them. This planning exercise differed quite fundamentally from the attempts at planning in the 1960s, in that there was no question of trying to impose unrealistic plans and targets from above. A number of sector working parties were established, comprising representatives of Government, management and unions, to analyse their own industry in detail and to consider what obstacles might exist to an increase in growth and efficiency. These Sector Working Parties have since been busy analysing ways of improving their own particular industry and a number of potential production bottlenecks in industries like steel have been identified and steps have been taken to deal with them.

Since 1975 the Government has given financial assistance to encourage investment in various sectors—for example, in July 1978 a five-year support programme was announced for the microelectronics components industry, particularly for those companies making silicon integrated circuits, commonly referred to as chips.

Suggested Further Reading

Hoyle, K., and Whitehead, G., *Business Economics Made Simple*, Heinemann, London, 1980.

Lee, D., *Regional Planning and Location of Industry* (3rd edition), Heinemann, London, 1980.

Lobley, D., *Applied Economics Made Simple*, Heinemann, London, 1980.

Morris, D. (Ed.), *The Economic System in the U.K.*, O.U.P., London, 1979.

Exercises

1. In Britain monopolies are regulated rather than controlled. Discuss with reference to U.K. competition policy since the war.
2. Outline the development of regional policy since the war. What have been its main aims and achievements?
3. What do you consider are the main arguments for and against specific intervention by government in industry?

Summary

1. Britain's poor comparative industrial performance in recent years has encouraged more analysis and discussion of industrial policy.
2. The root cause of Britain's poor industrial performance is low productivity, which has caused low wages, low profits, low investment, low growth and high inflation.
3. Competition policy has been developed since the war to control monopolies, mergers and restrictive practices with the aim of increasing economic efficiency.
4. In Britain monopolies are regulated rather than prohibited, with the benefits of monopoly in each case weighed against the possible economic and social disadvantages.
5. Regional policy has evolved to correct the imbalance of resources between different parts of the country, brought about largely by the decline of the old staple industries and the growth of new industries.
6. Increasingly, both Labour and Conservative Governments have over the years been called upon to give selective aid to industry by baling out so-called 'lame ducks'.
7. Since the mid-1970s a new industrial strategy has evolved which brings together leaders of Government, unions and management to discuss Britain's economic and industrial problems and ways of overcoming them.

CHAPTER TWENTY-THREE

POST-WAR INDUSTRIAL DEVELOPMENTS

Britain's balance of payments position at the end of the war necessitated the making of vigorous efforts to rebuild the export trade. This task was greatly aided in the early post-war years by the imposition of controls on the home market to limit demand. Thus for several years after the ending of the war important products earmarked for export, such as motor vehicles of all kinds, were in scarce supply for domestic use.

The export trade was further stimulated by the buoyancy of world demand and the temporary absence of formidable foreign competitors such as Germany and Japan. These circumstances provided the opportunity for some of the newer industries such as cars, chemicals, oil refining, aircraft, and machinery of all kinds, to gain a foothold in the world export markets. Thus the character of British exports changed resulting in the substantial expansion of some sectors of the economy, whilst other sectors either stagnated or declined. Coal and cotton were the two casualties amongst the pre-war staple export industries, whereas shipbuilding and iron and steel, which had been expanded during the war, were encouraged to continue their expansion when the war was over. Some idea of the changing pattern of British exports in the post-war world can be acquired by comparing the ten leading British exports in 1938 with the ten leading exports in 1957.

Table 43. Leading British Export Industries

Industry	*Percentage of total British exports by value (1938)*	*Industry*	*Percentage of total British exports by value (1957)*
Machinery (other than electric)	11	Machinery (other than electric)	17
Cotton goods	10	Vehicles and aircraft	12
Coal	9	Chemicals	8
Iron and steel	6	Electric machinery, apparatus, etc.	7
Chemicals	6	Manufactures of metals	5
Manufactures of metals	5	Woollen goods	3
Vehicles and aircraft	5	Petroleum and petroleum products	3
Miscellaneous textiles	5	Cotton goods	3
Electric machinery, apparatus, etc.	5	Miscellaneous textiles	3
Woollen goods	4		

Source: A. J. Youngson, *Britain's Economic Growth*, 1920–1966.

Nationalisation

Clause 4 of the Labour Party Constitution of 1918 committed the Labour Party to work towards the common ownership of all the means of production, distribution and exchange. Already at that time there was some measure of public control in the economy. The Post Office, for example, was run by the State, and many local authorities were responsible for the provision of water, gas, electricity and suburban transport in their areas. This trend towards the control of public utilities by local authorities was further extended between the wars, and in addition several public corporations were established. The coming of the Second World War and the extension of Government involvement in the economy provided the right psychological atmosphere for more State control of industry when the war was over. This coincided with the success of the Labour Party in the 1945 General Election, which meant that they were able to implement their cherished ideal of nationalising certain key industries, and during the next six years the Bank of England, the coal industry, inland transport, electricity, gas, and iron and steel were nationalised. Kelf-Cohen described this nationalisation programme as 'a political and economic revolution, forced through after a generation of waiting'.

Thus, by 1951, a large part of the British economy had been placed under direct Government control. The main economic arguments put forward in favour of nationalisation were that competition within certain industries was wasteful, and in the case of a monopoly there was also the danger of consumer exploitation. Certain industries had in the past been badly mismanaged by private enterprise and investment had failed to keep pace with the marginal efficiency of capital. There were many people, therefore, who were doubtful whether private enterprise could be entrusted with important decisions concerning investment and future planning in industries. Mismanagement and lack of investment in the coal industry had, for example, produced a situation of strife and confrontation between the wars. Hence, many people had high hopes of the benefits to be derived from the socialisation of industry, but, as A. J. Youngson remarked, 'the difference between making money and acting in the public interest was smaller than most people had imagined'. The Conservatives for their part saw other ways of remedying the defects of the capitalist system and promptly set about denationalising iron and steel and road transport when they were returned to power in 1951.

There is no doubt that the nationalisation of coal, electricity and railways during this first major phase of British nationalisation demonstrated that certain sections of economic activity ought to be conducted by Government, since some of the old sense of hopelessness and stagnation in these industries disappeared.

During the 1950s the nationalised industries represented 18 per cent of the country's gross domestic capital formation, and employment in public corporations continued to grow, thus making a significant contribution towards total public sector employment.

The return of a Labour Government in 1964 led to the renationalisation of steel in 1967, but the introduction of a bill to nationalise all ports

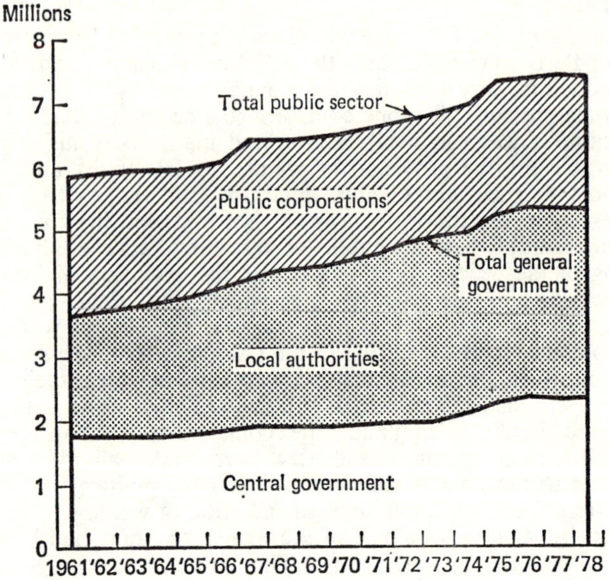

Fig. 33. Total public sector employment in the United Kingdom (mid-year 1961–78).

(Source: *Economic Progress Report*, February 1980)

failed to become an Act before the General Election of 1970. Since then British Aerospace was nationalised, largely because through grants and favourable contracts it was already effectively part of the public sector, and British Shipbuilding became operational as a public corporation from July, 1977, because of a growing recession, since under State control the rate of decline in the industry could be more easily planned. In addition, Government has acquired significant interests in a number of manufacturing companies, including British Leyland and Rolls-Royce. Thus by 1979 the nationalised section of the economy employed 8 per cent of the labour force and accounted for 16 per cent of total investment. After 1979, the trend has been towards the slimming down of the public sector, as was illustrated by the offering to the public of British Aerospace shares in February, 1981.

Progress of the Main Industries

Coal

During the Second World War the coal industry suffered a number of new problems, the chief of which were the loss of export markets and a decline in the industry's labour force. This shortage of labour, together with bigger demands from industry, resulted in a fuel crisis in 1942. This led to the Government taking over responsibility for the general direction of the industry during the last two years of war, and some 20,000 'Bevin Boys' were directed into the industry. Output, however, continued to decline in spite of increased mechanisation so that by 1945 the industry was incapable of meeting the demands required of it. In 1945, the Reid Technical Advisory Committee reported on the poor technical and organisational state of the industry and recommended the reorganisation of the industry on a coal-field or area basis.

When the post-war Labour Government began its programme of nationalisation, the coal industry, with its long history of neglect and conflict, became an obvious target for state ownership. Thus the Coal Industry Nationalisation Act of July, 1946, established public ownership of the industry, and on January 1, 1947, the National Coal Board took over control of the nation's coalmines. 'The Board became the largest single employer of labour in the western world, responsible for nearly 800,000 workers, and a business with an annual turnover at 1946 prices of £360 million. The inherited problems were equally immense: the industry at that time was being called upon to supply just over 90 per cent of the country's total energy needs, and yet some two thirds of all coal output was being produced from mines which dated back to the last half of the nineteenth century. It was the greatest transfer of industrial Victorianism ever recorded.' (J. Platt, *British Coal*, p. 20).

The demand for coal increased slightly during the 1950s, reaching a peak of 229 million tons in 1954 and 1955. Since then there has been a progressive decline in both demand and output. This decline was brought about by competition from more convenient fuels, such as oil and gas, and by the more efficient use of coal itself. Thus, with the exception of the electricity supply industry, demand from the coal industry's best customers fell away.

Table 44. Coal Supply and Consumption (million tons)

	1949	*1960*	*1972*
Total supply	215·2	201·2	124·1
Total consumption,	214·4	202·2	121·7
of which			
Electricity supply	30·0	51·9	65·6
Gas supply	25·3	22·6	0·6
Railways	14·3	8·9	0·1
Iron and steel	8·2	3·8	0·3
Large industrial consumers	30·1	27·9	9·9
Domestic	29·2	29·1	10·4

Source: *Annual Abstract of Statistics.*

Since 1948 the industry's labour force has fallen from 724,000 to 234,900 in 1978/79, whilst increased capital investment has led to an increase in productivity from 1·1 tonnes per man shift in 1948 to 2·24 tonnes per man shift in 1978/79.

The rundown of the coal industry during the 1960s was short sighted, as events were later to show, but at the time Governments considered that the country could manage with less coal and rely increasingly on what seemed like endless supplies of cheap gas, oil and nuclear energy. The industry's decline would have been even greater, however, had it not been for the imposition of an embargo on coal imports, and increased duties on fuel oil. In addition, the Government encouraged the public sector of industry to burn coal in preference to other fuels. Nevertheless, uneconomic pits continued to be closed down and the future prospects of the industry seemed dim. This trend was arrested, however, following the quadrupling of the price of oil in the winter of 1973/4, when it was realised that failure to develop indigenous coal resources efficiently would add substantially to future balance of payments burdens.

With recoverable reserves of coal estimated at 45,000 million tons (27,000 million tons oil equivalent), a 'Plan for Coal' was unveiled in 1973 which planned £1,400 million of investment for the industry up to 1985 to increase output and productivity per worker. This estimate of planned investment has since been revised upwards and in 1979 stood at £3,150 million. Part of the 'Plan for Coal' is to exploit new, more productive seams, such as those in the Selby district of Yorkshire and the Vale of Belvoir in North Leicestershire, whilst many of Britain's existing 223 pits are to be run down as they approach their expected average lifespan of 70 years during the 1980s. Therefore, without continuing investment in new capacity, colliery production would have fallen to around 80 million tons by the end of the century. It is expected that coal production on the Selby field will have built up to 10 million tons by 1987–88, whilst the Vale of Belvoir field should be producing 7 million tons by 1988. Thus, the industry's fortunes were changed during the 1970s and miners became amongst the best-paid workers in the country, with their jobs more secure at a time when many other workers in British industry were being threatened with redundancy. However, attempts at increasing production during the 1970s were disappointing. Production rose between 1974 and 1975 from 98·7 to 116·8 million tons, but after that it declined steadily, falling to 105·4 million tons in 1979.

North Sea Oil and Gas

Exploitation of the North Sea's oil and gas reserves is a relatively new industry in Britain, with natural gas production beginning in 1965 and oil production in 1975. Since then production has increased rapidly, with North Sea oil production reaching 78 million tonnes (1·6 million barrels a day) in 1979, and natural gas production reaching 35 million tonnes of oil equivalent in 1976, and remaining at about that level for the duration of the 1970s. In addition to the North Sea oil, small amounts of crude oil (100,000 tons in 1978) are taken from the inland fields in the East Midlands and Dorset.

In 1964 full-scale offshore exploration for natural gas began in the Southern Basin of the North Sea, off the coast of East Anglia and Yorkshire, and the first gas came ashore in 1967. Since then the Southern Basin reserves have become somewhat depleted and new gas fields in the northern North Sea and other offshore waters are increasingly contributing to our needs, with further supplies being imported from the

Table 45. U.K. Oil and Natural Gas Production

	Oil or oil equivalent					
	Oil			*Natural gas*		
	Million metric tonnes	*As % of U.K. oil consumption*	*As % of U.K. primary fuel consumption*	*Million metric tonnes of oil equivalent*	*As % of U.K. natural gas consumption*	*As % of U.K. primary fuel consumption*
1974	0·4	—	—	30·6	98·1	14·2
1975	1·6	2·0	—	31·8	97·5	15·6
1976	12·1	13·1	5·8	33·7	97·4	16·2
1977	38·2	41·1	18·1	35·3	95·7	16·7
1978	54·0	57·3	25·4	33·7	88·0	15·9

Source: *Economic Progress Report*, August, 1979.

Norwegian part of the Anglo-Norwegian Frigg gasfield (8 million tonnes oil equivalent in 1979). It is estimated that remaining recoverable reserves of gas in the British fields are 600 to 1,800 million tonnes oil equivalent.

During the 1970s the major oil discoveries were in the Northern Basin of the North Sea, the first significant discovery being the B.P. Forties Field in 1970, and the first British oil to flow ashore was from the Argyll field in 1975. By the end of the 1970s there were 14 North Sea oil fields in operation, but in fact about half the oil produced came from the Forties field. The remaining recoverable reserves of oil are officially estimated to be 2,000 to 4,200 million tonnes; production is therefore expected to be stepped up in the foreseeable future.

Table 46. U.K. Oil Production Forecasts (million tonnes)

1979	70– 80
1980	85–105
1981	95–115
1982	115–140
1983	115–140

Source: *Economic Progress Report*, August 1979.

Britain is expected to become self-sufficient in oil during the 1980s, but there will nevertheless continue to be substantial imports and exports due to the different types of oil required by refineries and consumers. In the late 1970s about half of North Sea oil was exported, with approximately 50 per cent going to other E.E.C. countries, 30 per cent to America, and the remaining 20 per cent to Norway, Sweden and Finland.

The benefits of North Sea oil and gas to the National Income have been quite profound and much faith and hope has been placed in the part that North Sea energy resources will play in Britain's future economic prospects. In 1977, the value of North Sea oil and gas was £2,800 million, representing 1·8 per cent of the Gross Domestic Product; in 1979 the value was about £5,000 million, which was just under 3·0 per cent of G.D.P.; and it is estimated that in 1985 the value of North Sea oil and gas will be £8,600 million at 1978 prices, representing 6·0 per cent of G.D.P. However, much concern was shown in the late 1970s as to whether or not North Sea oil would be used as collateral to finance current consumption or whether it would be used to regenerate British industry through capital investment, and/or provide tax cuts in the future. Certainly North Sea oil and gas have helped Britain's balance of payments and will provide future governments with the opportunity to pursue domestic policies less constrained by concern about the balance of payments.

Iron and Steel

The iron and steel industry was reorganised and modernised during the war in order to meet unprecedented demands for its products. This involved a greater use of home ores and scrap in steelmaking, thus reducing Britain's longstanding dependence on high-grade foreign ores. The strategic importance of iron and steel in the war effort led to the Government taking over control of the industry, though early in the war it was decided against any expansion of steel capacity and steel consumption was limited to essential requirements. Any deficiencies in home production were made good by imports from the United States and any new capacity that was developed was generally used for the production of specialised products which could not be imported.

Government control was extended after the war by the setting up of the Steel Board in 1946 for the purpose of maintaining supplies and continuing the wartime policy of price control. For several years after the war the demand for iron and steel products ran ahead of supply. This reflected chiefly the growth of the engineering industry in general, and the motorcar industry in particular. In these circumstances the steel industry was rapidly expanded, and by 1960 capacity had been roughly doubled.

The nationalisation of iron and steel in 1949 came at the end of the first post-war Labour Government's nationalisation programme. This measure caused a storm of protest, for whilst most people could see a good case for nationalising coal, electricity, gas and transport, the case for nationalising steel, which was making reasonable progress at the time, was less convincing, and many people thought the move was based on Socialist dogma rather than on sound economic principles. The Socialists for their part argued that nationalisation was in the long-term interests of the industry, and that it would lead to more efficient and better planned schemes for the industry as a whole. Steel nationalisation thus became a controversial political issue which led to its denationalisation by the Conservatives in 1953, and its subsequent renationalisation by Labour in 1967. It must be pointed out, however, that when the Conservatives returned the steel industry to private ownership in 1953, they were not content to leave the industry entirely to its own devices. Instead they set up an Iron and Steel Board, appointed by the Minister of Supply, 'to provide for the reorganisation of the iron and steel industry under free enterprise with an adequate measure of public supervision'. Included in the Board's general supervisory powers was some degree of control over the determination of prices.

The process of rationalisation begun during the inter-war years was continued throughout the post-war years. In ironmaking, for example, although output increased from 7·8 million tons in 1946 to 17·5 million tons in 1965, the average number of furnaces in blast was reduced from 98 to 66 and the number of works involved was reduced from 53 to 30. In steelmaking, although output increased from 12·7 million tons in 1946 to 27·0 million tons in 1965, the number of ingot-making works, excluding works which were primarily steel founders, was reduced by five and the number of existing steel furnaces fell from 567 to 468.

In 1967, 14 major steel companies were renationalised and formed into the British Steel Corporation, which by the late 1970s was producing over 85 per cent of Britain's crude steel and was the largest steel undertaking in Europe. The major strategy for modernisation of the industry during the 1970s was the replacement of open-hearth steelmaking (for bulk production) and the electric arc process (for more specialised tasks), and the concentration of bulk steelmaking at five main sites (at Port Talbot and Llanwern in Wales, Ravenscraig near Glasgow, Lackenby in Cleveland, and at Scunthorpe), which have good access to deep water for iron ore imports.

The iron and steel industry in the past has been traditionally vulnerable during times of economic recession, and it is therefore not surprising that the British industry, with its relatively low productivity, fared very badly during the economic recession of the late 1970s. In 1979, B.S.C. still had an average output per man of just over 100 tonnes a year, against 225 tonnes in France and 250 tonnes in West Germany; therefore when B.S.C.'s big customers at home in the motor, shipbuilding, engineering and construction industries were hit by recession, B.S.C. found itself in deep trouble. By 1979 the Corporation was losing £1 million a day and the entire crude steel output for 1980 was unlikely to reach 11 million tonnes, which was the lowest level since the late 1930s. Attempts to turn the corporation into a more commercially orientated organisation have included slimming down the labour force and closing down plants such as the Consett works in 1980, whilst making every effort to keep the five big new or modernised plants going at Ravenscraig, Redcar, Llanwern, Port Talbot and Scunthorpe, even at reduced output.

Engineering

Engineering in the broadest sense has been considerably expanded in the post-war period. The following branches of this industry are worthy of special note.

Shipbuilding. The potential output capacity in British shipyards was raised during the Second World War, largely through improved productivity brought about by more mechanisation and changes in equipment and plant, instead of by laying down additional berths, as had been the case during the First World War.

After the war, the British shipbuilding industry found itself faced with an immense and persistent demand, so that output was pushed even higher than it had been in wartime. Part of this demand was to replace ships destroyed during the war; 20 million gross tons of allied ships had been sunk, of which 11·5 million gross tons were British. Demand was also stimulated by the general lack of specialised ships required for the rebuilding of peacetime trade. Thus in the absence of competition from countries such as Germany and Japan, the British shipyards were producing about half of the world's ships.

By 1960 this post-war boom had come to an end, and British yards were becoming increasingly uncompetitive on both price and delivery dates. Work under construction at the end of June, 1960, totalled 1·87 million gross tons, the lowest figure since September 1946, and some of the smaller yards were beginning to experience a shortage of work. Part of the responsibility for Britain's increasingly poor competitive performance in shipbuilding was due to the long history of strained industrial relations stemming from the period of decline between the wars when unemployment had been so high. Shipbuilding workers were notorious for their sectionalism and their inclination towards spinning the work out for as long as possible. Demarcation lines were finely drawn by workers who were determined to protect their insecure skills from dilution at almost any cost.

Part of Britain's problem also lay in the structure and organisation of the industry. The British industry should have moved towards building a limited range of specialised ships instead of remaining as jobbing builders, capable of making all sorts of ships. The comparatively large numbers of independent companies, frequently run by proud and autocratic families, made it more difficult for a single shipyard to develop a speciality, because of a fear of being vulnerable to market changes. The Japanese, however, who by the early 1980s were producing 40 per cent of the world's ships, went in for building a limited range of ships—for example, large numbers of oil tankers during the 1960s. Furthermore, productivity in some of the Japanese yards has been increased by being located near to steel mills. By the 1970s output per shipyard worker in Britain was found to be 50 per cent worse than in other Western European yards, and even farther behind the productivity performance achieved in Scandinavia and the Far East.

In 1966, the Geddes Report on the British shipbuilding industry urged the need for mergers, rationalisation and massive investment in the industry in order to stop the stagnation and promote expansion. As a result of the Report, the Government, rather than nationalising the industry as was urged in some quarters, made money available to help those firms who were prepared to rationalise and become part of larger groups.

The problem that emerged for the British shipbuilding industry during the 1970s was one of world excess capacity in the face of shrinking trade and economic recession. During the sixties and early seventies world trade had trebled in response to expanding economies and world shipbuilding capacity had been correspondingly increased to meet the demand, but following the big rise in oil prices after 1972, the world shipbuilding industry faced a prolonged period of massive overcapacity, to which British yards were particularly vulnerable. Thus, the British shipbuilding industry became a symbol of Britain's industrial problems during the seventies, requiring Government aid from time to time. Between 1972 and 1978, the State provided more than £201 million in grants and subsidies to the industry, with a further £223 million in credits to induce British shipowners to place their orders in British yards.

In July 1977 the shipbuilding industry formally passed into public ownership when 19 of the larger shipbuilding companies were formed into a public corporation, known as British Shipbuilders. This was thought necessary by the Labour Government at the time in order to prevent the possibility of widespread closure as well as providing proper planning for the future. It was also argued that British defence needs its own shipbuilding capability and British companies need the security of a British merchant fleet which can be built in British yards. Hence, the Government declared its determination to maintain in the future an efficient and competitive industry by securing more orders, concentrating on the sectors where Britain was most competitive, and seeking an international solution to the problems of world overcapacity.

In the first year of operation of the British Shipbuilders Corporation, the U.K. share of the world market rose from about 3 per cent to 4 per cent, whilst many of our competitors in Western Europe found their share shrinking. Some people, however, expressed scepticism at this achievement because the largest single order, involving a £115 million Polish deal for 24 ships, had a large subsidy element attached to it. Since then the situation has worsened with the order books dwindling, and there seems the prospect of further decline well into the 1980s.

The Motor Industry. The development of motor vehicles for both the home and world markets became a striking aspect of industrial development in the post-war period. Vehicle production recovered rapidly from the dislocation caused by the war, and in 1950 car output passed the half million mark for the first time.

Table 47. The British Motor Industry

Year	*Cars*	*Commercial vehicles*	*Exports*
1946	219,000	148,000	121,000
1950	523,000	263,000	542,000
1955	898,000	341,000	629,000
1960	1,353,000	458,000	716,000
1965	1,722,000	455,000	786,000
1972	1,921,000	408,000	776,000

Motor vehicle exports became a major feature of the immediate post-war British export drive, and by 1950 exports represented about 76 per cent of total production, after which this proportion gradually fell. Meanwhile, competition in the world markets has gradually grown, particularly from France, West Germany, Italy and Japan, with the result that Britain's percentage share of total world production has fallen, and competition in both the home and foreign markets has become exceedingly severe.

The industry continued the pre-war trend for concentrating production in a few large groups, and by 1974 the British motor industry was dominated by four groups which accounted for 99 per cent of car production and almost 98 per cent of commercial vehicle output. These were British Leyland, Ford, Chrysler United Kingdom and Vauxhall. Part of these groups were in turn connected to world-wide industrial interests, with Ford and Chrysler of Britain being subsidiaries of Ford and Chrysler of America, and Vauxhall being a subsidiary of General Motors; thus any development plans by these American companies in Britain had to be viewed in terms of world-wide interests. Since then, American interests in the British motor industry have been slimmed down somewhat. In August 1978 the financially pressed Chrysler Corporation of America announced agreement to sell its British, French and Spanish car and commercial vehicle interests to Peugeot Citroen who, in turn, subsequently reduced their U.K. interests in Britain by announcing in January 1981 that they were closing down their Linwood works in Scotland.

Table 48. Major Vehicle Manufacturers in 1974

	Cars					
	Home		*Export*		*Total*	
	'000	%	*'000*	%	*'000*	%
British Leyland	416·0	44·4	322·5	54·1	738·5	48·1
Ford	290·6	31·0	93·2	15·6	383·7	25·0
Chrysler	117·8	12·6	144·0	24·2	261·8	17·1
Vauxhall	108·3	11·5	28·6	4·8	136·9	8·9
Others	5·3	0·6	7·9	1·3	13·2	0·9
	Commercial vehicles					
British Leyland	76·0	32·7	49·3	29·0	125·3	31·1
Ford	73·7	31·7	57·6	33·8	131·3	32·6
Chrysler	18·2	7·8	6·8	4·0	25·0	6·2
Vauxhall	56·6	24·4	55·5	32·6	112·2	27·9
Others	7·9	3·4	1·0	0·6	8·9	2·2

Source: S.M.M.T.

Competition for the British market intensified in the late 1970s, with British manufacturers taking a dwindling share, and British Leyland, with its poor productivity performance and out-of-date models, tottering on the verge of bankruptcy. Only the injection of massive Government help has saved the company and much hope is now pinned on the new models being built by B.L., such as the Mini Metro, the

LC-10, and the B.L.-Honda Bounty, which is being built in cooperation with the Japanese Honda Motor Company. A further incursion by the Japanese into the British and European car markets has been the decision in 1981 of the Japanese car company, Nissan, to build a plant in the U.K., at a cost of between £200 million and £300 million, for the production of Datsun vehicles, which will provide 4,000–5,000 jobs and produce 200,000 vehicles a year by 1986.

The Aircraft Industry. This industry was rapidly expanded during the Second World War, and by 1944 the aircraft and associated engineering industries were employing 1·8 million workers, compared with 355,000 in 1939, which represented a bigger labour force than agriculture and the coal industry combined.

A major reappraisal of strategy following the Korean War in 1951 led to a new defence policy, which stimulated the industry by increasing the demand for military aircraft, both for the home and foreign markets. Civil aviation also established itself as a major British industry in the post-war period. Amongst the successful civil aircraft produced by British firms in the 1950s were the Comet, Viscount and Britannia, whilst the 1960s saw the introduction of the V.C.10, the B.A.C. One-Eleven and the Trident. Britain also became jointly committed with France during the 1960s to the development of the world's first supersonic civil aircraft, the Concorde.

The impact of aviation upon the world of the 1950s and 1960s was probably greater than it will be henceforth. The rationale for providing huge sums of Government money for the development of aerospace was the balance of payments argument and the so-called technological 'spin-off' effects. Now the balance of payments benefit is vitiated by the huge cost of sustaining the industry and microelectronics and microbiology could arguably have a greater impact upon life through technological spin-off benefits than further aircraft development.

Developing new aircraft is a risky and expensive business; therefore a close link has been forged between the Government and the aircraft industry. The Government thus became very concerned in the late 1950s with the fragmented nature of the industry, and made any future help for the development of civil aviation dependent upon rationalisation. This led to a series of amalgamations and the emergence of two major groups, Hawker Siddeley and the British Aircraft Corporation. Because of Governments' increasing involvement in the aircraft industry during the 1970s, a strong case emerged for the nationalisation of the major companies in the aircraft industry, and in 1976 the public corporation of British Aerospace was formed. By this time Britain's aerospace industry had emerged as the largest and most comprehensive in Europe, producing civil and military aircraft, helicopters, aero-engines, guided weapons, hovercraft, space vehicles and a comprehensive range of aircraft and airfield equipment and systems. Amongst the main civil aircraft being produced in the late 1970s were the B.A.C. One-Eleven airliner and the Anglo-French Concorde supersonic transport, nine of which were in service by the end of 1977, whilst the most prominent military aeroplane being produced was the Hawker-Siddeley Harrier vertical/short take-off and landing aircraft, which has achieved substantial sales to the United States. The British aerospace industry is also a major producer of guided weapons, which include a number of export successes—particularly the Rapier ground-to-air missile.

The Chemical Industry. This was another growth industry which made rapid technological progress both during and after the war. The most important areas of growth were in oil refining and the production of petrochemicals.

Oil refining in Britain in 1945 was virtually a new industry, but with the commencement of work at the Shell plant at Stanlow in Cheshire in 1947 and at the Esso refinery at Fawley near Southampton in 1951, Britain rapidly became an important oil-refining centre. Investment in the industry was heavy and much of this was undertaken by Dutch and American interests. The labour force, however, remained comparatively small in relation to the amount of investment; therefore productivity per man was high.

Petroleum chemicals are now used in the manufacture of plastics, synthetic detergents, synthetic fibres, paint solvents, fertilisers and insecticides. Thus, a cluster of industries, collectively known as the petro-chemical industry, grew up alongside the oil-refining industry, and formed the basis of much modern manufacture.

Demand on both the home and foreign markets grew rapidly during the 1950s and 1960s for chemicals of all kinds, and the chemical industry became the third largest industrial sector in the United Kingdom. This expansion continued into the 1970s and by 1976 the industry had become the second largest in Europe and the fourth largest in the Western world, with exports totalling £3,200 million and accounting for 12·5 per cent of total British exports, thus making Britain one of the top five chemical exporting nations in the world.

Since petrochemicals are so important to the development of a chemical industry, the North Sea oil and gas exploitations have bolstered up prospects for the future of the British chemical industry. However, developments in this direction have been disappointingly slow, and a report for the Economic Development Council in 1977 said that Britain's petrochemicals industry would have to invest in more capacity for basic plastics if Britain were to have a chance of using North Sea oil as a petrochemical feedstock to gain a bigger share of the European plastics market. There will also be the need in the future to build more 'crackers' to make ethylene, which is the basic petrochemical building block for the production of plastics, paints and fibres, etc.

Cotton. The cotton industry staged a temporary recovery after the war and for a time it looked as though some of its old prosperity had been restored. This was wishful thinking, however, because once world production revived the industry sank into a sharp decline.

The turning point for the industry came in 1951 when demand began to fall and foreign competition increased. The decline continued throughout the 1950s and between 1954 and 1959, 25 per cent of the capacity of the industry was forced out of business. After considerable lobbying for Government aid, the Government passed the Cotton Industry Act in 1959 which compensated redundant workers, paid manufacturers for scrapping redundant plant and subsidised modernisation. This rationalisation increased the industry's efficiency by improving productivity, but the industry continued to decline in importance.

In recent years the cotton industry has suffered increasingly from the competition of man-made fibres, the two main types of which are still those first developed—the cellulosic fibres, such as rayon, and the synthetic fibres, such as nylon and polyester—made wholly by chemical processes. Britain's balance of trade in textiles generally and related products went into deficit in 1973, and since then, in the face of increasing competition from 'low wage' countries like Hong Kong, South Korea and Taiwan, there has been a general rundown of textile capacity.

Agriculture. World agriculture prices after the Second World War were rising rather than falling, as they had done between the wars. The rapidly growing world population meant that there was no longer a surplus capacity amongst the primary producing countries but instead shortages existed in the world which meant that the era of cheap imported food was over. This situation, together with the fact that Britain had been caught out twice with food shortages through war within the relatively short period of 25 years, persuaded the post-war Labour Government to pursue a policy of maintaining a healthy agricultural sector in the economy. Thus, the Agricultural Act of 1947 declared a policy of 'promoting and maintaining, by the provision of guaranteed markets and assured prices . . . such part of the nation's food and other agricultural produce as in the national interest it is desirable to produce in the United Kingdom, and of producing it at minimum prices consistent with proper remuneration and living conditions for farmers and workers in agriculture and an adequate return on capital invested in the industry'.

The implementation of this policy, which involved an annual price review and the fixing of prices for two years ahead to help farmers plan their output, led to increasing output and a rise in agricultural incomes. This pricing system changed when Britain joined the Common Market and prices for most U.K. farm products came to depend to a large extent on intervention support prices agreed by the European Community Council of Ministers each year as part of the Common Agricultural Policy. In the early years of Britain's membership of the Community, however, British agricultural prices were prevented from rising to the common E.E.C. level by an artificially high agricultural exchange rate, the 'green pound'. This benefited the British housewife but was a source of complaint to farmers whose incomes were depressed as a result. The green pound has since been devalued several times, and the normal exchange rate has risen, so that the gap has now vanished.

In recent years British farmers have enjoyed relative prosperity compared with earlier years in the century, with agricultural output rising on average by 2·4 per cent per year between 1970 and 1980, which was slightly faster than the Gross Domestic Product. However, Britain's agricultural sector appears comparatively small when compared with some of her European partners. In 1979 agriculture in Britain accounted for 2·5 per cent of the Gross Domestic Product, whereas in France the proportion was 9 per cent and in West Germany it was 6·5 per cent. By the early 1980s, 78 per cent of the U.K. land surface area was in agricultural use, with 30 per cent of it used as arable farmland and 48 per cent as grass and woodland. Table 49 shows the main agricultural products produced in Britain and the degree of self-sufficiency in 1979.

Table 49. Food Production and Self-sufficiency, 1979

Products	*'000 tonnes*	*Quantity as per cent of new supplies*
Wheat	7,045	74
Barley	9,680	107
Sugar (refined)	1,065	45
Potatoes	6,121	90
Beef and veal	1,034	83
Mutton and lamb	235	60
Pork	683	98
Bacon and ham	212	42
Poultry	757	100
Butter	161	42
Cheese	236	69
Eggs	1,175 (m. dozen)	101
Liquid milk	7,357 (m. litres)	100

Source: Lloyds Bank, *Economic Profile of Britain.*

Transport Developments

Striking changes in transport have taken place since the war both in terms of the amount of travelling done and the means of transportation. The main features of these changes are the big increase in passenger traffic and the continuation of the inter-war trend of the movement of passenger and goods traffic away from the railways towards the roads (see Tables 50 and 51).

Table 50. Passenger Transport in the United Kingdom (1,000 million passenger miles)

	1959	*1969*
Air	0·4	1·2
Rail	25·5	18·4
Road (public service vehicles)	44·1	35·7
Road (private transport)	82·1	184·0
Total	152·1	239·3

Table 51. Goods Traffic in the United Kingdom

	Million tons		*Thousand million ton miles*	
	1959	*1969*	*1959*	*1969*
Rail	234	206	17·7	15·1
Road	1,146	1,506	28·1	14·5
Coastal shipping	43	48	9·5	14·8
Inland waterways	9	7	0·1	0·1
Pipelines	3	43	0·1	1·6

Source: *Annual Abstract of Statistics.*

The Transport Act of 1953 denationalised road transport and sold a large part of the industry back to private enterprise, whilst a small section was retained under public ownership. The railway executive was also abolished and replaced by six area boards which were given greater freedom in deciding policy and fixing charges.

The Transport Act of 1962 decentralised the whole industry by abolishing the British Transport Commission and replacing it with the British Railways Board, the London Transport Board, the British Transport Docks Board, the British Waterways Board, and the Transport Holding Company. This Act thus ran directly contrary to the philosophy of integration behind the 1947 Act and encouraged competition between the different forms of transport.

The Transport Act of 1968 differentiated between passenger transport, which was to remain the responsibility of British Rail, and freight, which became the responsibility of the newly established National Freight Corporation. This new corporation was to be used as a means of extending the publicly owned sector of the road haulage industry, without resorting to outright renationalisation. Its main duties in conjunction with the Railways Board were:

(i) To provide, secure or promote the provision of properly integrated services for the carriage of goods within Great Britain by road and rail.

(ii) To secure that, in the provision of these services, goods are carried by rail wherever such carriage is efficient and economic.

By 1969 the Corporation was only carrying 5 per cent of the nation's freight, but the Government hoped that its streamlined modern image of carrying container freight would ensure that within a few years its share of the market would grow appreciably bigger.

The chief developments in the different branches of the transport industry were as follows.

Road Motor Transport

To own a motorcar before the war was a luxury invariably reserved for the better-off classes of society. During the war the industry's resources became geared to the war effort and private cars became even scarcer, whilst for several years after the war Britain's balance of payments position led to the strict rationing of motor vehicles on the home market in order to earmark the major part of production for the export drive. By 1953, however, Britain's balance of payments position had improved and the restrictions on the home market were lifted. It was this fact, together with steadily rising real incomes, which led to a big increase in the domestic demand for cars, which from the late 1950s onwards reached boom proportions.

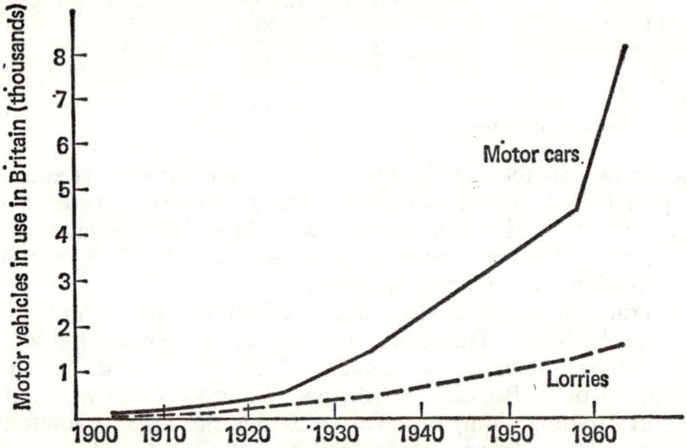

Fig. 34. The transport revolution: cars.

(courtesy Penguin Books)

Thus the motorcar became more than a rich man's toy and for many people became an economic and social necessity. In 1939 there had been one car to every 24 people: by 1959 the percentage of households having use of a car was 51·2 per cent and by 1979 the percentage had grown to 58 per cent. This huge increase in domestically owned motor-cars affected most people's lives at countless points and represented nothing less than an economic and social revolution.

Rail Transport

The two outstanding events affecting railways after the war were nationalisation in 1948, and the Beeching Report in 1963.

Railways had undergone a long period of stagnation and decline since 1914 and there was much apathy and a sense of hopelessness in the industry. There could therefore be little disputing of the need for their nationalisation, and on January 1, 1948, the Railway Executive assumed responsibility for the administration, maintenance and operation of British Railways.

Since nationalisation, railways have consistently been run at a loss. This has caused much public abuse, yet it is abuse that derives largely from the confusion in the mind of the public between the railways as a public service and the railways as a paying industry; and it is often forgotten that most railway systems in the world are run at a loss. Many of the same people who complain when the railways announce a deficit also denounce any reduction in services or alteration of prices designed to reduce the deficit.

In 1963 the Beeching Report recommended that the way to cut losses was by a reorganisation of the railway system and the closure of unprofitable lines. The Report recommended the closure to passenger traffic of more than 5,000 route miles, and 2,363 stations out of some 7,000. It also recommended that traffic should be carried in full train loads and that the number of liner trains should be expanded.

These proposals were not carried out to the letter, though the route mileage has been reduced by about 30 per cent through the elimination of duplicate lines and uneconomic services. The railways modernisation programme was also speeded up. Already in 1963 steam power had ceased to be the main form of traction, and by 1968 diesel engines had completely replaced the traditional steam engines. British Rail continued its programme of investment throughout the 1970s, extending its electrification programme, and making improvements in inter-city services through the introduction of high-speed trains.

Air Transport

In 1946, the Civil Aviation Act set up British European Airways and British South America Airways, though the latter was merged with B.O.A.C. in 1949. In theory B.O.A.C. and B.E.A. (later merged) were entirely free to compete with each other but in practice they tended to specialise on particular air services. In addition, there are a number of independent airlines operating on scheduled routes, the most prominent of which are Britannia, British Caledonian, Dan Air, Laker, British Midland and the new Air U.K.

In recent years there has been a rapid expansion of air travel, particularly on the profitable and expanding Atlantic, Far East and African routes. The leisure section of the business has been the area of fastest growth, and Freddie Laker's company has the big advantage here since it was structured from the start as a leisure airline. Laker saw that the leisure traveller deserved better than to be used as a means of filling up space on scheduled services, and proposed a transatlantic service designed specifically for the traveller who is paying for himself. The transatlantic route was one of the fastest growing routes in the late 1970s: 3·9 million passengers crossed the Atlantic between the U.K. and the U.S. in the year ending August 1977, and by the following year the total had grown by 22 per cent to 4·75 million. Air fares were subsequently slashed on the Atlantic route and vigorous competition for business ensued, with one-way tickets becoming available by 1980 at less than £90. Since then the struggle for cheaper air fares has spread to one of the most overpriced networks in the world—the European airlines—and British airline operators hope to extend European air travel by substantial reductions in fares.

Development of Trade Unionism

The whole labour movement was strengthened during the war when Churchill sought the full cooperation of labour for the war effort.

Trade union membership rose from 6¼ million in 1939 to 8 million in 1945, and trade union leaders were drawn more and more into active cooperation with the Government. Some members of the Labour Party were invited to join the war cabinet and Ernest Bevin, the trade union leader, became Minister of Labour.

This trend in the growth of the power and influence of trade unions has continued since the war and is seen both by the growth in the size of trade unions brought about by mergers, and by the increasing size of

Table 52. Trade Union Membership in Britain

Year	*Membership*	*Number of Unions*
1945	7,875,000	781
1950	9,289,000	732
1955	9,726,000	694
1960	9,821,000	654
1970	10,302,000	555
1975	11,755,000	407

their membership. One example of a union growing rapidly in recent years has been Clive Jenkins's Association of Scientific, Technical and Managerial Staffs, whose membership in 1976 stood at 374,000.

The growing power brought about by the increased membership and better organisation of the trade union movement has enabled it to play an increasingly important part in the economic, political and social affairs of the nation. Their advice has been frequently sought by successive governments but they have tended to identify themselves most with the Labour Party, with which their history is inextricably linked.

The unions have over the years been frequently criticised for contributing towards Britain's poor economic performance by resisting technological change, engaging in restrictive practices and above all frequently disrupting production through strike action.

Table 53. Total Number of Trade Union Stoppages

1950	1,339	1965	2,354
1955	2,419	1970	3,906
1960	2,832	1975	2,263

Trade union powers have been a source of constant debate since the war, and their legal status has been frequently changed, with Labour Governments in general being favourably disposed towards increasing the powers and privileges of trade unions, whilst Conservative Governments have been inclined towards curbing their powers.

In the distant past there was no doubt that the trade movement was heavily discriminated against as far as the law was concerned; however, over the years they have achieved certain legal rights which has left the status of the trade union unique in the British legal system and gave to trade unionists an extraordinary legal immunity. It was the 1906 Trade Disputes Act more than any other measure which bestowed this immunity on trade unions by freeing them from liability either under civil or criminal law for their action in pursuit of an industrial dispute, which meant that the trade unions were not responsible in law for loss or hardship caused by a strike.

The law affecting trade unions has been changed several times since the Second World War. The Trade Disputes Act, 1946, repealed all the main provisions of the 1927 Trade Disputes Act which had restricted picketing, made political strikes illegal, and ruled that union members could pay the political levy to the Labour Party only if they took the positive step of contracting in.

The Trade Disputes Act of 1965 followed the Rookes v. Barnard case, where union leaders at B.O.A.C. had threatened to strike unless the management sacked a worker who was not a union member. The ruling was that the union leaders could be prosecuted for conspiracy, which seemed to imply that to threaten a strike was to threaten an illegal act. The 1965 Act legalised such a threat if it was connected with a trade dispute.

When the Conservatives took office in 1970, they considered that the law as it then stood was balanced too much in the favour of trade unions, and they passed the 1971 Industrial Relations Act in an attempt to redress the balance. Under this act a series of 'unfair industrial practices' were laid down, and anyone found guilty of indulging in these 'unfair industrial practices' would be open to claims for damages. This meant that such actions as unofficial strikes or sympathetic strikes could be deemed 'unfair industrial practices', and therefore the Act was looked on by many trade unionists as an affront to their established rights, and was strongly resisted. When a Labour Government was subsequently returned to office they passed the 1974 Trade Unions and Labour Relations Act, which largely restored the legal position of the trade unions existing before the Industrial Relations Act. Also, the Labour Government was determined to end the strife and confrontation between unions and Government which had existed in the previous administration and replace it with cooperation. This was the background to the birth of the so-called 1975 'Social Contract', in which the T.U.C. and Labour Government arrived at a consensus on the broad social and economic policies to be implemented by Government and in return the T.U.C. agreed to support a pay policy which limited pay increases to an across-the-board increase of £6 per week with no increases being received by those earning £8,500 or more per annum.

The Government's contribution to the Social Contract was to introduce, mainly through the 1975 Employment Protection Act, far-reaching measures to safeguard the rights of employees and further the aims of independent trade unions.

The Employment Protection Act, 1975

The following are the most important changes brought about by the Act.

Recognition. This part of the Act was concerned with the recognition of an independent trade union, which might have no links with an employer. Under the Act, an Advisory Conciliation and Arbitration Service (A.C.A.S.) was set up which was an independent service responsible for drawing up Codes of Practice on particular issues. Basically, A.C.A.S. took over the former conciliation functions of the Department of Employment and provided the service of persuading reluctant employers to recognise independent trade unions. An employer must negotiate in good faith with a union which the A.C.A.S. recommends for recognition, and should an employer fail to comply with an A.C.A.S. recommendation, then the trade union can refer the complaint to the Central Arbitration Committee set up under the Act whose recommendations on wages or improvements on the contractual conditions of employment in the firm are enforceable at law. The new law relating to recognition disputes was quickly put to the test in the Grunwick dispute in 1976 when the film processing firm refused to recognise the clerical union A.P.E.X. This case was a good example of the potential difficulties facing A.C.A.S. in recognition disputes when an employer is determined by litigation to resist trade union pressure for recognition, since it developed into a long and bitter wrangle bringing the authorities into conflict with trade unionist pickets not directly involved in the dispute.

Guarantee Payments. Hourly paid workers were to be made less vulnerable in the future by receiving £6 per day when laid off because of lack of work, up to a maximum of five days in every quarter.

Maternity Benefits. An employee who is expecting a baby is provided with three important rights:

(i) Protection from dismissal because of pregnancy.
(ii) Return to work with her employer after a period of absence on account of pregnancy or confinement. This may involve the dismissal of a temporary employee when the mother resumes work.
(iii) Maternity pay.

Time Off Work. Paid leave was to be given to union officials to carry out their industrial relations activities and to receive training, which was a practice already operating in many firms when the Act was passed.

Insolvency. This provided protection for workers to be paid any outstanding pay or redundancy money in the event of a firm being unable to pay due to bankruptcy. Payment was to be made out of the Redundancy Fund.

Unfair Dismissal. This part of the Act provides employees with the right not to be dismissed unfairly and enables employees who think that they have been unfairly dismissed to seek remedy by complaining to an industrial tribunal.

The Act also laid down procedures for handling redundancy and spelled out the rights of an individual to belong to a union and to engage in trade union activities free from intimidation. In addition to the

Employment Protection Act, the Government in 1975 passed the Sex Discrimination Act, which aimed at providing women with more equal employment opportunities and promotion.

Thus by the second half of the 1970s the trade union movement found itself in a more secure legal position than ever before, with all its pre-1971 rights restored and more in addition, whilst employees were given extensive safeguards of employment. The supporters of the employment protection legislation claim that it has provided greater stability at work and has resulted in improved procedures, greater training of personnel officers, higher standards of recruitment, and more serious concentration on the industrial relations consequences of business decisions, whilst the critics argue that it has contributed to the rising unemployment problem by making managers grow cautious in their recruitment programmes with the result that companies employ fewer people.

Suggested Further Reading

Benson, D., and Whitehead, G., *Transport and Distribution Made Simple*, Heinemann, London, 1975.

Maunder, P. (Ed.), *The British Economy in the 1970s*, Heinemann, London, 1980.

Morris, D. (Ed.), *The Economic System in the U.K.*, O.U.P., London, 1979.

Williamson, H., *The Trade Unions*, Heinemann, London, 1979.

Exercises

1. Would you agree that Britain is the classic case of a 'mixed economy'? Illustrate your answer with reference to the period after 1945.
2. Outline the history of any one of Britain's major industries since the war.
3. Give an assessment of the effect on agriculture of Britain's membership of the Common Market.
4. Give a critical account of Government transport policy since the war.
5. Trace the growth in the power and influence of trade unions since 1939.

Summary

1. Since the war a large slice of industry has been taken into public ownership, and Britain has evolved into a mixed economy, seeking to get the best advantages of both private and public enterprise.
2. During the 1960s, the British coal industry was in decline, but new investment following the rise in oil prices in 1972 has given the industry brighter prospects for the future.
3. The development of North Sea oil and gas has brought a new dimension to the British economy and Britain is expected to become self-sufficient in oil during the 1980s.
4. Both the iron and steel industry and the shipbuilding industry are traditionally vulnerable during times of economic recession; therefore both industries, with their relatively low productivity, have fared badly during the economic recession of the 1970s.
5. The motor industry has suffered badly from poor organisation, low productivity and foreign competition during the 1970s, but Government aid to British Leyland and the development of new models has given the industry new hope for the future.
6. The British aerospace industry has emerged as the largest and most comprehensive in Europe but its fortunes have varied in the past and it has relied on much Government support.

7. The chemical industry has become the third largest industrial sector in the United Kingdom and accounts for 12·5 per cent of total British exports.

8. The cotton industry, after a brief period of recovery following the war, has experienced a continuation in the general run-down of the industry.

9. British agriculture has experienced a prosperous period since the war and agricultural output during the 1970s rose faster than the gross domestic product.

10. Trade unions have grown rapidly since the war and have played an increasingly important role in the nation's economic, social and political life. Legally, they hold a status unique in the British legal system, giving trade unionists an extraordinary legal immunity.

11. The 1975 Employment Protection Act introduced far-reaching measures to safeguard the rights of employees and further the aims of independent trade unions.

Index